Institutional and Social Dynamics of Growth and Distribution

# Institutional and Social Dynamics of Growth and Distribution

*Edited by*

Neri Salvadori

*Professor of Economics, University of Pisa, Italy*

**Edward Elgar**

Cheltenham, UK • Northampton, MA, USA

Published by
Edward Elgar Publishing Limited
The Lypiatts
15 Lansdown Road
Cheltenham
Glos GL50 2JA
UK

Edward Elgar Publishing, Inc.
William Pratt House
9 Dewey Court
Northampton
Massachusetts 01060
USA

A catalogue record for this book
is available from the British Library

Library of Congress Control Number: 2009936755

ISBN 978 1 84844 228 3

Printed and bound by MPG Books Group, UK

# Contents

# Contributors

Martin Baur, *Federal Tax Administration, Switzerland*
Nikos Benos, *University of Ioannina, Greece*
Samuel Bowles, *University of Siena, Italy*
David de la Croix, *Université catholique de Louvain, Belgium*
Pasquale Commendatore, *University of Naples Federico II, Italy*
Corrado Di Guilmi, *University of Technology, Sydney, Australia*
Luciano Fanti, *University of Pisa, Italy*
Piero Ferri, *University of Bergamo, Italy*
Valerio Filoso, *University of Naples Federico II, Italy*
Mauro Gallegati, *Polytechnic University of Marche, Italy*
Christian Henning, *University of Kiel, Germany*
Mimmo Iannelli, *University of Trento, Italy*
Davide Infante, *University of Calabria, Italy*
Stelios Karagiannis, *Centre of Planning and Economic Research, Greece*
Simone Landini, *Socioeconomic Research Institute of Pindemont, Italy*
Piero Manfredi, *University of Pisa, Italy*
Joel Mokyr, *Northwestern University, USA*
Edward Nell, *New School For Social Research, USA*
Carlo Panico, *University of Naples Federico II, Italy*
Antonio Pinto, *University of Naples Federico II, Italy*
Volker Saggau, *University of Kiel, Germany*
Neri Salvadori, *University of Pisa, Italy*
Janna Smirnova, *University of Calabria, Italy*
Anna Maria Variato, *University of Bergamo, Italy*

# Introduction

## Neri Salvadori

Interest in the study of economic growth has experienced remarkable ups and downs in the history of economics. It was central in classical political economy from Adam Smith to David Ricardo, and then in the critique of it by Karl Marx, but was moved to the periphery during the so-called 'marginal revolution'. John von Neumann's growth model and Roy Harrod's attempt to generalise Keynes's principle of effective demand to the long run re-ignited an interest in growth theory. Following the publication of papers by Robert Solow and Nicholas Kaldor in the mid 1950s, growth theory became one of the central topics of the economics profession until the early 1970s. After a decade of dormancy, since the mid 1980s, economic growth has once again become a central topic in economic theorizing. The recent 'new' growth theory (NGT) is also called 'endogenous growth theory', since the growth rate is determined accordingly from within the model and is not given as an exogenous variable.

Since Adam Smith, social and economic institutions have been considered as exerting a significant influence on the historical patterns of growth and distribution of nations. More recently, economists have also emphasized that the process of growth and distribution in turn shape the evolution of institutions. Growth and distribution are lenses through which we can investigate the complex interplay of the birth, life and decline of social and economic institutions. And institutional and social dynamics, in turn, are important elements in comprehending the interaction between growth and distribution. A conference held in Lucca in December of 2007 was a forum for presenting and discussing different approaches to the issues of the institutional and social dynamics of growth and distribution, with all their theoretical, empirical, historical and methodological implications. This book is the main product of the conference. Other papers will soon appear in a special issue of *Metroeconomica* (2010). The conference was hosted by a research group, and several of the papers elaborated by members of the group were delivered at the conference. The main products of the research group are companion books on *Geography, Structural Change and Economic Development: Theory and Empirics* (Salvadori, Commendatore and Tamberi, 2009) and on *Long-run Growth, Social Institutions and Living Standards* (Salvadori and Opocher, 2009). There is, of course, no overlap among the mentioned publications, which constitute the proceedings of the conference. The papers most directly related to the conference title have been inserted in this volume, which shares the same title as the conference itself. The result is that the book analyses recent developments in the interplay of economic growth and social and economic institutions.

The book opens with two chapters devoted to the relationship between growth and institutions from an historical and theoretical point of view. The first, by Joel Mokyr, analyses the beginnings of economic growth in eighteenth-century Britain and argues that formal institutions have been traditionally over-emphasized, and that the enforcement of property rights by the state was less crucial than other interpretations have suggested: the importance of institutions extended beyond politics and formal institutions; cultural beliefs need to be considered since they created an environment in which inventors and entrepreneurs got the opportunity to operate and cooperate freely; attention is also to be paid to those institutions that stimulated and encouraged technological progress and not just the growth that depends on well-functioning markets. The second chapter, by Samuel Bowles, concentrates on the coevolution of institutions and preferences, both from an historical and theoretical perspective; it proposes a model of the coevolution of cultures (modelled as the distribution of types of preferences in a population) and institutions (the distribution of types of contracts). The chapter specifies an underlying game which has as its possible outcomes a number of different ways that the participants might interact. The outcomes of this underlying game are institutions; the process of institutional change is then studied as a change from one to another of these outcomes.

The next five chapters deal with political institutions and the interplay of these institutions with growth and income distribution. Chapter 3 by Martin Baur reviews the literature concerning the connection between politics and income distribution and tests a number of propositions derived from it. Chapter 4 by Piero Ferri and Anna Maria Variato deals, like the previous one, with income distribution, but focuses on the interaction between cycles and growth. Chapter 5 by Davide Infante and Janna Smirnova deals with an undesired aspect of public activity, namely bureaucrats' rent-seeking activity, like bribery, red tape and corruption. The chapter argues that in the presence of a weak institutional environment the aim is not so much the elimination of opportunistic activities, but that of establishing an equilibrium between State inefficiencies and market distortions. Chapter 6 by Pasquale Commendatore, Carlo Panico and Antonio Pinto attempts a dynamic analysis of the role played by different kinds of government expenditure in alternative post-Keynesian theories. The aim of Chapter 7, by Nikos Benos and Stelios

Karagiannis, is to estimate the impact of human capital on regional economic growth in Greece, and analyse the implications for economic policy.

The next three chapters deal with demographic aspects and the role played by institutions like the family. Chapter 8 by David de la Croix argues that longevity is a key factor of growth; it provides four arguments using various data sets: Geneva and Venice longevity data before the Industrial Revolution, mortality data of English aristocrats, evidence on the rise in medical knowledge, and the height of Swedish soldiers data. Chapter 9 by Luciano Fanti, Mimmo Iannelli and Piero Manfredi explores the implications of age structure for macroeconomic growth models. It provides a general framework embedding the age structure of the population in descriptive growth models and uses it to investigate dynamic implications. This gives an insight on issues such as the optimum population growth rate and the overall structure of balanced growth equilibria. Chapter 10 by Valerio Filoso is an empirical study of multidimensional mating in the marriage market. It shows that the marriage market jointly determines assortative mating on schooling and on wages, that wage has predictive power in forecasting educational mating and that education also helps predict wage sorting.

Finally, three chapters deal with social aspects. Chapter 11 by Christian Henning and Volker Saggau offers an agent-based modelling approach to model the process of knowledge spillovers and knowledge accumulation; it derives a model that focuses on the role of global network structures as determinants of knowledge diffusion and its implied impact on knowledge accumulation in a network of firms. Chapter 12 by Edward Nell explores a tool which is able to capture the interactions between economic growth and change, on the one hand, and changes in social, environmental, political and population variables, on the other. Such a tool, the transformational growth matrix, is presented and the kinds of relationships between economic advances and social, political and demographic variables that it can capture are outlined. Chapter 13 by Corrado Di Guilmi, Mauro Gallegati and Simone Landini explores a model in which the interaction of heterogeneous agents in conditions of uncertainty gives rise to economic fluctuations.

Almost all the chapters of this book as well as all the papers included in the special issue of *Metroeconomica* have been peer-reviewed (the exceptions are the invited lectures to the conference). I would like to take this opportunity to thank all the referees who contributed to improving the published papers and advised me of their publishability. The following scholars helped me with this task: Lutz G. Arnold, (University of Regensburg, Germany), Nelson Barbosa (New School for Social Research, USA), Leonardo Becchetti (University of Rome Tor Vergata, Italy), Luciano Boggio (Catholic University of Sacro Cuore at Milan, Italy), Elise Brezis (Bar-Ilan University), Sebastian I. Buhai (University of Aarhus, Denmark),

Herbert Dawid (University of Bielefeld, Germany), Giovanni Dosi (Sant'Anna School of Advanced Studies at Pisa, Italy), Davide Dottori (Catholic University of Louvain, Belgium), Amitava Krishna Dutt (University of Notre Dame, USA), Steven Fazzari (Washington University in St. Louis, USA), Piero Ferri (University of Bergamo, Italy), Davide Fiaschi (University of Pisa, Italy), Valerio Filoso (University of Naples Federico II, Italy), Günther Fink (Harvard University, USA), Reto Foellmi (University of Bern, Switzerland), Eugenio P. Giolito (Carlos III University at Madrid, Spain), Orlando Gomes (Escola Superior de Comunicação Social at Lisbon, Portugal), David Greasley (University of Manchester, UK), Gregorio Impavido (International Monetary Fund), Davide Infante (University of Calabria at Cosenza, Italy), Stephen Knowles (University of Otago, New Zealand), Peter Kriesler (University of New South Wales at Sydney, Australia), Dorothea Kuebler (Technical University Berlin, Germany), Shiro Kuwahara (University of Tsukuba, Japan), Andrea Mario Lavezzi (University of Palermo, Italy), Marc Lavoie (University of Ottawa, Canada), Dunia Lopez-Pintado (Autonomous University of Barcelona, Spain), John S. McCombie (University of Cambridge, UK), Aashish Mehta (University of California at Santa Barbara, USA), Felix Meschke (University of Minnesota, USA), Branko Milanovic (World Bank), Marco Missaglia (University of Pavia, Italy), Chiaki Moriguchi (Northwestern University, USA), Edward Nell (New School for Social Research, USA), José Luis Oreiro (University of Brasilia, Brazil), Les Oxley (University of Canterbury, New Zealand), Chris Papageorgiou (International Monetary Fund), Carmelo Pierpaolo Parello (University of Rome La Sapienza, Italy), Rowena A. Pecchenino (National University of Ireland at Maynooth, Ireland), Margaret Polski (George Mason University, USA), Alexia Prskawetz (Vienna University of Technology, Austria), Srinivas Raghavendra (National University of Ireland at Galway, Ireland), Michelle Rendall (University of Oslo, Norway), Barkley Rosser (James Madison University, USA), Pier Paolo Saviotti (University Pierre Mendès-France at Grenoble, France), Mark Setterfield (Trinity College at Hartford, USA), John Smithin (York University at Toronto, Canada), Claudio Socci (University of Macerata, Italy), Serena Sordi (University of Siena, Italy), Robert Stehrer (Vienna Institute for International Economic Studies, Austria), Ken Tabata (Kobe City University of Foreign Studies, Japan), Massimo Tamberi (Polytechnic University of Marche, Italy), Robert Tamura (Clemson University, USA), Aysit Tansel (Middle East Technical University at Ankara, Turkey), Lance Taylor (New School for Social Research, USA), Andrea Vindigni (Princeton University, USA), Jacob Louis Weisdorf (University of Copenhagen, Denmark), Katsunori Yamada (Osaka University, Japan), Hiroshi Yoshikawa (University of Tokyo, Japan),

Giulio Zanella (University of Siena, Italy), Gennaro Zezza (University of Cassino, Italy), Jie Zhang (University of Queensland, Australia).

Last but not least, I wish to thank the members of the Scientific Committee of the Lucca Conference who shared with me the responsibility of selecting the papers to be given at the meeting, namely Sam Bowles (Santa Fe Institute, USA, and Università di Siena, Italy), David de la Croix (Université catholique de Louvain, Belgium), Oded Galor (Brown University, USA, and Hebrew University of Jerusalem, Israel) and Stephen J. Turnovsky (University of Washington, USA).

## REFERENCES

Salvadori N., P. Commendatore and M. Tamberi (2009), *Geography, Structural Change and Economic Development: Theory and Empirics*, Cheltenham, UK and Northampton, MA, USA: Edward Elgar.

Salvadori N. and A. Opocher (2009), *Long-run Growth, Social Institutions and Living Standards*, Cheltenham, UK and Northampton, MA, USA: Edward Elgar.

# 1. Institutions and the beginnings of economic growth in eighteenth-century Britain*

**Joel Mokyr**

## 1.1. INTRODUCTION

The new institutional economics has, so far, had little to say about the Industrial Revolution. In their survey of Institutions and Modern Growth, Acemoglu et al. (2005) acknowledge eighteenth-century Britain as a successful economy and much like North and Weingast (1989) before them search for the institutional causes in seventeenth-century political developments and in the constraints placed on the British executive (the monarchy and the royal bureaucracy) by Parliament before and after the Glorious Revolution. In this framework a grand coalition of merchants and landowners emerged, keen on protecting commerce and property. For the first time in British history, the commitment problem, in which property rights were enforced by a suitably constrained entity, approached solution.

While neither Acemoglu et al. nor North and Weingast actually say so explicitly, they imply that these reforms paved the road to the British Industrial Revolution.[1] Others are not so prudent. Mancur Olson (1982, pp. 78–83, 128) had no doubt that 'a few decades after stable and nationwide government had been established in Britain, the Industrial Revolution was on its way'. The accounts pointing to the formal political institutions established in late Stuart and Williamite Britain rely on the notion of credible commitment: the crown deliberately relinquished many of its prerogatives to Parliament, and thus committed itself to pay its debts and to respect the property of its citizens. At the same time, Parliament made its own commitment to sound public finance credible by not removing all of the Crown's power. One way or another, if institutions were the key to economic growth and 'rule' in the formulation of Rodrik et al. (2004), they should have played a major role in the central event that triggered modern economic growth: the British Industrial Revolution. Adam Smith, in a widely-cited line that does not appear in his *Wealth of Nations* but was reported posthumously by Dugald Stewart, thought that 'Little else is requisite to carry a state to the highest degree of opulence from the lowest barbarism but peace, easy taxes, and a tolerable administration of justice, all the rest being brought about the natural course of things'.[2]

Yet, surprisingly, there has been little effort to apply the new insights of institutional analysis to the central event of modern economic history to date, and the institutional origins of the Industrial Revolution remain poorly understood. The reason for this gap in the literature relates to two sources of confusion. One is the distinction between the events in *Britain,* which made it the leading economy in the Industrial Revolution, and developments in the larger North Atlantic economy, which refer to the Industrial Revolution in a wider area and the origins of modern growth in the West. One approach stresses the the exceptionalism of Britain, in trying to explain why it was the pioneer of the Industrial Revolution, and thus focuses on events such as the Glorious Revolution, the British Empire, or the fortunate mineral endowment of Britain (Prados de la Escosura, 2004). The alternative extreme approach regards Britain as a chance leader in a European phenomenon in which cultural phenomena such as the Enlightenment were decisive (Jacob, 1997; Mokyr, 2002). Institutional analysis falls somewhere in between those two approaches. Each country had its own national and local institutions, but certain institutional elements were shared, imitated, and spilled over so that a 'European mode' may be discerned in the continent-wide pressures toward reform after 1750. Institutional changes were inspired by Enlightenment thought that affected much of the Western World (Mokyr, 2006b). The analysis in this chapter will be concerned with the 'smaller' question of Britain's leadership and will thus focus primarily on the institutional environment in Great Britain. In other Western societies, however, institutional changes before 1850 helped create the convergence club as it existed in 1914.

The second source of confusion is that the new Institutional Economics literature focuses on formal institutional transformations, in which the Crown committed to respect the property rights of the landowning and mercantile classes, made contracts more enforceable, and reduced transactions costs and uncertainty. Such an account explains growth in an economy in which institutions lubricated the wheels of commerce, finance, agriculture, and premodern artisanal manufacturing and cottage industries. It led to an improvement in the allocation of resources and the accumulation of more capital. In this fashion such changes provide an explanation of Smithian Growth, in an economy with a static technology. The Industrial Revolution, however, rested on key technological breakthroughs and their application to production by a class of successful industrial entrepreneurs. These successes did not, moreover, lead to a new technological equilibrium but made room for the far more astonishing phenomenon of the non-convergence of technology to a new set of dominant designs. Instead, continued improvement in technology after 1800 became the rule. How are we then to link the essence of the British Industrial Revolution to the events of 1688 and beyond, and how did institutional factors, broadly defined, help elevate Britain to the leading position it took in the Industrial Revolution?

Below I argue that the traditional emphasis on *formal* institutions has been over-emphasized, and that the enforcement of property rights by the state was less crucial than the Northian interpretation has suggested. The importance of institutions extended beyond politics and formal institutions. We need to take account 'cultural beliefs' as defined by Greif (2005), which created an environment in which inventors and entrepreneurs could operate and cooperate freely. Equally important, we need to pay attention to those institutions that stimulated and encouraged technological progress and not just the growth that depends on well-functioning markets. Formal institutions such as state-enforced patent rights may have been overestimated at the expense of informal private order institutions

## 1.2. LAW, ORDER, AND INSTITUTIONS

Economic growth depends on law and order (Smith's 'tolerable administration of justice'), but the two are not identical. Law is enforced by public-order formal institutions. The issue then becomes one of credible commitment between a Hobbesian entity with a monopoly of violence, and its subjects. The subjects want the state to enforce the rules of the game but not to accumulate so much power that the state can threaten those very rights it is asked to protect. 'Order' in the sense of the protection of property and contract enforcement can be attained through norms reflecting the willingness of individuals to voluntarily overcome their tendency to behave opportunistically. In that fashion they create what can be called an *economic civil society* in which reputational or other mechanisms support a world in which most people believe that it is proper to behave in a cooperative way. The key to successful economic exchanges here is not necessarily an impartial and efficient third-party enforcing agency, but the existence of a level of trust or other self-enforcing institutions within relevant networks of commerce, credit, wage-labor, and other contractual relations that support free market activities. In other words, the state is neither necessary nor sufficient. The simple model in which it is *only* the state and threat of its justice and police systems that makes people behave cooperatively seems a poor description of any known situation.

How much of a 'law and order society' was Britain before the Industrial Revolution? Crime was of course a serious problem in this society, though it is not easy to quantify it. Yet the admittedly somewhat tenuous evidence suggests that violent crime was declining over the eighteenth century and that crimes against property moved more or less pari passu with population growth (Beattie, 1974; Beattie, 1986). There was also collective crime. Local rioting, either for economic or political grievances, was common. Machine breaking, bread riots, turnpike riots, or rioting against some unpopular group like Catholics, Irish immigrants, or dissenters were common. Turnpike riots, the Gordon riots of 1780, and the Bristol Bridge riot of 1793 all sowed fear in the hearts of property-owning classes. Food rioters, forgers, thieves, and those who resisted enclosures and new machinery forcibly were all threatened by execution and transport. However, daily crime that seriously endangered the accumulation of capital and the proper conduct of commerce was on the whole rare. To be sure, eighteenth-century Britain passed a myriad of draconic laws protecting property by imposing ferocious penalties on those who infringed on it.[3] The harshness of the penalties seems to suggest that violent crime and crimes against property were regarded as serious issues. Yet it also meant that the authorities were reluctant to spend resources on law-enforcement, hoping that the harsh punishments could deter would-be criminals.[4]

Moreover, in Hanoverian Britain law enforcement was largely farmed out to the private sector. It had no professional police force comparable to the constabulary that emerged after 1830, and the court system was unwieldy, expensive, and uncertain.[5] Britain depended on the deterrent effect of draconian penalties because it had no official mechanism of law-enforcement, prosecution was mostly private, and crime prevention was largely self-enforcing, with more than 80 per cent of all prosecutions carried out by the victims. Few victims were willing to proceed with the costly and burdensome tasks of prosecuting a crime (Emsley, 2005, pp. 183–6). Patrick Colquhoun noted in 1797 that 'not one in one hundred offences that is discovered or prosecuted' (1797, p. vii). The growing volume of both domestic and international commerce and credit was supported less by formal law and order and third-party arbitration than by private-order institutions.

If formal law enforcement was a last resort in the enforcement of contracts and the protection of property rights, how did markets function? What made transactions costs and opportunistic behavior mushroom to the point where they jeopardized the levels of exchange and division of labor required for a sophisticated economy? A different way of posing the same question was expressed by the young French economist Adolphe Blanqui (1824, p. 326) visiting London who wondered how a town twice the size of

Paris (nearly a million people) could maintain order with only a handful of watchmen and constables. He seemed less than satisfied by the answer that the English go to bed and lock up their shops early, and was more inclined to believe that they were harder-working and more enlightened.

At closer examination, day-to-day security depended more on social conventions and self-enforcing modes of behavior than on the administration of justice by an impartial judiciary. Commercial disputes rarely came to court and were often settled through arbitration.[6] Even patent litigation was rare: out of almost 12,000 patents issued between 1770 and 1850, only 257 ever came before the courts (Dutton, 1984, p. 71). Indeed, the number of civil cases that came to court in the eighteenth century declined precipitously relative to their mid-seventeenth-century levels: the number of cases heard at the King's Bench and Common Pleas in 1750 was only a sixth of what it was in 1670 (Brooks, 1989, p. 364). As Figures 1.1–1.3 demonstrate, there can be little doubt that the British as a whole were becoming less litigious in the eighteenth century before things picked up again in the nineteenth century. Interpreting this fact seems less than straightforward. Does it support the view that legal institutions were becoming less important as a contract enforcement mechanism? One could argue that if courts were extremely efficient, they might be used less.[7] Or was there a deeper social transformation? Historians such as Lawrence Stone (1985) have indeed argued that the social tensions and violence of the English world before 1650 gradually transformed it into a kinder and gentler environment in which contentiousness declined. Some contemporary commentators felt that in the late eighteenth century, behavior was slowly changing.[8]

Whether eighteenth-century Britain was really becoming a kinder and gentler place is a difficult issue, but at least within the circles of commerce, finance and manufacturing, trust relations and private settlement of disputes seem to have prevailed over third party enforcement. Most business was conducted through informal codes of conduct and relied on local reputation and religious moralizing to imbue honesty and responsibility. Voluntary compliance and respect for property and rank as social norms (private-order institutions, in Greif's terminology) may have been as important as formal property rights in turning the wheels of the British economy. These norms involved a variety of signalling devices associated with 'gentlemanly' codes and were commented on by contemporaries as 'politeness' in a variety of contexts (Langford, 2000). Economics suggests that such behavior is often associated with attempts to signal one's trustworthiness to potential partners in the market. These norms applied only to the middling classes. The laboring classes and the unwashed poor remained outside this society, so the norms did not apply to them. Hence, these classes had to be controlled by force, and the draconian laws protecting property from them reflected this need.

Observant contemporaries noted that informal institutions, that is, customs, traditions, and conventions delineating acceptable behavior were at least as important as a formal rule of law An increasing number of people were bargaining 'in the shadow of the law', that is, the parties in disputes knew what the stakes were and the (substantial) loss they would incur in case they went to trial. Yet the law itself set a guideline to dividing up the resources in dispute, and thus made the bargaining process more likely to result in cooperation, since knowledge of the law, as well as the costs of going to trial, were common to both sides, and the legal process may have become more conducive to private ordering by discouraging people to go to trial and compromise.[9] The Hobbesian view, that insists that order can only be achieved through firm third-party enforcement, may well be true for many societies (depending on many parameters, delineated by Cooter et al., 1982), but it appears that for Britain in the century following Hobbes's death (1679), it was becoming an increasingly less apt description of social reality in Britain. What this means is that we cannot really place the efficiency of the State at the center of the stage of institutional explanations of the British economic miracle.

Indeed, North's belief that Britain's advantage in leading the Industrial Revolution was due to its efficient enforcement of property rights after 1688 needs to be revisited. For one thing, property rights were not sacrosanct. Secure property rights in land may have been important in a technologically static commercial economy, whereas a more technologically dynamic economy required the flexibility provided by eminent domain and even the option to extinguish some traditional property rights if need be, such as happened through enclosure and railway acts. The rent-seeking institutions of the mercantilist economy had established monopoly rights, exclusionary rents, privileges and sinecures (known in the quaint terminology of the time as 'freedoms') were all property rights of one kind or another, but they had to be extinguished if the economy was to modernize and shake itself loose from the 'old corruption' that plagued the British state for much of the eighteenth century.

How, then, did commerce and credit work in this society in the absence of strong third-party enforcement? What mattered was that within the merchant and artisan classes there existed a level of trust that made it possible to transact with non-kin, and increasingly with people who were, if not strangers, certainly not close acquaintances. In an age when the costs of legal action went up, its availability and efficiency declined, fewer and fewer people took recourse to the law and it was replaced by common behavioral cultural norms among people belonging to the same class and the same social circles.[10] We might have expected the reverse: the growing integration of goods and factor markets and the widening of the domestic market, and especially the increase in transactions at arm's length throughout the period of the Industrial Revolution eventually necessitated a formal system of law enforcement. This is what eventually happened during the Victorian age. But in the eighteenth century matters were quite different.

Most enlightenment thinkers believed that the correlation between people cooperating and behaving honestly was caused by a mechanism running from prior commercialization to behavior. It was thought that commerce led to more trustworthy behavior, much like Montesquieu's influential notion of *doux commerce* which established an association between the 'gentle ways of man' and the establishment of trade (Hirschman, 1977, p. 60).[11] But it seems more plausible that the causal arrow went primarily in the other direction, that is, certain forms of behavior led to cooperative behavior that made market transactions possible, even at arm's length, and thus encouraged economic development.

The central concept that determined these concepts was a set of 'bourgeois virtues' (to use McCloskey's term) ironically known as 'gentlemanly behavior'. By 1700, 'gentleman' had come to mean quite different things, one a socio-economic status, the other a code of behavior.[12] A gentleman, Asa Briggs (1959, p. 411) notes, was someone who accepted the notion of progress but was always suspicious of the religion of gold. An individual signaled that he was trustworthy and would not behave opportunistically because, like a true gentleman, he was not primarily motivated by greed and was not maximizing short-term profits. Instead, he was primarily concerned with his reputation.

Gentlemanly Capitalism was a way in which opportunistic behavior was made sufficiently taboo that only in a few cases was it necessary to use the formal institutions to punish deviants, since the behavior is to a large extent internalized.[13] The notion that eighteenth-century landowners were scrupulously honest or indifferent to money is a myth, but the pretension was a good signal for behavior that was less than maximally opportunistic and could thus sustain more readily cooperative trust-equilibria. The idea of a gentlemanly culture is traditionally associated with an aristocratic aversion to business and is thus often held to be antithetical to economic development.[14] But in a different sense, being a gentleman meant that one could be trusted and Gentlemanly Capitalism provided a shared code, based on honor and obligation, which acted as a blueprint to prevent opportunistic behavior (Cain and Hopkins, 1993). In eighteenth-century Britain, a businessman's most important asset was perhaps his reputation as a 'gentleman' even if he was not a gentleman by birth or occupation.

Economists and other social scientists have come to the conclusion that social norms of cooperation and decency can prevail even in societies with ineffective formal law enforcement (Ellickson, 1991). This happens in tightly knit groups in which reputational mechanisms work effectively and social remedial norms can be applied. One such model (for example, Spagnolo, 1999) is supported by the linkage of two types of games, one a social game that lasts for a very long time and the other a one-shot economic game. If two agents face one another in both spheres, the punishment in one game may be used to induce cooperation in the other.[15] This is in some sense a formalization of the importance of trustworthiness through social networking and its effect on market efficiency. These models point to the likelihood that trust can be transferred from a social relationship into an economic relation and thus sustain cooperative outcomes in which exchange can take place and disputes are resolved even without the strict enforcement of contracts by a powerful system of impartial courts or arbiters. It is this kind of environment, whether or not one wants to refer to it as 'social capital', that created the possibility of cooperation even when standard behavior in finite games would suggest that defection and dishonest behavior might have been a dominant strategy.

In sum, then, in Britain during the Industrial Revolution, the social norms of what was perceived to be a gentlemanly culture with an emphasis on honesty and meeting one's obligations, supported cooperative equilibria that allowed commercial and credit transactions to be consummated and partnerships to survive without overly concern about possible defections and other forms of opportunistic behavior. Gentlemen (or those who aspired to become gentlemen) moved in similar circles and faced one another in a variety of linked contexts. Blackstone referred to Britain as a 'Polite and Commercial People'. Politeness was widely equated with law-abiding behavior, and it was intuitively sensed that commercial success depended a great deal on politeness. A market economy depended on people constraining their inclination to behave opportunistically. In other words, economic agents did not play necessarily 'defect' (even if that might have been in their immediate interest) and expected others to do the same. Modern economics teaches that if this is to be effective, agents need to send out costly signals that indicate to others that they are reliable and trustworthy because they belong to a class of reliable and trustworthy agents (see for example, Posner, 2000). Such signals were what 'politeness' were all about: gentlemanly customs in dress, manners, housing, transportation, and speech observed by the British upper classes, and their gradual adoption by the commercial and skilled artisanal classes in the eighteenth century marks the change in British society. They helped created a gentlemanly capitalism and thus an environment in which businessmen and entrepreneurs could deal with one another and with their subordinates in a cooperative fashion that made commerce work even without the heavy hand of third-party law enforcement. In other words, what made commerce and credit possible was that middle class people increasingly absorbed and imitated a set of behavioral norms that made them eschew opportunistic behavior that might have been personally advantageous in the very short run but socially destructive.

This kind of behavior was observed and blessed by Enlightenment thinkers.[16] The Enlightenment view associated with Montesquieu cited above that commerce made people more virtuous and honest must be seen to operate in reverse: it is a sense of honesty and the importance of maintaining a gentlemanly reputation that allowed a market economy to function effectively. To be sure, the ideal of 'gentleman' was not static and changed over the course of the eighteenth century, and the relation between ideal and norm on the one hand and reality on the other is always problematic. The question is not whether the preponderance of British middle-class economic agents invariably behaved like this, as much as whether it affected their behavior (and the way other expected them to behave) sufficiently to make a growing market economy feasible without the need for incessant litigation.[17]

One issue is whether the cooperative norms of behavior were the result of the fear of social sanctions and loss of reputation, or whether they had been 'internalized' into a belief in virtue and good behavior (McCloskey, 2006, *passim)*. Intellectual Historians seem to favor the internalization hypothesis. Pocock (1985, p. 49) feels that 'manners' (that is, cooperative codes of behavior) combined ethical behavior with legal concepts, 'with the former predominating'. Yet the importance of a good reputation in the business world of eighteenth-century Britain was clearly paramount, and Daniel Defoe was only one of many to realize this when he compared the reputation of a tradesman to that of a maiden, easily damaged by evil tongues and almost impossible to repair and describes how such reputations were made and lost around the coffee house through slander (Defoe, 1738, Vol. I, p. 197). Elsewhere he notes (ibid., p. 361) that a shopkeeper may borrow at better terms than a prince 'if he has the reputation of an honest man'. An illustration is the career of William Stout (1665–1752), whose autobiography appeared in 1851, and whose economic success was largely fueled by his meticulous reputation for honesty and generosity.[18] He covered the debts incurred by a dissolute apprentice as well as a nephew. As a Quaker, Stout may have been an unusual case, but his success in business was clearly consistent with the notion that cooperation was a remunerative strategy.

In order to function, a reputation-based system needed good information and communications, and these were provided through the many networks of friendly societies and masonic lodges that emerged all over Britain in the eighteenth century (Jacob, 1997, pp. 92–4). Such networks exist in every society, but the ones established in the eighteenth century were open and accessible to middle class men and thus were an ideal vehicle for the transmission of the information that supports reputational mechanisms. The number of associations and clubs of a variety of nature increased at an astounding rate in the eighteenth century, leading the expert of the topic to refer to it as the 'associational society' (Clark, 2000). Many of these clubs were purely social, eating and drinking clubs, or devoted to common interests and hobbies, but they clearly functioned as clearing houses for information as well.[19] From the point of view of commercial and financial development, what mattered was the emergence of networks of merchants, professionals, industrialists, engineers, and financiers whose interactions and information exchanges (much of it in the form of gossip and rumor-mongering) were critical to the emergence of these social norms.[20] This was clearly an elite phenomenon, encompassing perhaps no more than 15 or 20 percent of British adult male society. The unskilled workers and paupers were not part of these circles and thus not expected to behave the same way, but harsh as this may sound, they did not matter much in this context.

## 1.3. COOPERATION AND THE INDUSTRIAL REVOLUTION

As noted, institutions that foster cooperative behavior are conducive to efficiency and well-functioning markets, which are clearly growth-enhancing. However, it is not clear how they would be instrumental in bringing about an Industrial Revolution, which was driven by *innovation*. How does cooperation foster technological progress? One way to connect social norms and technological progress is to realize that social norms determined the way entrepreneurs interacted with their economic environment, with customers, suppliers, workers, and competitors, and to stress that within a competitive economy, many of the most successful actors were actually more cooperative than we would like to expect. These were norms that were increasingly important in determining the behavior of the inventors, skilled craftsmen, financiers, merchants, and the owners of the new mills and mines that defined the Industrial Revolution.

An emphasis on middle class social norms provides us with answers to some long-debated issues regarding entrepreneurship in the British Industrial Revolution (Mokyr, 2008). How was the scarce resource called venture capital generated? The answer is in part that personal trust allowed partnerships and other credit-relations to develop. This meant that investors often spread their interests over different projects and even different sectors.

A tell-tale sign of that is the diversified projects in which many of them engaged, investing in local improvements and subscribing to projects such as roads, bridges, canals, dockworks, and later railroads.[21] They could diversify their portfolios by investing in sectors they knew little about because they felt they could trust their partners (Pearson and Richardson, 2001). Cotton masters and other textile producers in Manchester, Leeds, and Liverpool could be found as directors of insurance companies, canal- and turnpike companies, gas companies, banks, and other sectors. Country banks were the diversifying instrument par excellence, and many bankers were diversified in a variety of business, and thus so were their partners. It may thus be the case that an entrepreneurial explanation of Britain's early success has some value, but rather than look only at the incentives and characteristics of individuals, we may be advised to see how they dealt with one another.[22] The typical successful British entrepreneur in the Industrial Revolution was not so much a self-absorbed obsessive monomaniac as much as a networked and connected member of a community, his behavior constrained by its moral codes.

Another interesting possibility for a connection from cooperation to innovation is through the idea of cooperation in technological progress itself. Economic historians have found some examples of what Allen (1983) has termed collective invention, that is, the main actors in technological innovation freely sharing information and claiming no ownership to it. There are three reasonably well-documented cases of successful collective invention: the case documented by Allen (1983) of the Cleveland (UK) iron industry between 1850 and 1875; the case documented by MacLeod (1988, pp. 112–13, 188) of the English clock- and instrument makers, and the case documented by Nuvolari (2004) of the Cornish steam-engine makers after 1800. Examples of such cases are not many and they required rather special circumstances that were not common, and collective invention in its more extreme form, to judge from its short lifespans, was vulnerable and ephemeral.

On a more general level, however, Gentlemanly Capitalism generated a great deal of cooperation in the generation of technological progress. The main point to keep in mind is that many and perhaps most of the people who generated useful knowledge during the British Industrial Revolution did not do so *primarily* to make money. This does not mean that they were indifferent to money (though a few were independently wealthy) but rather that the game they were in was not a profit-maximizing project but a signaling game in which individuals tried to demonstrate to their peers their intellectual and technical capabilities. Useful knowledge that was not immediately patentable (and some that was) was placed in the public realm.[23] Scientific discoveries of any kind were to be published and communicated.[24]

When the unusual case occurred that an eccentric scientist (for example John Flamsteed, the first astronomer royal, or the pathologically shy Henry Cavendish, a leading chemist of the second half of the eighteenth century) refused to do so, others would take exception.

Open science, much like open source technology, was not practiced primarily by idealistic altruists whose objective was the warm glow from seeing humanity enriched by their knowledge (though there were some of those). It was run by ambitious and hard working people who had clear objectives in mind. Yet the standard pecuniary incentive system central to the economic interpretation of technological change must be supplemented by a more complex one that includes peer recognition and the sheer utility of being able to do what one desires. Credit was given in terms of reputation, which correlated with university positions, court-related appointments, public honors, and sometimes a pension from a ruler or a rich citizen. But scientists, in order to be trusted and believed, had to establish reputations as gentlemen as well (Shapin, 1994). Even those scientists who discovered matters of significant importance to industry, such as Claude Berthollet, Count Rumford, Joseph Priestley, or Humphry Davy, usually wanted credit, not profit.[25]

Berthollet willingly shared his knowledge of the bleaching properties of chlorine with some savvy Scots, who soon were able to turn his discovery into a profitable venture. ‘When one loves science’, wrote Berthollet to one of those Scots, James Watt, ‘one had little need for fortune which would only risk one’s happiness’ (cited by Musson and Robinson, 1969, p. 266). The great engineer John Smeaton took only one patent in his entire illustrious career, his colleague John Rennie none at all. Some entrepreneurs, too, refused to take out patents out of principle. Abraham Darby II declined to take out a patent on his coke-smelting process allegedly saying that ‘he would not deprive the public from such an acquisition’ (cited by MacLeod, 1988, p. 185) and Richard Trevithick, a century later, likewise failed to take out a patent on his high pressure engine. William Godwin noted in 1798 that ‘Knowledge is communicated to too many individuals to afford its adversaries a chance of suppressing it. The monopoly of science is substantially at an end. By the easy multiplication of copies and the cheapness of books, everyone has access to them’ (Godwin, 1798, pp. 282–3). In that more general sense, social norms did have an effect on technology, though it is hard to quantify them.

A third mechanism linking trust and ‘culture’ to technological progress in eighteenth-century Britain concerns the formation of human capital. As I have argued elsewhere, what set Britain apart from other European countries was not its capacity to accumulate more and better science or even a higher propensity to invent, but the much higher level of *competence* of its skilled workers. Britain could draw on a large cadre of highly skilled craftsmen and technicians. These people might not have been the flashy inventors who came up with the revolutionary insights, but they were those who could read a blueprint, understood practical technicalities such as tolerance, lubrication, tension, and torque, and had experience with the qualities of iron, wood, leather and other materials (Mokyr, 2009).[26] Harris (1992, p. 33) describes them as 'unanalysable pieces of expertise, the "knacks" of the trade', that is to say, knowledge that is primarily tacit and could not be learned except through experience and imitation. Harris's view may be conditioned by his expertise of the coal and iron industry, but much of the same was true in hardware, textiles, instrument-making, and engineering. He notes that such skills were taken for granted at home and thus were noted mostly by foreign visitors, including industrial spies (ibid., p. 26, see also Harris, 1998).[27] It was understood that these skills could not be readily transferred from country to country.[28]

The evidence that Britain's comparative advantage was in the skills and competence of her workmen as much as in the characteristics of her entrepreneurs is above all that it imported technological ideas and exported machines and skilled workmen, even if there were legal restrictions on those exports.[29] When it imported an invention, such as the Jacquard loom or chlorine bleaching, Britain improved them by a sequence of microinventions. The reverberatory furnace, first described by Vanoccio Biringuccio in 1540 in glassblowing , was adopted in Britain in the early seventeenth century. By 1700, this device had been adapted successfully to non-ferrous metals by unknown British skilled workmen before its famous adaptation to iron-puddling. The British paper industry, imported the Frenchman Nicolas Robert's paper-making machinery, but British mechanics such as Bryan Donkin and Henry Fourdrinier made important improvements in it. Chlorine bleaching, invented in France, was perfected by the Scotchman Charles Tennant, who made a fortune in the process.

What were the institutional causes of Britain's high level of competence? It had preciously little to do with institutions of formal education, even if some of the dissenting academies were increasingly committed to teach practical skills. There were no engineering schools until about 1830, and even then they were limited in range. Instead, it was almost entirely the result of apprenticeships. It was the product of a process of human capital formation that relied precisely on the kind of trust that contracts would be honored even if the fine details of daily contact between master and apprentice were impossible to specify, much less monitor. Britain's increasingly weak guilds had little to do with this enforcement, and indeed there is some evidence from court cases that in many cases the process went awry. All the same, while courts provided some kind of protection of last resort, the normal case was clearly for the contract to be carried out and most apprentices completed their terms. It has been estimated that in the eighteenth century about two thirds of all British lads completed their apprenticeships.

Those who did on average benefitted economically. Despite the fact that apprenticeship relationships lent themselves to opportunistic behavior (such as hold-up strategies by both master and apprentice, depending on the timing pattern of the training), the system served Britain well and supplied it with a layer of skilled artisans like no other because apprenticeship contracts were largely self-enforcing and efficient (Humphries, 2003).[30] Apprenticeship took place within a 'traditional network of friends, neighbours, co-religionists, and next of kin' (Humphries, 2007, p. 11).[31] The apprentices themselves had quite a few incentives to complete their contract: only an apprentice with a completed term received the right of settlement in a county, and in those areas and trades controlled by guilds, they were barred from practicing a trade if they did not complete their term.[32] This stricture was repealed in 1814, but the institution of apprenticeship survived. It was obviously to a large extent self-enforcing rather than dependent on the letter of the law or the power of the guild. In the later nineteenth century apprenticeship as an institution was weakened, yet it was sufficiently flexible to withstand the changes and survive until deep into the twentieth century. Apprenticeship was ideal to transmit the kind of tacit artisanal knowledge that was the essential component of competence. It was not perfect, but by all appearances it worked as a self-enforcing institution rather than as one that relied entirely on third party enforcement (though for the social norms to work, a recourse to legal action as a *pis aller* was necessary).

To summarize, it is the complementary relation between the human capital and the social capital that explains Britain's leadership in the Industrial Revolution. The economy that could produce the technical acumen to follow up on new ideas and turn them into an economic reality was also able to create a group of entrepreneurs to exploit it, people with the ability to take advantage of the opportunities that the inventors and the mechanics created. This relationship appears up in the many pairings of technical ability and businessmen. Boulton found his Watt, Clegg his Murdoch, Marshall his Murray, and Cooke his Wheatstone. These pairings were made possible by a network of information flows and personal relationships that made trust and cooperation *within a certain class of people* the default. Here, too, the importance of private order seems predominant, and while they, too, existed in the shadow of the law, the success of the institutions was determined by its self-enforcing properties.

## 1.4. INSTITUTIONS, POLITICS, AND ECONOMIC PROGRESS

Why did sustained economic growth not occur more often and in more places before the nineteenth century? One standard argument is that technology was constrained by the poor understanding of the fundamental principles of the natural regularities that made certain technologies work (Mokyr, 2002). The alternative argument is one of negative feedback. In one version, Malthusian dynamics undid any gains in technology, institutions, and even favorable environmental shocks (Clark, 2007). To that, however, we should add the underappreciated problem of negative institutional feedback and institutional inertia, which held back pre-industrial societies. Jones (1988) has gone so far as to argue that growth might well have been the normal state in pre-industrial societies had not institutional blockages again and again terminated it.

Before 1800 economic growth was more of a regional than a national phenomenon; throughout the pre-industrial past there were some areas and cities that did well for a variety of reasons. Such local wealth gave rise to two kinds of negative institutional feedback: *internal* feedback, in which local priests, rulers, and powerful strongmen tried to extricate the rents for their own use and *external* feedback, generated by strong but poor neighbors or more remote predators. One way or another, regions that did well through trade or manufacturing were likely to attract predators like flies to honey. Time and again, prosperous regions in Germany, Central Europe, the Low Countries, and Northern Italy, had their wealth physically destroyed through war, their trade impeded by tariffs, navigation acts, and privateers, or were forced to spend crippling amounts on defense. In this world growth, in an almost dialectical way, generated the mechanisms that undid it.

In the eighteenth century, the political culture of Britain gradually turned away from the zero-sum approach and slowly became more liberal and more enlightened. Two political phenomena were at the center of this process. One was the centralization of rent-seeking and lobbying. By allowing growing domestic market integration (through turnpike and canal bills, for instance), Parliament oversaw the gradual disappearance of local monopolies. By the late eighteenth century, Prime Minister William Pitt refused to meddle in local matters, which were 'large areas of policy in which ministers and party politicians need not involve themselves' (Langford, 1991, p. 205). Rent-seeking and redistribution remained an essential part of the Hanoverian state until the closing years of the eighteenth century, but it became more nation-wide and coordinated. Mercantilist practices had been mostly part of a complex rent-seeking alliance between crown and mercantile interests (Ekelund and Tollison, 1997). Once centralized, however, the process was more amenable to changes from the top down (Mokyr and Nye, 2007). The striking fact is that the Industrial Revolution was accompanied, on the whole, by a growing liberalization of economic activity.

The other was the growing backlash against rent-seeking. Why and how did redistribution fall on hard times in Europe during and after the Industrial Revolution? Part of the reason must have been that these institutions had been very much part of the zero-sum mentality of the pre-enlightenment world. The notion that exclusionary rents were on the whole Pareto-dominated did not come naturally to most actors, either on the giving or the receiving end of rent-generating privileges. The areas against which British (and continental) policy makers particularly aimed their arrows were monopolies, subsidies, labor market restrictions, tariffs, poor relief, and price controls. By 1850, much of this regulatory machinery had been dismantled. Foreign trade, too, was regarded differently with eighteenth-century enlightenment thought foreshadowing the insights of political economy.[33] The growing influence of the beneficial effects of trade promulgated by Smith and Ricardo made their mark on policy makers (Grampp, 1987; Mokyr, 2006b).[34]

Enlightenment-induced changes in ideology and beliefs on the part of policy makers in charge of writing the rules played a central role in the American and French Revolutions, as well as the various reforms attempted in various European nations before 1789 (Scott, 1990). Reforms in Britain did not always come easy even if they did not require a Bastille. The liberal reforms of the 1780s (including the Eden treaty with France in 1786) made room for the more conservative and reactionary 1790s and early1800s, when war with Revolutionary France caused a retrenchment. But it was *reculer pour mieux sauter*. After Waterloo, the reform movement picked up steam led by both Whigs and so-called liberal Tories, and within a few decades had dismantled much of the remaining rent-seeking apparatus. Thus, the Statute of Artificers was abolished in 1814, the enumeration clauses (that forced British colonial goods to be shipped to third markets through Britain) in the Navigation Acts were repealed in 1822, the monopoly of the East India company was ended by two parliamentary acts in 1813 and 1833, the law prohibiting the emigration of artisans was repealed in 1824, the export prohibition on machinery was weakened in 1824 and repealed in 1843, the Bubble Act thrown out in 1825.[35] Other exclusionary arrangements that fell out of favor were serfdom and colonial slavery, prohibitions restricting the use of certain kinds of machinery, usury laws (repealed as late as 1854 but rarely enforced long before), and similar rent-seeking relics. As Nye (2007) has argued, protection was the last vestige of privilege and the ancient regime economy to go. By the middle of the nineteenth century, it is hard to find many instances of the kind of age-of-mercantilism rent-seeking that still predominated in 1721 when Robert Walpole became the first Prime Minister.

Perhaps the most telling proof of the change in political culture is the sharp decline in patronage and sinecures, that in 1750 still had been very much part of the power structure. The transition from Walpole to Pitt marks one of the most notable shifts in political culture. The forms of government spending that constituted a possible source of corruption and waste (pensions, fees, and the salaries of corrupt officers) in the 1780s and 1790s constituted at most 2 percent of annual spending, less than a quarter than in France (Brewer, 1988, p. 73). These figures do not, of course, include further corruption and waste in military spending and the appointment of officers, but still indicates that British government was turning away from ancien régime rent-seeking modes of government. By 1830, the Duke of Wellington said that as prime minister he commanded virtually no patronage (cited by Rubinstein, 1983, p. 57). By the mid-1830s, the total cost of all unreformed sinecures was estimated at under £17,000, down from £200,000 two decades earlier (Harling, 1995, p. 136). Rent-seeking in all its manifestations had become socially and politically unacceptable in early nineteenth-century Britain. There is no good explanation for this decline except to attribute it to the impact of Enlightenment thought, filtering through many layers and channels to the minds of the members of the British political elite in both parties. In England the influence of the Enlightenment had been more mixed with religious sentiment than in Scotland or on the Continent. Evangelical beliefs of what was moral mixed with Enlightenment notions of what was socially desirable to produce a regime that cultivated a governing style of disinterested public service. When the process was complete, by the second third of the nineteenth century, the British economy was as free of distributional institutions as any economy can ever hope to be.

A similar change happened, if somewhat belatedly, to international economic relations. Predatory warfare between the major European nations, continental and colonial, remained the rule during much of the eighteenth century and was a direct outgrowth of the zero-sum ideology that underlay Mercantilist-Cameralist policies. After the defeat of Napoleon, such predatory wars within Europe became rare, although Europeans obviously did not include non-western nations in their more enlightened approach to foreign policy. Whether the century of the *Pax Britannica* was entirely attributable to a new and less aggressive political outlook in Europe or the result of a new balance of power is unclear, but the few wars fought on European soil after 1815 (or elsewhere in the world between European colonial powers) were less predatory, destructive, and costly to the industrializing powers. As a result, the fruits of economic growth were not wasted on military spending and wars until the disasters of 1914 and beyond.

The enforcement of property rights through private-order institutions reflects something deep and supremely important about British institutions in the eighteenth century. The culture of respectability and gentility helped, if only for a while, solve the standard collective action problems that bedevil the production of public goods. The emergence of a plethora of networks, clubs, friendly societies, academies, and associations created a civil society, in which the private provision of public goods became a reality. What was true for property right enforcement was true for other projects where elsewhere in Europe the State played a major role. Roads, harbors, bridges, lighthouses, river navigation improvements, drainage works, and canals were initiated through private subscriptions. In some case, of course, there was the hope of making a profit, but commonly the entrepreneurs were motivated by the desire to improve local trade and employment. Voluntary associations founded hospitals, schools, orphanages, prosecution societies, charitable relief committees, as well as turnpike and canal trusts.[36] The belief that an improvement in the condition of the poor required knowledge of social conditions necessitated the collection of information and data about social conditions, and this knowledge, too, became a central tenet of the later Enlightenment. A typical institution was the Society for Bettering the Condition of the Poor, founded in 1797. Its founder wrote 'let us make the inquiry into all that concerns the poor and the promotion of their happiness into a science' (cited by George, 1966, p. 25). These philanthropic projects, typical of the age: a project that elsewhere was carried out by the State or the Catholic Church, they were voluntary and patterned after a commercial organizations, replete with a board of directors.

The way British society overcame the paradoxes of collective action in the eighteenth century was through reputation mechanisms. People wanted to do good, because they wanted to be seen as good, and that was to their advantage. This was particularly true in the new industrial urban areas, where the old poor law was less effective. Collective action to palliate the effects of economic crises were particularly necessary and effective in the new industrial cities. Middle class people wanted to take part in a community of socially-minded individuals (Lewis, 2001, pp. 250–55). Many of these organizations were subsequently confirmed by statutory authority acts, but they were initiated and managed by the spontaneous organization of private individuals, who banded together voluntarily to accomplish a common goal. These organizations formed a substitute for a more powerful and aggressive central government and they go some way toward explaining how an economy with a weak state was, all the same, so successful in transforming its economy faster and smoother than its rivals in Europe.

To sum up, what is most striking is what did not happen. The British state may have had the theoretical capability to be more predatory and repressive, but was generally constrained from doing so. Taxes, while heavy in the eighteenth century and even more so during the French Wars, were levied primarily on consumption of the middle classes, whereas landowners (who had the political power to block progress) saw their relative tax burden lighten and entrepreneurs had no real worry that the government would in some way expropriate their profits. The Industrial Revolution began to generate large surpluses and profits for entrepreneurs and those who owned the resources they needed, though their exact timing and magnitude are not quite clear. These surpluses could have readily been expropriated by the powerful political factions that controlled British government, and used for their own benefit or perhaps to bankroll colonial adventures. Nothing of the sort happened. Once the distractions of the Napoleonic Wars were over, the income tax was abolished with great glee, and real government spending per capita was sharply contracted.[37] After Waterloo a more liberal creed began to replace the mercantilist instincts that had still ruled during much of the Hanoverian years. Neither the British government nor powerful special interests had more than a nibble from the gains that improving technology generated.

Another blockage to economic progress before the Industrial Revolution was resistance by vested interests, who had large fixed capital invested in the technological and political status quo. Acemoglu et al. (2005) raise a central question: if the income distributions in all societies were closely associated with the distribution of political power, why would anyone in a position to block change ever agree to give it up? In Britain, the landed classes had traditionally controlled much of Parliament, after 1688 in an informal coalition with the resurgent mercantile interests. Both of these groups had a lot to gain from maintaining the status quo in which mercantilist measures channeled rents to merchants and shipping interests and landlords received bounties on farm exports. How did this cosy arrangement slip between their fingers in the nineteenth century? In terms of political economy, the astonishing fact remains that the coalition that controlled parliament until deep in the nineteenth century, the large landlords and the merchant-financial elite, did not block the process that was to end their grip on power and enfranchised the middle class. Indeed, in a series of measures starting in the early 1820s and culminating in the great reform acts of 1829 and 1832, they opened the political process and provided increased political power to groups that had previously been excluded from de iure power.

Part of the answer must simply be that nobody saw it coming: the technological innovations of the Industrial Revolution transformed the British economy to a degree that was completely unforeseeable in the mid eighteenth century. Part of the answer was that the old coalition was given a soft landing, and that eventual losers were compensated and bribed to cooperate: the Corn Laws were renewed in 1815 to maintain the income of those classes in a position to block economic reforms and some of the old arrangements were phased out gingerly and gradually. A third part of the answer is that the old landowning class benefitted from the development, in part because of the continued rise in rents until 1815, but also because many of them were able to profit from the rise in value of urban properties, mining areas, and other real estate.[38] Economic losers who were not political losers, as Acemoglu et al. (2005, p. 435) maintain, would have been able to redistribute the incremental income to themselves if they retained political power. Indeed, the powerful British political elite did so, at least for a transition period long enough to absorb the shock and weaken their resistance. Finally, of course, there was the fear of rebellion. Commercial and industrial interests acquired *de facto* power during the Industrial Revolution, and obviously at some point those who wrote the rules had to heed their desires. Acemoglu and Robinson (2006, p. 350) argue that the concessions made after 1832 (they had actually started in the mid 1820s, with the repeal of the Combination Acts), were in large part motivated by a desire to pre-empt a rebellion or the need to repress it violently. Such pre-emptive action seems plausible (the British had closely followed the unfolding events in Paris in 1830), and it is clear that the Reform Crisis of 1831–32, including the rather serious Bristol riots in October 1831, was instrumental in bringing about reform (Stevenson, 1979, p. 221).

But the exact magnitude of the threat to overthrow the existing order remains unknown. The modest scale of British political riots, and the poor coordination between different groups suggests that the likelihood of success was never overwhelming. The reforms enfranchised the middle classes, but did little for the unskilled working poor, the displaced domestic workers, and paupers. Archer (2000, p. 93) concludes that the middle classes were as fearful of a violent revolution as any hard-line conservative. The Chartist movement, which was largely middle class and which in its early stages prompted a few outbreaks of local violence, actually followed rather than preceded the 1832 electoral reforms and led to no further franchise enlargements.[39] The year 1848 passed by relatively peacefully in Britain. On the other hand, any serious threat to the existing order would have been suppressed harshly. During the biggest threats, in the late 1790s and early 1800s, the government clamped down hard on dissidents through both legal and violent methods.

A separate role for changing ideology among the ruling elites therefore cannot be dismissed. Economic interests were important, but people at that time (or any other) do not vote *just* their pocketbook. The abolition of the profitable slave trade in 1807 was clearly a moral, not an economic choice.[40] The impact of liberal political economy, the Enlightenment's proudest offspring, on many of the policy makers of the epoch is visible simply by examining the beliefs of the leadership. The dominant figure in the 'liberal Tory' government of Lord Liverpool of the 1820s was William Huskisson, an avowed Smithian, who passed a series of tariff reductions and was instrumental in re-energizing the reform movement in the 1820s.[41] The Enlightenment led to the more extreme radical reform movement of the 1820s in which ideologues like Joseph Hume and Francis Place fought for reform legislation informed and inspired by Political Economy as they interpreted it. The astonishing historical fact is not that such radicals were tolerated (though Place was dubbed 'a bad man' for his outrageous advocacy of contraceptives; he himself sired sixteen children), but how successful they eventually proved to be in implementing their liberal programs.

The other potentially important institutional impediment to the Industrial Revolution was resistance by the interests most directly affected by the technological changes affecting various industries after 1750. Resistance to new technology by organized or unorganized workers was a major issue in the eighteenth century and remained so during the Industrial Revolution. The groups that were on the losing end were above all domestic-industry workers who were being out-competed by factories, artisans of various levels of skills whose human capital was threatened by obsolescence, and small-scale farmers, the victims of the enclosure movement. These groups had access to a variety of effective means that were a times quite successful: from peaceful petitions to Parliament to legal strikes, to illegal rioting and machine-breaking, skilled and semi-skilled workers found ways to signal their disapproval. Many of these struggles had short-term or local effects, and may well have slowed down the path of technological change in some regions.[42] The struggle over 'employment' can be seen in part as one over the sunk cost in specific human capital, and in part over threatened local market power. In fact, if there was ever a serious chance of popular uprising (Acemoglu and Robinson's *de facto* power), this may have been it. But the state did not make many concessions; it cracked down mercilessly on rioters, siding unilaterally with innovating employers.

In the 1790s and early 1800s the world was inevitably viewed by British policy makers in harsher terms than the peaceful harmony between cooperative nations that Enlightenment writers dreamed about. The implication of this new outlook was that in a hostile world Britain could not afford to pass on technological opportunities and supported employers against workers. In 1806, a Committee was appointed to decide the complaints of the West Country clothiers into the new gig mills that they felt threatened their livelihood. It is telling that the final report of the committee was written by William Wilberforce, M.P., better known for his successful moral campaign against the slave trade. These principles supported the employers' rights without any hesitation. There can be no doubt that the concern about foreign competition was the main motive of the men in power to refuse the demands of the anti-innovation lobbies.[43] While the *Report* piously reiterated its conventional recognition of the 'merits and value of the domestic system,' it also felt that the 'apprehensions about it being rooted out by the Factory System were *at present at least* wholly without foundation' (Great Britain, 1806, p. 10, emph. added). Above all, however, Wilberforce and his colleagues regarded as gospel that 'the right of every man to employ [his] Capital according to his own discretion... is one of those privileges every Briton considers his birthright' (Wilberforce, 1838, p. 12).[44] The resistance movement went underground, but with enough determination and force on the part of the State, it had little chance to prevail. The people in power had made up their minds – the eighteenth century was over. The determined and sometimes harsh policy in support of innovation was not entirely due to enlightened beliefs in the salutary effects of technological progress. Nationalism (and especially the fear of France) played as important a role. But liberal political economy had assigned to government a well-defined role, and redistributing income was not one of them.

There are other answers to the question why the lower classes, both the working and the indigent poor, did not rebel more. British institutions provided something no other state did, a mandatory outdoor poor-relief system that remained in force until 1834. Its net effects on industrialization remains a matter of dispute (Solar, 1995). The Poor Law provided a big carrot next to a large stick of violent suppression and achieved its main goal, namely domestic order. The British government, more than in any other state West of the Elbe river, was able to keep its laboring poor in their place. The Poor Law, by providing the poorest workers with a safety net and thus reducing the need to cling to land at all costs, contributed to the creation of a proletariat needed for the factories and the railroad. It also helped in smoothing the labor supply both cyclically and seasonally. In addition, the Poor Law supported the practice of so-called pauper apprenticeships. The provision of young factory workers from workhouses run by local Poor Law guardians provided an important source of unskilled labor for the factories, especially in rural and small-town mills before 1800.[45] All the same, the magnitude of these effects is hard to ascertain and in all probability was second order.

## 1.5. CONCLUSION

What were the institutional origins of the Industrial Revolution? As argued, this question only makes sense if we distinguish the 'big question' (why

Europe?) from the 'small question' (why Britain?).We should emphasize that the differences between Britain and its European competitors was one of degree and of timing. The question is what kind of institutional environment, formal and informal, was most fertile to the successful sprouting of the seeds of the Industrial Revolution? The commercial environment and incentives that institutions created for the innovators and entrepreneurs who made the Industrial Revolution may have been central to Britain's leadership, even if they are harder to observe and measure than differences in the availability of coal. In part, its success was due to adaptive flexibility: the formal institutions of the British polity, rather than being 'right' or 'wrong,' proved to be sufficiently agile to change with the changing needs of the economy. Eventually, many of these advantages that gave Britain its lead were weakened and the lead that it had in the Industrial Revolution was lost. To the extent that the Enlightenment and its political and economic effects were important, other European nations could take equal advantage of them.

The solution to 'the commitment problem' after 1688 and the role of Parliament in constraining the executive have been at the center of the literature until now. We need, however, to be concerned with a wider set of issues than just the matter of 'who shall guard the guardian'. In part, the answer to the question of economic success in this age is about the informal social norms that defined the cultural beliefs of the elites, and allowed market exchange and innovation to operate in a regime of low transactions costs and reasonably self-enforcing norms of what Greif has called private-order contract-enforcement institutions. Hence, we need to consider the cultural beliefs of the political and technological elites. Cooperative behavior and trust based on gentlemanly codes allowed not just market exchange to operate but also created opportunities for new technology by allowing partnerships between inventors and entrepreneurship, and by providing Britain with a large contingent of highly skilled and dexterous craftsmen through well-functioning apprenticeships.

Institutional analysis is an important component of the emergence of modern economic growth and not just its continuation at later because the British Industrial Revolution occurred in a society that overcame successfully and at comparatively low cost the institutional obstacles to sustained economic growth in earlier times. Technological inertia, negative feedback, and opportunistic behavior at both the micro and the macro level were gradually overcome in Britain in the century after the Glorious Revolution. In addition, formal institutions, above all the changing role and orientation of Parliament, complemented the changes in informal institutions, to create an unexpected confluence of factors and circumstances that created the British Industrial Revolution. Enlightenment ideas, through a variety of mechanisms, influenced decision makers and legislators, hence real outcomes.

Assessing the 'importance' of institutions relative to other factors such as geography or demography assumes a separability that may be ahistorical. The synergy created by the interaction between the growth of useful knowledge in the eighteenth century and the formal and informal institutions that emerged side-by-side suggests a strong complementarity. With just technological progress but no institutional change, the process would have hit barriers that would have aborted the take-off, as in nineteenth century Russia. Had there been only better institutions, but no technological advances, the system would have similarly run out of steam and asymptoted off into a new stationary state (Mokyr 2006a). Sustainable and continuous economic growth needed both.

## NOTES

* A slightly different version of this chapter has been published in Helpman (2008). Parts of this essay are also based on Mokyr (2009) and other essays as cited in the text. The comments of Avner Greif, Elhanan Helpman, Deirdre McCloskey, Michael Silver and Joachim Voth on an earlier version are acknowledged with gratitude.

1. North (1981, p. 166) comes close to linking the institutional changes of the late eighteenth century with the Industrial Revolution when he maintains that it was explained by 'a combination of better-specified and enforced property rights and increasingly efficient and expanding markets'. North and Weingast (1989, p. 831) are more prudent and wonder if arguing that without the Glorious Revolution the British economy would have followed a very different path and would not have experienced an Industrial Revolution would be 'claiming too much'.
2. Stewart (1794, p. 72), who adds that the sentence appears in a small manuscript that was now in his possession, but which was not to be published.
3. By 1760, the great legal scholar Blackstone complained that 'Yet, though ... we may glory in the wisdom of the English law, we shall find it more difficult to justify the frequency of Capital Punishment to be found therein, inflicted ... by a multitude of successive independent statutes upon crimes very different in their natures'. He added that the list was so dreadful that crime-victims were reluctant to press charges and juries reluctant to convict (Blackstone, 1765–69, Vol. 4, p. 18).
4. This argument has been made with great emphasis by Hay (1975), who stressed the strong class-bias in eighteenth-century British criminal law. For a critique, see Langbein (1983), who has argued effectively that the bark of these draconian criminal codes was worse than their bite.
5. Eighteenth-century law enforcement was in the hands of local magistrates and a part-time local parish constables. For the rest, justice had to rely on volunteers, local informers, vigilante groups, and private associations specializing in prosecutions of felons. Some 450 such organizations were established in England between 1744 and 1856. London developed its first constables after Henry Fielding was appointed magistrate at Bow Street in 1748, and his professional assistants or thieftakers became known as 'Bow Street Runners'. Yet it was

not until after 1830 that anything remotely resembling a professional police force began to emerge in the rest of Britain and as late as 1853, half the counties in Britain were still without police. In fact, the eighteenth-century idea of 'police' was quite different from ours: the word meant something like a series of regulations and regulatory agencies for the supervision of the manners, morals, and health of society rather than a body of officers (Paley, 2004).

6. Small debts could be settled through courts of voluntary arbitration known as Courts of Conscience (also known as Courts of Requests), which became increasingly popular after 1750 for settling debts without the burden of expensive court cases. These courts, significantly, were unpopular among working people who objected to the way they dealt with tallies run up in ale houses — a tell-tale sign that they were effective.
7. The most likely alternative to a decline in litigiousness is that courts became less accessible and more costly. On the other hand, courts enforced contracts (both written and verbal) increasingly through procedures called 'actions on the case' (such as assumpsit for debt) in which courts enforced contracts without a formal trial (though such trials could sometimes still result). Brooks (1989, p. 91) adds that it is even possible that the high volume of trials in the seventeenth century may have exerted a 'pedagogic effect' on debitor–creditor relationships.
8. Francis Place (1771–1854), the radical politician and reformer, for instance, noted that 'the progress made in refinement of manners and morals seems to have gone on simultaneously with the improvement in arts, manufactures and commerce ... we are a much better people than we were [half a century ago], better instructed, more sincere and kind-hearted, less gross and brutal' (cited by George, 1966, p. 18). Beattie (1986, pp. 138–9) concurs with this view, and concludes that in 1800 British cities, and especially London, were less violent and dangerous places than in 1660.
9. The term 'bargaining in the shadow of the law' originates with Mnookin and Kornhauser (1979).
10. As Brewer (1982, p. 214), who was one of the first to point to the importance of this phenomenon, noted, 'reliability, fairness and generosity were the qualities most highly valued ... these attitudes oiled the wheels of commerce and enabled men to make greater profits'.
11. Adam Smith, in his *Lectures of Jurisprudence*, thought he had the answer: 'Whenever commerce is introduced into any country, probity and punctuality always accompany it. These virtues in a rude and barbarous country are almost unknown. Of all the nations in Europe, the Dutch, the most commercial, are the most faithfull to their word ... There is no natural reason why an Englishman or a Scotchman should not be as punctual in performing agreements as a Dutchman. It is far more reduceable to self interest, that general principle which regulates the actions of every man, and which leads men to act in a certain manner from views of advantage, and is as deeply implanted in an Englishman as a Dutchman. A dealer is afraid of losing his character, and is scrupulous in observing every engagement ... Where people seldom deal with one another, we find that they are somewhat disposed to cheat, because they can gain more by a smart trick than they can lose by the injury which it does their character' ([1757]1958, p. 327).
12. Defoe (1703, p. 19) famously wrote that 'Wealth, however got, in England makes lords of mechanics, gentlemen of rakes; Antiquity and birth are needless here; Tis impudence and money makes a peer'. Dr. Johnson, in the same spirit, noted that 'An English tradesman is a new species of gentleman' if he prospered sufficiently (Porter, 1990, p. 50). McCloskey (2006, pp. 294–6) traces the transformation of the word 'honor' in English and French from its aristocratic sense ('reputation') to its more capitalist sense of 'honesty' (reliability, truth-telling) and 'politeness' ('doing the right thing') when the importance of these concepts

began to increase in the eighteenth century, and discovers that the same change occurred in the Dutch language.

13. By the mid-Victorian times, this was expressed almost as a caricature by Samuel Smiles describing what really mattered for the gentleman: 'The true gentleman has a keen sense of honour – scrupulously avoiding mean actions. His standard of probity in word and action is high. He does not shuffle or prevaricate, dodge or skulk; but is honest, upright, and straightforward. His law is rectitude – action in right lines. When he says YES, it is a law ... Above all, the gentleman is truthful. He feels that truth is the "summit of being", and the soul of rectitude in human affairs' (Smiles, 1859).
14. As Daunton (1989, p. 125) summarizes the traditional argument, 'the more an occupation or a source of income allowed for a life style which was similar to that of the landed classes, the higher the prestige it carried and the greater the power it conferred. The gentleman-capitalist did not despise the market economy but he did hold production in low regard and avoided full-time work'.
15. An example of this kind of arrangement existed in Manchester in the 1820s, where the Manchester Fire and Life Assurance Company's boardroom provided 'interconnected circuits of political, business, and social activities' to generate not only information underlying collective action but also regarding the reputations of the major players. Similar conditions were noted among Bristol sugar refiners in 1769 (Pearson, 1991, p. 388).
16. John Locke, for instance, wrote in 1693 that a gentleman's upbringing should endow him with a love of virtue and reputation to make him from within 'a good, a vertuous, and able man' and with 'Habits woven into the very Principles of his Nature', not because he feared retribution but because this defined his very character (Locke, [1693]1732, pp. 46–7). Many decades later, the French historian Hippolyte Taine, who stayed in London in 1858, summarized the concept of a gentleman as 'the three syllables that summarize the history of English society' (Taine [1872], 1958, p. 144). The essence of the gentleman as Locke and his successors saw him 'was to be his integrity' (Carter 2002, p. 335). Paul Langford (2000, p. 126) observes that one of the British aristocracy's prime characteristics was the belief in fair play and that a cheating lord was a traitor to his class.
17. The French traveler Pierre Jean Grosley noted the 'politeness, civility and officiousness' of citizens and shopkeepers 'whether great or little' (Grosley, 1772, Vol. 1, pp. 89, 92). The eighteenth-century Italian writer and philosopher Alessandro Verri felt that London merchants were far more trustworthy than their Paris counterparts (cited by Langford, 2000, p. 124). One French visitor to early-nineteenth-century London noted that British shopkeepers were fundamentally honest, and that a child could shop as confidently as the most street-wise market shopper (Nougaret, 1816, vol. ii, p. 12). Charles Dupin (1825, pp. xi–xii) went as far as to attribute Britain's economic successes to the 'wisdom, the economy and above all the probity' of its citizens. Reputation was critical. Prosper Mérimée, commenting on the open access policies in the British Museum Library in 1857, observed that 'The English have the habit of showing the greatest confidence in everyone possessing character, that is, recommended by a gentleman ... whoever obtains one is careful not to lose it, for he cannot regain it once lost' (1930, pp. 153–4).
18. 'At my begining I was too credulos and too slow in caling, and seldom made use of atturney, except to write letters to urge payments, being always tender of oppressing poor people with law charges, but rather to loose all or get what I could quietly, than give it to atturnies. And I never sued any to execution for debt, nor spend 20s in prosecuting any debter, and to loose all was more satisfaction to me than getting all to the great cost of my debtor, and to the preservation of my reputation' (Stout, 1967, pp. 120–21).

19. The extent of the spreading of these clubs is reflected by the founding of the Sublime Club of Beefsteaks' devoted to carnivory in 1735. The total number of friendly societies membership in 1800 is estimated at 600,000 (Porter, 1990, pp. 156–7).
20. Pearson (1991) documents in details the interconnected political, social, and financial networks of Manchester's cotton elite in the post 1815 period. These tight circuits were more effective in provincial towns, where information flowed more easily than in the metropole, and may have been a contributor to the advantage that provincial towns had over the capital.
21. The great ironmonger John Wilkinson, who played such a strategic role in helping Watt cast his cylinders, invested widely outside his field of expertise such as banks, agricultural improvements, mines, and the many canals promoted by his friend and fellow ironmaster, Richard Crawshay. Profits made in shipbuilding and banking were invested in breweries (Mathias, 1959, p. 240). Abraham Darby III invested not only in turnpike trusts but also in the great hotel built to face his great iron bridge in Coalbrookdale. The woolen manufacturer Edward Pease became George Stephenson's partner and a major entrepreneurial force in the early railroad enterprises.
22. Recent work on the history of entrepreneurs in the United States seems to have come to the same conclusion that networks and trust-through-connections are as important in entrepreneurial success as talent and ambition. See Laird (2006).
23. Other early examples of such priority disputes can be cited such as the dispute between Newton and Hooke (about the inverse-square force law) or the battle between two Dutchmen, Jan Swammerdam and Reinier de Graaf, on the discovery of certain aspects of female reproduction.
24. This process has been documented in great detail by Eamon (1994, pp. 319–50) who pointed to the influence of Francis Bacon and his followers in establishing this rule, as they realized that any progress was going to be the result of a cooperative effort. More recently Paul David (2004) has argued that open science established the quality of intellectual superstars, much in demand by courts and universities for prestige reasons.
25. A recent survey (Bowler and Morus, 2005, pp. 320–21) refers to the class of 'gentlemanly specialists', men who led the development of useful knowledge but did not make their living from it and were suspicious of anyone who did. At the same time, those who were not independently wealthy needed to find patronage either as University Professors or from government, industry, or wealthy individuals.
26. Josiah Tucker, a keen contemporary observer, pointed out that 'the Number of Workmen [in Britain] and their greater Experience excite the higher Emulation, and cause them to excel the Mechanics of other Countries in theses Sorts of Manufactures' (Tucker, 1758, p. 26). He must have thought of men like John Whitehurst, William Murdoch, Bryan Donkin, John Wilkinson, John Kay, Edward Troughton, not quite hall of fame inventors, but brilliant craftsmen.
27. Harris singles out the competence of the British iron puddler, requiring not only skills but experience and 'almost artistic judgement,' and adds that foreigners would have had a hard time importing this competence, because it was the British skilled worker who was the repository of the knowledge. He absorbed the skills needed to work with coal and iron 'with the sooty atmosphere in which he lived' and would find it hard to know even what needed to be explained (Harris, 1992, pp. 28, 30)

28 The French scientists and industrialists Jean-Antoine Chaptal noted that in many branches of manufacturing the British had become dominant, but that even after importing the machinery the French could not compete and sold at twice the price of the British because they lacked the immense details, the customs, and the 'turns of hand' (dexterity) and that

while the slow progress of industry could be accelerated by learned men, there was no substitute for experience (Chaptal, 1819, Vol. 2, pp. 430–31).

29. The French political economist Jean-Baptiste Say, a keen observer of the economies of his time, noted in 1803 that 'the enormous wealth of Britain is less owing to her own advances in scientific acquirements, high as she ranks in that department, as to the wonderful practical skills of her adventurers in the useful application of knowledge and the superiority of her workmen' (Say [1803], 1821 Vol. I, pp. 32–3). Another Swiss visitor, De Saussure, had noticed the same seventy-five years earlier: 'English workmen are everywhere renowned, and justly. They work to perfection, and though not inventive, are capable of improving and of finishing most admirably what the French and Germans have invented' (de Saussure, 1902, p. 218, letter dated May 29, 1727). The great engineer John Farey, who wrote an important treatise on steam power, testified a century later that 'the prevailing talent of English and Scotch people is to apply new ideas to use, and to bring such applications to perfection, but they do not imagine as much as foreigners'.
30. Local studies have concluded that in the eighteenth century while masters had an incentive and opportunities to exploit and abuse the young, few apparently did so (Rushton, 1991, p. 101). Reputation effects seem to have been important here, since apprentices without parents protecting them were in greater jeopardy of being in some way cheated by their masters.
31. Humphries (2007, pp. 22–3) recounts a number of cases in which disputes between master and apprentice were resolved by social and reputational pressures, many of them supported by the need of the master to maintain his social relations with the parents. Her sample of hundreds of autobiographical accounts of working class people, provides a unique picture of the centrality of apprenticeship in the intergenerational transfer of human capital.
32. In 1777 the calico printers admitted that fewer than 10 percent of their workers had served because 'the trade does not require that the men they employ should be brought up to it; common labourers are sufficient' (Mantoux, 1928, p. 453).
33. Thus Jean-François Melon, a friend of Montesquieu's, wrote in the 1730s that the 'the spirit of commerce and of polity are inseparable ... the spirit of conquest and the spirit of commerce mutually exclude each other in a nation' and added that it was commerce, not violence that supplied the 'wisdom for preservation' (Melon, 1738, pp. 136–9).
34. Kindleberger (1978, p. 52) who admits that in some cases 'free trade is the hypocrisy of the export interest' felt that 'in the English case it was more a view of a world at peace, with cosmopolitan interests served as well as national'.
35. As Harris (2000) has shown, the Bubble Act was primarily used as an exclusionary tool by incumbents to reduce entry and competition.
36. The example of Thomas Coram, described eloquently by Colley (1992, pp. 56–60) is illustrative: a successful merchant, he became a leading philanthropist particularly concerned with foundlings and orphans, and established a famous foundling hospital in London in 1741. The Marine Society, established by Jonas Hanway in 1756, similarly was a project run by merchants.
37. Total government gross income went from a peak of £69.2m in 1817 to a trough of £56.3m in 1854. The national debt peaked at £844 m in 1819 and then fell to £774m in 1854. Nominal GDP went from £322m in 1821 to £718m in 1854, thus reducing per capita taxation by 57 percent and national indebtedness by 59 percent.
38. Rubinstein's rather heroic estimate of landed and non-landed millionaires and half millionaires dying between 1809 and 1859 shows 179 landed millionaires vs. 10 non-landed millionaires, and 338 landed half-millionaires as compared to 54 non-landed ones (Rubinstein, 1981, pp. 60–5). As Rubinstein (ibid., p. 61) remarks, 'an observer entering a

room full of Britain's 200 wealthiest men in 1825 might be forgiven for thinking that the Industrial Revolution had not occurred'.

39. William Lovett's Charter dated from 1838 and fizzled out after 1848, twenty tears before the next big electoral reform. The most serious outbreak of violence was the 1838 Newport riot that left fifteen people dead.
40. Scottish serfdom, a quaintly anachronistic institution in the eighteenth century that involved miners and salters was abolished in 1774 (the last traces were removed as late as 1799). These Acts, declared Parliament, would 'remove the reproach of allowing such a state of servitude to exist in a free country' (cited by Smout, 1969, p. 406).
41. Huskisson 'zealously and consistently subscribed to the theories of Adam Smith. Smith's teaching, reflected in practically every reform in the twenties' (Brady, 1967, p. 133). Equally well-documented is the enormous influence that *Wealth of Nations* had on other policy makers, especially after Dugald Stewart, Smith's successor at Edinburgh, turned the book into a fountainhead of wisdom (Herman, 2001, pp. 229–30; see also Rothschild, 2001). Among Stewart's pupils were two future Prime Ministers, Palmerston and John Russell. His program was to remove all state support and protection for manufacturing and agriculture.
42. Thus, in Wiltshire, shearmen through the 'Wiltshire outrages' of 1802 were able to prevent the introduction of gig mills until after 1815; the machinery destroyed during the Luddite riots took some years to replace; and as late as 1830, the Captain Swing riots delayed the introduction of agricultural machinery into the South of England by many years. Randall (1991, p. 289) feels that the resistance, at least in some areas, gave the artisans 'many extra years respite'.
43. The language used by the committee is telling: 'If Parliament had acted on such principles [on which the use of these particular machines is objected to] 50 years ago, the Woollen Manufacture would never have attained to half its present size ... its Augmentation is principally to be ascribed to the general spirit of enterprize and industry among a free and enlightened people ... It is likewise an important consideration ... that we are at this day surrounded by powerful and civilized Nations, who are intent on cultivating their Manufactures and pushing their Commerce' and specifically mentioned the worrisome evidence of such an establishment being set up in Paris. See Great Britain, B.P.P. 1806 No. 3 ('Select Committee on State of Woollen Manufacture of England'), p. 7.
44. As the biography written by his sons recalls, Wilberforce had to mediate between the valuable men 'of small capital who, with the aid of their own families, prepared the goods at home' and 'enterprising capitalists'. He laid down the 'clear principles on which trade must be conducted' (Wilberforce, 1838, Vol. 3, pp. 263–7).
45. Some of the transactions between Poor Law authorities and mill owners resembled the slave trade; for example, the purchase of seventy children from the parish of Clerkenwell by Samuel Oldknow in 1796 (Mantoux, 1928, p. 411).

## REFERENCES

Acemoglu, D. and J. Robinson (2006), *Economic Origins of Dictatorship and Democracy*, Cambridge: Cambridge University Press.

Acemoglu, D., S. Johnson and J. Robinson (2005), 'Institutions as a Fundamental Cause of Economic Growth', in P. Aghion and S. Durlauf (eds), *Handbook of Economic Growth*, Amsterdam: Elsevier, pp. 385–465.

Allen, R.C. (1983), 'Collective Invention', *Journal of Economic Behavior and Organization*, **4**(1), 605–33.
Archer, J.E. (2000), *Social Unrest and Popular Protest in England, 1780–1840*, Cambridge: Cambridge University Press.
Beattie, J.M. (1974), 'The Pattern of Crime in England, 1660–1800', *Past and Present*, **62**(Feb.), 47–95.
Beattie, J.M. (1986), *Crime and the Courts in England, 1660–1800*, Princeton: Princeton University Press.
Blackstone, W. (1765–69), *Commentaries on the Laws of England*, 1st Edition, Oxford: Clarendon Press. http://avalon.law.yale.edu/subject_menus/blackstone.asp.
Blanqui, A.-J. (1824), *Voyage d'un jeune Français en Angleterre et en Ecosse, pendant l'automne de 1823*, Paris: Dondey-Dupré père et fils.
Bowler, P.J. and I.R. Morus (2005), *Making Modern Science*, Chicago: University of Chicago Press.
Brady, A. (1967), *William Huskisson and Liberal Reform: an Essay on the Changes in Economic Policy in the Twenties of the Nineteenth Century*, London: Oxford University Press.
Brewer, J. (1988), *The Sinews of Power: War, Money and the English State, 1688–1783*, New York: Alfred A. Knopf.
Briggs, A. (1959), *The Age of Improvement*, London: Longman.
Brooks, C.W. (1989), 'Interpersonal Conflict and Social Tension: Civil Litigation in England, 1640–1830', in A.L. Beier, D. Cannadine and J.M. Rosenheim (eds), *The First Modern Society: Essays in English History in Honor of Lawrence Stone*, Cambridge: Cambridge University Press.
Cain, P. and A.G. Hopkins (1993), *British Imperialism: Innovation and Expansion*, Harlow, Essex: Longman.
Carter, P. (2002), 'Polite Persons: Character, Biography, and the Gentleman', *Transactions of the Royal Historical Society*, **12**, pp. 333–54.
Chaptal, J.-A.-C. (1819), *De l'industrie Françoise*, Paris: Chez A.-A. Renouard, 2 vols.
Clark, G. (2007), *Farewell to Alms: a Short Economic History of the World*, Princeton: Princeton University Press.
Clark, P. (2000), *British Clubs and Societies, 1580–1800: the Origins of an Associational World*, Oxford: Clarendon Press.
Colley, L. (1992), *Britons: Forging the Nation, 1707–1837*, New Haven: Yale University Press.
Colquhoun, P. (1797), *A Treatise on the Police of the Metropolis; Containing a Detail of the Various Crimes and Misdemeanors*, 5th edition, London: Printed by H. Fry, Finsbury-Place.
Cooter, R., S. Marks and R. Mnookin (1982), 'Bargaining in the Shadow of the Law: a Testable Model of Strategic Behavior', *Journal of Legal Studies*, **11**(2), 225–51.
Daunton, M.J. (1989), 'Gentlemanly Capitalism and British Industry 1820–1914', *Past and Present*, **122**(Feb.), 119–58.
David, P.A. (2004), 'Patronage, Reputation, and Common Agency Contracting in the Scientific Revolution', Stanford University, mimeo.

Defoe, D. (1703), *A Collection of the Writings of the Author of the True-born English-man*, London (no publisher listed).

Defoe, D. (1738), *The Complete English Tradesman*, 4th edition, 2 Vols, London: C. Rivington.

Dupin, C. (1825), *The Commercial Power of Great Britain: Exhibiting a Complete View of the Public Works Of this Country*, London: Printed for C. Knight, 2 vols.

Dutton, H.I. (1984), *The Patent System and Inventive Activity during the Industrial Revolution*, Manchester: Manchester University Press.

Eamon, W. (1994), *Science and the Secrets of Nature*, Princeton, N.J.: Princeton University Press.

Ekelund, R.B. Jr. and R. Tollison (1997), *Politicized Economies: Monarchy, Monopoly, and Mercantilism*, College Station: Texas A&M University Press.

Ellickson, R.C. (1991), *Order Without Law: How Neighbors Settle Disputes.* Cambridge, MA: Harvard University Press.

Emsley, C. (2005), *Crime and Society in England, 1750–1900*, 3rd edition, Harlow: Pearson Longman.

George, M.D. (1966), *London Life in the Eighteenth Century*, 2nd edition, Harmondsworth: Penguin Books.

Godwin, W. (1798), *Enquiry Concerning Political Justice and its Influence on Morals and Happiness*, 3rd edition, corrected, London: Paternoster-Row, printed for G.G. and J. Robinson.

Grampp, W.D. (1987a), 'How Britain Turned to Free Trade', *Business History Review*, **61**(1), 86–112.

Great Britain, B.P.P. (1806), no. 3, 'Select Committee on State of Woollen Manufacture of England'.

Greif, A. (2005), *Institutions and the Path to the Modern Economy: Lessons from Medieval Trade*, Cambridge: Cambridge University Press.

Grosley, P.J. (1772), *A Tour to London; or, New Observations on England, and its Inhabitants*, by M. Grosley, Translated from the French by Thomas Nugent, London: printed for Lockyer Davis.

Harling, P. (1995), 'Rethinking "Old Corruption"', *Past and Present*, **147**(May), 127–58.

Harris, J.R. (1992), 'Skills, Coal and British Industry in the Eighteenth Century', in *Essays in Industry and Technology in the Eighteenth Century*, Aldershot, UK: Ashgate.

Harris, J.R. (1998), *Industrial Espionage and Technology Transfer: Britain and France in the Eighteenth Century*, Aldershot, UK: Ashgate.

Harris, R. (2000), *Industrializing English Law: Entrepreneurship and Business Organization, 1720–1844*, Cambridge: Cambridge University Press.

Hay, D. (1975), 'Property, Authority and the Criminal Law', in D. Hay, P. Linebaugh, J. Rule, E.P. Thompson and C. Winslow (eds), *Albion's Fatal Tree: Crime and Society in Eighteenth-century England*, New York: Pantheon, pp. 17–63.

Helpman, E. (ed.) (2008), *Institutions and Economic Performance*. Cambridge, MA: Harvard University Press.

Hirschman, A.O. (1977), *The Passions and the Interests*, Princeton: Princeton University Press.
Humphries, J. (2003). 'English Apprenticeships: a Neglected Factor in the First Industrial Revolution', in P.A. David and M. Thomas (eds), *The Economic Future in Historical Perspective*, Oxford: Oxford University Press, pp. 73–102.
Humphries, J. (2007), *Through the Mill: Child Labour and the British Industrial Revolution*, Cambridge: Cambridge University Press, in press.
Jacob, M.C. (1997), *Scientific Culture and the Making of the Industrial West*, 2nd edition, New York: Oxford University Press.
Jones, E.L. (1988), *Growth Recurring Economic Change in World History*, Oxford: Oxford University Press.
Kindleberger, C.P. (1978), *Economic Response: Comparative Studies in Trade, Finance, and Growth*, Cambridge, MA: Harvard University Press.
Laird, P.W. (2006) *Pull: Networking and Success since Benjamin Franklin*, Cambridge, MA: Harvard University Press.
Langbein J.H. (1983), 'Albion's Fatal Flaws', *Past and Present*, **98**(Feb.), 96–120.
Langford, P. (1991), *Public Life and the Propertied Englishman, 1689–1798*, Oxford: The Clarendon Press.
Langford, P. (2000), *Englishness Identified: Manners and Character, 1650–1850*, Oxford: Oxford University Press.
Lewis, B. (2001), *The Middlemost and the Milltowns: Bourgeois Culture and Politics in Early Industrial England*, Stanford, CA: Stanford University Press.
Locke, J. ([1693]1732), *Some Thoughts Concerning Education*, 9th edition, London: printed for A. Bettesworth.
MacLeod, C. (1988), *Inventing the Industrial Revolution: the English Patent System, 1660–1880*, Cambridge: Cambridge University Press.
Mantoux, P. ([1928]1961), *The Industrial Revolution in the Eighteenth Century*, New York: Harper Torchbooks, revised edition.
Mathias, P. (1959), *The Brewing Industry in England, 1700–1830*, Cambridge: Cambridge University Press.
McCloskey, D.N. (2006), *The Bourgeois Virtues: Ethics for an Age of Commerce*, Chicago: University of Chicago Press.
Melon, J.F. (1738), *A Political Essay upon Commerce*, translated with some annotations and remarks by David Bindon, Dublin: printed for Philip Crampton.
Mérimée P. (1930), 'Études Anglo-Americaines', in P. Trahard and É. Champion (eds), *Oevres Complètes*, Vol. 8, Paris: Librairie Ancienne Honoré Champion.
Mnookin, R.H. and L. Kornhauser (1979), 'Bargaining in the Shadow of the Law: the Case of Divorce', *Yale Law Journal*, **88**(5), 950–97.
Mokyr, J. (2002), *The Gifts of Athena: Historical Origins of the Knowledge Economy*, Princeton: Princeton University Press.
Mokyr, J. (2006a), 'The Great Synergy: the European Enlightenment as a Factor in Modern Economic Growth', in W. Dolfsma and L. Soete (eds), *Understanding the Dynamics of a Knowledge Economy*, Cheltenham, UK and Northampton, MA, USA: Edward Elgar, pp. 7–41.
Mokyr, J. (2006b), 'Mercantilism, the Enlightenment, and the Industrial Revolution', paper presented to the Conference in Honor of Eli F. Heckscher, Stockholm, May

2003, in R. Findlay, R. Henriksson, H. Lindgren and M. Lundahl (eds) (2006), *Eli F. Heckscher (1879–1952): a Celebratory Symposium*, Cambridge, MA: MIT Press, pp. 269–303.

Mokyr, J. (2007), 'The Market for Ideas and the Origins of Economic Growth in Eighteenth-century Europe' [Heineken Lecture], *Tijdschrift voor Sociale en Economische Geschiedenis*, **4**(1), 3–38.

Mokyr, J. (2008), 'Entrepreneurship and the Industrial Revolution in Britain', in W. Baumol, D.S. Landes and J. Mokyr (eds), *Entrepreneurship in History*, Princeton: Princeton University Press.

Mokyr, J. (2009), *The Enlightened Economy: an Economic History of Britain, 1700–1850*, New Haven, CT: Yale University Press and Penguin Press.

Mokyr, J. and J. Nye (2007), 'Distributional Coalitions, the Industrial Revolution, and the Origins of Economic Growth in Britain', *Southern Economic Journal*, **74**(1), 50–70.

Musson, A.E. and E. Robinson (1969), *Science and Technology in the Industrial Revolution*, Manchester: Manchester University Press.

North, D.C. (1981), *Structure and Change in Economic History*, New York: Norton.

North, D.C. and B.R. Weingast (1989), 'Constitutions and Commitment: the Evolution of Institutions Governing Public Choice in Seventeenth-century England', *Journal of Economic History*, **49**(4), 803–32.

Nougaret, P.J.-B. (1816), *Londres: La Cour et Les provinces d'Angleterre*, 2 Vols, Paris: Chez Briand.

Nuvolari A. (2004), 'Collective Invention during the British Industrial Revolution: the Case of the Cornish Pumping Engine', *Cambridge Journal of Economics*, **28**(3), 347–63.

Nye, J. (2007), *War, Wine, and Taxes: the Political Economy of Anglo–French Trade, 1689–1900*, Princeton: Princeton University Press.

Olson, M. (1982), *The Rise and Decline of Nations*, New Haven, CT: Yale University Press.

Paley, R. (2004), 'Colquhoun, Patrick (1745–1820)', in H.C.G. Matthew and B. Harrison (ed.), *Oxford Dictionary of National Biography*, Oxford: Oxford University Press.

Pearson, R. (1991), 'Collective Diversification: Manchester Cotton Merchants and the Insurance Business in the Early Nineteenth Century', *Business History Review*, **65**(2), 379–414.

Pearson, R. and D. Richardson (2001), 'Business Networking in the Industrial Revolution', *Economic History Review*, **54**(4), 657–79.

Pocock, J.G.A. (1985), *Virtue, Commerce, and History*, Cambridge: Cambridge University Press.

Pomeranz, K. (2000), *The Great Divergence: China, Europe, and the Making of the Modern World Economy*, Princeton, NJ: Princeton University Press.

Porter, R. (1990), *English Society in the 18th Century,* London: Penguin Books, 2nd edition.

Posner, E.A. (2000), *Law and Social Norms*, Cambridge, MA: Harvard University Press.

Prados de la Escosura, L. (2004), *Exceptionalism and Industrialization: Britain and its European Rivals, 1688–1815*, Cambridge: Cambridge University Press.
Randall, A. (1991), *Before the Luddites*, Cambridge: Cambridge University Press.
Rodrik, D., A. Subramanian, and F. Trebbi (2004), 'Institutions Rule: the Primacy of Institutions over Geography and Integration in Economic Development', *Journal of Economic Growth*, **9**(2), 131–65.
Rothschild, E. (2001), *Economic Sentiments: Adam Smith, Condorcet, and the Enlightenment*, Cambridge: Harvard University Press.
Rubinstein, W.D. (1981), *Men of Property: the Very Wealthy in Britain Since the Industrial Revolution*, London: Croom Helm.
Rubinstein, W.D. (1983), 'The End of "Old Corruption" in Britain 1780–1860', *Past and Present*, **101**(Nov), 55–86.
Rushton, P. (1991), 'The Matter in Variance: Adolescents and Domestic Conflict in the Pre-industrial Economy of Northeast England, 1600–1800', *Journal of Social History*, **25**(1), 89–107.
Saussure, C. (de), (1902), *A Foreign View of England in the Reigns of George I and George II: the Letters of Monsieur César de Saussure to his Family, tr. and ed. by Madame Van Muyden*, London: J. Murray.
Say, J.-B. ([1803]1821), *A Treatise on Political Economy*, 4th edition, Boston: Wells and Lilly.
Scott, H.M. (ed.) (1990), *Enlightened Absolutism: Reform and Reformers in Later Eighteenth-century Europe*, Houndsmill, Basingstoke: Palgrave MacMillan.
Shapin, S. (1994), *The Social History of Truth*, Chicago: University of Chicago Press.
Smiles, S. (1859), *Self Help*, http http://www.emotionalliteracyeducation.com/classic_books_online/selfh10.htm.
Smith, A. ([1757]1958), *Lectures on Jurisprudence*, Oxford: Clarendon Press.
Smout, T.C. (1969), *A History of the Scottish People, 1560–1830*, New York: Charles Scribner's and Sons.
Solar, P. (1995), 'Poor Relief and English Economic Development Before the Industrial Revolution', *Economic History Review*, **48**, 1–22.
Spagnolo, G. (1999), 'Social Relations and Cooperations in Organizations', *Journal of Economic Behavior and Organizations*, **38**(1), 1–25.
Stevenson, J. (1979), *Popular Disturbances in England, 1700–1870*, London: Longman.
Stewart, D. (1794), *Account of the Life and Writings of Adam Smith ... from the Transactions of the Royal Society of Edinburgh*, no publisher.
Stone, L. (1985), 'The History of Violence in England: some Observations', *Past and Present*, **108**(Aug), 216–24.
Stout, W. (1967), *The Autobiography of William Stout of Lancaster, 1665–1752*, edited by J.D. Marshall, Manchester: Manchester University Press.
Taine, H. ([1872]1958), *Notes on England. Translated with an Introduction by Edward Hyams*, Fair Lawn, NJ: Essential Books.
Tucker, J. (1758), *Instructions for Travellers*, Dublin: printed for William Watson at the Poets Head in Carpel-Street.
Wilberforce, S. and R.I. (1838), *The Life of William Wilberforce, by his sons, Robert Isaac Wilberforce and Samuel Wilberforce*, London: John Murray.

# 2. The coevolution of institutions and preferences: history and theory*

**Samuel Bowles**

## 2.1. INTRODUCTION

Memorable titles, *The Protestant Ethic and the Spirit of Capitalism* (Weber, 1958) or *Nations and Nationalism* (Gellner, 1983) for example, at once capture a historical commonplace and pose a theoretical challenge, namely that the emergence of new institutions is often accompanied by cultural innovation. The appearance of private property in the means of production that was coincident with the domestication of plants and animals 11 thousand years ago and the concomitant eclipse of the egalitarian and collectivist cultures of hunting and gathering bands exhibits this co-evolutionary dynamic. So too does twentieth-century transformation in family structure and the spread of feminist values.

The theoretical challenges posed by these and similar cultural–institutional dynamics are the following.

First, the processes of institutional and cultural change are frequently the result of a very large number of substantially uncoordinated actions. The novel institutions and cultures that are observed historically are the emergent properties of these decentralized processes, more akin to the evolution of language than to the deliberate social engineering by mechanism design or the dyadic strategic interactions of classical game theory. Leon Trotsky (1970) exaggerated when he wrote that history is 'the natural selection of accidents' but his quip captures an important aspect of human social dynamics that is missing from most economic models.

Second, while entire schools of thought are formed around the purported direction of historical causation connecting culture and institutions – as Weber's and Marx's contrasting views on religion suggest – the examples mentioned above implicate a simultaneous dynamic in which complementary cultures and institutions may jointly emerge and proliferate when neither could survive in isolation.

Third, the very long term persistence of dysfunctional cultural and institutional systems catalogued by Edgerton (1992) casts doubt on the 'efficient design' assumption invoked in biology and by some economists such as Williamson (1985, p. 394): 'viable modes of economic organization ... ordinarily possess an efficiency advantage'.

Finally, the cultural and institutional innovations mentioned above exhibit a striking pattern of long term stasis punctuated by brief periods of rapid change.

To address these challenges I draw on both stochastic evolutionary game theory and biologically-inspired models of cultural evolution (Cavalli-Sforza and Feldman, 1981; Boyd and Richerson, 1985; Young, 1998) to develop a model of the coevolution of cultures (modeled as the distribution of types of preferences in a population) and institutions (the distribution of types of contracts).

Institutions are sometimes modeled as games; the firm, for example is represented by a principal–agent model of employer–employee interaction. If we are interested in the process of institutional evolution, however, we need to depict institutions not as exogenously given constraints but rather as the *outcome* of individual interactions. In other words, we want to go 'behind' the game describing the institution to investigate the interactions from which it evolved. To do this we specify an underlying game which has as it as its possible outcomes a number of different ways that the participants might interact (Aoki, 2001; Bowles, 2004). The outcomes of this underlying game are thus institutions; the process of institutional change will then be studied as a change from one to another of these outcomes.

An insightful way to describe the outcomes of the underlying game is to say that they are conventions, that is, Nash equilibria of an n-person game in which individual adherence to the conventional behavior is a best response as long as the individual believes that a sufficient number of others will also adhere to the convention (Lewis, 1969; Young, 1995). Institutional change occurs when one convention is displaced by another. Thus, institutional innovation and change becomes a problem of *equilibrium selection*. An advantage of this apporoach is that it represents institutional change as the emergent property of the actions taken by very large numbers of people with a characteristic pattern of long term stasis interrupted by brief periods of transition. The very long term persistence of customs governing crop shares and wealth inheritance, their occasional rapid change and their striking pattern of local homogeneity and global heterogeneity are all consistent with this modeling approach (Cowlishaw and Mace, 1996; Young and Burke, 2001).

I model cultural change in a similar decentralized manner. We acquire preferences through genetic inheritance and cultural learning. Because both are influenced by economic and other institutions, preferences are endogenous. The model I develop highlights the way that structures of social interaction influence the direction and pace of the evolution of preferences. Preferences may be endogenous in other ways. For example, religious or political indoctrination and advertising are undoubtedly important. But the available empirical studies of preferences for brands of food, soap, movies, and other consumption items for which one would expect an important deliberate inculcation effect show that advertising appears to be less important than one's personal contacts and other influences. Preferences are like accents; we can try to acquire them – learning to love Prokofiev and escargot, or adopting an 'upper class accent' – but for the most part we are only dimly aware of how we acquired them. For this reason the model below is patterned after studies of language change. On the basis of intensive empirical study of linguistic change in Philadelphia, for example, William Labov concluded that

> linguistic traits are not transmitted across group boundaries simply by exposure in the mass media or in schools. ... Our basic language system is not acquired from school teachers or from radio announcers, but from friends and competitors: those who we admire, and those who we have to be good enough to beat (Labov, 1983, p. 23).

The inference is not that institutions such as schools and churches are unimportant, but that we can understand their evolutionary importance may be enhanced by seeing them – along with markets, firms, families, and neighborhoods – as distinct patterns of social interaction affecting the differential replication of behavioral traits rather than simply transmitting the explicit message of the curriculum or the canon (Bowles and Gintis, 1976).

I begin with four historical cases of cultural–institutional change before attempting a model capable of illuminating their main features.

## 2.2. CULTURAL AND INSTITUTIONAL DYNAMICS: EXAMPLES

In October 1989, the general secretary of the East German Communist Party, Erich Honecker, grandly celebrated the fortieth anniversary of the founding of the German Democratic Republic as a 'historical necessity' and a 'turning point in the history of the German people'. Parades and demonstrations commemorated the event. Anti-regime protesters had mounted a dozen or so demonstrations over the summer months, but they had attracted fewer than 10,000 participants in all. But twelve days after his address, Honecker resigned, as anti-regime demonstrations mounted first in Leipzig and then throughout the country, with a million and a half participating in October and twice that number in November (Lohmann, 1994). Within a month, East and West Germans danced on the Berlin Wall, and then dismantled it. Less than a year after Honecker's commemoration of the German Democratic Republic, it passed out of existence, its territory joining the Federal Republic of Germany. As a result, the citizens of the former Communist nation passed from one system of governance to another with an entirely new set of property rights and political processes. Few had anticipated the suddenness and extent of these and the other dramatic changes in institutions which took place throughout most of the formerly Communist world over the same period.

A less heralded but equally dramatic process of institutional and cultural change concerns the painful and dangerous practices of female circumcision and other forms of female genital cutting (FGC) in many parts of Africa (Mackie, 1996, 1999). Like foot binding, which was once widely practiced in China, in parts of Africa FGC is a convention to which families adhere in order to ensure that daughters will be able to marry. The spread of schooling and other modernizing influences on the continent during the twentieth century had left FGC intact; in some regions it was spreading. At the turn of the twenty-first century, it was estimated that two million African girls suffered the practice every year.

But at a meeting in 1997 in the small Bambara village of Malicounda in Senegal, residents pledged they would *all* reject FGC. The about face in Malicounda had been prompted not by an anti-FGC campaign but rather by a non-governmental organization which had brought women together to promote literacy and to consider community development and health problems. In nearby Keur Simbara, villagers prudently decided to consult with all of the other villages in the relevant marriage pool; eventually all 13 of these villages collectively pledged to abandon the practice. After village-level meetings, representatives of another cluster of 18 villages of the Fulani ethnic group did the same. Pledge groups spread from village to village. Within a year of the Fulani declaration, the Government of Senegal outlawed FGC.

A third example of institutional and cultural change comes from the Philippines, where the traditional contract governing the rice harvest is called *hunusan* ('sharing' in Tagalog). According to the *hunusan* system, any members of the community may participate in the harvest of a farmer's fields, receiving one-sixth of the amount they personally harvest (Hayami, 1998; Hayami and Kikuchi, 1999). The farmer may not rightfully deny anyone this right, and by custom his own family members may not participate, nor may he or they supervise the work. During the 1960s, the one-sixth share provided a return to an hour's harvesting work on a par with wage-earning opportunities in rural areas, constituting a kind of equilibrium between traditional and modern contracts. However, the increased use of high yielding varieties of rice during the 1970s and 1980s (the Green Revolution) nearly doubled yields and thus greatly increased the value of the one-sixth of the harvest stipulated by the *hunusan* system. As a result, by the end of the 1970s, harvesting under the *hunusan* system earned a substantial rent above the laborer's next best alternative (wage labor).

Some of the large landowners sought to take advantage of the change by reducing the crop share to one-ninth, but this violation of custom caused much indignation among the harvesters, perhaps explaining the suspicious nighttime burning of unharvested crops. The larger farms subsequently invested heavily in both mechanical threshers and in the supervision of harvest labor. Smaller farms, however, continued to offer the one-sixth share, but added to it a traditional obligation that had long been common in some adjacent regions. This was the restriction of harvest labor to those who had performed unpaid weeding services throughout the prior growing season. In contrast to the strategy adopted by the large owners, the new obligation imposed by the smaller farmers did not violate the reciprocity-based *hunusan* system. Hayami (1998, p. 45) reports that 'in the minds of the villagers weeding with no direct payment is considered. ... an expression of gratitude by laborers for the goodwill of the farmer patron who provides them with a guaranteed stable income ... at a time honored share'. By amalgamating two traditional contracts, the modified *hunusan* system depressed the de facto remuneration of harvest labor to almost exactly the rate for equivalent wage work, thus eliminating the rents introduced by the Green Revolution.

A final example. The labor market aspects of South African *apartheid* were a convention (or a set of conventions) regulating the patterns of racial inequality which had existed throughout most of South Africa's recorded history and had been formalized in the early twentieth century and especially in the aftermath of World War II. For whites, the convention was: Offer only low wages for menial work to blacks. For blacks: Offer one's labor at low wages, do not demand more. These actions represented mutual best responses: As long as (almost) all white employers adhered to their side of the convention, the black workers' best response was to adhere to their aspect of the convention, and conversely. Apartheid can be described as a convention because other non-racial and more egalitarian mutual best responses were in principle feasible even if inaccessible by means of individual action.

The power of apartheid labor market conventions is suggested by the fact that real wages of black gold miners did not rise between 1910 and 1970, despite periodic labor shortages in the mines and a many-fold increase in productivity (Wilson, 1972: Wood, 2000). But a series of strikes beginning in the early 1970s and accelerating after the mid 1980s signaled a rejection of the convention by increasing numbers of black workers. In doing this, of course, workers and others were not conforming to the best responses of the *status quo* apartheid convention. Their deviation from the convention provoked further defections; many business leaders concluded that the old convention was no longer a best response, leading them to alter their labor relations, raising real wages and promoting black workers. Non-best-response actions by black workers had altered the employers' best responses; as a result the convention unraveled. Within a decade the entire system of apartheid had been abandoned and an ethic of multi-racialism proliferated among whites.

As in the case of the abandonment of FGC in Senegal, the official end of apartheid – the release of Nelson Mandela from prison and the first all-race elections – was the consequence, not the cause of the de facto cultural and institutional rejection of racism by businesses and workers.

## 2.3. STATIONARY INSTITUTIONS AND PREFERENCES

The acquisition of new preferences may be modeled as a cultural evolution process in which individuals periodically update their behavioral norms (perhaps frequently, perhaps only during adolescence) after having taken into account information about the frequency distribution of various behavior in the population, the payoffs associated with various behaviors in recent periods, and other facts (Bowles, 1998). Equilibrium (that is, stationary) preferences will depend on the nature of the updating rules and the structure of social interactions given by the society's institutions. The latter are important as they determine who meets who to do what tasks and with what benefits. Among the institutions making up this cultural environment are the structure of markets, contracts, legislation and other aspects of society affected by public policy. A consequence is that differing economic institutions support different equilibrium preferences.

This cultural evolution model provides a dynamic setting for the processes studied by Brown et al. (2004). They designed a market experiment to explore the effects of contractual incompleteness on the pattern of trading. The good to be exchanged varied in quality, with higher quality more costly to provide. In the complete contracting condition, the level of quality promised by the supplier was enforced by the experimenter, while in the incomplete contracting condition the supplier could provide any level of quality (irrespective of any promise or agreement with the buyer). Buyers and sellers knew the identification numbers of those they were interacting with, so they could use information they had acquired in previous rounds as a guide to whom they would like to interact with, the prices and quality to offer, and the like. Buyers had the opportunity to make a private offer (rather than broadcasting a public offer) to the same seller in the next period, thus attempting to initiate an ongoing relationship with the seller.

Very different patterns of trading emerged under the complete and incomplete contracting conditions. In the first, 90 percent of the trading relationships lasted less than three periods (most of them were single-shot). By contrast, only 40 percent of the relationships were this brief under the incomplete contracting condition and most traders formed trusting relationships with their partners. Buyers in the incomplete contracting condition offered prices considerably in excess the supplier's cost of providing quality. When buyers were disappointed by the quality supplied, they terminated the relationship, thereby withdrawing the implied rent from the supplier. The differences in behavior under the two treatments were particularly pronounced in later rounds of the game, suggesting that the traders learned from their experiences, and updated their behaviors accordingly.

These results suggest that trust and reciprocity may depend on the form of the contract, contractual incompleteness sometimes supporting trusting and reciprocal behaviors. The converse is also true: expectations of lower levels of trust and reciprocity would plausibly lead those designing contracts to be willing to pay more for more complete contracts. The implication is that changes in the legal and policy environment that more closely approximate the ideal of complete contracting may have deleterious effects due to their influence on preferences. Behavioral experiments and evidence from natural settings suggests that because explicit economic incentives and other regarding preferences are often sub-modular (substitutes rather than complements) these 'crowding out' effects may be pervasive and substantial (Bewley, 1999; Frey and Jegen, 2001; Bowles, 2008; Bowles and Polania Reyes, 2009).

Based on this evidence of non-separability of other regarding preferences and economic incentives I model an interaction similar to that in Brown et al. (2004) embedded in a dynamic cultural evolutionary environment. As in Bohnet et al. (2001), the underlying process jointly determines the distribution of contracts and the distribution of behavioral norms in the population, a dynamic sometimes termed the *co-evolution of institutions and preferences*

Consider a population of buyer and sellers who are paired randomly for a single interaction. They trade a good or service whose quality (high (H) or low (L)) is determined by the seller and is costly for the buyer to determine *ex ante*. Buyers offer a contract, following which sellers determine the quality of the good they will provide. The buyer may offer one of two contracts. If the complete (C) contract is offered, the seller receives a fixed compensation just sufficient to offset the costs of providing low quality. These are C-type buyers. According to the incomplete (I) contract, the buyer pays the cost of producing low quality, plus half of the net profits resulting from the transaction. These are I-type buyers.

Sellers are also of two types. R-type sellers interpret the I-contract as a sign of trust on the part of the buyer, and reciprocate by providing high quality, incurring an additional cost of $\delta_H$ as a result. When offered a C-contract, however, R-type sellers feel mistrusted, experiencing a subjective cost $\delta_C$, and they retaliate, providing low quality. S-type sellers are completely self-regarding and provide low quality irrespective of the contract. The net surplus of the transaction (net of compensating the seller sufficient to offset the cost of low quality) are $\pi^H$ and $\pi^L$ for high and low quality respectively. Those offering a C-contract must pay a cost for monitoring and contractual enforcement, and this cost is greater when interacting with an (offended) R-type ($\mu_R$) than with an S-type ($\mu_S$) with $\mu_R > \mu_S$. Those offering an I-contract make themselves vulnerable to an expected loss of $\kappa$ through theft should they interact with an S-type seller who gains an additional amount $\kappa$ as a result.

To exclude cases in which only one of the pairs of contracts and preferences is a Nash equilibrium, I further assume that $\pi^H > 2\,(\pi^L - \mu_R)$, $\pi^H - \pi^L > 2\,(\kappa - \delta_H)$ and $\pi^L > 2\,(\kappa - \mu_S)$. The payoffs appear in Table 2.1. From these assumptions we know that {I,R}, that is, the I-contract matched with the R-seller is the joint surplus maximizing outcome. Thus buyers will offer I contracts if there are sufficiently many R-sellers in the population, and sellers will remain reciprocal if there are sufficiently many I-buyers in the population. But that does not guarantee that {I,R} will be observed in practice in a dynamic setting.

*Table 2.1. Row player's payoffs first*

| Seller → / Buyer ↓ | Reciprocator (*R*) | Selfish (*S*) |
|---|---|---|
| Incomplete contract (I) | $\boldsymbol{\pi^H/2, \pi^H/2 - \delta_H}$ | $\pi^L/2 - \kappa, \pi^L/2 + \kappa$ |
| Complete contract (C) | $\pi^L - \mu_S - \delta_C$ | $\boldsymbol{\pi^L - \mu_A, 0}$ |

*Note*: Those in bold refer to the two pure strategy Nash equilibria of this game.

## 2.4. THE DYNAMICS OF PREFERENCES AND INSTITUTIONS

At the beginning of each period with a given probability each member of the sellers and buyers sub-populations may update their strategy upon exposure to a 'model' (a competitor, a teacher, a co-worker, or a neighbor, for example) drawn respectively from the sub-population of seller and buyers, respectively. If the model and the individual have the same strategy, it is retained by the individual. But if the individual and the model have different strategies then the individual may switch if the other strategy would have gained higher payoffs given the distribution of play in the previous period, the probablity of a switch occuring increasing in the difference in the payoffs of the two strategies.

Writing the fraction of the sellers who are reciprocators as ω, the expected payoffs to buyers offering the I- and C-contracts are:

$$v^I = \frac{\omega\pi^H}{2} + (1-\omega)\frac{\pi^L}{2-\kappa}$$

$$v^C = \omega(\pi^L - \mu_R) + (1-\omega)(\pi^L - \mu_S) = \pi^L - \omega\mu_R - (1-\omega)\mu_S$$

Similarly, writing the fraction of the buyers offering incomplete contracts as $\varphi$, the expected payoffs to the R- and S-sellers are

$$v^R = \omega\frac{\pi^H}{2-\delta_H} + (1-\omega) - \delta_C$$

$$v^S = \omega\frac{\pi^L}{2+\kappa}$$

These payoff functions are illustrated in Figure 2.1. What kinds of contracts and behaviors would we expect to observe in this population? One's intuition is that likely outcomes would include a high frequency of both incomplete contracts and reciprocating sellers or the opposite: a predominance of both complete contracts and self-interested sellers. These correct intuitions are readily formalized.

The dynamical system we want to study concerns the state space defined by all possible combinations of contractual and behavioral strategies or $\varphi \in [0,1]$ and $\omega \in [0,1]$. We wish to explore the movement of both $\varphi$ and $\omega$ over time. Letting $\beta$ be a positive constant that converts payoff differences into the probability that an individual will switch strategies, it is easily shown (Bowles, 2004) that this process gives the familiar replicator dynamic equations

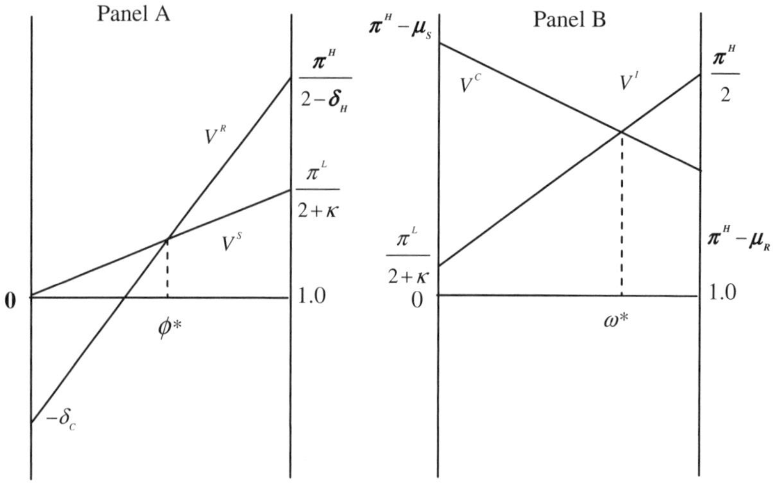


*Note*: φ is the fraction of buyers offering incomplete contracts while ω is the fraction of sellers who are reciprocal.

*Figure 2.1. Expected payoffs to reciprocal and self-regarding preferences (left panel) and complete and incomplete contracts*

$$\frac{d\varphi}{dt} = \varphi(1-\varphi)\beta(v^I - v^C)$$

$$\frac{d\omega}{dt} = \omega(1-\omega)\beta(v^R - v^S)$$

The terms $\varphi(1-\varphi)$ and $\omega(1-\omega)$ measure (for the buyers and seller respectively) the expected frequency of pairings with 'unlike' models, while $\beta(v^I - v^C)$ and $\beta(v^R - v^S)$ capture the payoff monotone probability of a switch when unlikes meet.

The stationary values of $\varphi$ and $\omega$ in this dynamic are:

$$\frac{d\varphi}{dt} = 0 \text{ for } \varphi = 0, \varphi = 1 \text{ and } \omega = \omega^* = \frac{\pi^L + 2(\kappa - \mu_S)}{\pi^H - \pi^L + 2(\kappa + \mu_R - \mu_S)}$$

and

$$\frac{d\omega}{dt} = 0 \text{ for } \omega = 0, \omega = 1 \text{ and } \varphi = \varphi^* = \frac{2\delta}{\pi^H - \pi^L - 2\kappa}$$

The resulting dynamical system is illustrated in Figure 2.2, with $\omega$ and $\varphi$ the fractions of R-sellers and I-buyers in the previous period and the arrows indicating the out of equilibrium adjustment given by the equations immediately above. The state ($\varphi^*$, $\omega^*$) is stationary but it is a saddle: perturbations away from $\varphi^*$ or $\omega^*$ are not self-correcting. The asymptotically stable states are CS (that is, $\omega^* = 0 = \varphi^*$) and IR ($\omega^* = 1 = \varphi^*$), confirming the above intuition.

In this deterministic setting, the initial state determines which of these two asymptotically stable states occurs, and once at either of these states the population remains there (they are absorbing). But historically such 'lock-in' outcomes are not forever.

To take account of the possibility of escape from 'lock-in' a more realistic dynamic would include stochastic influences on payoffs and occasional idiosyncratic updating of preferences or contracts (that is, acquiring lower rather than higher payoff preferences or contracts through error or experimentaiton.) In a plausible version of this process (for example, Young, 1998), transitions between IR and CS will occur, but the system will spend more (and depending on the technical details, possibly virtually all) of the time in the one with the larger basin of attraction.

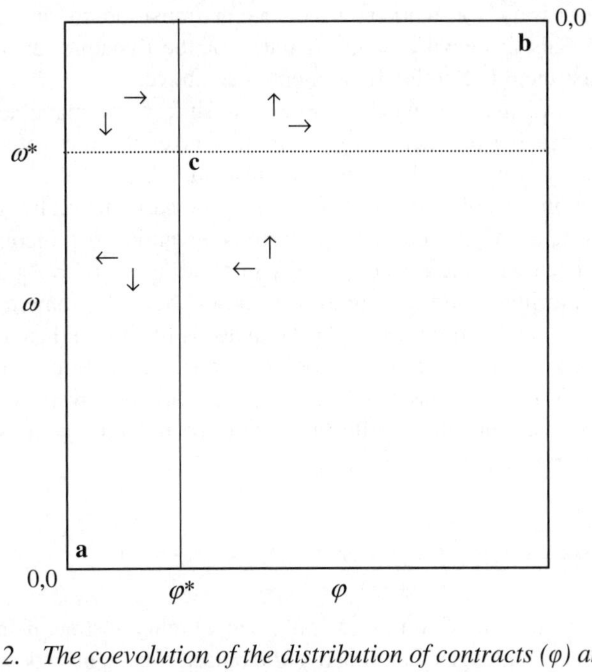


*Figure 2.2. The coevolution of the distribution of contracts (φ) and preferences (ω)*

## 2.5. CLASS CONFLICT, TECHNICAL CHANGE AND CULTURAL-INSTITUTIONAL DYNAMICS

Deliberate idiosyncratic may take the form of refusal of the terms of the status quo contract or collective changes in preferences under as a result of religous or political movements. Like accidents or experimentation, these non-best responses may also account for shifts among the two culture-institutional conventions. Suppose for concreteness that the sellers are workers selling their labor time (the effort they provide may be of high or low quality), while those offering contracts are their employers. If the payoffs are as depicted in Figure 2.1 the two classes have different preferences over the two conventions, workers preferring IR while their employers prefer CS. At the CS equilibrium ($\omega^* = 0 = \varphi^*$) employers capture the entire surplus produced when low quality effort is provided by sellers. At the IR equilibrium the larger surplus is shared between the two classes. If for reasons external to the model a fraction of workers greater than $\omega^*$ were to become reciprocal, however, the best-responding employers would abandon their preferred arrangements, offering incomplete contracts and thereby inducing best-responding workers also to reject self-interest in favor of reciprocity. Thus $\omega^*$ can be interpreted as a kind of collective action threshold necessary for workers to induce a transition to their preferred convention. This framework captures much of the dynamic leading to the demise of apartheid in South Africa, mentioned above.

Suppose now that technical change – a shift from manufacturing to knowledge-intensive production for example – takes the form of increasing the productivity of high quality labor. Because $d\omega^*/d\pi^H < 0$, the consequence is a reduction in the collective action barrier to be surmounted by workers in order to induce a transition to their preferred convention. An increase in $\mu_S$ or $\mu_S$ associated with increased difficulty in securing even low quality labor through monitoring would (as Figure 2.1 shows) have the same effect. The model thus provides a framework for the analysis of Marx's insight that the dynamism of knowledge and technology may create conditions under which collective action by a class that stands to benefit may overthrow inertial institutions that are unable to fully implement the potential gains associated with technological change.

## 2.6. CONCLUSION

The model proposed here addresses – albeit in a highly abstract manner – the four theoretical challenges mentioned at the outset: it presents a decentralized process whereby culture and institutions co-evolve, each providing conditions affecting the dynamic of the other, and in which inefficient institutions may persist over very long periods only to be abandoned as a result of a rapid cultural–institutional transition. The model also provides a framework for analyzing what might be termed quasi-decentralized historical dynamics, namely those involving minimally coordinated collective action by members of the same class or other groups.

Public policy may also affect the long run outcome by altering the two critical values $\varphi^*$ and $\omega^*$. Consider two possibilities. First, the government imposes the rule of law, reducing theft and setting $\kappa = 0$. Because $d\varphi^*/d\kappa > 0$ and $d\omega^*/d\kappa > 0$ the effect will be to lower the critical fractions of I-types and R-types required to propel the population the surplus maximizing outcome. This is a case of crowding in: an institutional innovation (the rule of law) generates a cultural environment in which reciprocal preferences and hence efficient incomplete contracts may proliferate.

Suppose, as a second example also beginning with the CS status quo, that judicial reforms designed to perfect property rights reduced the costs of contract enforcement, lowering $\mu_S$ and $\mu_R$. The effect is to reduce $\omega^*$ and to leave $\varphi^*$ unaffected, so this improvement in property rights enforcement environment increases the critical fraction of suppliers who are R-types necessary to propel dynamic to the efficient equilibrium. In this case crowding out has occurred: a contractual improvement has made an efficient outcome more difficult to attain by raising the barrier to the cultural transition that it requires.

This case illustrates a cultural-institutional analogue to the second best theorem of Lipsey and Lancaster (1956–57) that may be stated as follows: where contracts are incomplete (and hence socially beneficial values may be important in attenuating market failures), public policies and legal practices designed to more 'improve property rights' so as to more closely align self-regarding preferences and public objectives may exacerbate the underlying market failure (by undermining social values such as trust or reciprocity) and may result in a less efficient equilibrium allocation (Bowles and Hwang, 2008).

A similar model has been used in Belloc and Bowles (2009) to study the effects of international economic integration on the evolution of institutions and culture. We show that two otherwise identical countries will specialize and benefit from gains to trade if their cultural–institutional conventions differ (one at the CS and the other at the IR convention). We also find that the economic integration does not induce convergence to the superior IR convention even when it is Pareto-efficient, but instead renders the institutional–cultural transitions that would accomplish this more costly and hence less likely. Finally, if as above, the sellers are workers and the buyers their employers, in a country at an inferior CS convention, the employers (but not workers) benefit from trade integration (by contrast to autarchy) while workers benefit from a transition to the 'superior' institutions (but not necessarily their employers).

There are two major lacunae. Both are easily rectified, but not in the short space of a single chapter. First, I have abstracted from competition between territorially based groups such as nations and ethno-linguistic units. This dynamic, essential (if sometimes only implicit) in the contributions of many evolutionary thinkers (Parsons, 1964; Hayek, 1988) may be captured by embedding the model presented here in a standard model of equilibrium selection by warfare or other kinds of between-group competition (Bowles, 2006, 2009; Choi and Bowles, 2007). If, as is plausible, the probability of success in intergroup contests is increasing in the average payoffs of the group this group selection dynamic will favor the selection of conventions that maximize the joint surplus, providing a second (conflictual but non-revolutionary) mechanism by which Marx's dynamic of institutional change might come about. The model (with or without the group selection addendum) thus provides a mechanism that could implement a kind of selection of efficient institutions, albeit one brought about with long lags by class and inter-group conflict rather than individual accommodation to new technological possibilities.

The second shortcoming is that other than specifying a collective action barrier, the model does not explain how collective action – rather than stochastic experimentation or error – could be the mechanism by which transitions may come about. This can be done by representing non-best response play as a public good among those members who may benefit from a transition should it occur (for example a strike against employers offering complete contracts). The resulting joint model of the stability of conventions and the process of collective action generating non-best response play (Bowles, 2004) illuminates conditions under which risk dominance or other plausible individual behavioral rules would allow for transitions.

## NOTE

* Thanks to Larry Blume, Robert Boyd, Herbert Gintis, Peyton Young and the other participants in the past decade's meetings of the Santa Fe Institute's seminar on the 'Coevolution of Preferences and Institutions' and to the Behavioral Science Program of the Santa Fe Institute, the University of Siena and the U.S. National Science Foundation, for support of this project.

# REFERENCES

Aoki, M. (2001), *Towards a Comparative Institutional Analysis*, Cambridge, MA: MIT Press.

Belloc, M. and S. Bowles (2009), 'International Trade and the Persistence of Cultural-Institutional Diversity', *Santa Fe Institute Working Paper*, no. 09-03-005.

Bewley, T.F. (1999), *Why Wages Don't Fall During a Recession*, Cambridge: Harvard University Press.

Bohnet, I., B. Frey and S. Huck (2001), 'More Order with Less Law: On Contractual Enforcement, Trust, and Crowding', *American Political Science Review*, **95**(1), 131–44.

Bowles, S. (1998), 'Endogenous Preferences: the Cultural Consequences of Markets and Other Economic Institutions', *Journal of Economic Literature*, **36**(1), 75–111.

Bowles, S. (2004), *Microeconomics: Behavior, Institutions, and Evolution*, Princeton: Princeton University Press.

Bowles, S. (2006), 'Group Competition, Reproductive Leveling and the Evolution of Human Altruism', *Science*, **314**(5805), 1569–72.

Bowles, S. (2008), 'Policies Designed for Self Interested Citizens May Undermine "the Moral Sentiments": Evidence from Experiments', *Science*, **320**(5883), 1605–9.

Bowles, S. (2009), 'Did Warfare among Ancestral Hunter-gatherer Groups Affect the Evolution of Human Social Behaviors?', *Science*, in press.

Bowles, S. and H. Gintis (1976), *Schooling in Capitalist America: Educational Reform and the Contradictions of Economic Life*, New York: Basic Books.

Bowles, S. and S.-H. Hwang (2008), 'Social Preferences and Public Economics: Mechanism Design when Preferences Depend on Incentives', *Journal of Public Economics*, **92**(8–9), 1811–20.

Bowles, S. and S. Polania Reyes (2009), *Economic Incentives and Social Preferences: a Preference-based Lucas Critique of Public Policy*, Santa Fe Institute, mimeo.

Boyd, R. and P.J. Richerson (1985), *Culture and the Evolutionary Process*, Chicago: University of Chicago Press.

Brown, M., A. Falk and E. Fehr (2004), 'Relational Contracts and the Nature of Market Interactions', *Econometrica*, **72**(3), 747–80.

Cavalli-Sforza, L.L. and M.W. Feldma. (1981), *Cultural Transmission and Evolution: a Quantitative Approach*, Princeton, NJ: Princeton University Press.

Choi, J.-K. and S. Bowles (2007), 'The Coevolution of Parochial Altruism and War', *Science*, **318**(5850), 636–40.

Cowlishaw, G. and R. Mace (1996), 'Cross-cultural Patterns of Marriage and Inheritance', *Ethology and Sociobiology*, **17**(2), 87–97.

Edgerton, R.B. (1992), *Sick Societies: Challenging the Myth of Primitive Harmony*, New York: The Free Press.

Frey, B. and R. Jegen (2001), 'Motivation Crowding Theory: a Survey of Empirical Evidence', *Journal of Economic Surveys*, **15**(5), 589–611.

Gellner, E. (1983), *Nations and Nationalism*, Ithaca: Cornell University Press.

Hayami, Y. (1998), 'Norms and Rationality in the Evolution of Economic Systems: a View From Asian Villages', *The Japanese Economic Review*, **49**(1), 36–53.

Hayami, Y. and M. Kikuchi (1999), 'Technology, Market, and Community in Contract Choice: Rice Harvesting in the Phillipines', *Economic Development and Cultural Change*, **47**(2), 371–86.

Hayek, F.A. (1988), *The Fatal Conceit: the Errors of Socialism*, Chicago: University of Chicago Press.

Labov, W. (1983), 'De Facto Segregation of Black and White Vernaculars', in D. Sankoff (ed.), *Diversity and Diachrony*, Amsterdam: John Benjamins, pp. 1–24.

Lewis, D.K. (1969), *Convention: a Philosophical Study*, Cambridge: Harvard University Press.

Lipsey, R. and K. Lancaster (1956–57), 'The General Theory of the Second Best', *Review of Economic Studies*, **24**(1), 11–32.

Lohmann, S. (1994), 'Dynamics of Informational Cascades: the Monday Demonstrations in Leipzig', *World Politics*, **47**(1), 42–101.

Mackie, G. (1996), 'Ending Footbinding and Infibulation: a Convention Account', *American Sociological Review*, **61**(6), 999–1017.

Mackie, G. (1999), *Female Genital Cutting: the Beginning of the End*, Oxford: St. John's College.

Parsons, T. (1964), 'Evolutionary Universals in Society', *American Sociological Review*, **29**(3), 339–57.

Trotsky, L. (1970), *My Life*, New York: Pathfinder (original Russian edition, 1930).

Weber, M. (1958), *The Protestant Ethic and the Spirit of Capitalism*, New York: Charles Scribner's Sons.

Williamson, O.E. (1985), *The Economic Institutions of Capitalism*, New York: Free Press.

Wilson, F. (1972), *Labour in South African Goldmines*, Cambridge: Cambridge University Press.

Wood, E.J. (2000), *Forging Democracy From Below: Insurgent Transitions in South Africa and El Salvador*, Cambridge: Cambridge University Press.

Young, P. (1995), 'Economics of Conventions', *Journal of Economic Perspectives*, **10**(2), 105–22.

Young, H.P. (1998), *Individual Strategy and Social Structure: an Evolutionary Theory of Institutions*, Princeton, NJ: Princeton University Press.

Young, H.P. and M. Burke (2001), 'Competition and Custom in Economic Contracts: a Case Study of Illinois Agriculture', *American Economic Review*, **91**(3), 559–73.

# 3. Politics and income distribution*

**Martin Baur**

## 3.1. INTRODUCTION

The relationship between growth and income distribution as well as political structure and economic performance has long been a subject of scrutiny for researchers. Whereas the reciprocal links between growth and income distribution have gained considerable attention in the last decades, the link between political and institutional variables and income distribution has not gained much emphasis so far. There are only a few studies investigating the connection between institutions, political variables and income distribution and most of them analyse the connection between aggregate democracy measures and income distribution with ambiguous results (Gradstein and Milanovic, 2000).

Considering the generally important role of transfers and redistributive policies in modern economies, the interactions between politics and income distribution deserve more detailed attention. The redistribution literature agrees that redistribution generally benefits politically influential groups. Therefore, the distribution of political influence determines the income distribution in a society.

The present chapter has two aims. In a first step, the research literature dealing with the connection between politics and income distribution is reviewed. In a second step, different propositions concerning the connection between political influence and income distribution are derived from the research literature and empirically tested.

The chapter is organised as follows: Section 3.2 gives a short overview of the most important theoretical and empirical findings concerning the connection between growth and income distribution. Section 3.3 deals with the literature on the relationship between politics and income distribution. In Section 3.4 the hypotheses are presented. The empirical analysis follows in Section 3.5. Section 3.6 concludes with a short summary of the most important results and possible strands for further research.

## 3.2. INCOME DISTRIBUTION AND GROWTH

Questions of growth and income distribution have always been a major concern for economists. In his seminal article (Kuznets, 1955) Kuznets proposed his hypothesis of an 'inverted-U' relationship between growth and income distribution. After examining empirical data for different industrial and developing countries, Kuznets found that income inequality increases in a first stage of economic growth and then begins to decrease after a certain point of growth. According to Kuznets the reason for this phenomenon lies in labour migration between a traditional agricultural sector and a modern, urban industrial sector. On the one hand, the inequalities between these two sectors rise during the development process, on the other hand, the share of the more unequal industrial sector, where wages differ more than in the agricultural sector, increases. According to Kuznets (1955, p. 17), the growing political power of the urban low-income groups, their political participation and the better chances for organisation lead to a variety of protective and supportive legislation by the state. This means that income inequality begins to decrease when all sectors of the working class are integrated into the political and economic structure of a country and have begun to gain political influence.

In the following years many economists have tried to find evidence for the Kuznets curve and to answer the question of how growth and income distribution affect each other (Adelman and Morris, 1973; Chenery et al., 1974; Ahluwalia, 1976; Papanek and Kyn, 1986; Fields, 1987; Ram, 1988; Bourgignon and Morrisson, 1990; Anand and Kanbur, 1993; Deininger and Squire, 1996; Li et al., 1998; Barro, 2000). Although many of the older cross-sectional studies found evidence for the Kuznets hypothesis, the more recent investigations working with newer and better data material and using time series data did not find proof for a systematic relationship between growth and income distribution (Deininger and Squire, 1996, p. 583–9; Li et al., 1998).

A new strand of research literature looks at the long-term evolution of the income distribution in particular countries (Piketty, 2003, 2005; Piketty and Saez, 2003; Atkinson, 2003; Dell et al., 2005; Atkinson and Piketty, 2007). These studies report a strong decrease of income inequality throughout the first half of the 20th century, whereas the recent experience is quite diverse across countries, with some countries experiencing an increase in inequality since the 1970s. In general, the studies found no gradual, Kuznets type explanation for the decline of inequality but attributed most of the explanation of declining inequality to severe shocks to capital holdings between 1914 and 1945 (Piketty, 2005, p. 386). Whereas skill-based technological change and globalisation affect the income distribution everywhere (Glaeser, 2005), economic structure, pursued policies and the geographic and historical heritage of the investigated countries play a more important role in explaining the differences in income distribution between countries than the level of development.

In the last few years interest in Kuznets' hypothesis decreased and the relationship between growth and income distribution was newly analysed from another point of view, that is, the impact of income inequality on the growth rate of an economy (for a survey, see Alesina and Perotti, 1994; Perotti, 1996 and Bertola et al., 2006). Most of these studies came to the conclusion that a more equal distribution of income has a positive impact on the growth rate of an economy, whereas an unequal income distribution can affect growth negatively. These new findings contradicted the notion of inequality as a prerequisite for development ensuring the adequate incentives for work, savings and investment. Different channels were identified as possible links connecting income distribution and economic growth. The fiscal policy channel predicts that income distribution affects growth through the negative distortionary effects of government expenditures and taxes on investment and savings decisions (Persson and Tabellini, 1992, 1994; Perotti, 1993; Alesina and Rodrik, 1994). The endogenous fiscal policy approach, with its basis on the Median-voter theorem where the amount of government expenditures and the tax rates are decided, is theoretically persuasive but empirically problematic, not least because the correlation between inequality and tax rates was found to be negative and taxation and redistributive expenditures are often positively associated with growth (Saint Paul and Verdier, 1996; Perotti, 1996 and Josten and Truger, 2003). Furthermore, initial inequality is found to be associated with lower growth in non-democratic countries only, indicating that in the absence of democratic rights the high-income minority has the resources to protect their wealth and to lobby for policies which are beneficial to them but may be harmful to the rest of the economy and to growth (Li et al., 1998, a similar argument is pursued by Rodriguez, 2004). Another strand of literature identified the security of property rights as a link between inequality and growth, with higher income inequality turning property rights less secure through social polarisation, resulting in negative growth impacts (Knack and Keefer, 2000). Related approaches stress the impact of inequality on socio-political stability and its influence on growth with higher inequality leading to less socio-political stability which is considered detrimental for growth (Venieris and Gupta, 1986; Alesina and Perotti, 1996; Perotti, 1996 and Bourgignon, 1998). Non-political models of the link between income distribution and growth consider factors such as education and fertility (Perotti, 1996; De la Croix and Doepke, 2003) credit market imperfections and human capital investments (Galor and Zeira, 1993; Bertola et al., 2006), market size, demand effects and innovations (Murphy et al., 1989; Matsuyama, 2002; Foellmi and Zweimüller, 2006) and aspects of globalisation (Cornia, 2003; Dreher and Gaston, 2006).

The proposition that initial inequality seems to be associated with lower growth rates has gained much empirical support in recent years (Bénabou, 1996). But many new studies drawing on the Deininger–Squire database (Deininger and Squire, 1996), which is superior to data available to older studies, have questioned the supposed new consensus. Forbes (2000), for example, finds a significant and positive impact of inequality on economic growth. Knack and Keefer (2000) found the only surviving link between income inequality and growth to be the property rights channel. The coefficients for political violence, redistribution, capital market and market size all lose their significance when tested with higher-quality income distribution data. Deininger and Squire (1998) find the negative coefficient on initial income inequality in their regressions insignificant when a variable for asset inequality (the Gini coefficient for land ownership) is introduced into the model. Some subsequent studies found negative growth impacts of human capital inequalities (Birdsall and Londono, 1997; Castello and Domenech, 2002) and land inequality (Deininger and Olinto, 2001).

The current state of the debate can be summarised as follows: while it is not certain whether initial income inequality directly affects economic growth (Bourgignon, 2004), it is a proxy for more fundamental wealth and human capital inequalities. Once measures for wealth inequalities are included in the empirical analysis, there seems to be a significant negative relationship between asset inequality and economic growth. On the other hand, there seem to be no systematic links between the level of development and income distribution. Nevertheless, the research literature was able to identify certain factors affecting the income distribution such as land tenure, education and population growth (Kanbur, 2000, p. 818). In addition, most studies agree that not the level of development but economic structure and, most importantly, pursued policies are the most important factors determining income distribution.

## 3.3. POLITICS, INSTITUTIONS AND INCOME DISTRIBUTION

Income distribution and growth are definitely influenced by pursued policies and political institutions. However, the analysis of the relationship between institutions, the political process and income distribution has not gained much emphasis so far. While the impact of economic and political liberties on the economic growth performance of a country has been extensively investigated (Scully, 1992; Przeworski and Limongi, 1993, 2003; Knack and Keefer, 1995; Baum and Lake, 2003; Halperin et al., 2004), only a few studies deal with the relationship between political institutions and income distribution (Meltzer and Richard, 1981; Olson, 1982; Scully, 1992; Li et al., 1998; Acemoglu and Robinson, 2000, 2002; Gradstein et al., 2001; Mueller and Stratmann, 2003; Reuveny and Li, 2003; see also Gradstein and Milanovic, 2000 for a survey).

It has long been recognised that a more egalitarian distribution of political rights in the form of a political democracy should, according to the Median-voter model, be accompanied by a more equal income distribution (Meltzer and Richard, 1981). The model shows that the poorer the median voter is relative to the average voter, the higher his preferred tax rate and therefore the higher the amount of redistribution. So, inequality and the expansion of suffrage (with the assumption that the new voters are poorer than the median voter) lead to more redistribution from rich to poor and, accordingly, to a more equal income distribution. Empirical evidence, however, does not support the Median-voter model (Milanovic, 2000). Not only does redistribution from rich to poor constitute only a small fraction of existing redistribution (Tullock, 1997; Mueller, 2004), furthermore, higher inequality does not necessarily lead to more redistribution because different income groups have different political weights and political participation is endogenous with the poor having a lower participation than the rich, making the decisive voter richer than the median voter (Saint Paul and Verdier, 1996; Bassett et al., 1998; Bénabou, 2000; Josten and Truger, 2003 and Rodriguez 2004).

Another strand of literature, pioneered by Olson (1982) investigates the impact of interest groups on income distribution. The studies found that, since the possibility of organising interest groups is far more unequally distributed than productive abilities and the control of free-riding requires enough resources, poor-to-rich redistribution is the likeliest consequence of interest group activity (Olson, 1982; Mueller and Murrell, 1986; Tollison, 1997; Rodriguez, 2004). Therefore, the presence of interest groups and the inherent logic of their formation are assumed not only to lead to redistribution from poor to rich and from unorganised to organised, but also to increased income inequality in general. As of to date, there are no empirical studies investigating these theoretical assumptions.

There are some, albeit few, studies dealing with the impact of democratic institutions and participation on income distribution. Scully (1992) presents empirical evidence that politically open countries that are committed to the rule of law, respect private property and have a market allocation of resources have more equal income distributions than countries where these rights are restricted. Li et al. (1998) show that in the absence of democratic rights and civil liberties the high-income groups are able to protect their resources and lobby for policies which are beneficial to them but detrimental for the economy as a whole. This leads to persisting inequality and a negative impact of inequality on the growth rate. According to Acemoglu and Robinson (2000, 2002), the experience of some industrial countries between the middle of the 19th and the beginning of the 20th century shows that increasing inequality caused by industrialisation led to rising political instability. This forced the elite of the respective countries towards democratisation which then caused redistribution measures and a reduction of inequality. Analysing the historical experiences of these countries, the authors find support for a Kuznets curve with democratisation being the link between growth and income distribution. The reduction of inequality therefore depends on political participation. Gradstein et al. (2001) empirically show that the democratisation effect on income distribution works through ideology. In Judeo–Christian societies increased democratisation leads to lower inequality, whereas in Muslim and Confucian societies, which rely on informal transfers to reach the desired level of inequality, democratisation has an insignificant effect on inequality. Mueller and Stratmann (2003) present cross-national evidence that high levels of democratic participation in the form of high voter turnout at elections are associated with more equal distributions of income. Their reasoning shows that high voter participation rates affect government policies, which in turn affect the distribution of income. The reduction of income inequality is caused by larger government sectors, resulting in slower economic growth. Reuveny and Li (2003) investigate the effects of democracy and economic openness on income distribution. Their cross-country evidence shows that democracy has a positive effect on income distribution. The same applies to trade openness, whereas the level of foreign direct investment leads to more inequality.

The results from studies dealing with the connection between political institutions and inequality indicate that institutions seem to matter in the determination of the income distribution of a country. A few studies find democratic constitutional environments and participation to have an influence on income distribution whereas the supposed impact of interest groups on income distribution has so far not been empirically tested. Since political participation is endogenous and different income groups have different political weights in the political process, the voting process as modelled by the Median-voter model does not necessarily lead to an equalisation of the income distribution. Low-income individuals very often do not only stand outside of the economic market but they also have, for different reasons, a weak position in the political marketplace because their political participation is low. The important role of political participation (and political representation) was already stressed by Kuznets (1955, p. 17) stating that increasing political participation and better chances for organisation of low-income groups constitute a necessary condition for falling inequality. Keeping this in mind, it is easy to see that for a concise analysis of income inequality in a society and between countries the political process, and especially political participation, has to be investigated more thoroughly.

## 3.4. HYPOTHESES

There is little empirical evidence so far regarding the connection between political variables and income distribution. The studies measuring the impact of aggregate regime variables on income distribution are at best inconclusive. The few studies investigating the relationship between participation and the income distribution on a more disaggregated level suggest that increasing participation leads to decreasing income inequality. The impact of interest groups on income distribution has so far not been empirically analysed.

The distribution of political income such as monetary transfers, favourable legislation (protection of markets, price subsidies, favourable wages and working conditions, tax exemptions), governmental expenditures on education, housing, health care, agriculture and the like, rents, patronage, jobs and many more is determined by activities of politicians, voters, interest groups and bureaucrats on the political marketplace. Only people who are represented in the political structure of a country can influence the decisions regarding the political income distribution and thus the overall income distribution. People can only become integrated into this political structure and gain influence through some sort of political participation. The amount of participation depends on the individual income situation and educational status with educated and high-income persons participating more than uneducated and low-income persons (Saint Paul and Verdier, 1996; Tullock, 1997; Bassett et al., 1999). From this it follows that uneducated and low-income individuals are more likely to stand outside the political marketplace in which the political income distribution is determined. Increasing participation would therefore lead to more people from lower-income groups to participate in the political marketplace, being able to influence the political income distribution. This can be considered to be a necessary condition for equalising the income distribution in general. Participation influences the integration of the population into the political structure of a country, therefore influencing the political income distribution and the general income distribution. Defined in purely political terms, participation involves voting, campaigning, interest group activity and lobbying (Ayee, 2000, p. 2), in other words, activities to get people involved collectively in efforts to influence policy decisions. Political participation thus means taking part in elections and organising interest groups with the aim of influencing policy. Therefore, in the following empirical investigation, political participation and the integration into the political structure will be measured by the number of interest groups and voter turnout.

### 3.4.1. Interest Groups and Income Distribution

Interest groups are a means of promoting the interests of a certain group of people, focusing their energy on the redistribution of income. Common interests are only a necessary, but not a sufficient reason for successful group formation. In general, the possible formation of a group depends on group size, with small groups having less difficulty to overcome the free-rider problem than large groups (Olson, 1992, p. 5ff.). In addition, the control of free-riding depends on the availability of necessary resources to bear the coordination costs. Therefore groups with higher income are assumed to be organised more easily than poorer income groups (Rodriguez, 2004). The impact of the number of interest groups on the income distribution is not clear however. On the one hand, a large number of pressure groups means that a lot of different small groups get rents at the expense of the large unorganised population, thus resulting in an unequal income distribution (Olson, 1982). On the other hand, the rising number of interest groups enhances the possibility that an individual voter is represented by such a group and therefore gains more influence in the political process. A large number of pressure groups could therefore lead to more political participation and thus to a better integration of the population in the political structure of a country with the possibility of influencing the political income distribution. As a consequence, the political income distribution would be more equal and so would the general income distribution. From this follows, that the number of interest groups can have two opposing effects on the income distribution, which are both tested empirically:

- The 'rent-seeking approach' predicts that a larger number of interest groups leads to a less equal income distribution.
- The 'political participation approach' predicts that a larger number of interest groups leads to a more equal income distribution

### 3.4.2. Voter Turnout and Income Distribution

Voter turnout is a key element of democratic participation. Voters that do not bother or are not allowed to vote are likely not to be represented and have no influence in the political process. Although there are other ways to participate in the political process of a country (for example, through interest groups, public opinion, etc.), the most obvious way is to take part in elections. The higher the participation of a certain group, the higher is its influence in the political process. Voter turnout is different for different groups, depending on factors such as income and education (Mueller and Murrell, 1986, p. 139f.; Saint Paul and Verdier, 1996, p. 720f.; Bassett et al., 1999, p. 208), with high income classes participating more in the political process than low income classes. A higher level of participation would, ceteris paribus, lead to more people from lower-income groups taking part in the political process and influencing the political income distribution. The hypothesis with regard to voter turnout which will be tested later in this chapter is:

- More participation in the form of a higher voter turnout leads to a more equal income distribution.

### 3.4.3. The Importance of Institutions

The extent of integration of the population into the political structure and the degree of their influence on the political income distribution depends on the institutional arrangements of the respective country. Thus, the integration of the population represents a link between institutions and income distribution. Freedom of speech, freedom of association and the right to vote are fundamental conditions for the representation and participation of groups and individual voters in the political process. Countries that curtail these rights are assumed to have lower representation and participation rates than countries where these rights are guaranteed. In addition, even if more authoritarian countries know some kind of forced political participation (for example, compulsory voting, elections with no/limited alternatives, mandatory interest group membership) the restrictions of the political systems ensure that the political income distribution remains unaffected by political participation. Therefore, political participation (voting, organisation of interest groups) is assumed to have no impact on the income distribution in authoritarian states. Democratic institutions such as civil liberties and political rights are assumed to lead to high rates of integration of the population. The responsiveness of politicians who want to be re-elected ensures that the growing influence of lower-income classes translates into legislative and redistributing policy measures. Therefore, in a democratic setting, political participation leads to a more equal political income distribution and thus to a more equal general income distribution. The validity of these arguments can be tested by the following hypotheses:

- The more civil liberties and political rights in a country, the more equal its income distribution.

- In a democratic setting political participation (voting, organising interest groups) has an equalising effect on the income distribution.
- In a non-democratic setting political participation (voting, organising interest groups) has no effect on the income distribution.

## 3.5. EMPIRICAL ANALYSIS

### 3.5.1. The Data

In the following section, the six propositions about the connection between institutions, participation and income distribution will be tested empirically. A sample of 59 countries at three points in time with 156 observations in total is used. The choice of countries was influenced by the availability of the necessary data, with available data for all variables for a least two points in time being the necessary condition for inclusion of the respective country.

*Table 3.1. Data and sources*

| Variable name | Variable description | Variable source |
|---|---|---|
| GINI | Gini coefficient, decade average 1970, 1980, 1990 | Easterly 1999 |
| IGP | Interest groups per 100'000 population, 1970, 1980, 1990 | Coates, Heckelman & Wilson 2007 |
| NOIG | Absolute number of interest groups, 1970, 1980, 1990 | World Guide to Trade Associations 1973/4, 1985, 1999 |
| VT | Voter turnout as % of VAP (voting age population), decade average 1970, 1980, 1990 | www.idea.int |
| POLITY | Polity Score, decade average 1970, 1980, 1990 | Polity IV Project, www.systemicpeace.org |
| SECED | Gross enrolment ratio, secondary education, % of relevant age group, 1970, 1980, 1990 | Easterly 1999 and www.unesco.org |
| POPGR | Annual population growth rate, decade average 1970, 1980, 1990 | Penn World Tables 6.1. |
| GDPPC | GDP per capita, decade average 1970, 1980, 1990, in 1,000 USD | Penn World Tables 6.1. |
| GOVTR | Government transfers as % of GDP, for 1975, 1985, 1995 | www.heritage.org |
| OPEN | Sum of imports and exports as % of GDP, decade average 1970, 1980, 1990 | Penn World Tables 6.1. |
| COMP | Dummy variable, 1 for countries with some degree of obligation to vote | ww.idea.int |

The 59 countries in the total sample consist of 23 OECD-countries, 13 countries from Latin America and the Carribean, 12 countries from Africa and 11 Asian countries. Table 3.1 shows the variables employed in the empirical analysis. The source for data on the Gini coefficient (GINI) is Easterly (1999), who computed decade averages for the Gini coefficients for the 1970s, 1980s and 1990s using data compiled by Deininger and Squire (1996). Interest group data (IGP) is taken from Coates et al. (2007) and the World Guide to Trade Associations (1973, 1974, 1985 and 1999). The variable (IGP) is the number of interest groups per 100,000 population for 1970, 1980 and 1990. Whereas Coates et al. (2007) argue that group strength might depend on the number of interest groups relative to country size, Olson (1982) focuses on the absolute number of groups in a society. Therefore, in some regressions, the absolute number of interest groups in a country (NOIG) is used in addition to the relative number of interest groups. According to Olson (1982) the influence of groups depends not only on the number but also on their strength. However, the data employed here assume that each group is equally powerful, while in fact groups vary in their influence. As proxies for group influence, group budget or membership could be used, but unfortunately, no such data are available for a cross-section of countries. Data for voter turnout are from the International IDEA website (www.idea.int/vt). Political participation is measured as voter turnout (VT) as percentage of the voting age population ('VAP'), whereas the voting age population is an estimation of the number of all those citizens over the legal voting age. Average voter turnout for 1970, 1980 and 1990 is used for all countries in the sample. For the classification of countries according to their political and civil liberties, the combinded Polity score (POLITY) is used, which stems from the Polity IV project (Marshall and Jaggers, 2007). The Polity score is one of the most comprehensive and widely used measures of political regime characteristics. The Polity score ranges from 10 (strongly democratic) to –10 (strongly autocratic). Average values for 1970, 1980 and 1990 are used for all countries in the sample.

In addition to the main explanatory variables, several control variables which are frequently used in income distribution studies are included. GDP per capita, population growth and education are identified to affect income distribution in several studies (Kanbur, 2000). The average GDP per capita in a country (GDPPC, in 1,000 USD) for the 1970s, 1980s and 1990s from the Penn World Tables 6.1 (Heston et al., 2002) and $GDP^2$ are included to test for the Kuznets curve – a positive sign of GDP and a negative sign for $GDP^2$ are expected. The average enrolment ratio in secondary education (SECED) for the three decades from Easterly (1999) and UNESCO (http://www.unesco.org/) is expected to have a positive effect (that is, a negative coefficient) on the income distribution whereas the average population growth rate (POPGR) for the three decades from the Penn World Tables 6.1. should have a negative effect (that is, a positive sign). Following the arguments developed by the Globalisation literature (see Reuveny and Li, 2003 for an overview), trade is expected to influence the income distribution, but the results are inconclusive. Reuveny and Li (2003) found open countries to have a more equal income distribution. Therefore the average sum of imports and exports as percentage of GDP (OPEN), average for the 1970s, 1980s and 1990s from the Penn World Tables 6.1, is included in the equation and expected to have a negative sign. As a last control variable, government transfers (GOVTR) as percentage of GDP for the three decades from the Heritage Foundation (www.heritage.org) is included. Following the reasoning in Mueller and Stratmann (2003), governments affect the distribution of income in several ways (for example, through transfers and expenditures). A larger share of government transfers is thus expected to lead to a more equal income distribution (that is, a negative sign is expected). COMP is a dummy variable identifying countries with compulsory voting (www.idea.int). It serves to control for the impact of a high voter turnout, which does not result from an integration of the population into the political structure of a country but simply results from a legal obligation.

Table 3.2 presents the summary statistics for all variables used in this study. The table shows that the OECD countries do not only have a larger GDP than the non-OECD countries, but also higher secondary education enrolment, slower population growth, larger voter turnout, more interest groups and less inequality. The mean for the Polity variable also shows that

*Table 3.2. Means and standard deviations*

| Variable | Full sample | | | OECD countries | | | Non-OECD countries | | |
|---|---|---|---|---|---|---|---|---|---|
| | Mean | S.D. | n | Mean | S.D. | n | Mean | S.D. | n |
| GINI | 40.48 | 9.28 | 156 | 34.03 | 6.51 | 62 | 44.74 | 8.34 | 94 |
| IGP | 2.18 | 3.59 | 155 | 4.62 | 4.63 | 62 | 0.56 | 0.84 | 93 |
| NOIG | 458.14 | 1012.26 | 155 | 1051.42 | 1407.31 | 62 | 62.61 | 81.83 | 93 |
| VT | 66.19 | 17.18 | 151 | 76.26 | 11.87 | 62 | 59.18 | 16.87 | 89 |
| POLITY | 3.91 | 6.59 | 154 | 8.26 | 4.08 | 62 | 0.99 | 6.34 | 92 |
| GDPPC | 6.02 | 6.10 | 156 | 11.06 | 6.61 | 62 | 2.69 | 2.28 | 94 |
| SECED | 53.37 | 28.86 | 156 | 79.84 | 18.15 | 62 | 35.91 | 19.91 | 94 |
| POPGR | 1.68 | 1.02 | 156 | 0.76 | 0.65 | 62 | 2.28 | 0.73 | 94 |
| GOVTR | 9.91 | 8.73 | 147 | 17.44 | 7.70 | 62 | 4.41 | 4.10 | 85 |
| OPEN | 60.63 | 42.52 | 156 | 55.91 | 27.04 | 62 | 63.75 | 50.08 | 94 |
| COMP | 0.18 | 0.39 | 156 | 0.21 | 0.41 | 62 | 0.16 | 0.37 | 94 |

the OECD countries are on average more democratic than the non-OECD countries. Thus, the propositions are expected to receive more support in the OECD countries because the institutional structure is more open and the integration of the population into the political structure therefore appears to be easier. Differences in the variables for political participation are therefore hypothesised to have a stronger effect in the high-income countries where the democratic institutions are more developed than in the low-income countries.

### 3.5.2. Empirical Estimation and Results

The propositions will be tested empirically by using the following regression equation:

$$GINI = \alpha_1 + \alpha_2 IGP + \alpha_3 NOIG + \alpha_4 VT + \alpha_5 POLITY + \alpha_6 SECED + \alpha_7 POPGR + \\ + \alpha_8 GDPPC + \alpha_9 GDPPC^2 + \alpha_{10} GOVTR + \alpha_{11} OPEN + \alpha_{12} COMP + \varepsilon \qquad (3.1)$$

This specification follows the standards set in other income distribution studies (Kanbur, 2000), where the income distribution is modelled as being linearly dependent on different exogenous variables such as the participation variables (interest groups, voter turnout), the institutional variable (openness of political institutions) and control variables (enrolment in secondary education, population growth, GDP government transfers and trade openness) plus a dummy variable for compulsory voting.

This unbalanced panel is estimated using Least Squares regression with fixed effects to control for bias resulting from omitted variables which are constant over time. In the present case of cross-country comparisons these fixed effects could account for historical and cultural differences between the investigated countries. Fixed effect specification is a way of dealing with endogeneity problems that can be traced to unobservable time-invariant country fixed effects. Heteroskedasticity is accounted for by using White-type robust standard errors.

Tables 3.3–3.5 show the regression results for different specifications of equation (3.1) and different samples. Table 3.3 presents the results for the full sample, including all 59 countries.

The coefficient of the interest group variable (IGP) has a statistically significant negative sign in all equations. This result indicates that more interest groups lead to less income inequality. The 'participation and integration' aspect of interest groups thus seems to be stronger than the 'rent-seeking' aspect. The relative number of interest groups appears to be the decisive variable, with the absolute number of interest groups (NOIG) not having a statistically significant impact on the income distribution. Voter

*Table 3.3. Regression results (dependent variable GINI, different specifications, full sample)*

| Variable | Full sample | | | | | | | | |
|---|---|---|---|---|---|---|---|---|---|
| | 1 | 2 | 3 | 4 | 5 | 6 | 7 | 8 | 9 |
| Constant | 41.27<br>(6.77) | 42.16<br>(6.82) | 41.14<br>(6.54) | 42.00<br>(6.55) | 39.74<br>(7.70) | 41.22<br>(6.66) | 39.81<br>(8.00) | 42.32<br>(6.71) | 42.93<br>(6.70) |
| IGP | −0.37***<br>(−2.62) | −0.24**<br>(−2.08) | −0.36**<br>(−2.53) | −0.24**<br>(−2.05) | −0.34**<br>(−2.48) | | | −0.34**<br>(−2.36) | −0.23*<br>(−1.89) |
| NOIG | | | | | | | | −0.0006<br>(−1.21) | −0.0004<br>(−0.93) |
| VT | −0.02<br>(−0.29) | −0.03<br>(−0.45) | −0.01<br>(−0.24) | −0.02<br>(−0.38) | | −0.02<br>(−0.28) | | −0.03<br>(−0.44) | −0.03<br>(−0.55) |
| POLITY | 0.07<br>(0.39) | 0.09<br>(0.54) | | | | | 0.02<br>(0.13) | 0.07<br>(0.42) | 0.09<br>(0.56) |
| SECED | −0.12***<br>(−2.71) | −0.13***<br>(−2.79) | −0.12***<br>(−2.68) | −0.12***<br>(−2.74) | −0.13***<br>(−2.97) | −0.13***<br>(−2.84) | −0.13***<br>(−3.09) | −0.12**<br>(−2.57) | −0.12***<br>(−2.68) |
| POPGR | 3.23**<br>(2.58) | 3.09**<br>(2.52) | 3.21**<br>(2.40) | 3.06**<br>(2.31) | 3.68***<br>(2.73) | 3.48***<br>(2.72) | 3.89***<br>(3.05) | 3.05**<br>(2.41) | 2.96**<br>(2.37) |
| GDPPC | 1.06<br>(1.50) | 0.98<br>(1.39) | 1.08*<br>(1.66) | 1.03<br>(1.56) | 1.10*<br>(1.71) | 1.04<br>(1.62) | 1.07<br>(1.53) | 1.07<br>(1.52) | 0.99<br>(1.40) |
| $GDPPC^2$ | −0.04<br>(−1.48) | −0.03<br>(−1.36) | −0.04<br>(−1.64) | −0.04<br>(−1.53) | −0.04<br>(−1.61) | −0.04<br>(−1.59) | −0.04<br>(−1.44) | −0.04<br>(−1.43) | −0.03<br>(−1.32) |
| GOVTR | −0.16<br>(−1.56) | −0.21**<br>(−2.26) | −0.15<br>(−1.53) | −0.20**<br>(−2.25) | −0.13<br>(−1.41) | −0.20**<br>(−2.31) | −0.20**<br>(−2.07) | −0.17*<br>(−1.65) | −0.22**<br>(−2.30) |
| OPEN | 0.004<br>(0.29) | 0.0006<br>(0.04) | 0.003<br>(0.20) | −0.001<br>(−0.06) | 0.003<br>(0.20) | −0.002<br>(−0.14) | 0.0002<br>(0.02) | 0.002<br>(0.13) | −0.001<br>(−0.06) |
| COMP | | 3.03**<br>(1.99) | | 2.91*<br>(1.84) | | | | | 2.93*<br>(1.89) |
| *n* | 141 | 141 | 142 | 142 | 146 | 143 | 145 | 141 | 141 |
| $R^2$ adj. | 0.48 | 0.50 | 0.49 | 0.50 | 0.52 | 0.48 | 0.50 | 0.48 | 0.49 |

*Notes*:
T-statistics in parentheses:
*** statistically significant on the 99% level
** statistically significant on the 95% level
* statistically significant on the 90% level

turnout has the expected negative sign, indicating that a stronger voter turnout leads to less inequality. However, the coefficient is not statistically significant. The coefficient of the institutional variable (POLITY) does not have the expected negative sign and is not statistically significant. With the exception of the variable measuring openness towards trade, all the other control variables have the expected signs and the coefficients of the education and population growth variable even have strong statistical significance, which is in line with the findings of other income distribution studies. The coefficients of the two GDP variables hint at a Kuznets-type relationship between state of development and income distribution, but the results are in general not significant (with two exceptions). In addition, government transfers are found to lead to lower income inequality (expected sign in all and statistical significance in six of nine equations).

In regressions 2, 4 and 9 a dummy variable for countries with compulsory voting regimes was added. The coefficient has a statistically significant positive sign in all equations indicating that countries with some sort of obligation to vote have a more unequal income distribution. In addition, the dummy variable for compulsory voting has an impact on some of the other coefficients, most notably the coefficients for voter turnout and government transfers, which both increase in absolute size and in their statistical significance. Countries with compulsory voting seem to have a more unequal income distribution, but government transfers have a stronger income equalising effect in these countries compared to countries without compulsory voting. A first tentative explanation for the findings in Table 3.3 could be that they are an indicator that unequal countries try to ensure that all parts of its diverse population take part at elections. The significant role of government transfers in reducing income distribution in countries with compulsory voting might be an indicator for the attempt of governments in unequal societes to mitigate inequality. This explanation would be in line with some results from the research literature finding that compulsory voting not only leads to higher welfare spending but that compulsory voting has mainly been adopted by countries with commitments to social democratic outcomes (Jackman, 2001; Chong and Olivera, 2005). In general, the research literature on compulsory voting is, until now, inconclusive, especially with regard to the origins and impacts of compulsory voting and its connection to income distribution (Jackman, 2001; Chong and Olivera, 2005; Helmke and Meguid, 2008). To be able to consider compulsory voting adequately in models of income distribution (for example, through instrumental variable estimation), more research is needed to clarify the reasons for introduction of compulsory voting and its connection to income distribution (see Section 3.6).

Overall, the regressions for the full sample are able to explain around 50 percent of the total variation of the Gini coefficient through the variation of the independent variables, which is a good result for models trying to explain the income distribution. Generally, the t-statistics and the coefficients of determination are mostly satisfactory and heteroscedasticity is accounted for. The problem of omitted variables is considered by estimating a model with fixed effects.

In Table 3.4 the sample is divided along OECD membership. As noted above, the propositions are expected to receive more support in OECD countries because their institutional structure is more open and therefore integration of the population into the political structure is assumed to be easier. However, the results presented in Table 3.4 do not support this assumption. The voter turnout variable still has the expected sign but is still not statistically significant. The interest group variable has the expected and (in 3 of 4 cases) significant sign in the OECD sample, but in the non-OECD sample, the coefficient becomes positive and even statistically significant in equation 16. The compulsory voting variable is positive for both samples and statistically significant in the non-OECD sample. The other variables do not much differ from the results in the full sample, with the exception of the variables measuring state of development (GDPPC and $GDPPC^2$), which become strongly significant, indicating a Kuznets-type relationship between GDP and income distribution at least in less industrialised countries.

*Table 3.4. Regression results (dependent variable GINI, different specifications, OECD/non-OECD sample)*

| Variable | OECD sample | | | | | Non-OECD sample | | |
|---|---|---|---|---|---|---|---|---|
| | 10 | 11 | 12 | 13 | 14 | 15 | 16 | 17 |
| Constant | 48.54 | 51.04 | 48.36 | 44.60 | 48.83 | 35.64 | 36.28 | 34.53 |
| | (7.44) | (6.47) | (7.34) | (12.16) | (7.49) | (4.55) | (4.68) | (4.30) |
| IGP | –0.14* | –0.07 | –0.13* | –0.14* | | 2.32 | 3.45* | 1.32 |
| | (–1.67) | (–0.53) | (–1.67) | (–1.66) | | (1.20) | (1.74) | (1.08) |
| VT | –0.05 | –0.09 | –0.05 | | –0.05 | –0.01 | –0.009 | –0.006 |
| | (–0.83) | (–1.21) | (–0.83) | | (–0.84) | (–0.18) | (–0.13) | (–0.08) |
| POLITY | 0.07 | 0.01 | | | | –0.007 | 0.02 | |
| | (0.49) | (0.08) | | | | (0.04) | (0.13) | |
| SECED | –0.10** | –0.08 | –0.10** | –0.10** | –0.09** | –0.11 | –0.12* | –0.13* |
| | (–2.13) | (–1.59) | (–2.14) | (–2.16) | (–2.04) | (–1.63) | (–1.81) | (–1.98) |
| POPGR | 4.32*** | 4.02** | 4.24*** | 4.56*** | 4.42*** | 2.42 | 2.57* | 2.49 |
| | (3.46) | (2.83) | (3.66) | (4.56) | (3.80) | (1.55) | (1.78) | (1.52) |
| GDPPC | –0.73 | –0.78 | –0.64 | –0.61 | –0.80 | 5.24*** | 4.66*** | 5.90*** |
| | (–1.34) | (–1.27) | (–1.06) | (–1.01) | (–1.32) | (3.07) | (2.80) | (3.65) |
| $GDPPC^2$ | 0.02 | 0.01 | 0.01 | 0.01 | 0.01 | –0.39*** | –0.35*** | 0.46*** |
| | (1.12)+ | (0.90) | (0.85) | (0.88) | (0.99) | (2.92) | (–2.69) | (–3.73) |
| GOVTR | 0.02 | 0.04 | 0.03 | 0.008 | 0.03 | –0.11 | –0.26 | –0.05 |
| | (0.15) | (0.35) | (0.26) | (0.08) | (0.35) | (0.49) | (–1.41) | (–0.23) |
| OPEN | –0.02 | –0.03 | –0.02 | –0.03 | –0.03 | –0.02 | –0.03* | –0.01 |
| | (–0.79) | (–0.89) | (–0.89) | (–1.05) | (–1.46) | (–1.57) | (–1.80) | (–1.08) |
| COMP | | 1.91 | | | | | 4.15** | |
| | | (1.14) | | | | | (2.12) | |
| *n* | 62 | 62 | 62 | 62 | 62 | 79 | 79 | 80 |
| $R^2$ adj. | 0.68 | 0.68 | 0.69 | 0.69 | 0.69 | 0.13 | 0.15 | 0.16 |

*Notes*:
T-statistics in parentheses:
*** statistically significant on the 99% level
** statistically significant on the 95% level
* statistically significant on the 90% level

In general, the separation of the sample into OECD and non-OECD countries does not shed more light into the relationship between institutions, participation and income distribution. It is nevertheless possible that the participation propositions receive more support in more democratic countries, as the division of the sample into OECD and non-OECD countries might not be accurate enough. If we look at OECD members closely, we see that there are countries such as Mexico, Turkey and South Korea which are not labelled as free and democratic countries for the period 1970–1990. Other OECD members such as Spain, Portugal and Greece did not get rid of their authoritarian regimes until the middle of the 1970s. On the other hand, non-OECD countries include countries with a long democratic tradition such as India, Mauritius and Costa Rica. To better account for the assumed differences of the impact of the participation variables on the income distribution in democratic and non-democratic countries, the sample will now be divided into 'strong democratic' and 'weak democratic' countries according to the score of the Polity index for political rights and civil liberties (countries with a value of 7 and more are labelled 'strong democratic', the others are termed 'weak democratic'). This differentiation allows for a better separation of democratic from non-democratic countries because it now includes the non-OECD countries with a long democratic tradition whereas some OECD members with a less democratic history are excluded. In addition, to control for the robustness of the results, two interaction terms between institutions and participation (POLITY*IGP and POLITY*VT) are tested as well.

The results are presented in Table 3.5. In the strong democratic sample, voter turnout and interest groups now both have a statistically significant equalising impact on the income distribution. The impact of voter turnout on income distribution slightly increases when compulsory voting is controlled for, on the other hand, the coefficient of the interest group variable loses its significance. In the weak democratic sample, the coefficients of the voter turnout variable and the interest group variable both have a positive insignificant sign. The equations with interaction terms (equations 22 and 23) support these results. The total marginal effect of the number of interest groups and voter turnout on the Gini coefficient is determined by adding the respective marginal effects of the individual coefficients and the coefficients of the interaction terms multiplied by the value of the Polity variable (Brambor et al., 2006). The results indicate, albeit weakly, that the impacts of interest groups and voter turnout on income distribution depend on the extent of democracy in a country. Only in countries which are very strongly democratic (Polity score at least 9 in equation 22 or 9.6 in equation 23), do interest groups have an equalising effect on the income distribution. If democratic institutions are not strong enough, interest groups have a negative impact on the income distribution. The marginal effect of voter turnout on the Gini coefficient is negative for all countries with a democracy score of more than 1 (equation 22) or 0 (equation 23), that is, voter turnout has an equalising effect on the income distribution in countries with democratic institutions. Even though statistical significance is at best weak, the results nevertheless support the results found in equations 18–21. All other variables remain relatively stable and have the expected signs indicating the robustness of the model.

*Table 3.5. Regression results (dependent variable GINI, different specifications, strong democratic/weak democratic sample)*

| Variable | Strong democratic sample | | Weak democratic sample | | Full Sample | |
|---|---|---|---|---|---|---|
| | 18 | 19 | 20 | 21 | 22 | 23 |
| Constant | 42.49 | 44.16 | 28.65 | 28.77 | 38.05 | 38.52 |
| | (5.20) | (5.54) | (3.10) | (3.01) | (6.36) | (6.40) |
| IGP | –0.29* | –0.24 | 2.41 | 3.64 | 2.70 | 3.05 |
| | (–1.84) | (–1.59) | (0.94) | (1.43) | (1.36) | (1.56) |
| VT | –0.10** | –0.13** | 0.05 | 0.05 | 0.002 | –0.007 |
| | (–2.13) | (–2.25) | (0.64) | (0.65) | (0.03) | (–0.13) |
| POLITY | | | | | 0.72* | 0.89** |
| | | | | | (1.92) | (2.35) |
| POLITYIGP | | | | | –0.30 | –0.32* |
| | | | | | (–1.52) | (–1.64) |
| POLITYVT | | | | | –0.009 | –0.01* |
| | | | | | (–1.27) | (–1.65) |
| SECED | –0.05 | –0.06 | –0.18*** | –0.17*** | –0.11*** | –0.11*** |
| | (–1.01) | (–1.15) | (–3.09) | (–2.91) | (–2.78) | (–2.85) |
| POPGR | 3.71*** | 3.54*** | 4.79*** | 5.06*** | 3.66*** | 3.59*** |
| | (2.94) | (2.77) | (2.94) | (3.03) | (3.25) | (3.27) |
| GDPPC | 0.66 | 0.70 | 4.50** | 3.87** | 0.99 | 0.92 |
| | (0.69) | (0.75) | (2.57) | (2.30) | (1.38) | (1.28) |
| $GDPPC^2$ | –0.03 | –0.03 | –0.31* | –0.27 | –0.04 | –0.034 |
| | (–0.93) | (–0.97) | (–1.81) | (–1.57) | (–1.45) | (–1.35) |
| GOVTR | –0.18 | –0.19 | 0.10 | –0.09 | –0.08 | –0.13 |
| | (–1.40) | (–1.52) | (0.49) | (–0.47) | (–0.71) | (–1.33) |
| OPEN | 0.05 | 0.05 | –0.01 | –0.02 | –0.003 | –0.007 |
| | (1.11) | (1.11) | (–0.86) | (–1.20) | (–0.21) | (–0.43) |
| COMP | | 2.09 | | 4.59* | | 3.70*** |
| | | (1.19) | | (1.75) | | (2.71) |
| n | 80 | 80 | 61 | 61 | 141 | 141 |
| $R^2$ adj. | 0.61 | 0.62 | 0.14 | 0.17 | 0.51 | 0.53 |

*Notes*:
T-statistics in parentheses:
*** statistically significant on the 99% level
** statistically significant on the 95% level
* statistically significant on the 90% level

These results suggest that in democratic countries participation of the population in the form of organising interest groups and taking part in elections has an equalising effect on the income distribution because it leads to a larger part of the population being integrated into the political structure of a country and being able to influence the distribution of political income. In weakly democratic/authoritarian states, elections are often symbolic and do not influence the composition of the government or the outcome of policies and therefore do not allow the population to influence the political income distribution. The same seems to be true with regard to the organisation of interest groups. In weakly democratic states the interest groups that matter are often informal groups which are not taken into account here. Therefore it is likely that the impact of interest groups on income distribution is underestimated especially in weakly democratic countries.

The results in general show that participation of the population constitutes a link between the institutional structure of a country and the income distribution. Participation per se is more important than the institutional structure in its effect on income distribution, but the institutional structure influences the size of the effect of participation on income distribution. A more democratic institutional structure of a country leads to a larger effect of political participation on income distribution. The general results support Kuznets' notion about the importance of the working class's integration into the political structure of a country as a necessary condition for falling income inequality. The formation of interest groups such as trade unions seems to have an important equalising effect on the income distribution because it integrates the population into the political structure and allows them to influence the political income distribution. The results for the government transfers variable indicate that the resulting government transfers have an equalising effect on the income distribution. So redistribution by the state seems to go from richer to poorer segments of the population. Voter turnout seems to be less important than interest group formation for integrating the population into the political structure and equalising the income distribution. However, in a strong democratic setting, voter turnout has a more significant effect on income distribution because the institutional structure allows for the impact of voting on the political income distribution.

## 3.6. CONCLUDING REMARKS

The results of this study show that democratic institutions, that is, civil liberties and political rights, alone are no guarantee for a more equal income distribution. Participation in the pure political term is more important for explaining income distribution differentials across countries than institutional variables. The coefficient of the number of interest groups is robust and almost always significant. The coefficient of voter turnout is robust and significant in the strong democratic sample. Democratic participation in the form of being organised through interest groups and to a lesser extent taking part in elections has an equalising effect on the income distribution. The effect of interest groups on the integration of the population seems to be far stronger than the distortionary effect of interest groups through redistribution to themselves. Even if the ability of forming interest groups is far more unequally distributed in a society than resource endowments, the presence of interest groups integrates the population into the political structure of a country and allows them to influence the political income distribution. This influence leads to a variety of policy responses (transfers, legislation etc.). As the political income distribution becomes more equal so does the general income distribution.

The study presented here is one of only a few studies dealing with the institutional determination of income distribution and the first to measure the impact of interest groups on income distribution for a panel of countries. Further research on the topic of institutions and income distribution could focus on a more detailed analysis of the underlying political process and the interactions between groups and politicians regarding the political income distribution, taking into account further factors such as the voting system (proportional or majority voting), the origins and impacts of compulsory voting with regard to income distribution, the political system (direct versus representative democracy) and institutionally determined restrictions (the budget restriction, the administrative restriction and so on).

## NOTE

* The author would like to thank Bruno Jeitziner, Marc Dubach, Alowin Moes, Dennis C. Mueller, Samuel Bowles, Neri Salvadori, two anonymous referees and the participants of the conference 'The Instutitional and Social Dynamics of Growth and Distribution' in Lucca in December 2007 for helpful feedback and comments.

## REFERENCES

Acemoglu, D. and J.A. Robinson (2000), 'Why Did the West Extend the Franchise? Democracy, Inequality, and Growth in Historical Perspective', *Quarterly Journal of Economics*, **115**(4), 1167–99.

Acemoglu, D. and J.A. Robinson (2002), 'The Political Economy of the Kuznets Curve', *Review of Development Economics*, **6**(2), 183–203.

Adelman, I. and C.T. Morris (1973), *Economic Growth and Social Equity in Developing Countries*, Stanford: Stanford University Press.

Ahluwalia, M.S. (1976), 'Inequality, Poverty and Development', *Journal of Development Economics*, **3**(4), 307–42.

Alesina, A. and R. Perotti (1994), 'The Political Economy of Growth: a Critical Survey of the Recent Literature', *World Bank Economic Review*, **8**(3), 351–71.

Alesina, A. and R. Perotti (1996), 'Income Distribution, Political Instability, and Investment', *European Economic Review*, **40**(6), 1203–28.

Alesina, A. and D. Rodrik (1994), 'Distributive Politics and Economic Growth', *Quarterly Journal of Economics*, **109**(2), 465–90.

Anand, S. and S.M.R. Kanbur (1993), 'The Kuznets Process and the Inequality-Development Relationship', *Journal of Development Economics*, **40**(1), 25–52.

Atkinson, A.B. (2003), 'Income Inequality in OECD Countries: Data and Explanations', *CESifo Working Paper*, no. 881.

Atkinson, A.B. and F. Bourgignon (eds) (2000), *Handbook of Income Distribution*, vol. 1, Handbooks in Economics, 16, Amsterdam: North-Holland.

Atkinson, A.B. and T. Piketty (eds) (2007), *Top Incomes over the Twentieth Century: a Contrast Between Continental Europe and English-speaking Countries*, Oxford: Oxford University Press.

Ayee, J.R.A. (2000), 'Participation', paper presented at DPMF and International IDEAs workshop 'Democracy, Poverty and Social Exclusion: Is Democracy the Missing Link', Addis Ababa.

Barro, R.J. (2000), 'Inequality and Growth in a Panel of Countries', *Journal of Economic Growth*, **5**(1), 5–32.

Bassett, W.F., J.P. Burkett and L. Putterman (1999), 'Income Distribution, Government Transfers, and the Problem of Unequal Influence', *European Journal of Political Economy*, **15**, 207–28.

Baum, M.A. and D.A. Lake (2003), 'The Political Economy of Growth: Democracy and Human Capital', *American Journal of Political Science*, **47**(2), 333–47.

Baur, M. (2002), 'Political Institutions and Income Distribution', Dissertation, University of Vienna.

Bénabou, R. (1996), 'Inequality and Growth', in B. Bernanke and J. Rotemberg (eds), *NBER Macro Annual*, Cambridge, MA: MIT Press, pp. 11–76.

Bénabou, R. (2000), 'Unequal Societies: Income Distribution and the Social Contract', *American Economic Review*, **90**(1), 96–129.

Bertola, G., R. Foellmi and J. Zweimüller (2006), *Income Distribution in Macroeconomic Models*, Princeton, NJ: Princeton University Press.

Birdsall, N. and J.L. Londono (1997), 'Asset Inequality Matters: An Assessment of the World Bank's Approach to Poverty Reduction', *American Economic Review Papers and Proceedings*, **82**(2), 32–37.

Bourgignon, F. (1998), *Crime as a Social Cost of Poverty and Inequality: A Review Focusing on Developing Countries*, Paris: DELTA.

Bourgignon, F. (2004), 'The Poverty–Growth–Inequality Triangle', Washington, D.C.: World Bank, mimeo.

Bourgignon, F. and C. Morrisson (1990), 'Income Distribution, Development, and Foreign Trade', *European Economic Review*, **34**, 1113–32.

Brambor, T., W.R. Clark and M. Golder (2006), 'Understanding Interaction Models: Improving Empirical Analyses', *Political Analysis*, **14**, 63–82.

Castello, A. and R. Domenech (2002), 'Human Capital Inequality and Economic Growth: Some New Evidence', *Economic Journal*, **112**(478), C187–C200.

Chenery, H., M.S. Ahluwalia, C.L.G. Bell, J.H. Duloy and R. Jolly (eds) (1974), *Redistribution with Growth*, London: Oxford University Press.

Chong, A. and M. Olivera (2005), 'On Compulsory Voting and Income Inequality in a Cross-section of Countries', *Research Working Paper Series*, no. 533, Washington, D.C.: Inter-American Development Bank.

Coates, D., J.C. Heckelman and B. Wilson (2007), 'Special-interest Groups and Growth', *Department of Economics Working Paper*, no. 01/2007, John Cook School of Business, Saint Louis University.

Cornia, G.A. (2003), 'The Impact of Liberalisation and Globalisation on Income Inequality in Developing and Transitional Economies', *CESifo Working Paper*, no. 843.

Deininger, K. and L. Squire (1996), 'A New Data Set Measuring Income Inequality', *World Bank Economic Review*, **10**(3), 565–91.

Deininger, K. and L. Squire (1998), 'New Ways of Looking at Old Issues', *Journal of Development Economics*, **57**(2), 259–87.

Deininger, K. and P. Olinto (2001), 'Asset Distribution, Inequality and Growth', *World Bank Working Paper*, no. 2375.

De la Croix, D. and M. Doepke (2003), 'Inequality and Growth: Why Differential Fertility Matters', *American Economic Review*, **93**(4), 1091–113.

Dell, F., T. Piketty and E. Saez (2005), 'Income and Wealth Concentration in Switzerland over the 20th Century', *CEPR Discussion Paper*, no. 5090.

Dreher, A. and N. Gaston (2006), 'Has Globalisation Increased Inequality?', *KOF Working Paper*, no. 140.

Easterly, W. (1999), 'Life During Growth', *Journal of Economic Growth*, no. 4, 239–75.

Fields, G.S. (1987), 'Measuring Inequality Change in an Economy with Income Growth', *Journal of Development Economics*, no. 26, 357–74.

Foellmi, R. and J. Zweimüller (2006), 'Income Distribution and Demand-induced Innovations', *Review of Economic Studies*, no. 73, 941–60.

Forbes, K.J. (2000), 'A Reassessment of the Relationship Between Inequality and Growth', *American Economic Review*, **90**(4), 869–87.

Galor, O. and J. Zeira (1993), 'Income Distribution and Macroeconomics', *Review of Economic Studies*, **60**(1), 35–52.

Glaeser, E.L. (2005), 'Inequality', *Harvard Institute of Economic Research Discussion Paper*, no. 2078.

Gradstein, M. and B. Milanovic (2000), 'Does Liberté=Egalité? A Survey of the Empirical Links Between Democracy and Inequality with some Evidence on the Transition Economies', *Policy Research Working Paper*, no. 2875, Washington, D.C.: The World Bank.

Gradstein, M., B. Milanovic and Y. Ying (2001), 'Democracy and Income Inequality: an Empirical Analysis', *World Bank Working Paper*, no. 2561.

Halperin, M.H., J.T. Siegle and M.M. Weinstein (2004), *The Democracy Advantage: How Democracies Promote Prosperity and Peace*, New York: Routledge.

Helmke, G. and B.M. Meguid (2008), 'Endogenous Institutions: the Origins of Compulsory Voting Laws', Paper prepared for the Political Institutions and Economic Policy Conference at Princeton University on 10 May 2008, Department of Political Science, University of Rochester.

Heston, A., R. Summers and B. Aten (2002), *Penn World Tables Version 6.1*, Center for International Comparisons at the University of Pennsylvania.

Jackman, S. (2001), 'Voting: Compulsory', in N.J. Smelser and P.B. Baltes (eds), *International Encyclopedia of the Social and Behavioral Sciences*. Amsterdam: Elsevier, pp. 16314–18.

Josten, S.D. and A. Truger (2003), 'Inequality, Politics and Economic Growth. Three Critical Questions on Politico-Economic Models of Growth and Distribution', *Department of Economics Discussion Paper*, no. 3, Hamburg: University of the Federal Armed Forces.

Kanbur, R. (2000), 'Income Distribution and Development', in A.B. Atkinson and F. Bourgignon (eds), *Handbook of Income Distribution*, vol. 1, Handbooks in Economics 16, Amsterdam: North-Holland, pp. 791–841.

Knack, S. and P. Keefer (1995), 'Institutions and Economic Performance: Cross-Country Tests Using Alternative Institutional Measures', *Economics and Politics*, **7**(3), 207–27.

Knack, S. and P. Keefer (2000), 'Polarization, Politics, and Property Rights: Links between Inequality and Growth', *Policy Research Working Paper*, no. 2418, Washington, D.C.: The World Bank.

Kuznets, S. (1955), 'Economic Growth and Income Inequality', *American Economic Review*, **45**(1), 1–28.

Li, H., L. Squire and H. Zou (1998), 'Explanining International and Intertemporal Variations in Income Inequality', *Economic Journal*, **108**(446), 26–43.

Marshall, M.G. and K. Jaggers (2007), 'Polity IV Project. Political Regime Characteristics and Transitions 1800–2006. Dataset Users' Manual', Centre for Systemic Peace (www.systemicpeace.org).

Matsuyama, K. (2002), 'The Rise of Mass Consumption Societies', *Journal of Political Economy*, **110**(5), 1035–70.

Meltzer, A. and S. Richard (1981), 'A Rational Theory of the Size of Government', *Journal of Economy*, **89**(5), 914–27.

Milanovic, B. (2000), 'The Median-voter Hypothesis, Income Inequality, and Income Redistribution: an Empirical Test with the Required Data', *European Journal of Political Economy*, **16**(3), 367–410.

Mueller, D.C. (2004), *Public Choice III*, Cambridge and New York: Cambridge University Press.

Mueller, D.C. and P. Murrell (1986), 'Interest Groups and the Size of Government', *Public Choice*, **48**(2), 125–45.

Mueller, D.C. and T. Stratmann (2003), 'The Economic Effects of Democratic Participation', *Journal of Public Economics*, **87**(9), 2129–55.

Murphy, K.M., A. Shleifer and R. Vishni (1989), 'Income Distribution, Market Size, and Industrialization', *Quarterly Journal of Economics*, **104**(3), 537–64.

Olson, M. (1982), *The Rise and Decline of Nations: Economic Growth, Stagflation and Social Rigidities*, New Haven, CT: Yale University Press.

Olson, M. (1992), *Die Logik des kollektiven Handelns*, 3. Aufl., Tübingen: Mohr.
Papanek, G.F. and O. Kyn (1986), 'The Effect on Income Distribution of Development, the Growth Rate and Economic Strategy', *Journal of Development Economics*, **23**(1), 55–65.
Perotti, R. (1993), 'Political Equilibrium, Income Distribution, and Growth', *Review of Economic Studies*, **60**(4), 755–76.
Perotti, R. (1996), 'Growth, Income Distribution and Democracy: What the Data Say', *Journal of Economic Growth*, **1**(2), 149–87.
Persson, T. and G. Tabellini (1992), 'Growth, Distribution and Politics', *European Economic Review*, **36**(2–3), 593–602.
Persson, T. and G. Tabellini (1994), 'Is Inequality Harmful for Growth?', *American Economic Review*, **84**(3), 600–621.
Piketty, T. (2003), 'Income Inequality in France 1901–1998', *Journal of Political Economy*, **111**(5), 1004–42.
Piketty, T. (2005), 'Top Income Shares in the Long Run: an Overview', *Journal of the European Economic Association*, **3**(2–3), 382–92.
Piketty, T. and E. Saez (2003), 'Income Inequality in the United States, 1913–1998', *Quarterly Journal of Economics*, **118**(1), 1–39.
Przeworski, A. and F. Limongi (1993), 'Political Regimes and Economic Growth', *Journal of Economic Perspectives*, **7**(3), 51–69.
Przeworski, A. and F. Limongi (2003), 'Political Regime and Economic Growth', in M.A. Seligson and J.T. Passe-Smith (eds), *Development and Underdevelopment: the Political Economy of Global Inequality*, Boulder: Lynne Reiner, pp. 435–48.
Ram, R. (1988), 'Economic Development and Income Inequality: Further Evidence on the U-Curve Hypothesis', *World Development*, **16**(11), 1371–76.
Reuveny, R. and Q. Li (2003), 'Economic Openness, Democracy, and Income Distribution', *Comparative Political Studies*, **36**(5), 575–601.
Rodriguez, F. (2004), 'Inequality, Redistribution and Rent-seeking', *Economics & Politics*, **16**(3), 287–320.
Saint Paul, G. and T. Verdier (1996), 'Inequality, Redistribution and Growth: a Challenge to the Conventional Political Economy Approach', *European Economic Review*, **40**, 719–28.
Scully, G.W. (1992), *Constitutional Environments and Economic Growth*, Princeton: Princeton University Press.
Tollison, R.D. (1997), 'Rent Seeking', in D.C. Mueller (ed.), *Perspectives on Public Choice*, Cambridge: Cambridge University Press, pp. 506–25.
Tullock, G. (1997), *Economics of Income Distribution*, 2nd edition, Dordrecht: Kluwver-Nijhoff Publishing.
Venieris, Y.P. and D.K. Gupta (1986), 'Income Distribution and Socio-political Instability as Determinants of Savings: a Cross-sectional Model', *Journal of Political Economy*, **94**(4), 873–83.
World Guide to Trade Associations (1973), Part 1 Europe, München.
World Guide to Trade Associations (1974), Part 2 Africa, America, Asia, Oceania, München.
World Guide to Trade Associations (1985), 3rd edition, München, New York, London, Paris.
World Guide to Trade Associations (1999), Vol. I and II, 5th edition, München.

# 4. Income distribution and the interaction between cycles and growth*

**Piero Ferri and Anna Maria Variato**

## 4.1. INTRODUCTION

Although the integration of demand and supply was present in the beginning of formal growth theory (see Harrod, 1939), it was largely absent in the mainstream growth models that followed (see also Dutt, 2006 and Palley, 1997). These models mainly focused upon the supply side and upon a deterministic trend (see, for instance, Solow, 1956). This one-sidedness, however, runs the risk of leading to paradoxes or to wrong conclusions. If a long-run time series of growth rates is considered, for example, the hypothesis of interdependence between short-run and long-run movements can be reasonably put forward, as is done by the stochastic trend hypothesis (see Prescott, 1986). Within this hypothesis, which has been largely supported by real business cycle theories (RBC), there is the tendency to attribute an acceleration of growth to technical change, while leaving decelerations largely unexplained, unless the possibility of negative technology shocks is admitted. The advent of endogenous growth theory (Romer, 1986) has helped remove these counterfactual features, for instance by allowing monetary aspects to have long-run effects (see Stadler, 1990). The persistence of shocks has an important role in these kinds of explanations.

Our thesis is that an effective way of dealing with the interaction between cycles and growth is through explicit consideration of the interplay between demand and supply. In this perspective, four points deserve to be stressed. The analysis is based upon a Keynesian model integrated with supply considerations, on the one hand, and a link connecting income distribution, financial and institutional aspects, on the other. It is based on a macro model that is not strictly microfounded, but is compatible with other justifications (see, for instance, Akerlof, 2007). The analysis mainly refers to a medium-run period, rather than a long-run period, as is traditionally done, in which the analysis usually emphasizes the steady state. In this context, it is possible to detect both periods of rapid expansion and of relative decline that differ from those stressed in the business cycle literature and that are ignored by growth models. These phenomena are compatible with the existence of multiple equilibria, where there is dynamic regime switching and agents learn accordingly.

The analysis is carried out by means of simulations in the methodological spirit of Tesfatsion (2006). The results of the simulations show a variety of dynamic patterns that are particularly rich and complex because the model is not constrained to be linear. The simulations show that accelerations and decelerations are possible and that cyclical behaviour can be very persistent. In this context, one can distinguish between feasible and steady-state rates of growth. The former represent the averages that link cycles and growth and depend on the interaction between aggregate demand and supply. These averages can be far from the steady-state values that, according to the supply-side approach, necessarily lead to growth. This gap represents the role of business cycles and, through this channel, the impact of demand on growth dynamics. Its comparative dynamics are studied from an income distribution perspective.

The chapter is structured as follows. Section 4.2 illustrates the main stylized facts from a medium-run perspective. Section 4.3 introduces the multiple equilibria and the regime-switching hypotheses. Section 4.4 presents the relationship between income distribution, debt and the consumption function. Section 4.5 introduces the remaining equations of the model. Section 4.6 discusses the steady-state properties, while Section 4.7 introduces expectations. Section 4.8 analyzes the results of the simulations, and Section 4.9 discusses the concept of feasible growth. Section 4.10 examines the dynamic role of income distribution, while the final section concludes.

## 4.2. MEDIUM-RUN STYLIZED FACTS

When considering growth in the advanced industrialized countries over a long period, it is clear that the actual performance of the economies is far from the steady-state path suggested by the literature on long-run dynamics. The US economy, for example, experienced sustained output growth during the 1960s. From the early 1970s to the early 1980s, however, output growth was low on average, while since the mid-1990s, there has been, for the most part, a return to strong growth.

Three points are worth stressing. The first is that these ups and downs pertain not only to the US economy, but also extend to such economies as those of Europe and Japan. Although the details differ, the experience of these two areas is characterized by similar ups and downs. In the second place, these ups and downs manifest themselves over a time span that is longer than that expected for statistical business cycles. In the third place, these movements seem to be more consistent than those identified at shorter frequencies.

Comin and Gertler (2006) have tried to link the high and medium frequencies. The purpose of this chapter is to link the medium-run to lower frequencies. The possible link between medium-run fluctuations and growth is one of the least explored themes in the economic literature. One might wonder whether this is a relevant area of analysis since business cycles seem to be less relevant in recent experience. From a medium-run perspective, that is, a longer time perspective than is considered in conventional business cycle analyses, the record shows that many industrialized countries have tended to oscillate between periods of sustained growth and intervals of relative stagnation.

These records suggest that the long-run rate of growth may not depend only on technology and a few other parameters that reflect the fundamentals, but also on the complex events that link economic policy, institutions and fundamentals.

## 4.3. MULTIPLE EQUILIBRIA AND REGIME SWITCHING

The oscillations between growth and stagnation can be studied with the hypothesis of multiple equilibria. In this perspective, the economy is characterized by a 'bad' state (state 1), with high unemployment and low growth and by a 'good' state (state 2), with the opposite situation of sustained growth accompanied by low unemployment. In order to obtain multiple equilibria, non-linear relationships are usually introduced (for this strategy, see for instance Evans et al., 1998). Alternatively, one might refer to a piecewise linear technique which assumes that certain functions change discontinuously when they reach a threshold. This is the strategy followed in this chapter (see also Ferri et al., 2001).

It is important to stress that in a regime-switching model, growth depends on: i) what happens within each state and between the two states and ii) the time spent in each regime. In this case, history matters for the process of growth (see also Day and Walter, 1989) and hence for the relationships with income distribution.

In order to implement this approach, one needs to consider two further steps. First of all, a threshold must be identified. For instance, it can be represented by a particular rate of unemployment ($u^{th}$). [1] In this case, if

$$u_{t-1} > u^{th}$$

then the system enters Regime 1.

In the second place, one has to identify the equations that undergo changes when the threshold is reached.[2] In the present analysis, regime switching affects three equations:

i. labour productivity;
ii. income distribution;
iii. monetary policy.

The fundamental equation where the switch takes place is the dynamics of labour productivity which can be expressed in the following way:[3]

$$\tau_{tj} = \tau_{1j} + \tau_2 i_{tj} \tag{4.1}$$

where $j = 1, 2$ are the two regimes and $i_{tj}$ represents investment as a share of output:

$$i = \frac{I_t}{Y_{t-1}}$$

It is assumed that:

$$\tau_{11} < \tau_{12}$$

which implies that the exogenous component of labour productivity growth increases when 'Regime 2' is entered. This means that a regime with lower unemployment stimulates capital–labour substitution and hence labour productivity growth (see also Dutt, 2006 and Tripier, 2006).

Regime switching, however, is not only determined by the technological equation. There are at least two more equations to be considered. The first refers to income distribution. Initially, it will be considered exogenous. However, the labour share ($\omega$) may be assumed to have different steady-state values (always marked by a 0 after any variable) in the two regimes:

$$\omega_{01} \neq \omega_{02}$$

The sign of the inequality is not imposed *a priori* and this is a flexibility property of the analytical tool employed. Yet another switch may happen in monetary policy. Also in this case, one might start initially with the hypothesis that the two steady-state values of the monetary rate of interest $(R_{0j})$ are different in the two steady states:

$$R_{01} \neq R_{02}$$

so that a version of the Taylor equation can be written in the following way:

$$R_{tj} = R_j^* + \psi_1\left(\overline{E}\pi_{tj} - \pi_{0j}\right) + \psi_2\left(\overline{E}g_{tj} - g_{0j}\right) \tag{4.2}$$

where $\pi$ and $g$ represent, respectively, inflation and growth, a bar refers to expectations, and the subscript 0 refers to a steady state. This rule is strengthened by a regime-switching mechanism that is triggered by the deterministic threshold discussed above.[4] Changes in these steady-state values bring about variations in the steady state values of the other variables as well.

The dynamics of the model are generated by a non-linear system of equations supplemented by the regime-switching mechanisms described above. Technically, one should present two systems of equations, one for each state. However, in order to economize space, only the meta system will be presented, indexed by $j$ =1, 2. Furthermore, only parameters that switch, along with the steady states, will be indexed with $j$, while the endogenous variable is only indexed by time.

## 4.4. INCOME DISTRIBUTION, DEBT AND THE CONSUMPTION FUNCTION

The model is based upon two fundamental Keynesian features: saving and investment equations refer to different decision makers, and the labour market does not clear. In particular, the model includes most of the non-neutralities described by Akerlof (2007), which can be justified by 'social norms' and by uncertainty (see Ferri and Variato, 2007).[5]

Let us start from the equilibrium condition that aggregate demand equals supply. In dynamic terms, this equality implies that 1 plus the rate of growth of output $(g_t)$ must be equal to the sum of the investment ratio ($i_t = I_t / Y_{t-1}$) and the consumption ratio (in a closed economy without Government). The latter is a positive function of past and expected incomes and a negative function of the interest rate on accumulated debt ratio (deflated by expected inflation):

$$g_t = i_t + c_1\left(1 + \overline{E}_t g_t\right) + c_2 - c_3 \frac{R_t d_t}{1 + \overline{E}_t \pi_t} - 1 \tag{4.3}$$

where $c_1$ and $c_2$ represent the propensity to consume past and forecast income, while $c_3$ measures the impact of debt.

This consumption function stresses the relationship between income distribution, financial aspects and institutional factors.[6] In this formulation, debt increases from interest and consumption and diminishes because of wages received. In terms of last year output, the debt ratio

$$d_t = \frac{D_t}{P_{t-1}Y_{t-1}}$$

evolves according to the following formula:

$$d_t = \frac{d_{t-1}(1+R_{t-1})}{(1+g_{t-1})(1+\pi_{t-1})} - \frac{i_{t-1}}{(1+g_{t-1})} + (1-\omega_{t-1}) \tag{4.4}$$

where $R$ is the nominal rate of interest and ω stands for the labour income share. Since debt contracts are set in nominal terms, they may be affected by inflation. This is why $\pi$ appears in the denominator.[7]

## 4.5. CLOSING THE MODEL

The interdependence between real and financial aspects is mainly concentrated in the consumption function because we wish to pay tribute to the *Zeitgeist*, namely the tendency of consumers to borrow. Consequently, the investment function has been somewhat simplified; it depends on both the accelerator and the cost of capital:

$$i_t = \eta_1 + \eta_2 \overline{E} g_t - \eta_3 (r_t - r_{0j}) \tag{4.5}$$

Since this equation is expressed in terms of $Y_{t-1}$, it implies that a normalized output–capital ratio is assumed throughout the analysis. The real cost of capital is related to the nominal rate of interest by the Fisher formula:

$$r_t = \frac{(1+R_t)}{(1+\overline{E}_t \pi_t)} - 1 \tag{4.6}$$

We next introduce the labour market equations. Labour demand is given by the following equation:

$$l_t = l_{t-1}\frac{(1+g_t)}{(1+\tau)} \tag{4.7}$$

Two aspects of this formulation should be stressed. First, $l_t$ represents the employment ratio, referred to a normalized labour supply. Hence unemployment $(u_t)$ is given by

$$u_t = 1 - l_t \tag{4.8}$$

Finally, price inflation is determined by the following formula:

$$\pi_t = -\sigma_1 (u_t - u^*) + (1-\varphi)\overline{E}_t \pi_t \tag{4.9}$$

where, as in Akerlof (2000), $\varphi$ measures the percentage of people who are boundedly rational (in the current literature, $\varphi$ measures nominal rigidities, while $\sigma_1$ measures (inversely) real rigidities).

Finally, also the equation relative to income distribution is introduced so that the model is ready for future developments:

$$\omega = \omega_j^* \tag{4.10}$$

For given expectations, the model contains ten unknowns $(d_t, i_t, g_t, l_t, u_t, \pi_t, \tau_t, R_t, r_t, \omega_t)$ in ten equations. This holds true for each regime $j = 1, 2$.

## 4.6. STEADY STATES

As stressed by Solow (2000), the medium run is a sort of no-man's-land that is worth analyzing. It does not belong to the Marshallian tripartite classification (see Leijonhufvud, 2006) and from a statistical point of view it occupies a range between high frequencies (short run) and low frequencies (long run). In economics terms, its steady state is defined by the fulfilment of expectations

$$\overline{E}g_t = g_t$$
$$\overline{E}\pi_t = \pi_t$$

the constancy of growth and of the main ratios. In this perspective, unemployment is constant, as are the debt ratio and the investment ratio.

Two caveats are worth stressing. The first is that the model does not consider the relationship between investment and capital, and it assumes a normalized labour supply. Both assumptions would be untenable in the long run. Secondly, there is no single steady state, since the model is distinguished by the presence of two regimes. In this context, the steady state of growth is given by:

$$g_{0j} = \frac{\tau_{1j} + \tau_2 \eta_1}{1 - \tau_2 \eta_2}$$

and since

$$\tau_{11} < \tau_{12}$$

$$g_{01} < g_{02}$$

where 0 refers to the steady state, while 1 and 2 represent, respectively, the 'stagnation' and 'exuberant' states. This dichotomy influences the remaining values. The steady-state value of inflation is given by

$$\pi_{0j} = \frac{B_j + (1 + R_{0j})}{1 + g_{0j}} - 1$$

where $B_j$ is obtained by referring to equations (4.2), (4.3) and (4.6).

The steady state of unemployment is given by:

$$u_{0j} = u^* - \frac{1 - \varphi_1}{\sigma_1} \pi_{0j}$$

This is equal to the NAIRU when the sum of the coefficients $\varphi$ is equal to 1. The real rate of interest is obtained in the Fisher equation (4.6).

## 4.7. MARKOVIAN EXPECTATIONS

In this two-regime system, the decision makers know that the economy experiences periods of 'high' and 'low' growth, along with phases of deflation followed by periods of inflation. We make the assumption that in forming their expectations they follow a two-state Markovian regime switching process (see Hamilton, 1989 and Jamovich and Rebelo, 2006). In more detail, at the end of period $t - 1$, agents believe that the growth rate in period $t$ will be

$$g_t^e = \alpha_1 + \beta_1 s_t + (\rho_1 + \mu_1 s_t) g_{t-1}$$

where $s_t$ is a random variable that assumes the value 0 in the low state and 1 in the high state. It evolves according to the following transition probabilities:

$$\Pr(s_t = 0 | s_{t-1} = 0) = a_1$$

$$\Pr(s_t = 1 | s_{t-1} = 0) = 1 - a_1$$

$$\Pr(s_t = 0 | s_{t-1} = 1) = 1 - b_1$$

$$\Pr(s_t = 1 | s_{t-1} = 1) = b_1$$

Since $s_t$ is not known at time *t*, the expected value, conditional upon $s_{t-1}$, is taken as a forecast. If $s_{t-1}=0$, the conditional forecasting rule is:

$$\overline{E}(g_t|s_{t-1}=0)=\alpha_1+(1-a_1)\beta_1+[\rho_1+(1-a_1)\mu_1]g_{t-1}$$

where the operator *E* is written with a bar to indicate its subjective character, which is different from rational expectations. For $s_{t-1}=1$, the conditional forecasting rule is:

$$\overline{E}(g_t|s_{t-1}=1)=\alpha_1+b_1\beta_1+(\rho_1+b_1\mu_1)g_{t-1}$$

The general forecasting rule is given by:

$$\overline{E}g_t=E(g_t|s_{t-1})=\alpha_1+\beta_1[b_1s_{t-1}+(1-a_1)(1-s_{t-1})]+$$
$$+\{\rho_1+\mu_1[(1-a_1)(1-s_{t-1})+b_1s_{t-1}]\}g_{t-1}$$

With this formulation agents are supposed to form their expectations according to a particular form of bounded expectation (see Grandmont, 1998). Hommes and Sorger (1998) argue that expectations must be consistent with data in the sense that agents do not make systematic errors. This criterion implies that forecasts and data should at least have the same means and autocorrelations.

A similar forecasting rule can applied to inflation, where the random state variable is denoted by *z*. The forecast for this variable is

$$\overline{E}\pi_t=E(\pi_t|z_{t-1})=\alpha_2+\beta_2[b_2z_{t-1}+(1-a_2)(1-z_{t-1})]+$$
$$+\{\rho_2+\mu_2[(1-a_2)(1-z_{t-1})+b_2z_{t-1}]\}\pi_{t-1}$$

Although *s* and *z* are unobserved (latent) random variables that introduce regime switching, this does not imply that they have no economic meaning. Regime switching is interpreted as a convenient device to apply to the problem of forecasting and, in view of its popularity among forecasters, it may reflect their practices.

In the present model, we suppose that agents learn the value of these parameters by means of rolling regression,[8] which is another source of dynamics in the model. The assumption that all the agents have the same learning simplifies the coordination problem, as underlined by Howitt (2006).

## 4.8. DYNAMICS OF THE MODEL

The system of structural equations above, along with the forecasting rules, is non-linear and can be solved only by means of simulations. In this sense, our exercise is very close to the experiments suggested by Tesfatsion (2006). It differs in that heterogeneity of agents is considered in a macro version, and it is based upon a functional distinction (consumers, investors, firms, labour) rather than microeconomic heterogeneity.

The parameters of the simulations are presented in Table 4.1, where the threshold has been set at $u_{02} = 0.02$.

*Table 4.1. Simulation parameters*

| | | | | |
|---|---|---|---|---|
| $u^* = 0.08$ | $\varphi = 0.15$ | $\sigma_1 = 0.03$ | $\tau_{11} = 0.005$<br>$\tau_{12} = 0.01$ | $\tau_2 = 0.022$ |
| $\eta_1 = 0.201$ | $\eta_2 = 0.35$ | $\eta_3 = 0.60$ | $C_1 = 0.40$ | $c_2 = 0.405$ |
| $c_3 = 0.15$ | $\psi_1 = 1.80$ | $\psi_2 = 0.4$ | $\omega = 0.78$ | $R^*_1 = 0.001$<br>$R^*_2 = 0.003$ |

| Variables | $a_j$ | $b_j$ | $\beta_j$ | $\mu_j$ | $\rho_j$ |
|---|---|---|---|---|---|
| $\overline{E}g_t\,(j=1)$ | 0.4 | 0.6 | 0.001 | 0.43 | 0.55 |
| $\overline{E}\pi_t\,(j=2)$ | 0.45 | 0.8 | 0.0002 | 0.48 | 0.48 |

The simulation results (the last 50 runs over $N$ = 1000) are illustrated in Figure 4.1.

The dynamics of the model show persistent fluctuations in growth, unemployment and rate of interest in spite of the presence of a monetary rule that respects the Taylor principle. These fluctuations, however, do not explode but remain bounded after 1000 simulations. These complex results[9] depend on many factors that are worth considering.[10] First of all, they depend on the presence and the nature of the two regimes. In the present case, the values of the parameters guarantee the existence of two steady states with the desired characteristics, as appears from Table 4.2.[11] Secondly, the dynamics are a function of the value of the threshold, as will be discussed below. Thirdly, the dynamics are also a function of expectations. Since expected values are very close to the actual, the learning mechanism is working satisfactorily.[12] Finally, the role of endogenous forces generating the dynamics must be stressed.

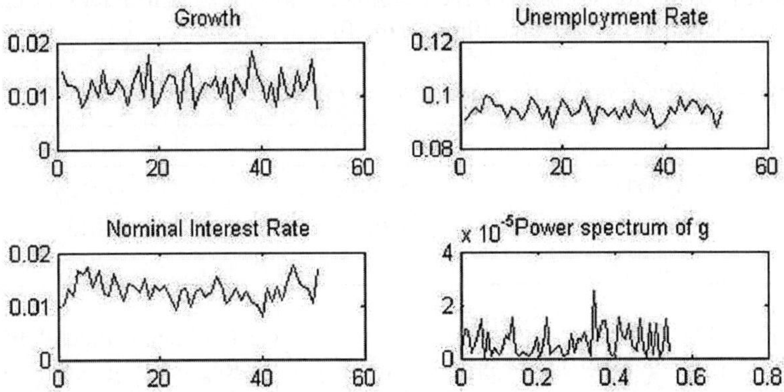


*Figure 4.1. Dynamics of the mode*

*Table 4.2. Steady-state values of the two regimes*

| Regime | $U$ | $\pi$ | $G$ |
|---|---|---|---|
| 1 | 0.1184 | –0.0077 | 0.0095 |
| 2 | 0.0739 | 0.0012 | 0.0145 |

## 4.9. THE FEASIBLE RATE OF GROWTH

Once fluctuations in growth that remain within bounds after a considerable number of runs have been obtained, some further discussion of the actual growth rate is worthwhile. For instance, the long-run rate of growth is hard to determine straightforwardly. It cannot be the steady-state value, because there are two of them. An alternative is to take a long-run average of actual growth rates to obtain 'a feasible rate of growth' (see Ferri, 2001). According to Solow (1997), one can argue whether 'it is best to think about the trend as passing through successive cyclical averages, defined one way or another, or best to think of it passing through cyclical peaks, or some other measure of 'potential' output' (p. 230). In the first alternative, there is a coupling between the short run and the long run. In other words, there is an interaction between cycles and growth. This is the strategy followed in this chapter.

The actual rate of growth depends on the dynamics of the model which, as has been already mentioned, depends on three factors: i) the values of the steady states that constitute a corridor within which actual rate of growth evolves; ii) the time spent in each regime;[13] iii) the actual values in each regime. Table 4.3 gives some hints on the first point.

*Table 4.3. Steady-state values and actual growth*

| $\tau_{01}$ | $\tau_{02}$ | $G$ |
|---|---|---|
| 0.0095 | 0.0145 | 0.0138 |
| 0.0100 | 0.0145 | 0.0137 |
| 0.0010 | 0.0150 | 0.0146 |

The table shows that the actual rate of growth (that is, the average of 1000 runs) depends on the rate of productivity growth in Regime 2, given $\tau_{01}$, the value of productivity in Regime 1. It follows that the greater the range of productivity values, the higher is, ceteris paribus, the feasible rate of growth.

The caveat arises because feasible growth is not a supply-side concept that depends on productivity, but also on other elements, such as the value of the threshold (see Table 4.4), where a non-linear, non-monotonic relationship is obtained. The reasons behind this relationship must be identified in the interrelationship between supply, demand and policy measures.

In this sense, feasible growth depends on history with its interplay of demand and supply factors

*Table 4.4. Growth and the threshold*

| Threshold | Growth | Regime 2: % |
|---|---|---|
| 0.1139 | 0.0136 | 0.8260 |
| 0.0959 | 0.0139 | 0.870 |
| 0.0789 | 0.0138 | 0.8430 |

## 4.10. THE ROLE OF INCOME DISTRIBUTION

Exogenous changes to income distribution can be a privileged angle from which to further study the dynamics of the model. In the first place, it may facilitate understanding of how the system works. Secondly, it is a sensitivity exercise that ascertains the degree of structural stability of the dynamics.

Some points are worth making. First of all, sensitivity analysis, performed by changing the value of $\omega$, shows that the model has structural stability, which is an important dynamic property that allows us to conduct exercises in comparative dynamics. In other words, by changing the values of $\omega$ within a certain range, fluctuations remain bounded. Secondly, in more economic terms, there is a non-linear negative relationship between labour share and growth, along with the percentage of times spent in Regime 2. This result stems both from the particular consumption function that was specified and the steady-state values of the model. An increase in the labour share impacts on debt and hence the steady-state value of inflation in Regime 2. This higher level of steady state inflation ($\pi_{02}$) increases the actual inflation rate which is related to unemployment and hence to the threshold.

*Table 4.5. Growth and exogenous distribution*

| Labour share | *G* | Regime 2:% |
|---|---|---|
| 0.78 | 0.0139 | 0.87 |
| 0.781 | 0.139 | 0.873 |
| 0.785 | 0.0138 | 0.836 |
| 0.79 | 0.0130 | 0.6980 |

Income distribution may be assumed to be endogenous. Endogenous income distribution can result from a wage dynamics that differs from inflation dynamics (see Asada et al., 2006). In this chapter, we theorize a reduced-form macro relationship of the kind:

$$\omega_t = \omega_{0j} - \gamma(u - u_{0j})$$

The results are similar to those obtained with an exogenous income distribution (see Figure 4.2). This implies that regime switching is a robust phenomenon that resists a large variety of changes in both the values of the parameters and the specification of the equations.

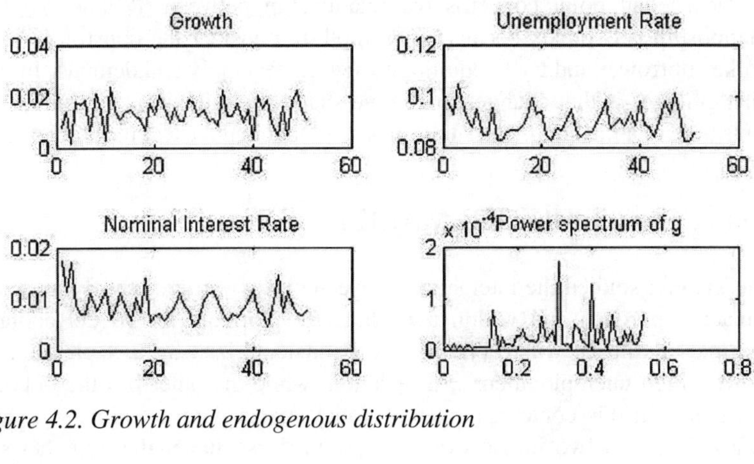


*Figure 4.2. Growth and endogenous distribution*

The new parameters are illustrated in Table 4.6, where different situations are contemplated.

*Table 4.6. Different hypotheses about income distribution*

| $\omega_{01}$ | $\omega_{02}$ | $\gamma$ (+) | $\gamma$ (–) | $g$ | Regime 2:% |
|---|---|---|---|---|---|
| 0.7803 | 0.7798 | 0.1 | | 0.0131 | 0.7120 |
| | | | –0.1 | 0.0140 | 0.8810 |
| 0.7798 | 0.7803 | | –0.1 | 0.0141 | 0.8870 |
| | | 0.1 | | 0.0130 | 0.6950 |

In the present case, persistent oscillations can be obtained with the opposite hypothesis concerning the dynamics of the labour share. While its steady-state value in Regime 2 can be either greater or smaller than that in Regime 1, its link with unemployment can go in either direction. This flexibility can be helpful when dealing with empirical studies where income distribution seems to have less clear-cut stylized facts than those illustrated above for the process of growth.

Two further points are worth considering. The first is that in the case of endogenous income distribution the stability of the system depends crucially on the relationship between $\omega$ and $\gamma$, whereby any increase in the former must be accompanied by a simultaneous decrease in the latter if one wants to obtain the same kinds of persistent fluctuations. The reason for this negative relationship depends on the implicit constraints present in equation (4.4), where a worker–borrower situation is represented. The model does not consider a switch from a worker–lender to worker–borrower situation.[14]

The second point concerns the relationship between $\tau_2$ and $\gamma$. This relationship is complex because it has both to consider the constraint of the worker-borrower and try to equilibrate aggregate supply and demand. In fact, what emerges is that changes in income share through an increase in $\gamma$ can contribute to adjusting the system subject to endogenous technical change.[15]

## 4.11. CONCLUDING REMARKS

This chapter studied the interaction between cycles and growth. By means of a macro approach and within a medium-run horizon, the model contains multiple equilibria, where one regime is characterized by low productivity growth, high unemployment and deflation, while the other has the opposite properties. In this context, monetary policy reacts with a regime-switching policy. This has two impacts on the system. First, under the hypothesis of endogenous productivity growth, steady-state values are not independent of aggregate demand. Second, the regime-switching mechanism constitutes a check on endogenous dynamics, where consumers, investors and workers adjust expectations according to a Markov learning device.

The actual rates of growth can diverge from both steady-state values, which are the focus of most growth theories. Indeed, determination of actual growth is rather complex and depends, in addition to the steady-state values, on the time spent in each regime and on the economic factors that determine the growth rate within each regime. In particular, the results depend very much on the existence of a relationship between consumption, income distribution and debt. In this context, a higher labour share, both in the exogenous and endogenous versions of productivity growth, seems to lead to a smaller average rate of growth.

This average rate can be defined as the feasible rate of growth, a concept that is more compatible with a range rather than a single point and that depends on technological, economic, institutional and policy factors. The fact that average growth can differ from steady-state values indicates the importance of the interplay between business cycles and growth and therefore, indirectly, the role of aggregate demand beyond the very short run.

There is a different way to extend the analysis. First of all, one could extend the link between income distribution and debt to other functions (such as the investment function). Secondly, the relationship between income share, income inequalities, consumption and debt should be developed. This more disaggregated view can bring new insight into the recent developments of the economy. Finally, more long-run forces should be considered in order to move the medium-run horizon towards the long run. Physical capital along with human capital are the obvious candidates. In this perspective, also the problem of creative destruction, that is, the cleansing mechanism present in recessions, along with the possible feedback from growth to cycle, could be considered. Schumpeterian concepts could enrich the multi-phase approach suggested by Day and Walter (1989) where different regimes under different institutional settings can produce complex dynamics in the long run.

## NOTES

* We are grateful to S. Fazzari and E. Greenberg (Washington University) for sharing the scientific project and to Serena Sordi (University of Siena) as an excellent discussant. Finally, special thanks are due to two anonymous referees for stimulating suggestions. A financial contribution from the University of Bergamo is acknowledged. A preliminary version of this paper was discussed at the SEA Annual Meeting, New Orleans (2007)

1. In this medium-run model, an alternative threshold could be given by a longer-run rate of growth.

2. Changes can also be smooth as happens in the so-called STAR models. See Tong (1990).
3. On the relationship with Kaldorian hypotheses, see Ferri (2007). For a general discussion, see Aghion and Howitt (1998) and Velupillai (2004).
4. This behaviour is different from that suggested by Davig and Leeper (2007), where the switching is Markovian and refers to the values of the parameters $\varphi$.
5. Even though the origin of social norms and uncertainty is different, the effects may be similar. Indeed, both create some kind of 'conventional environment' where individuals can take meaningful decisions.
6. These relationships have been justified by Cynamon and Fazzari (2007) along the lines suggested by Akerlof (2007).
7. One must consider that this formula is different from the situation where the debt pertains to the firm and therefore to investment.
8. See Gilchrist and Saito (2006) for the use of a Kalman filter in the case of learning. For an introductory exposition, see Turnovsky (2000). It must be stressed that in our model the agents do not learn the probabilities, but this option can be accomplished.
9. On the different asymptotic results in the case of a non-linear system, see Kuznetsov (2004). On complex dynamics, see Arthur, Durlauf and Lane (1997).
10. Were the threshold given too high a value, it would be as if there were no regime switching. In this case, the dynamics become explosive.
11. In Regime 1, a steady-state nominal rate of interest equal to 0 was assumed, while in Regime 2 a steady-state real rate of interest of 0.001 was fixed.
12. The mean values of $g$ and $Eg$ are respectively 0.0130 and 0.0131, while for $\pi$ and $E\pi$ *they* are 0.0066 and 0.0064.
13. The ergodic probabilities that govern this aspect differ according to the different hypotheses. For Markov regime-switching, see Hamilton (1994). In the case of regime-switching based upon different stochastic processes, see Tong (1990). The reason why the long-run rate of growth is not equal to the steady-state value of growth weighted by ergodic probabilities of the Markov process is due to the presence of deterministic regime-switching.
14. An alternative approach would consist in modifying the constant in the investment equation.
15. More specifically, if $\tau_2$ increases, for instance, to 0.024, then $\gamma$ can reach the value of 0.12 in order to obtain the same kinds of fluctuations. If $\tau_2$ is assumed to be 0.024, then $\gamma$ can be equal to 0.14.

# REFERENCES


Aghion, P. and P. Howitt (1998), *Endogenous Growth Theory*, Cambridge, MA: The MIT Press.

Akerlof, G.A. (2000), 'Behavioral Macroeconomics and Macroeconomic Behavior', *American Economic Review*, **92**(2), 411–33.

Akerlof, G.A. (2007), 'The Missing Motivation in Macroeconomics', *American Economic Review*, **97**(1), 5–36.

Arthur, W.B., S.N. Durlauf and D.A. Lane (eds) (1997), *The Economy as an Evolving Complex System II*, Proceedings Volume XXVII, Santa Fe Institute Studies in the Sciences of Complexity, Reading, MA: Addison-Wesley.

Asada, T.P., C. Chen, C. Chiarella and P. Flaschel (2006), 'Keynesian Dynamics and the Wage–Price Spiral: a Baseline Disequilibrium Model', *Journal of Macroeconomics*, **28**(1), 90–130.

Comin, D. and M. Gertler (2006), 'Medium-term Business Cycles', *American Economic Review*, **96**(3), 523–51.

Cynamon, B.Z. and S.M. Fazzari (2007): 'Household Debt in the Consumer Age: Source of Growth – Risk of Collapse', Washington University, St Louis, MO, mimeo.

Davig, T. and E.M. Leeper (2007), 'Generalizing the Taylor Principle', *American Economic Review*, **97**(3), 607–35.

Day, R.H. and J.L. Walter (1989), 'Economic Growth in the Very Long Run: On the Multiple-phase Interaction of Population, Technology and Social Infrastructure', in W.A. Barnett, J. Geweke and K. Shell (eds), *Economic Complexity*, Cambridge: Cambridge University Press.

Dutt, A.K. (2006): 'Aggregate Demand, Aggregate Supply and Economic Growth', *International Review of Applied Economics*, **20**(3), 319–36.

Evans, G.W., S. Honkapohja and P. Romer (1998), 'Growth Cycles', *American Economic Review*, **88**(3), 495–515.

Ferri, P. (2001), 'Ceilings and Floors, Growth and the Nairu', in R. Bellofiore and P. Ferri (eds), *Financial Fragility and Investment in the Capitalist Economy: the Economic Legacy of Hyman Minsky*, Cheltenham, UK and Northampton, MA, USA: Edward Elgar, pp. 53–68.

Ferri, P. (2007), 'The Labor Market and Technical Change in Endogenous Cycles', *Metroeconomica*, **58**(4), 609–33.

Ferri, P., E. Greenberg and R.H. Day (2001), 'The Phillips Curve, Regime Switching, and the Nairu', *Journal of Economic Behavior and Organization*, **46**(1), 23–37.

Ferri, P. and A.M. Variato (2007), 'Investment and the Taylor Rule in a Boundedly Rational Model', *Quaderni del Dipartmento di Scienze Economiche*, Università di Bergamo (Italy).

Gilchrist, S. and M. Saito (2006), 'Expectations, Asset Prices and Monetary Policy: the Role of Learning', *NBER Working Paper*, no. 12442.

Grandmont, J.M., (1998), 'Expectations Formation and Stability of Large Socioeconomic Systems', *Econometrica*, **66**(44), 741–81.

Hamilton, J.D. (1989), 'A New Approach to the Economic Analysis of Non-stationary Time Series and Business Cycle', *Econometrica*, **57**(2), 357– 84.

Hamilton, J.D. (1994), *Time Series Analysis*, Princeton: Princeton University Press.

Harrod, R.F. (1939), 'An Essay in Dynamic Theory', *Economic Journal*, **49**(193), 14–33.

Hommes, C. and G. Sorger (1998), 'Consistent Expectations Equilibria', *Macroeconomic Dynamics*, **2**, 287–321.

Howitt, P. (2006), 'Coordination Issues in the Long-run Growth', in L. Tesfatsion and I. Judd (eds), *Handbook of Computational Economics*, Volume 2, pp. 1606–24.

Jaimovich, N. and S. Rebelo (2006), 'Can News about the Future Drive the Business Cycle', *NBER Working Paper*, no. 12537.

Kuznetsov, Y.A. (2004), *Elements of Applied Bifurcation Theory*, New York: Springer.

Leijonhufvud, A. (2006), 'Agent-based Macro', in L. Tesfatsion and I. Judd (eds), *Handbook of Computational Economics*, Volume 2, pp. 1626–37.

Palley, T.I. (1997), 'Aggregate Demand and Endogenous Growth: a Generalized Keynes–Kaldor Model of Economic Growth', *Metroeconomica*, **48**, 161–76.

Prescott, E.C. (1986), 'Theory Ahead of Business Cycle Measurement', *Federal Reserve Bank of Minneapolis Quarterly Review*, Fall, 9–22.

Romer, P.M. (1986), 'Increasing Returns and Long-run Growth', *Journal of Political Economy*, **94**(5), 1002–37.

Stadler, G.W. (1990), 'Business Cycle Models with Endogenous Technology', *American Economic Review*, **80**(4), 763–78.

Solow, R.M. (1956), 'A Contribution to Growth Theory', *Quarterly Journal of Economics*, **70**(1), 65–94.

Solow, R.M. (1997), 'Is There a Core of Usable Macroeconomics We Should All Believe in?', *American Economic Review, Papers and Proceedings,* **87**(2), 230–32.

Solow, R.M. (2000), 'Towards a Macroeconomics of the Medium Run', *Journal of Economic Perspectives*, **14**(1), 151–58.

Tesfatsion, L. (2006), 'Agent-based Computational Economics: a Constructive Approach to Economic Theory', in L. Tesfatsion and I. Judd (eds), *Handbook of Computational Economics*, Volume 2, pp. 832–80.

Tong, H. (1990), *Non-linear Time Series,* Oxford: Oxford University Press.

Tripier, F. (2006), 'Sticky Wages, Fair Wages and Co-movements of Unemployment and Labor Productivity Growth', *Journal of Economic Dynamics and Control,* **30**(12), 2749–74.

Turnovsky, S.J. (2000), *Methods of Macroeconomic Dynamics*, Cambridge, MA: MIT Press.

Velupillai, K.V. (2004), 'A Disequilibrium Macrodynamic Model of Fluctuations', National University of Ireland, Galway, mimeo.

# 5. Market failures within poor institutions: the effects of bureaucrats' rent-seeking activity

**Davide Infante and Janna Smirnova**

## 5.1. INTRODUCTION

Recent research has demonstrated that institutions play a fundamental role in economic performance. The establishment of an appropriate institutional infrastructure has been shown to be essential for achieving economic development. Indeed, the presence of solid institutions such as constitutional order, political and financial stability, market securities, competition policies and solid legal systems are necessary components for successful economic growth in developed countries as well as in those undergoing development.

Empirical research has shown that institutional quality continues to improve among developing countries, mainly in transition economies (see, amongst others, Havrylyshyn and van Rooden, 1999; Campos, 2000; Djankov et al., 2003). Likewise, recent studies (Campos 2000; Recanatini and Ryterman, 2000; EBRD, 2002; Di Tommaso et al., 2007) have demonstrated that institutions should be considered important determinants of economic activity since high institutional quality sustains and improves economic performance. However, while there is much agreement regarding the importance of establishing strong institutions for successful economic outcomes, the question as to how a better institutional environment might be created and what its characteristics should be remains still undefined. Indeed, many developing countries are unable to establish strong institutions which can go beyond the embedded poor institutional environment. As some authors argue (Waller et al., 2002; Djankov et al., 2003; Shi and Temzelides, 2004; Acemoglu, 2006; Rajan and Zingales, 2006), societies may continue to harbour weak institutions for various reasons, such as unsuccessful institutional adoption, poor initial distribution of factor endowments, fundamentals of society or the persistence of the elites' preference for a poor institutional environment. In such weak contexts with poor institutions and market distortions, some mechanisms which would otherwise not work for strong economies could actually improve economic outcomes. One such controversial mechanism is the positive effect of rent-seeking activities. While rent-seeking is normally considered harmful for economic performance, some scholars (Shleifer and Vishny, 1994; Acemoglu and Verdier, 2000; McChesney, 2001; Méon and Sekkat, 2005; Infante and Smirnova, 2007; Ahlin and Bose, 2007) have demonstrated that activities such as bribery, red tape and corruption may actually play a positive role when economic and institutional conditions are weak.

Rent-seeking activities are frequent when a weak government attempts to implement its objectives, as asymmetric information between the State and its agents leaves ample room for opportunistic behaviours. However, despite the high opportunity costs, state-sector interventions are clearly necessary due to the production of positive externalities which cannot be introduced by the private sector, particularly in the presence of market failures or in the process of public goods provision. In these situations, government failure, for example, corruption, lobbying, bribery and red-tape, could be tolerated. The issue is therefore not so much the elimination of such opportunistic activity, but of establishing an equilibrium between State inefficiencies and market distortions (Aidt, 2003).

The purpose of this chapter is to analyse the beneficial contribution of rent-seeking activity on economic performance in the presence of a weak institutional environment. In particular, we explore how rent-seeking may influence the allocation of resources in State and production sectors in an institutional environment where bureaucrats enjoy discretional powers when the State attempts to correct market failures. Our analysis is based on two strands of literature, one dedicated to institutions and their role in economic relations and the other to the effects of rent-seeking during State intervention in the economy.

The importance of institutions for economic performance is quite a new area of research with much empirical work carried out, but little from the theoretical point of view. The main difficulties to be tackled by theoretical research dealing with institutions lie in what constitutes an institution and in the complexity of the relationship between various types of institutions and economic theory, making it complicated to introduce institutional indicators into models (Nelson and Sampat, 2001). Most papers studying institutions analyse a single institution or a set of similar institutions within an economic framework. One approach is to analyse the organisational aspect of institutions. A good example is Huang and Xu's (1999) model which shows how economic growth rates depend on whether the financial institutions are organised as merged or centralised bodies. A similar approach is the analysis of the quality of a single institution. Likewise, Skaperdas and Syropoulos (2001) modelled economic performance as a function of a single institution, such as trade security, which can be considered an informal institute necessary for economic development.

Another way to evaluate functionality of institutions is to analyse how efficiently they have been introduced into economic systems. Using this approach, Jack (2002) demonstrated the effect the introduction of a new institution has on social welfare in transition economies, analysing the interaction between operating enterprises and a new institute introduced by government, and comparing the levels of welfare. The actual development of new institutions was considered by Grossman (2001) in terms of the creation of property rights.

Finally, an alternative way to include institutions in theoretical models is to introduce indicators that reflect not a single institution, but a set of them. This approach, although not commonly used in theoretical modelling, has proved to be a good tool in undertaking a broad analysis of the role of institutional environment in the economy. Using this approach, Esfahani (2000) introduced a parameter representing the strength of the institutional environment and showed a way whereby institutions influence the relationship between State and enterprises. The analysis demonstrated how institutional factors such as evaluation of public funds by private agents, reliability of government policies, corruption etc. influenced the ownership of enterprises and the degree of State intervention in the industrial sector. A further developed structural growth model (Esfahani and Ramírez, 2003) examined the mutual effects of infrastructure and economy, using an institutional parameter that encompasses the variables that influence the adjustment rate for capital and infrastructure. Similarly, Brezis and Verdier (2003) constructed a model that studied the diffusion of democracy as well as the process of privatization among former socialist countries, introducing parameters which measure the effectiveness of a 'repression apparatus'. In our model, this approach is applied utilising the institutional parameter, similar to that of Esfahani (2000), to demonstrate the effects of institutional environmental change on resource allocation in neutralising market failure.

The second strand of literature, on which our research is based, regards the theoretical considerations of how the presence of rent-seeking activities influences the relationship between the State and the market. Many studies have examined the effect of rent-seeking in the context of State interventions, exploring the emergence of rent-seeking, government control over rent-seeking behaviour, the interaction of rent-seeking on different levels of hierarchies, and the implication of rent-seeking in State–market relationships. The latter is of great interest to economists who have generated extensive empirical evidence and theoretical proof regarding the negative effect of rent-seeking on government intervention. However, starting from the research of Leff (1964) and Huntington (1968), some have shown that legal and illegal rent-seeking, in certain circumstances, may have a positive influence on economic performance. We focused on theoretical models dedicated to this approach which is mainly based on situations regarding correction of market failures, provision of public goods and other processes where State intervention in the market is required.

An interesting contribution, demonstrating the positive effects of rent-seeking, was made by Auriol and Benaim (2000) who analysed the consequences of public sector corruption in a growth model, showing that equilibrium with corruption may be preferred over one where corruption is absent as corruption mechanisms bypass bureaucratic red tape. Likewise, Coppier and Michetti (2006) demonstrated that higher corruption can be associated with greater production when the State is unable to invest in proper monitoring mechanisms.

Guriev (2004) presented a model that deals with market failures, introducing corruption and red tape and evaluating the mechanism of their integration. The author showed that, at general equilibrium, the level of red tape is above the socially optimal level due to the presence of corruption. It is demonstrated that, even though corruption may have positive effects, its overall effect is destructive and it reduces social welfare. A similar result is obtained by Infante (1999) who presented a growth model in which the presence of rent-seeking is determined endogenously and depends on the different reward structures of the technologies used in the production and rent-seeking sectors.

Rent-seeking usually appears in the relationship between the principal and the agent, with the former being more often the victim of corruption, due to the financial gains the agents obtain from the principal. Olsen and Torsvik (1998) presented an alternative model, demonstrating that the prospective corruption can actually benefit the principal.

Corruption in both private and public sectors was also considered by Acemoglu and Verdier's (1998) general equilibrium model where the State has the role of reinforcing contracts in the private sector. As the authors showed, preventing corruption can actually be very costly and optimal allocation may involve some degree of corruption. This result, as they argue, confirms the experience of developing countries that do not have sufficient sources to prevent rent-seeking activities.

In addition to the abovementioned papers, particular attention is merited by Acemoglu and Verdier's (2000) seminal paper on the positive effects of corruption when the second-best equilibrium has to be chosen. In their model the government neutralises market failure by allocating agents between the State and production sectors. The model uses the principal–agent approach that involves the interaction between two kinds of agents: entrepreneurs and bureaucrats. Bureaucrats are designed as a mechanism to increase system efficiency by controlling market externalities produced by entrepreneurs. The model demonstrates that the second-best allocation requires some level of corruption when the externality in question is considerable.

To explore the interaction between changes in the institutional environment and optimal resources allocation we build a model introducing Esfahani's (2000) institutional parameter into the Acemoglu and Verdier (2000) framework. In our model, bureaucrats are able to enjoy high rent when institutions are weak as opposed to where little rent can be derived when institutions are strong. However, while Acemoglu and Verdier (2000) deal with illegal rent-seeking such as corruption, in our model we consider bureaucrats' rent-seeking as not being necessarily illegal. Bureaucrats obtain economic rent through tools and mechanisms that do not necessarily contradict the rules of society. Although some of our findings are in line with those of Acemoglu and Verdier (2000), that is some illegal rent-seeking (corruption) activity may be preferable to a situation with no illegal rent-seeking, our model pursues a different objective and analyses the links between the strength of the institutional environment and the State intervention to correct market failures. Following the authors, we demonstrate that under a weak institutional environment self-interested bureaucrats have stronger positive effects on market failure corrections by improving the second-best allocation of agents. However, the institutional approach that we adopted permits us to go further and show that, in a weak institutional environment, rent-seeking not only stimulates the agents to opt for good production technology, but also enlarges the range of the positive externality generated by good technology adoption, increasing social surplus. We also argue that rent-seeking in a poor institutional context becomes beneficial only in the case when the State can perceive and utilise the opportunistic behaviour of agents to improve economic performance.

The remainder of the chapter is organised as follows. In Section 5.2, we discuss how the institutional environment is introduced into Acemoglu and Verdier's model (2000) and what transformations were necessary for such a modification. The basic model is presented in Section 5.3, whereas Section 5.4 discusses its implications and derives some propositions. Section 5.5 extends the model, analysing the outcome when rent-seeking activities from different sources are incorporated. In Section 5.6, conclusions are drawn.

## 5.2. MODEL SETTINGS

We start by constructing a model based on that of Acemoglu and Verdier (2000), where the government aims to neutralise market failure by introducing bureaucrats into the production sector. Market failure occurs due to the fact that entrepreneurs opt for bad production technology as good technology is more costly. As a consequence, the positive externality that would have been produced through the use of good technology is not generated.

To induce the production sector to adopt good technology, some of the agents become bureaucrats when called on by the government to monitor and report on the technology choices made by entrepreneurs. The government, in turn, imposes taxes on those entrepreneurs who use bad technology and, at the same time, transfers subsidies to those who use good technology, modifying their pay-offs. This mechanism establishes an allocation of agents such that a positive externality is generated and thus social surplus is increased.

At this point, we introduce a parameter into Acemoglu and Verdier's (2000) model, which reflects the institutional environment in order to analyse how changes in the strength of the institutions influence allocations of agents and production of positive externalities. To provide the analysis, however, some of the settings in the original model need to be modified.

It is first necessary to suppose that when the institutional environment weakens, bureaucrats are prone to practise rent-seeking activity. To introduce rent-seeking into the model, it is assumed that the government gives subsidies and collects taxes through the bureaucrats, giving them direct access to funds and allowing them to extract a 'premium' or personal rent during the transfer of public funds to/from a production sector. As discussed in Section 5.1, this mechanism was proposed by Esfahani (2000) who argues that, for self-interested bureaucrats, each dollar under government control is worth more than a dollar, because it can be utilised for private purposes and thus increases the bureaucrats' rents. According to Esfahani (2000), the premium size depends on various institutional factors, such as financial and economic stability, efficiency of the legal system, market security etc.; poor institutional quality permits the extraction of high rents by bureaucrats, while within strong institutions, rent is negligible or null. The premium level also reflects the administrative capability of the government which refers to a set of bureaucratic institutions developed to control and promote the activities of entrepreneurs. If the government is administratively capable, it collects taxes and issues subsidies with less distortions and bureaucratic costs, decreasing the volume of the premium.

For the sake of simplicity, in our model the premium is expressed as in terms of the delay in the transfer of specific taxes from bad technology entrepreneurs to the government and of the subsidies from the government to good technology entrepreneurs. Hence, the subsidies and taxes become available after a time lag,[1] with a short delay considered welfare-increasing. Therefore, the bureaucrats are involved in rent-seeking activity and extract rent from the subsidies and taxes, which does not represent an illegal action. The amount of rent that bureaucrats can extract depends on the strength of the institutional environment: in a weak institutional environment, where the government is not administratively capable and the institutional quality is poor, the bureaucrats can extract a high premium while, in a strong institutional environment, the premium is negligible. A similar approach introducing institutional quality is described by Ellis and Fender's (2006) growth model.

In our model, another assumption must be added to overcome the problem of negative subsidy which was identified by Acemoglu and Verdier (2000). In their model, income from the State budget, which was used to pay the wages of bureaucrats and subsidies to good technology entrepreneurs, comes from the taxes extracted from bad technology entrepreneurs. Consequently, the presence of bad technology entrepreneurs is necessary to balance the State's budget. However, in the final equilibrium, bad technology is completely eliminated. Such an allocation of agents could not therefore be supported by a State which has no funds to pay the bureaucrats and good technology entrepreneurs. To overcome this problem, Acemoglu and Verdier (2000) allowed for a negative subsidy, whereby good technology entrepreneurs were also taxed. In our model, both positive and negative subsidies can be applied to achieve a final equilibrium by introducing an additional source of income for the State in the form of a general tax paid by all entrepreneurs. We suppose that the general tax is paid when the entrepreneurs are monitored by the bureaucrats,[2] that is, it depends on the probability of bureaucrats monitoring. The State budget therefore consists of both the specific tax paid by bad technology entrepreneurs, as well as the general tax paid by all entrepreneurs.

Based on the above assumptions, we can now construct a model that analyses how changes in the strength of the institutional environment can influence the allocation of agents in both State and production sectors, supporting the neutralisation of market failure and the generation of positive externalities.

## 5.3. MODEL

The model considers two types of production technologies chosen by the entrepreneurs ($n$). Good production technology generates a positive externality ($\beta$) together with an output ($y$) that provides benefits for the other agents (with the total number of agents normalised to unity), and requires cost ($c$). Bad production technology does not produce any externality and does not require any cost, producing the same amount of output as good technology. As the entrepreneurs are interested in maximising the pay-off that they can extract from production and since the application of bad production technology means a greater pay-off, they are not motivated to choose the good technology and no positive externality is therefore generated.

To incentivize the choice of good technology, the government induces some of the entrepreneurs to become bureaucrats $(1 - n)$ to monitor the technological choices of the entrepreneurs, transferring subsidies $(s)$ to the entrepreneurs who use good technology $(x)$ and collecting taxes $(\tau)$ from the entrepreneurs using bad technology $(n - x)$. By delaying the transferring of subsidies and taxes, the bureaucrats extract a premium $(\gamma)$. Both types of entrepreneurs pay the government a general tax $(t)$.

As in Acemoglu and Verdier's (2000) model, bureaucrats monitor entrepreneurs randomly with the probability given by:

$$p(n) = \frac{1-n}{n}$$

When bureaucrats monitor entrepreneurs, the pay-offs of the good and bad entrepreneurs are given by:

$$\pi_{good} = y + \beta x - c + p(n)(s - t) \tag{5.1}$$

$$\pi_{bad} = y + \beta x - p(n)(\tau + t) \tag{5.2}$$

Pay-offs thus depend on the output produced, the positive externality received and on the taxes paid or the subsidies received after being monitored.

The government is interested in maximising the social surplus (*SS*) that is positively correlated to the entrepreneurs' output and the positive externality. As in Acemoglu and Verdier (2000), this is:

$$SS = ny + (\beta - c)x \tag{5.3}$$

With no government intervention, when entrepreneurs do not apply good technology, the allocation of agents is given by $n = 1,\ x = 0$. Once the government intervenes, it aims to allocate agents such that $n = x$, so as to obtain the adoption of only good technology and thus maximise social surplus.

Given the above settings, the following sections analyse how changes in the premium that bureaucrats put on subsidies and specific taxes influence both the allocation of agents at the second-best equilibrium point and the amount of positive externality which can be generated by good technology entrepreneurs.

### 5.3.1. Allocation of Entrepreneurs Between Good and Bad Technology

We start by analysing how the premium which bureaucrats extract from public funds influences the allocation of entrepreneurs between good and bad technologies. To maximise the social surplus, the government has to respect the following set of constraints:

1. *Liability constraint.* The total amount of the general and specific taxes paid to the government does not exceed the value of entrepreneurs' output:

$$\tau \leq y - t \tag{5.4}$$

2. *Technology constraint.* To induce the entrepreneurs to use good production technology, the pay-off of good technology entrepreneurs is greater than that of bad technology entrepreneurs, implying the following inequality:

$$y + \beta x - c - \frac{1-n}{n}t + \frac{1-n}{n}s \geq y + \beta x - \frac{1-n}{n}t - \frac{1-n}{n}\tau \tag{5.5}$$

   where the good technology entrepreneurs' pay-off consists of the output produced, plus externality received and subsidies obtained, minus the cost of good technology and a general tax paid to the State, while that of bad technology entrepreneurs is given by the output produced, plus the positive externality received, minus the general and specific taxes paid to the State.

3. *Government budget constraint.* The government does not spend more than it earns; hence the amount of taxes it collects is at least equal to its total expenses:

$$\frac{1-n}{n}(n-x)\tau + \frac{1-n}{n}tn \geq (1-n)w + \frac{1-n}{n}xs \tag{5.6}$$

   where the amount of specific and generic taxes the State collects is on the left and the value of wages paid to bureaucrats plus the value of subsidies issued for good technology entrepreneurs is on the right.

4. *Allocation of talent constraint.* To induce some agents to become bureaucrats the pay-off of a bureaucrat is greater than the pay-off of a good technology entrepreneur:

$$w + \beta x + \frac{1-n}{n}(s+\tau)\gamma \geq y + \beta x - c - \frac{1-n}{n}t + \frac{1-n}{n}s \tag{5.7}$$

where on the left there is the wage and the positive externality a bureaucrat receives plus the premium $\gamma$, which is an exogenous parameter, that a bureaucrat extracts from specific taxes and subsidies.

Substituting the above inequalities (5.4, 5.5, 5.6 and 5.7) and solving them for $x$, we obtain the entire set of constraints the government must respect:

$$x \leq \frac{y(1-n)^2}{nc} + \gamma(1-n) \tag{5.8}$$

This constraint defines the allocation of entrepreneurs between good and bad technology and clearly shows that the number of good technology entrepreneurs is positively related to the premium which the bureaucrats can extract from subsidies and taxes.

Introducing the premium $\gamma$, that is, the legal rent-seeking activity of bureaucrats, directly into the constraint set (5.8) makes our approach different from that of Acemoglu and Verdier's (2000), who generate a separate illegal rent-seeking (corruption) constraint. This distinction makes any further comparison of our results with those of the authors inappropriate, given that our analysis also goes in another direction, concentrating on institutional environment aspects.

### 5.3.2. Allocation of Agents Between State and Production Sectors

To analyse how the premium extracted by bureaucrats affects the allocation of agents between entrepreneurs and bureaucrats, we first consider a State which is attempting to neutralise market failure given constraint (5.8). As in the Acemoglu and Verdier (2000) model, the constraint set is non-convex in $x$ and the social surplus is linear in $x$, such that maximisation of the social surplus has two solutions (see Figure 5.1). The first is given by $n = 1$ and $x = 0$, where none of the entrepreneurs uses good technology. This solution gives the level of social surplus that presumes market failure is inevitable:

$$SS_{MF} = y \tag{5.9}$$

The second solution corresponds to equality $n=x$, where all the entrepreneurs use good technology. In this case the social surplus is given by:

$$SS = n(y + \beta - c) \tag{5.10}$$

Clearly, the State intervenes in the production sector only when $SS_{MF} \leq SS$.

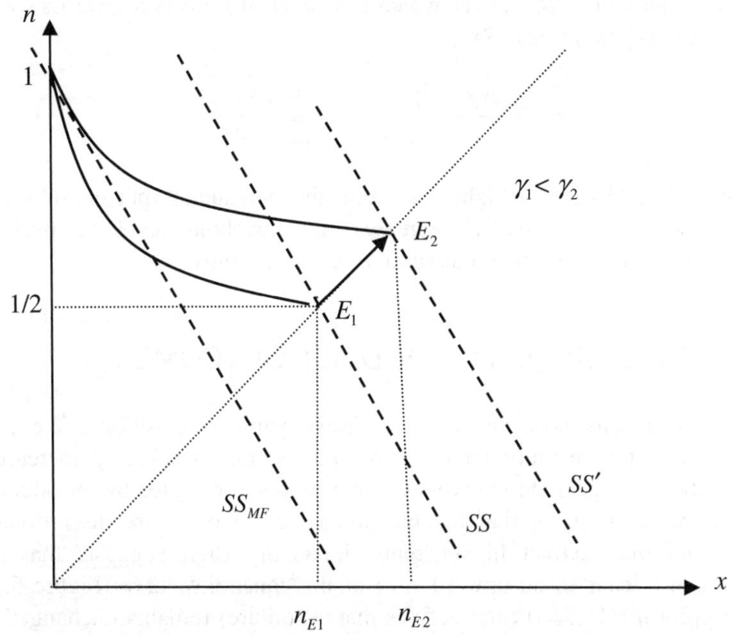


*Figure 5.1. The second-best allocation of agents in a weakening institutional environment*

As optimal outcome from State intervention requires $n=x$, substituting $x$ for $n$ in (5.8) we obtain the second-best allocation of agents ($n_E$):

$$n_E = \frac{-2y + c\gamma + \sqrt{4cy + c^2\gamma^2}}{2(c - y + c\gamma)} \tag{5.11}$$

Since $\partial n_E / \partial \gamma \geq 0$, the premium on public funds ($\gamma$) is positively related to the size of the production sector at the second-best allocation point. Clearly, the level of social surplus that corresponds to this allocation is also positively related to the premium $\gamma$.

### 5.3.3. Positive Externality Produced by Good Technology Entrepreneurs

Here we analyse the relationship between the level of positive externality produced by the adoption of good technology and the premium. To do so, we compare the level of social surplus when market failure has been neutralised ($SS$) to that with market failure ($SS_{MF}$) and define the *threshold* level of positive externality ($\beta_{TH}$) over which any level of $\beta$ gives a level of social surplus that is greater than $SS_{MF}$:

$$\beta_{TH} = \frac{cy\gamma + c^2\gamma + (c-y)\sqrt{4cy + c^2\gamma^2}}{-2y + c\gamma + \sqrt{4cy + c^2\gamma^2}} \tag{5.12}$$

Since $\partial\beta_{TH}/\partial\gamma \leq 0$, a higher premium the bureaucrats put on subsidies and specific taxes actually decreases the threshold level of positive externality over which State intervention in the economy is optimal.

## 5.4. ANALYSIS OF THE MODEL'S OUTCOMES

The above results now allow us to derive some propositions. We first suppose that the institutional environment becomes weaker ($\gamma$ increases) around the time the state intervenes in the production sector by introducing some bureaucrats, such that the bureaucrats can have more discretionary power and thus extract higher rents. Inequality (5.8) suggests that the increase in $\gamma$ leads to an upward shift of the constraint curve (Figure 5.1). While point $n = 1$, $x = 0$ (that defines market failure) remains unchanged in such a shift, the point of second-best solution moves up along the line $n = x$, passing from $E_1$ to $E_2$, demonstrating that there is an increase in the number of good technology entrepreneurs ($n_E$) in accordance with (5.11). Therefore, the increase in $\gamma$ leads to a better allocation of agents ($n_{E2} > n_{E1}$).

We can now analyse the mechanism of government intervention in detail. In order to operate with parameters the government controls, (5.11) can be re-written as:

$$n_E = \frac{\gamma(\tau + s) + (t + s)}{\gamma(\tau + s) + (s + t) + 2\tau} \tag{5.13}$$

Careful examination shows that since $n = x$, any increase in $\gamma$ requires changes in some endogenous parameters if an increase in $n_E$ is needed. To prove this, we rearrange the terms of the constraints the government must respect to satisfy (5.13). The technology constraint (5.5) thus takes the following form:

$$n \leq \frac{s + \tau}{c + (s + \tau)} \tag{5.14}$$

The budget constraint (5.6) can be presented as:

$$x \leq n\frac{\tau + t - w}{\tau + s} \tag{5.15}$$

The talent constraint (5.7) becomes:

$$w \geq y - c + \left[s(1-\gamma) - t - \tau\gamma\right]\frac{1-n}{n} \tag{5.16}$$

As (5.16) shows, growth in $\gamma$ reduces $w$. At the same time, from (5.15), it follows that the decrease in $w$ implies higher $x$. Since the State searches for $n = x$, when $x$ increases, $n$ increases automatically. However, as (5.14) shows, an increase in $n$ suggests changes in $s$, $\tau$, and/or $c$ ($\tau$, in turn, depends on the levels of $y$ and $t$).[3] As a result, increasing $\gamma$ in equation (5.13) does not suggest an automatic increase in $n_E$, but a change in government policy that leads to an increase in $n_E$.

Obviously, there is a wide range of policies the State may implement, such as changing general taxation, bureaucrats' wages and the value of subsidies. It is worth noting that the constraint set imposes precise links between some of these parameters, and changing one of them would automatically change others. For example, with an increase in $\gamma$, one of the reasonable strategies the State may choose is to reduce bureaucrats' wages.[4] In fact, in countries suffering from an 'institutional vacuum', the government has little control over increasing disorder and bureaucrats' rent-seeking become significantly profitable. Therefore, in such weak institutional contexts, government policy may use the increase in $\gamma$ to lower bureaucrats' wages, increasing subsidies in the production sector.

Applying our model, we can demonstrate the application of such a policy. Using the four constraints (5.4, 5.5, 5.6, 5.7 and the requirement $x = n$), the dependence of $w$ on $\gamma$ can be obtained for the second-best point:

$$w = y - \frac{c\gamma + \sqrt{(c\gamma)^2 + 4cy}}{2} \tag{5.17}$$

The second term of the above equation is positive, thus confirming that increasing $\gamma$ may permit a decrease in bureaucrat's wage.

It is now possible to evaluate whether a decrease in $w$ can lead to an increase in $s$. Rearranging the set of constraints, we derive the equation for $s$:

$$s + \tau = \frac{c\gamma + \sqrt{(c\gamma)^2 + 4cy}}{2} \tag{5.18}$$

which simply becomes $s + \tau + w = y$. Indeed, in lowering $w$, the State chooses a higher $s$, and the remaining variables are adjusted respectively.

Therefore, a decrease in bureaucrats' wages can be used to support an increase in the subsidies for good technology entrepreneurs.

We have demonstrated that a policy which reduces bureaucrats' wages to increase subsidies may represent a solution for neutralising market failure in a weakening institutional environment. This means that, in using an appropriate response to the increase in rent-seeking activity, the government can neutralise market failure with a better allocation of agents. Within rent-seeking activities and weak institutions, it is possible to increase the number of good technology entrepreneurs, employing fewer bureaucrats who are also paid lower wages. Such policy goes in the same direction as that outlined by McChesney (2001) who argues that the surest way to respond to rent-seeking activity is to reduce the size of the public sector. Having fewer bureaucrats, necessary for achieving a second-best allocation of agents, also reduces the bureaucratic costs resulting from the loss of output produced by entrepreneurs. It is therefore possible to give the following proposition:

**Proposition 1.** *In a weak institutional environment, the increase in rent-seeking activity of bureaucrats may enable the government, through suitable policies, to neutralise market failure with a larger production sector, lower bureaucratic costs thus increasing social surplus.*

Now we can analyse how rent-seeking influences the threshold level of positive externality which is required to induce the government to intervene in the production sector. As shown in Section 5.3, a higher premium put by bureaucrats on public funds implies a lower threshold level of positive externality produced by good technology (5.12). This mechanism is described by Figures 5.2 and 5.3. Figure 5.2 demonstrates that increasing bureaucrats' discretionary power ($\gamma_2 > \gamma_1$) leads to a better final allocation of agents $n_{E2} > n_{E1}$, shifting from point $E_1$ to $E_2$. This change leads to a higher social surplus, that is, $SS_2$, instead of $SS_1$ (Figure 5.3), that corresponds to a lower threshold level of positive externality ($\beta_{TH2} < \beta_{TH1}$). In fact, Figure 5.3 shows that the threshold level of positive eternality, over which State intervention becomes optimal, decreases with the rise in social surplus lines, generated by the premium increase.

This occurs since even with a lower level of $\beta_{TH}$, an increase in the number of good technology entrepreneurs, resulting from an increase in premium, establishes the level of social surplus beyond $SS_{MF}$. Therefore, in a weak institutional environment, it is possible to actually enlarge the range of feasible good technology adoption, such that even technologies offering a low positive externality become worthwhile for State intervention. The following proposition can thus be formulated:

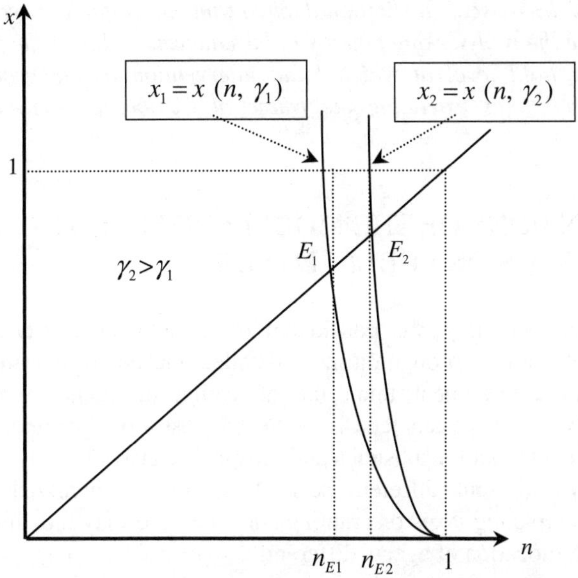


*Figure 5.2. Allocation of agents in a weak institutional environment*

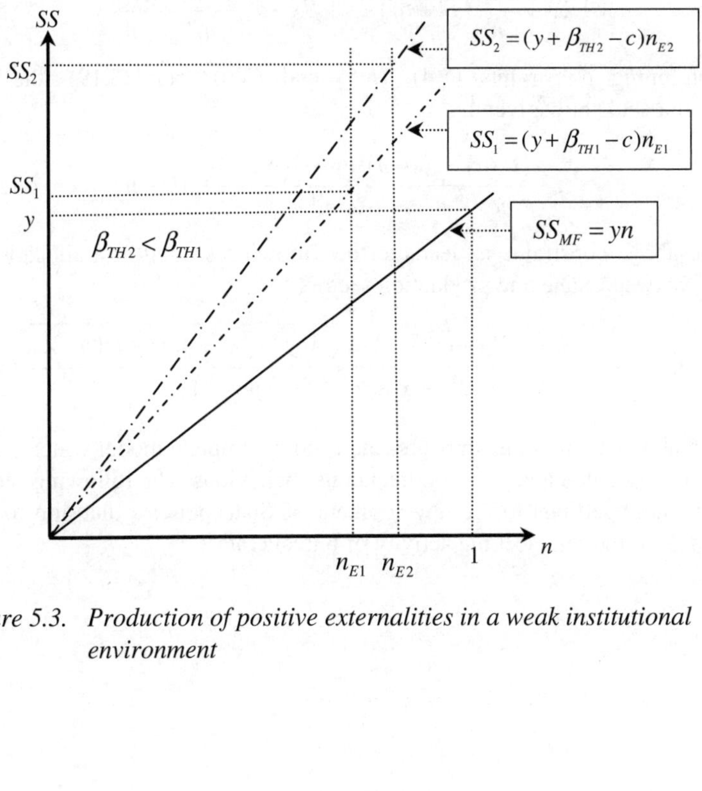


*Figure 5.3. Production of positive externalities in a weak institutional environment*

**Proposition 2.** *In a weak institutional environment, suitable government policies can use the rent-seeking activity of bureaucrats to lower the positive externality threshold level at which State intervention in the production sector is optimal, thus extending the range of feasible good technology adoption.*

## 5.5. EXTENSIONS OF THE MODEL: DIFFERENT PREMIUMS ON PUBLIC FUNDS

In the previous section, $\gamma$ was considered the sole parameter describing bureaucrats' behaviour. To obtain a more detailed analysis of the impact of the institutional environment upon the allocation of agents, $\gamma$ can be expressed by two new parameters $\lambda$ and $\delta$ that respectively represent the premium bureaucrats put on subsidies and on specific taxes. Clearly, distinct premiums may represent different sets of institutions involved in the mechanism of extracting taxes or granting subsidies and may thus influence the second-best allocation of agents differently.

Modifying the settings of the model with respect to the talent constraint, bureaucrats' pay-off is changed as follows:

$$w+\beta x+\frac{1-n}{n}(s\lambda+\tau\delta)\geq y+\beta x-c-\frac{1-n}{n}t+\frac{1-n}{n}s \tag{5.19}$$

Combining constraints (5.4), (5.5) and (5.6) with (5.19), the new constraint set is now given by:

$$x^{*}\leq\frac{y(1-n)^{2}}{nc}+\frac{(1-n)^{2}(y-t)(\delta-\lambda)}{nc}+\lambda(1-n) \tag{5.20}$$

The above constraint set leads to the following second-best allocation of agents between State and production sectors:

$$n_{E}^{\ *}=\frac{-2y+c\lambda-2(y-t)(\delta-\lambda)+\sqrt{4cy+c^{2}\lambda^{2}+4c(y-t)(\delta-\lambda)}}{2\left[c-y+c\lambda-(\delta-\lambda)(y-t)\right]} \tag{5.21}$$

The above expressions thus present a more complete model which allows for a more detailed analysis of bureaucrats' behaviour. The following section applies these settings to the development of State policies that aim to find responses to the rent-seeking activity of bureaucrats.

### 5.5.1. Rent-seeking as a Function of Premiums on Public Funds

Here we describe the comparative static of government intervention in the production sector to neutralise market failure, as a function of the different premiums which bureaucrats can extract from taxes and subsidies.

We first suppose that the government controls $n$ and $x$ by establishing $w$, $\tau$, $s$ and $t$, such that (5.21) is satisfied and the allocation of agents can reach point $E_1$ (Figure 5.4). In the initial stage where the allocation of agents moves from point $A$ to point $B$ and the number of bureaucrats starts growing, these bureaucrats first face bad technology entrepreneurs who must pay the specific tax $\tau$ to the government. The increasing number of bureaucrats, through the monitoring process, augments the pay-off of good technology entrepreneurs, incentivising their emergence. As seen from Figure 5.4, moving from point $A$ to point $B$, the number of good technology entrepreneurs would thus increase from 0 to $x_B$.

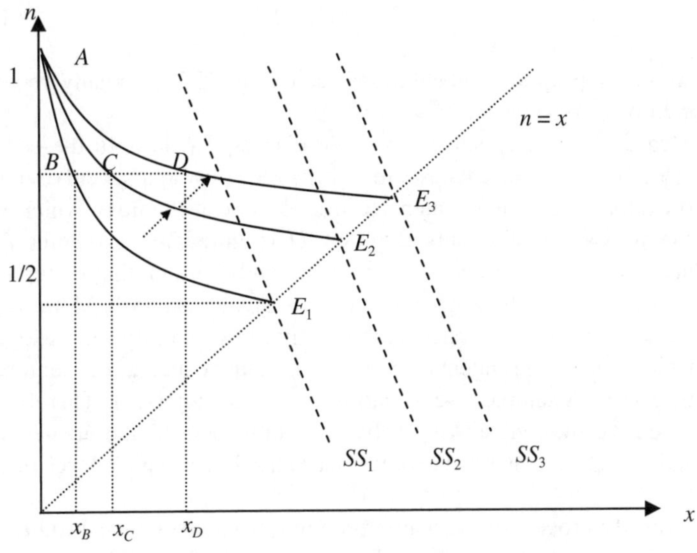


*Figure 5.4. The second-best allocation of agents in a weak institutional environment: a positive effect of rent-seeking, given different premiums on specific taxes and subsidies*

Subsequently, the bureaucrats increase their discretionary power since the institutional environment at point $B$ becomes weaker (that is, $\delta$ increases). Rearranging inequality (5.20) to mirror this increase in rent-seeking behaviour, we obtain:

$$x^* \leq \frac{y(1-n)^2}{nc} + \delta\frac{(1-n)^2(y-t)}{nc} + \lambda\left[(1-n) - \frac{(1-n)^2(y-t)}{nc}\right] \quad (5.22)$$

Therefore, $\partial x^* / \partial\delta \geq 0$ which means that the constraint curve moves forward with an increase in $\delta$. Hence, the allocation moves to point $C$ where the number of good technology entrepreneurs increases ($x_C$). The shift of the constraint curve also implies that point $E_1$ moves upward along line $n = x$ to the point $E_2$, as shown in Figure 5.4, representing a higher level of social surplus.

Once good technology entrepreneurs appear, the bureaucrats also begin to extract rent from subsidies. Referring to equation (5.22) and analysing the derivative $\partial x^* / \partial\lambda$, it becomes evident that the premium on subsidies may have either a positive or a negative influence on the allocation of entrepreneurs. In fact, $\partial x^* / \partial\lambda \geq 0$ when

$$c \geq \frac{1-n}{n}(y-t) \quad (5.23)$$

Applying appropriate substitutions, condition (5.23) actually represents the condition of positive subsidy, $s \geq 0$.

The case of negative subsidy will be discussed below. In the condition where (5.23) is valid, an increase in $\lambda$ shifts the constraint set curve upwards and corresponds to a more intensive use of good technology which would shift the allocation of agents to point $D$ (Figure 5.4). At point $D$, the bureaucrats continue extracting premiums $\lambda$ and $\delta$, prompting entrepreneurs to switch to good technology that offers a greater pay-off. Moreover, the State uses bureaucrats' rent-seeking activity to modify the exogenous parameters, allocating agents to $x_E = n_E$ and reducing the number of bureaucrats (for example, the situation moves to point $E_3$). Therefore, the more intensive the rent-seeking activity of bureaucrats,[5] the greater the $x_E$, and market failure actually becomes neutralised at a higher level of social surplus.

Clearly, the process of extraction premium from taxes and subsidies is not necessarily a gradual one. Indeed, the premium from subsidies may be already extracted at point $B$, as well as the premium on taxes, thus shifting the constraint set curve, after the increase in $\lambda$ and $\delta$, towards the equilibrium point $E_3$.

### 5.5.2. Negative Subsidy for Good Technology Entrepreneurs

In the situation where the subsidy is negative, that is, the case where (5.23) does not hold, modifying the constraints the government must respect (the liability constraint $\tau \leq y-t$ is maintained, since $s \leq \tau$), the constraint set becomes:

$$x^* \leq \frac{y(1-n)^2}{nc} + \delta\frac{(1-n)^2(y-t)}{nc} + \lambda\left[\frac{(1-n)^2(y-t)}{nc} - (1-n)\right] \quad (5.24)$$

The second term in inequality (5.24) shows that the increase in premium on bad technology for which entrepreneurs are taxed ($\delta$) increases the number of good technology entrepreneurs ($x^*$). At the same time, a rise in premium on subsidies of good technology entrepreneurs ($\lambda$) increases $x^*$ if the third term of inequality (5.24) is positive. Elaborating this expression and applying appropriate substitutions, we find that, as in the above case of positive subsidy, the condition of $\partial x^* / \partial \lambda \geq 0$ is only possible when $s \geq 0$. Hence, regardless of whether the subsidy on good technology entrepreneurs is negative or positive, the mechanism of rent-seeking may actually contribute to achieving a better allocation of agents (a greater $x$) in the production sector when institutions are weak.

While this result confirms that of Acemoglu and Verdier (2000), showing that it is possible to apply a negative subsidy to neutralise market failure, our model also shows that when good technology entrepreneurs are taxed, the number of good technology entrepreneurs is reduced compared to the case where good technology entrepreneurs are given subsidies. The following equality that describes the final allocation of agents in the case of negative subsidy demonstrates this result, compared to that in the case of positive subsidy, where all signs remain positive:

$$n_E^* = \frac{\tau - s}{c + \tau - s} \quad (5.25)$$

Therefore, using negative subsidies rather than positive ones with good technology entrepreneurs, the final allocation of agents is given by a lower number of good technology entrepreneurs and a greater number of bureaucrats. The following proposition can thus be formulated:

**Proposition 3.** *The State may use rent-seeking to improve the second-best allocation of agents, regardless of whether the subsidies on good technology entrepreneurs are positive or negative. However, a better second-best allocation of agents is obtained when the State gives positive subsidies.*

Interestingly, the second-best allocation of agents behaves differently to the change of the premium on subsidies or specific taxes. To demonstrate this, from (5.24) we find the ratio of the first derivative of both premiums:

$$\frac{\left(\partial x^*/\partial\lambda\right)}{\left(\partial x^*/\partial\delta\right)}=\frac{s}{\tau} \tag{5.26}$$

Equation (5.26) demonstrates that changes in $\lambda$ or $\delta$ do not elicit the same response in $x^*$, indicating that the State may have various policies at its disposal for correcting market failure since the second-best allocation of agents behaves differently to the change of the premium placed by bureaucrats on specific taxes or subsidies. This could be valuable in a situation when different institutions are involved in subsidisation and taxation. For example, subsidising may be given a primary role if the State does not intend to improve the corresponding institution in the near future, but intends to impose as much good technology as possible.

## 5.6. CONCLUSIONS

This chapter, starting from Acemoglu and Verdier's (2000) model, explored how changes in institutional environment strength affect the allocation of resources in both State and production sectors when the government intervenes to correct market failure. We treat the changes in the institutional environment with a parameter that accounts for both the rent-seeking activity of bureaucrats and the administrative capability of the government. It is supposed that bureaucrats, introduced to neutralise market failure, are involved in transferring subsidies or taxes to/from entrepreneurs who apply good or bad production technology. Subsidies and taxes therefore become a source of rent for bureaucrats. In a weak institutional environment, an increase in bureaucrats' discretionary power influences the choice of agents to become entrepreneurs or bureaucrats, as well as to adopt bad or good technology.

While our findings regarding the positive influence of rent-seeking activity are in line with those of Acemoglu and Verdier (2000), the institutional approach adopted in the present model makes it inappropriate to compare our overall results with those of the above authors. Our model demonstrates that, in a weak institutional environment, the State may actually use the bureaucrats' rent-seeking activity to achieve a second-best agents allocation, wherein more entrepreneurs opt for good technology. Indeed, by implementing suitable State policies as a feedback mechanism to guide rent-seeking behaviour, market failure can be neutralised with lower bureaucratic costs and with a higher level of social surplus. We show that the State may use bureaucrats' rent-seeking activity to extend the range of feasible good technology adoption in the production sector.

The model provides a detailed analysis that considers how differences in the rent which bureaucrats extract from taxes and subsidies influences the second-best agents allocation. In fact, we find that the second-best allocation of agents changes as a function of the rent which bureaucrats manage to obtain from different sources. Therefore, to neutralise market failure, the State may choose among various policies, depending on the strength of the institutions involved in taxation and subsidisation. Finally, our model demonstrates that while both positive and negative subsidies can be applied to good technology entrepreneurs to neutralise market failure, higher levels of good technology adoption and greater social surplus are achieved when the subsidy is positive.

As shown, in a weak institutional environment, bureaucrats' rent-seeking activity can actually work as a constructive mechanism to achieve a better allocation of resources. However, the positive effect of rent-seeking is not everlasting. Once the institutional environment is strong, the search for rent becomes a negative factor that exhausts economic resources and is detrimental to economic performance. The analysis of this aspect goes beyond our model. Further research would be required to consider how new institutional parameters can be incorporated so as to overcome this limit. As it is, the model offers a framework for guiding empirical research to test the propositions regarding the effect of rent-seeking on economic performance in a weak institutional environment.

## NOTES

1. An example of such rent-seeking activity can be the interest rate gained from delay in payments of subsidies and in the transfer of taxes, a common practice of government agencies in developing and transition countries (Saha, 2001).
2. The introduction of such taxes is in response to the reality surrounding weak institutions where tax evasion is common practice (Choi and Thum, 2005).
3. The cost of good technology ($c$) and the level of entrepreneur's output ($y$) cannot be considered under the State's policy.
4. Although, a usual policy response to the increase in bureaucrats' rent-seeking activities is to apply higher wages (Rose-Ackerman, 1999), Waller et al. (2002) demonstrate in their theoretical paper that the increase in bureaucrats' wages may neither reduce corruption itself, nor the number of corrupt state officers. Van Rijckeghem and Weder (2001) empirically prove that the increase in bureaucrats' wages must be very substantial to decrease the level of corruption, which is hard to achieve in a context of weak institutions.
5. The premium cannot increase indefinitely to reach the first-best allocation of agents ($n = x = 1$), since it would require bureaucrats to receive a negative wage. The maximum possible level of premium at the second-best allocation point is given by substituting $w = 0$ in the constraint set and setting $n = x$; therefore $\gamma_{max} = (y/c) - 1$.

# REFERENCES


Acemoglu, D. (2006), 'A Simple Model of Inefficient Institutions', *Scandinavian Journal of Economics*, **108**(4), 515–46.

Acemoglu, D. and T. Verdier (1998), 'Property Rights, Corruption and Allocation of Talent: a General Equilibrium Approach', *Economic Journal*, **108**(450), 1381–403.

Acemoglu, D. and T. Verdier (2000), 'The Choice Between Market Failures and Corruption', *American Economics Review*, **90**(1), 194–211.

Ahlin, C. and P. Bose (2007), 'Bribery, Inefficiency, and Bureaucratic Delay', *Journal of Development Economics*, **84**(1), 465–86.

Aidt, T.S. (2003), 'Economic Analysis of Corruption: a Survey', *Economic Journal*, **113**(11), F632–52.

Auriol, E. and M. Benaim (2000), 'Standardization in Decentralized Economies', *American Economic Review*, **90**(3), 550–70.

Brezis, E.S. and T. Verdier (2003), 'Political Institutions and Economic Reforms in Central and Eastern Europe: a Snowball Effect', *Economic Systems*, **27**(3), 289–311.

Campos, N. (2000), 'Context is Everything: Measuring Institutional Change in Transition Economies', *World Bank Policy Research Working Paper*, no. 2269.

Choi, J.P. and M. Thum (2005), 'Corruption and the Shadow Economy', *International Economic Review*, **46**(3), 817–36.

Coppier, R. and E. Michetti (2006), 'Corruption vs Production: a Non-linear Relationship', *Economic Modelling*, **23**(4), 622–37.

Di Tommaso, M., M. Raiser and M. Weeks (2007), 'Home Grown or Imported? Initial Conditions, External Anchors and the Determinants of Institutional Reform in the Transition Economies', *Economic Journal*, **117**(520), 858–81.

Djankov, S., E.L. Glaeser, R. La Porta, F. Lopez-de-Silanes and A. Shleifer (2003), 'The New Comparative Economics', *NBER Working Papers Series*, no. W9608.

EBRD (2002), *Transition Report*, London: EBRD.

Ellis, C. and J. Fender (2006), 'Corruption and Transparency in a Growth Model', *International Tax and Public Finance*, **13**(2–3), 115–49.

Esfahani, H.S. (2000), 'Institutions and Government Controls', *Journal of Development Economics*, **63**(2), 197–229.

Esfahani, H.S. and M.T. Ramírez (2003), 'Institutions, Infrastructure, and Economic Growth', *Journal of Development Economics*, **70**(2), 443–77.

Grossman, H.I. (2001), 'The Creation of Effective Property Rights', *American Economic Review*, Papers and Proceedings of the Hundred Thirteenth Annual Meeting of the American Economic Association, **91**(2), 347–52.

Guriev S. (2004), 'Red Tape and Corruption', *Journal of Development Economics*, **73**(2), 489–504.

Havrylyshyn, O. and R. van Rooden (2003), 'Institutions Matter in Transition, But So Do Policies', *Comparative Economic Studies*, **45**(1), 2–24.

Huang, H. and C. Xu (1999), 'Institutions, Innovations, and Growth', *American Economic Review*, **89**(2), 438–43.

Huntington, S.P. (1968), *Political Order in Changing Societies*, New Haven: Yale University Press.

Infante, D. (1999), 'Entrepreneurship, Rent-seeking and Economic Development', Federico Caffè Centre, Roskilde University, *Research Report*, 9/1999.

Infante, D. and J. Smirnova (2007), 'Institutional Environment and Transition Economies', in *Proceedings of the Sixth International Scientific and Practical Conference 'State Regulation of the Economy: a Regional Aspect'*, University of Nizhni Novgorod, Russia.

Jack W. (2002) 'Institutional Design and the Closure of Public Facilities in Transition Economies', *Economics of Transition*, **10**(3), 619–35.

Leff, N. (1964), 'Economic Development through Bureaucratic Corruption', *American Behavioral Scientist*, **8**(3), 6–14.

McChesney, F.S. (2001), 'Ever the Twain Shall Meet', *Michigan Law Review*, **99**(6), 1348–69.

Méon, P.G. and K. Sekkat (2005), 'Does Corruption Grease or Sand the Wheels of Growth?', *Public Choice*, **122**(1–2), 69–97.

Nelson, R.N. and B.N. Sampat (2001), 'Making Sense of Institutions as a Factor Shaping Economic Performance', *Journal of Economic Behavior and Organization*, **44**(1), 31–54.

Olsen, T. and G. Torsvik (1998), 'Collusion and Regulation in Hierarchies: a Case of Beneficial Corruption', *International Economic Review*, **39**(2), 413–38.

Rajan, R.G. and L. Zingales (2006), 'The Persistence of Underdevelopment: Institutions, Human Capital or Constituencies', *CEPR Discussion Papers*, no. 5867.

Recanatini, F. and R. Ryterman (2000), 'Disorganization or Self-organization?', *FEEM Working Paper*, no. 26.

Rose-Ackerman, S. (1999), *Corruption and Government: Causes, Consequences and Reform*, Cambridge: Cambridge University Press.

Saha, B. (2001), 'Red Tape, Incentive Bribe and the Provision of Subsidy', *Journal of Development Economics*, **65**(1), 113–33.

Shi, S. and T. Temzelides (2004), 'A Model of Bureaucracy and Corruption', *International Economic Review*, **45**(3), 873–908.

Shleifer, A. and R.W. Vishny (1994), 'Politicians and Firms', *Quarterly Journal of Economics*, **109**(4), 995–1025.

Skaperdas, S. and C. Syropoulos (2001), 'Guns, Butter, and Openness: On the Relationship between Security and Trade', *American Economic Review*, **91**(2), 353–57.

Van Rijckeghem C. and B. Weder (2001), 'Bureaucratic Corruption and the Rate of Temptation: Do Wages in the Civil Service Affect Corruption, and by How Much?', *Journal of Development Economics*, **65**(2), 307–31.

Waller, C.J., T. Verdier and R. Gardner (2002), 'Corruption: Top Down or Bottom Up?', *Economic Inquiry*, **40**(4), 688–703.

# 6. Government spending, effective demand, distribution and growth: a dynamic analysis

**Pasquale Commendatore, Carlo Panico and Antonio Pinto**

## 6.1. INTRODUCTION

This chapter deals with the role of different types of government expenditure in post-Keynesian analysis. This tradition of thought has proposed a formal treatment of these issues with significant delay, in spite of the crucial importance it attributes to government intervention and the fact that its founders paid great attention to the problem of the composition of government spending.[1]

Steedman (1972) made the first attempt to provide a formal treatment of the intervention of a government sector with a balanced budget in the post-Keynesian theory of growth and distribution. Some years later, Fleck and Domenghino (1987) and Pasinetti (1989) started an intense debate on the formal analysis of government deficit within this theory (see Panico, 1997 and Commendatore et al., 2003), while You and Dutt (1996), Lavoie (2000) and Commendatore et al. (2005) proposed a formal analysis of how government debt can affect income distribution and the rate of growth within alternative post-Keynesian approaches. Very recently some post-Keynesian analyses of growth and distribution have focussed on the role of government expenditure and on complex forms of dynamics, generating hysteresis, poverty traps and so on (see Skott, 2008; Hein et al., 2008; Commendatore, 2006; Commendatore et al., 2007 and 2009). These contributions have attained interesting results in the analysis of equilibrium conditions and have paved the way for dynamic treatment of these problems.

Commendatore et al. (2007, 2009) argue that it is important to distinguish different kinds of government expenditures, showing that in the Kaleckian analysis increases in what has been termed 'unproductive'[2] expenditure have a positive influence on growth and can generate hysteresis effects which permanently lead the economy out of the poverty trap. Increases in 'productive' expenditure produce the same positive effects, but may also reduce the degree of capital utilisation and the rate of growth depending on the distribution of the productivity gains between wages and profits. In the Classical–Harrodian analysis increases in 'unproductive' expenditure do not produce hysteresis effects and there can be both positive and negative influences on the degree of capital utilisation and the rate of growth. The same effects are produced by increases in 'productive' expenditure, with the difference that in this case their occurrence depends on whether after-tax profits rise or diminish.

In what follows we attempt a dynamic analysis of the role played by different kinds of government expenditure in these post-Keynesian theories. It is argued that in Kaleckian analysis increases in 'unproductive' expenditure have a positive influence on the stability of the system, such that the existence of a 'big government' favours both the growth and the controllability of the economy.[3] The influence of increases in 'productive' expenditure on the stability and controllability of the system are not so clear-cut, but depend on whether after-tax profits rise or fall. In the Classical–Harrodian analysis increases in 'unproductive' expenditure improve the controllability of the economic system when the size of the government sector is sufficiently large. In this case, however, the effects on growth can be both positive and negative. Examination of changes in 'productive' expenditure shows instead that increases positively affect the stability of the economy when the size of the government sector is sufficiently large, whereas reductions have the same effects when the government sector is sufficiently small. Moreover the controllability of the system improves when the size of the government sector approaches the level that maximises after-tax profits.

The chapter is organised as follows. Section 6.2 presents the analytical model. Sections 6.3 and 6.4 elaborate the Kaleckian and Classical–Harrodian analysis respectively. Section 6.5 summarises the main conclusions.

## 6.2. THE MODEL

The model used by Commendatore et al. (2007, 2009) refers to a single-good closed economy with two production inputs: labour, whose supply is perfectly elastic, and fixed capital, which does not depreciate. In this model technical progress is excluded, in each period the capacity of the capital stock is not fully utilised, such that the potential and current output do not coincide, and the production function is of a Leontief type:

$$Y^P = aK \quad and \quad Y = bL \tag{6.1}$$

where $Y^P$ is the potential output, $Y$ the current output, $K$ the stock of capital, $L$ the amount of labour employed in production, and $a$ and $b$ are the reciprocal of the capital and labour coefficients respectively.

The degree of capacity utilisation is defined as:

$$u = \frac{Y}{Y^P} \tag{6.2}$$

Income is distributed between wages and profits: $Y = wL + rK$, where $w$ is the wage rate and $r$ is the rate of profit. Normalising with respect to output, and taking into account expressions (6.1) and (6.2), this equation becomes

$$1 = \frac{w}{b} + \pi \tag{6.3}$$

where $w/b$ and $\pi \equiv r/au$ are respectively the share of wages and the share of profits in national income.

The model assumes that the wage rate is a function of labour productivity:

$$w = w(b) \quad with \quad w'(b) \geq 0$$

where the value of $w'(b)$ depends on the bargaining power of the unions. By letting the wage–productivity elasticity $\lambda \geq 0$ measure the ability of unions to capture labour productivity improvements, we write

$$w = w_0 b^{\lambda} \tag{6.4}$$

When $0 \leq \lambda < 1$, workers are not able to fully capture the increase in productivity; when instead $\lambda \geq 1$, wage increases are equal or higher than productivity improvements.

The model further assumes that the government sector operates under a balanced budget constraint:

$$\tau = \gamma \tag{6.5}$$

where taxation $\tau$ and public expenditure $\gamma$ are expressed in terms of income.

Although government expenditure can affect labour and capital productivity, the model focuses on the influence on average labour productivity $b$:

$$b = b(\gamma) \quad \text{with} \quad b(0) > 0, \; b' \geq 0 \quad \text{and} \quad b'' \leq 0 \tag{6.6}$$

When $b'=0$, government expenditure has no effect on the labour input coefficient; when $b'>0$, government expenditure reduces the labour coefficient and increases the productivity of this input.

Like in Barro (1990, p. S107), the model assumes that the government enhances input productivity by purchasing goods and services that are freely provided to the private sector. It describes these features by introducing a production function where government expenditure may reduce, as a positive externality, the labour and capital coefficients, instead of following Barro's choice to allow government expenditure to explicitly enter the production function as an argument.

When government expenditure affects labour productivity, the wage share may vary too, depending on the bargaining power of the unions, that is, on $\lambda$. This assumption makes it possible, using equations (6.3), (6.4) and (6.6), to describe the profit share as a function of government expenditure:

$$\pi=\pi(\gamma)=1-w_0\left[b(\gamma)\right]^{\lambda-1} \tag{6.7}$$

where

$$\pi'(\gamma)=(1-\lambda)w\frac{b'(\gamma)}{b}\geq(<)0 \quad for \quad \lambda\leq(>)1$$

If the wage rate increases less (more) than labour productivity, the profit share increases (decreases). In the analysis of the equilibrium condition developed by Commendatore et al. (2007, 2009) and in that proposed below, this relationship plays a crucial role.

As to the private sector, the model assumes that workers do not save and the investment function is not linear:[4]

$$s=s_\pi r(1-\tau)=s_\pi \pi au(1-\tau) \tag{6.8}$$

$$g=\alpha+\phi(u) \tag{6.9}$$

where $s$ is the saving to capital ratio and $s_\pi$ is the propensity to save out of profits while, according to equation (6.9), capital accumulation $g$ depends on an autonomous term $\alpha$ and on a non-linear term $\phi(u)$ enjoying the following properties:

$$\phi(\tilde{u})=0, \quad \phi'>0, \quad \text{and} \quad \phi''\geq(<)0 \quad \text{for} \quad u\leq(>)\tilde{u}$$

where $0<\tilde{u}\leq1$ is the *normal* degree of capacity utilisation that is interpreted as the optimal degree of capacity utilisation given the existing technology (for further details, see Commendatore et al., 2007, 2009).

The term $\alpha$ can be interpreted along a Kaleckian or a Classical–Harrodian line. In the first case, $\alpha$ reflects entrepreneurs' animal spirits and is taken as given like the state of long-term expectations in Keynesian models (see Rowthorn, 1981; Dutt, 1984; Amadeo, 1986; and Lavoie, 1992):

$$\alpha = \bar{\alpha} \tag{6.10}$$

In the second case, $\alpha$ represents the Harrodian 'warranted rate of growth', which depends on the saving generated at normal capacity utilisation (for a similar interpretation, see Commendatore et al., 2003; Shaikh, 2007):

$$\alpha = \tilde{g} \equiv s_\pi \tilde{r}(1-\tau) \tag{6.11}$$

where $\tilde{g}$ is the warranted rate of growth and $\tilde{r} \equiv \pi a \tilde{u}$ is the rate of profit corresponding to normal capacity utilisation.

The dynamics of the system is generated by the variations in the degree of capital utilisation in the face of discrepancies between demand and supply, i.e., between investment and saving. If in one period the economy is not in equilibrium, in the following period the degree of capacity utilisation changes:

$$u_{+1} = \psi(u) = u + \theta(g - s) \tag{6.12}$$

where '$x_{+1}$' denotes the one-period forwarded value of the variable $x$ and where $\theta > 0$ is the speed at which capacity utilisation adjusts to the discrepancy between saving and investment.

By imposing in each period the equilibrium condition $g = s$ and given that $r \equiv \pi a u$, Commendatore et al. (2007, 2009) show that the solutions for $u$ and $g$ correspond to:[5]

$$u^* = \frac{\alpha + \phi(u^*)}{s_\pi \pi a(1-\gamma)} \qquad g^* = s_\pi \pi a(1-\gamma)u^* \tag{6.13}$$

where '$x^*$' denotes the equilibrium value of the variable $x$. The existence of equilibrium solutions, whether single or multiple, depends on the value of the parameters.

An equilibrium solution is locally asymptotically stable or attracting if, and only if, it satisfies the following condition:

$$0 < \theta\left[s_\pi \pi a(1-\gamma) - \phi'(u^*)\right] < 2 \tag{6.14}$$

Expression (6.14) implies that a necessary condition for local stability is that at the equilibrium the slope of the saving function should be steeper than that of the investment function:

$$s_\pi \pi a(1-\gamma) > \phi'(u^*) \tag{6.15}$$

## 6.3. THE KALECKIAN INTERPRETATION

### 6.3.1. Equilibrium

In the Kaleckian interpretation $\alpha$ reflects entrepreneurs' animal spirits and represents the expected growth rate of demand. In this case the equilibrium solutions are

$$u^* = \frac{\bar{\alpha} + \phi(u^*)}{s_\pi \pi a(1-\gamma)} \qquad g^* = s_\pi \pi a(1-\gamma)u^* \tag{6.16}$$

Commendatore et al. (2007, 2009) present the diagram reported in Figure 6.1, which shows that, according to the value attributed to $\gamma$, there can be up to three equilibrium positions that the economy can reach, denoted by $e_L \equiv (u_L^*, g_L^*)$, $e_I \equiv (u_I^*, g_I^*)$ and $e_H \equiv (u_H^*, g_H^*)$.[6] The intermediate equilibrium $e_I$ is unstable, because condition (6.15) is violated. For the 'low' equilibrium $e_L$ and the 'high' equilibrium $e_H$, the slope of the saving function is steeper than that of the investment function. These equilibrium positions are locally stable if conditions (6.14) and (6.15) are satisfied.

Commendatore et al. (2007, 2009) also show that by changing the value of the parameters one or two equilibrium positions may disappear via a fold bifurcation. The bifurcation sequence depends on the impact of government expenditure on the labour coefficient. In Figure 6.1(a), when $\gamma$ does not affect labour productivity, there is one equilibrium position $e_L$. The rise of $\gamma$ generates a fold bifurcation and the appearance of the intermediate and high equilibrium positions, $e_I$ and $e_H$ (Figure 6.1b). Further increases in $\gamma$ end up

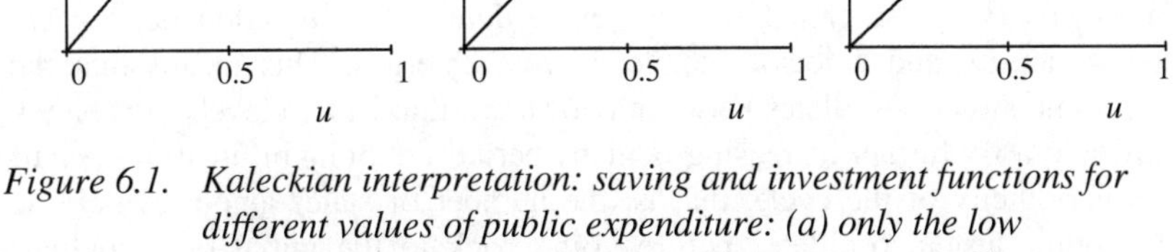


*Figure 6.1. Kaleckian interpretation: saving and investment functions for different values of public expenditure: (a) only the low equilibrium exists; (b) three equilibria are present (low, intermediate, high); (c) only the high equilibrium exists*

generating another fold bifurcation and the disappearance of the low and intermediate equilibrium positions (Figure 6.1c). Notice, however, that changes in $\gamma$ that affect labour productivity can also generate the opposite tendency, going from one high equilibrium position to one low equilibrium when $\gamma$ increases.

These findings (Commendatore et al., 2007, 2009) show that there can be hysteresis effects, which can lead the economy into a poverty trap or out of it, depending on the influence of government expenditure on labour productivity.

### 6.3.2. Dynamic Analysis

Let us now present a dynamic analysis, first investigating how changes in parameter $\theta$, representing the speed at which firms adjust capacity utilisation, affect the local stability of the equilibrium solutions and the long-term behaviour of the economy. The analysis then considers how changes in government expenditure, $\gamma$, affects the local stability of the equilibrium positions.

The difference equation (6.12) is revised as follows for the Kaleckian case:

$$\psi(u)=u+\theta\left[\alpha+\phi(u)-s_{\pi}\pi a(1-\gamma)u\right] \tag{6.17}$$

This map determines the long-term evolution of the state variable $u$ and of the economic system. $\theta$ does not affect the fixed point solution $\psi(u^*)=u^*$, which is determined by the equilibrium condition $g = s$, but it affects the local stability properties of the fixed points and the global stability properties of the map $\psi(u)$. For the fixed point $u^*$, a necessary and sufficient condition for local stability is

$$0<\theta<\theta^F \equiv \frac{2}{s_{\pi}\pi a(1-\gamma)-\phi'(u^*)}$$

As long as this inequality is satisfied, the fixed point $u^*$ is attracting. When $\theta>\theta^F$, a so-called flip or period doubling bifurcation occurs: $u^*$ loses stability and a locally stable 2-cycle emerges. This means that the economic system oscillates between two states, that is, two levels of capacity utilisation. By further increasing $\theta$, many period-doubling bifurcations occur: the periodicity of the cycle, that is, the number of states among which the economic system oscillates before going back to the initial one, doubles. Finally, for sufficiently high values of $\theta$, cycles of any periodicity and even chaos emerge.[7]

Figure 6.2 considers what happens when the values of $\gamma$ generate one equilibrium position and one attractor, as described in Figures 6.1(a) and 6.1(c). It presents two bifurcation diagrams, which describe the impact of the adjustment speed $\theta$ – changing within the interval $14.5 \leq \theta \leq 23.5$ – on the long-term behaviour of the state variable $u$.[8] A period-doubling route to chaotic behaviour can occur both for the low equilibrium $u_L^*$ (Figure 6.2(a)) and for the high equilibrium $u_H^*$ (Figure 6.2(b)).

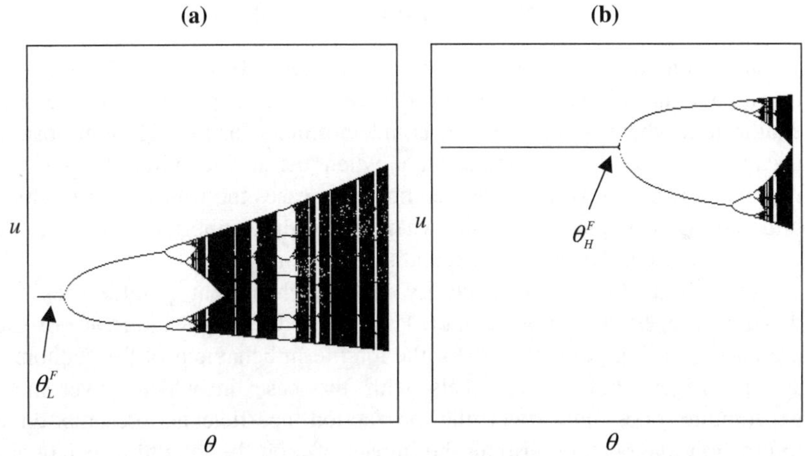


*Figure 6.2. Kaleckian interpretation: bifurcation diagrams showing the impact of the adjustment speed θ on the long-term behavior of the state variable u for different values of public expenditure γ: (a) only the low equilibrium exists; (b) only the high equilibrium exists*

$\theta_L^F$ and $\theta_H^F$ denote the flip bifurcation values of $\theta$ corresponding to the low and high equilibrium.

Instead, for values of $\gamma$ producing three equilibrium positions, as described in Figure 6.1(b), the following situation occurs: when $\theta$ is below the smaller of $\theta_L^F$ and $\theta_H^F$, the low and high equilibrium are both stable; for values of $\theta$ between $\theta_L^F$ and $\theta_H^F$ a stable fixed point and an attracting cycle coexist; finally, when $\theta$ is above the larger of $\theta_L^F$ and $\theta_H^F$, two attracting cycles that can be regular or chaotic coexist. The two attractors are asymmetric with respect to the intermediate equilibrium and do not generally have the same periodicity. Moreover, the basins of the two attractors, defined as the set of the initial values of the state variable $u$ that converge to an attractor, undergo substantial modifications as $\theta$ changes. For small values of $\theta$, the two basins are simple and correspond to the interval to the left and the interval to the right of the intermediate equilibrium $u_I^*$. As $\theta$ increases, they become increasingly disconnected and intermingled.[9]

Let us now explore the influence of a change in $\gamma$ on the dynamic properties of the map $\psi(u)$. Consider first the case in which government expenditure does not affect the labour input coefficient. For both $\theta_L^F$ and $\theta_H^F$ the following derivative holds:

$$\frac{d\theta^F}{d\gamma}=\theta^F\frac{s_\pi \pi a+\phi''(u^*)du^*/d\gamma}{s_\pi \pi a(1-\gamma)-\phi'(u^*)}.$$

Since condition (6.15) is satisfied and $du^*/d\gamma>0$ for both the low and the high equilibrium, the sign of the derivative is positive for the low equilibrium where $\phi''(u_L^*)>0$ and is indeterminate for the high equilibrium because $\phi''(u_H^*)<0$. This means that when the low equilibrium position prevails, a rise in government expenditure increases the values of $\theta$ at which bifurcations take place. Instead, when the high equilibrium prevails, the effects of a rise in government expenditure are ambiguous.

Some simulations further clarify how a change in $\gamma$ influences the dynamic properties of the map $\psi(u)$ and what the implications are of the presence of a 'big government' for the long-term behaviour of the economic system. Figure 6.3, which deals with the case in which government expenditure does not affect the production coefficients, presents three bifurcation diagrams describing the impact of $\gamma$ on the long-term behaviour of the degree of capacity utilisation for $0\leq\gamma\leq 0.4$ and for (a) $\theta=10$, (b) $\theta=15$ and (c) $\theta=20$.[10] Summarising the results achieved in Commendatore et al. (2007, 2009), Figure 6.3(a) shows that as $\gamma$ overtakes $\gamma^T$, a fold catastrophe takes place. The economic system rapidly moves from a low to a high equilibrium position and stays there even if $\gamma$ returns to its initial value. This phenomenon is known as *hysteresis*.

Figure 6.3(b) points out that at $\gamma_L^F$ a flip bifurcation point takes place. For $0\leq\gamma<\gamma_L^F$ a locally stable 2-cycle occurs. For $0\leq\gamma<\gamma_L^F$ the 2-cycle disappears and the economic system converges towards a unique equilibrium. Analysis of $0\leq\gamma<\gamma^T$ is also described by Figure 6.3(c) for $\theta=20$, which confirms that the low equilibrium position is locally unstable and shows that the economic system has a chaotic behaviour. Nonetheless, increases in $\gamma$ reduce the size of fluctuations, contributing to rid the economic system of chaotic behaviour. Figure 6.3(c) also shows that for $\gamma>\gamma^T$ two bifurcations occur. For $\gamma>\gamma^{F1}$ the economic system moves from a unique equilibrium position to a 2-cycle situation. For $\gamma>\gamma^{F2}$ the economic system returns to a unique equilibrium.

Figures 6.3(b) and 6.3(c) confirm that increases of $\gamma$ tend to produce a positive phenomenon of hysteresis. Moreover, they tend to reduce the

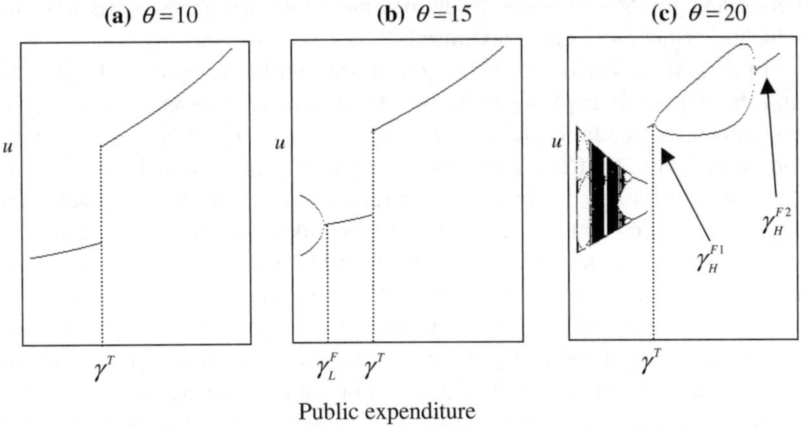


*Figure 6.3. Kaleckian interpretation: bifurcation diagrams showing the impact of 'unproductive' public expenditure γ on the long-term behaviour of the state variable u for different values of the adjustment speed θ*

complexity of the behaviour of the economic system, thus making it more controllable, and eventually lead the economic system to a unique and stable equilibrium.

To sum up, the previous analysis of the effects of changes of what has been called 'unproductive' government expenditure, that is, that generating $b'=0$, attributes to a 'big government' a positive influence on the growth, stability and controllability of the economic system. The influence of changes to what has been called 'productive' government expenditure, that is, that generating $b'(\gamma)>0$, depends instead on the effects of taxation on the disposable income of the private sector and on how the gains in productivity are distributed between profits and wages. These effects are captured by the following derivative, which holds for the flip bifurcation values of $\theta$ corresponding to the low and the high equilibrium positions:

$$\frac{d\theta^F}{d\gamma}=\theta^F\frac{s_\pi a[\pi(\gamma)-\pi'(\gamma)(1-\gamma)]+\phi''(u^*)\frac{du^*}{d\gamma}}{s_\pi\pi(\gamma)a(1-\gamma)-\phi'(u^*)} \tag{6.18}$$

The expression contained in the square brackets represents the impact of government expenditure on after-tax profits.

Commendatore et al. (2007, 2009) show that the relationship between after-tax profits and government expenditure is increasing for $0\leq\gamma<\bar{\gamma}$ and decreasing for $\gamma > \bar{\gamma}$, where $\bar{\gamma}$ defines the value of public expenditure for which after-tax profits are maximised.

In derivative (6.18) for $0 \leq \gamma < \bar{\gamma}$ after-tax profits are positively affected and the degree of capacity utilisation is negatively affected by changes in government expenditure, hence $d\theta_L^F / d\gamma < 0$ and $d\theta_H^F / d\gamma$ is indeterminate. On the contrary, if after-tax profits are negatively affected and the degree of capacity utilisation is positively affected by changes in government expenditure, $d\theta_L^F / d\gamma > 0$ and $d\theta_H^F / d\gamma$ is indeterminate. This means that when $\gamma < \bar{\gamma}$, increases in government expenditure have a destabilising effect on the low equilibrium since they reduce the value of $\theta$ at which a flip bifurcation takes place. When instead $\gamma > \bar{\gamma}$, increases in government expenditure have a stabilising effect on the low equilibrium. The effects are always indeterminate when the high equilibrium position prevails.

Some simulations further clarify the effects of changes in government expenditure on the long-term behaviour of the degree of capacity utilisation and of the economic system. They are described in Figure 6.4, where $0 \leq \gamma \leq 0.4$ and (a) $\theta = 15$, (b) $\theta = 17.5$ and (c) $\theta = 20$.[11]

Figure 6.4(a) summarises the findings of Commendatore et al. (2007, 2009). It shows that two-fold catastrophes occur for values of $\gamma = \gamma^{T1}$ and $\gamma = \gamma^{T2}$. For $\gamma \geq \gamma^{T1}$ the economic system rapidly moves from a high to a low equilibrium position and remains there even if $\gamma$ returns to its initial value. The opposite effect takes place for $\gamma \geq \gamma^{T2}$, where the economic system rapidly moves towards a high equilibrium position.

Figure 6.4(b) points out that two bifurcations occur for the low equilibrium positions. For $\gamma_L^{F1}$ the equilibrium loses stability and an attracting 2-cycle emerges. For $\gamma_L^{F2}$ the cycle disappears and the equilibrium becomes attracting again. The size of fluctuations increases up to $\bar{\gamma}$ and decreases afterwards.

Analysis of $\gamma^{T1} < \gamma < \gamma^{T2}$ is also described by Figure 6.4(c) for $\theta = 20$, which confirms that the low equilibrium position is locally unstable and shows that, if $\gamma < \bar{\gamma}$, increases in $\gamma$ generate many period-doubling bifurcations in the economic system up to chaos. On the contrary, if $\gamma > \bar{\gamma}$, increases in $\gamma$ reduce the period and the size of fluctuations, contributing to rid the economic system of chaotic behaviour. As to the high equilibrium position, for $\gamma^{F1} \leq \gamma < \gamma^{T1}$ the economic system moves from a 2-cycle situation to a unique equilibrium position. For $\gamma \geq \gamma^{F2}$ the opposite occurs and the economic system returns to a 2-cycle situation.

To sum up, analysis of the effects of changes in what has been called ‘productive’ government expenditure is more ambiguous than that of the effects of ‘unproductive’ expenditure. It shows that, for $e_H$, increases in government expenditure tend to have a positive influence on the stability and controllability of the economic system when they generate an increase in after-tax profits. This influence is however negative when government expenditure approaches the level that maximises after-tax profits. By contrast, when they reduce after-tax profits the influence on the stability and controllability of the economic system is positive up to a level, beyond which it becomes negative. As to the influence on growth, it is negative when after-tax profits increase and positive when they decrease.

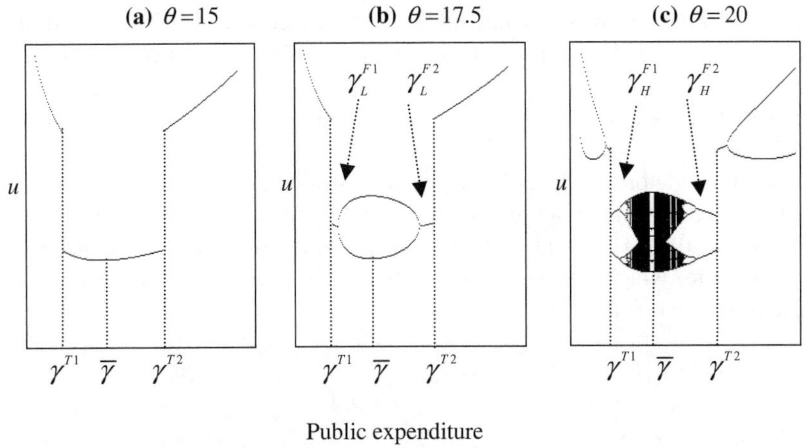


*Figure 6.4. Kaleckian interpretation: bifurcation diagrams showing the impact of 'productive' public expenditure $\gamma$ on the long-term behaviour of the state variable $u$ for different values of the adjustment speed $\theta$*

## 6.4. THE CLASSICAL–HARRODIAN INTERPRETATION

### 6.4.1. Equilibrium

The results of the Classical–Harrodian case may differ from those of the Kaleckian case because the rate of growth and the degree of capital utilisation may move in opposite directions when government expenditure changes. The former case interprets the expected growth rate of demand as the warranted rate of growth, that is, $\alpha = \tilde{g} \equiv s_\pi \pi a(1-\gamma)\tilde{u}$. The equilibrium solutions are

$$u^* = \frac{\tilde{g} + \phi(u^*)}{s_\pi \pi a(1-\gamma)} \quad \text{and} \quad g^* = \tilde{g} + \phi(u^*) \tag{6.19}$$

Commendatore et al. (2007, 2009) present the diagram reported in Figure 6.5, which refers to the case of 'unproductive' expenditure and shows that, according to the value attributed to $\gamma$, there can be either one or three equilibrium positions, $e_L \equiv (u_L^*, g_L^*)$, $\tilde{e} \equiv (\tilde{u}, \tilde{g})$ and $e_H \equiv (u_H^*, g_H^*)$.[12] In Figure 6.5(a) there is one equilibrium position, $\tilde{e}$, which is globally stable because condition (6.15) holds. In Figure 6.5(b) the increase in $\gamma$ generates a pitchfork bifurcation and the appearance of two new equilibrium positions, $e_L$ and $e_H$, which are symmetrical with respect to $\tilde{e}$. The equilibrium positions $e_L$ and $e_H$ are locally stable, while $\tilde{e}$ is unstable because condition (6.15) is violated. Notice that increases in 'productive' government expenditure, which raise after-tax profits, could reverse the direction of the bifurcation process.

Commendatore et al. (2007, 2009) also show that there are no hysteresis effects and that increases in 'unproductive' government expenditure lower the value of $u_L$ and raise that of $u_H$, while increases in 'productive' expenditure, which positively affect after-tax profits, raise the value of $u_L$ and lower that of $u_H$.

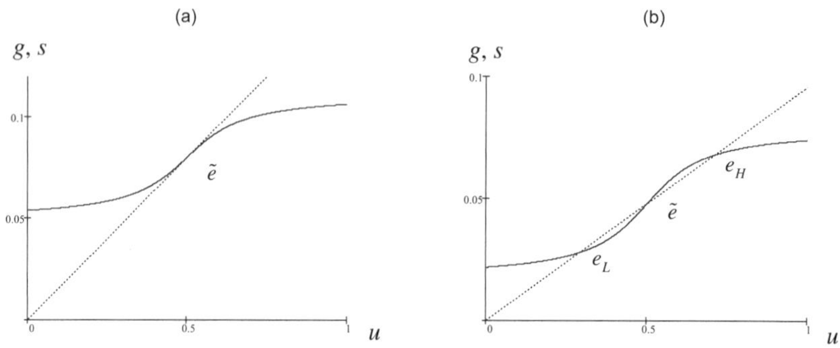


*Figure 6.5. Classical–Harrodian interpretation: saving and investment functions for different values of public expenditure: (a) only the Harrodian warranted growth equilibrium exists; (b) three equilibria are present (low, Harrodian and high)*

### 6.4.2. Dynamic Analysis

Let us now present the dynamic analysis, investigating how changes in $\theta$ affect the long-term behaviour of the economy. Subsequently we explore the influence of changes in government expenditure on the local stability of equilibrium positions.

The difference equation (6.12) is revised as follows for the Classical–Harrodian case:

$$\psi(u) = u + \theta\left[\phi(u) - s_\pi \pi a(1-\gamma)(u - \tilde{u})\right] \tag{6.20}$$

This map determines the long-term evolution of the state variable $u$. A crucial property of this map is that it is symmetric around the equilibrium $\psi(\tilde{u}) = \tilde{u}$.

The equilibrium positions $u_L$ and $u_H$ are stable for

$$\theta < \theta^F \equiv \frac{2}{s_\pi \pi a(1-\gamma) - \phi'(u^*)}$$

Due to the symmetry of map (6.12), the bifurcation point $\theta^F$ is the same for both equilibrium positions since $\phi'(u_L^*) = \phi'(u_H^*)$. When $\theta$ increases both equilibrium positions lose stability through a flip bifurcation and two locally stable 2-cycles emerge.[13] Further increases in $\theta$ generate first the appearance of two symmetric attractors of various periodicity and then the emergence of chaotic attractors. The attractors, located around the low and high equilibrium positions, enjoy the same periodicity. As $\theta$ increases, their basins become more intertwined up to when, for a sufficiently large $\theta$, a global bifurcation takes place and the two basins merge.

Figure 6.6 presents two bifurcation diagrams which describe the influence of changes in $\theta$ – varied within the interval $35 \leq \theta \leq 55$ – on the long-term behaviour of the state variable $u$ and on the stability properties of the low and high equilibrium positions.[14] Both diagrams confirm that a period-doubling route to complex behaviour occurs simultaneously for the low and high equilibrium positions. A multiplicity of symmetric attractors is created whose stability properties also follow a symmetric pattern.

Let us now examine the impact of a change in $\gamma$ on the dynamic properties of the map $\psi(u)$. Consider first the case of a change in 'unproductive' government expenditure and its effects on the bifurcation point $\theta^F$.

$$\frac{d\theta^F}{d\gamma} = \theta^F \frac{s_\pi \pi a + \phi''(u^*) du^*/d\gamma}{s_\pi \pi a(1-\gamma) - \phi'(u^*)}.$$

The sign of $d\theta^F/d\gamma$ is indeterminate because for the low equilibrium position $\phi''(u_L^*) > 0$ and $du_L^*/d\gamma < 0$ and for the high equilibrium position $\phi''(u_H^*) < 0$ and $du_H^*/d\gamma > 0$. Thus the effect of a change in government expenditure on the local stability is not unambiguous.

When government expenditure is 'productive', the effects of its changes on the bifurcation point $\theta^F$ are described by the following derivative:

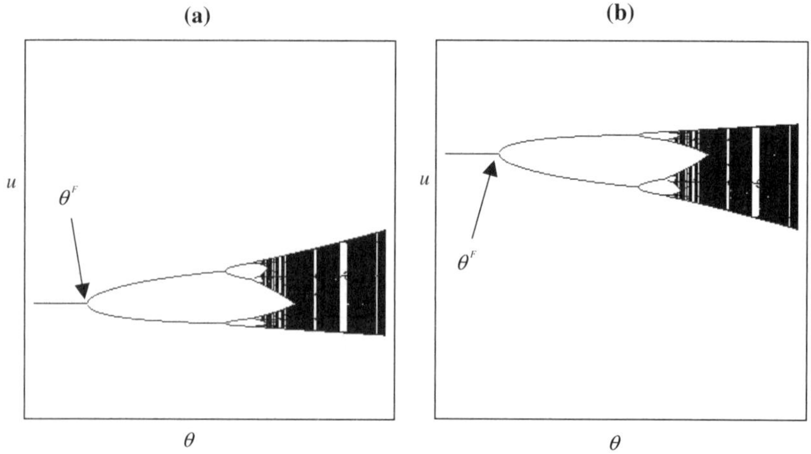


*Figure 6.6. Classical–Harrodian interpretation: bifurcation diagrams showing the impact of the adjustment speed $\theta$ on the long-term behaviour of the state variable u for different initial conditions: (a) the initial condition belongs to the basin of attraction of the low equilibrium; (b) the initial condition belongs to the basin of attraction of the high equilibrium*

$$\frac{d\theta^F}{d\gamma} \equiv \theta^F \frac{s_\pi a[\pi(\gamma)-\pi'(\gamma)(1-\gamma)]+\phi''(u^*)\dfrac{du^*}{d\gamma}}{s_\pi \pi(\gamma)a(1-\gamma)-\phi'(u^*)}$$

The sign of this derivative is also indeterminate. When after-tax profits are increased by the rise in government expenditure, that is, $\pi(\gamma)-\pi'(\gamma)(1-\gamma)<0$, for the low equilibrium $\phi''(u_L^*)>0$ and $du_L^*/d\gamma>0$, whereas for the high equilibrium $\phi''(u_H^*)<0$ and $du_H^*/d\gamma<0$. When instead $\pi(\gamma)-\pi'(\gamma)(1-\gamma)>0$, for the low equilibrium $\phi''(u_L^*)>0$ and $du_L^*/d\gamma<0$, whereas for the high equilibrium $\phi''(u_H^*)<0$ and $du_H^*/d\gamma>0$.

To explore further the effects of government expenditure on the local stability of the economic system some simulations were made.

Figure 6.7 presents the bifurcation diagrams, 6.7(a) and 6.7(b), showing the impact of $0 \leq \gamma \leq 0.5$ on the long-term behaviour of the degree of capacity utilisation for $\theta = 40$.[15] Figure 6.7(a) deals with the case of 'unproductive' government expenditure and Figure 6.7(b) with the case of 'productive' expenditure.

Figure 6.7(a) shows two flip bifurcations, occurring at $\gamma = \gamma^{F1}$ and $\gamma = \gamma^{F2}$, for the high equilibrium position. By symmetry two other bifurcations occur at the same values of $\gamma$ for the low equilibrium position.

For $0 \leq \gamma < \gamma^{F1}$ these equilibrium positions are stable. For $\gamma^{F1} < \gamma < \gamma^{F2}$ two locally attracting 2-cycles emerge. For $\gamma^{F2} < \gamma \leq 0.5$ the couple of 2-cycles disappear and the low and high equilibrium positions become locally attracting once again.

These results mean that, taking the bifurcation points as reference, small and big sizes of the government sector have stabilising effects on the economic system. Moreover, increases in 'unproductive' government expenditure have a positive effect on $u_H^*$ and, by symmetry, a negative effect on $u_L^*$. With respect to the Kaleckian case both 'small' and 'big' governments generate stabilising effects on the economy. Moreover, owing to the negative effect on $u_L^*$, increases in the size of the government sector may produce depressing effects on the economy.

Figure 6.7(b) shows four flip bifurcations for the high equilibrium position. By symmetry, four other bifurcations occur at the same values of $\gamma$ for the low equilibrium position. For $0 \leq \gamma < \gamma^{F1}$ the equilibrium positions are stable. For $\gamma^{F1} < \gamma < \gamma^{F2}$ two locally attracting 2-cycles emerge. For $\gamma^{F2} < \gamma < \gamma^{F3}$ the equilibrium positions are stable again. An attracting 2-cycle

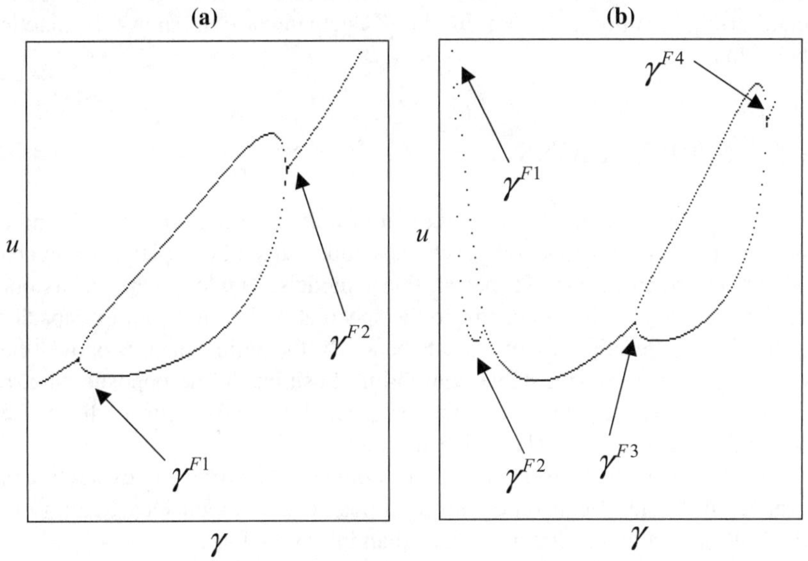


*Figure 6.7. Classical–Harrodian interpretation: bifurcation diagrams showing the impact of public expenditure γ on the long-term behaviour of the state variable u: (a) 'unproductive' public expenditure; (b) 'productive' public expenditure.*

emerges again for $\gamma^{F3} < \gamma < \gamma^{F4}$. For $\gamma^{F4} < \gamma \leq 0.5$ the pair of 2-cycles disappear and the low and high equilibrium positions become locally attracting once again.

These results mean that increases in 'productive' government expenditure have stabilising effects on the economic system when the government sector is 'big' enough to overtake $\gamma^{F4}$ and when it approaches the value that maximises after-tax profits, $\bar{\gamma}$. By contrast, reductions in 'productive' government expenditure have stabilising effects on the economic system when the size of the government sector is 'small', that is, it is less than $\gamma^{F1}$, and when, approaching $\bar{\gamma}$, it becomes less than $\gamma^{F3}$. Moreover, increases in 'productive' government expenditure have a negative effect on $u_H^*$ and, by symmetry, a positive effect on $u_L^*$ when after-tax profits rise. On the contrary, when after-tax profits diminish, increases in 'productive' government expenditure have a positive effect on $u_H^*$ and, by symmetry, a negative effect on $u_L^*$.

To sum up, the results of Classical–Harrodian analysis of changes in 'productive' government expenditure differ from those of the Kaleckian case because, when the size of the government sector approaches the level that maximises after-tax profits, the economic system converges to a stable equilibrium position whereas in the Kaleckian case it shows a chaotic behaviour.

## 6.5. CONCLUSIONS

Our analysis shows that the introduction of a discrete time framework and a nonlinear investment function generates a wide range of complex phenomena which are absent in post-Keynesian linear models. The long-term behaviour of the economic system depends on the speed at which firms adjust capacity utilisation in reaction to excess demand. If the adjustment is slow, the economy converges to a stable equilibrium position. In the opposite case, a period-doubling sequence to complex behaviour can occur both in the Kaleckian and Classical–Harrodian analysis.

What we called 'unproductive' and 'productive' government expenditures produce different effects on equilibrium positions and their local stability in the Kaleckian and the Classical–Harrodian interpretations.

In the Kaleckian interpretation, increases in 'unproductive' government expenditure have a stabilising effect on the low equilibrium position. They also have stabilising effects on the high equilibrium position as long as the size of the government sector is sufficiently large. The existence of a 'big government' favours a high degree of capital utilisation and high rates of growth.

Increases in 'productive' expenditure have destabilising effects on the low equilibrium position when after-tax profits rise and stabilising effects when after-tax profits diminish. The high equilibrium position is instead stabilised by the increase in 'productive' expenditure when after-tax profits rise and destabilised when after-tax profits diminish (see Commendatore et al., 2007, 2009).

In the Classical–Harrodian interpretation increases in 'unproductive' government expenditure stabilise the economic system when the government sector is sufficiently large. The existence of a 'big government', however, pushes the degree of capital utilisation further above its normal level for the high equilibrium position and further below it for the low equilibrium position.

The effects of increases in 'productive' expenditure are stabilising when the dimension of the government sector approaches the value that maximises after-tax profits and when it is sufficiently large. On the contrary, reductions in 'productive' expenditure have stabilising effects when the government sector is sufficiently 'small' and when it approaches the value that maximises after-tax profits. Moreover, unlike the Kaleckian case that shows chaotic behaviour, the economic system converges to a stable equilibrium position when the dimension of the government sector approaches the level that maximises after-tax profits. Finally, the effect of 'productive' expenditure on the degree of capacity utilisation, for both the low and high equilibrium, is ambiguous depending on the behaviour of after-tax profits (see Commendatore et al., 2007, 2009).

## NOTES

1. Keynes (1924) underlined the crucial role of the composition of government expenditure since he first called for the use of fiscal policy to stimulate the economy (see Harrod, 1951, chapter IX, para 3), while Kaldor (1958, pp. 136–7; 1966, 1967 and 1971) pointed out that the composition of government expenditure has important effects on long-run growth. For a review of Keynes' position on this topic see Pressman (1994).
2. The definition of 'unproductive' and 'productive' government expenditure is given in Section 6.2.
3. Mastromatteo (2009) reports that Minsky, following a Kaleckian theory of growth and distribution, argues for the positive effects of the existence of a 'big government' on the growth and controllability of the system.
4. For the sake of simplicity we do not incorporate the rate of profit into the investment function. Our results would not be substantially modified if we change this equation to include the profit rate.
5. We assume $\alpha + \phi(0) > 0$, that is the long-run expected growth of demand $\alpha$ is always high enough to induce positive investments even in correspondence of a low capacity utilisation in the current period (this assumption is standard in the Kaleckian literature: see Lavoie, 1996; see also Kaldor, 1940). Hence $u^* > 0$ and $g^* > 0$.

6. Figure 6.1 assumes that $\gamma$ takes the following values: (a) $\gamma = 0$, (b) $\gamma = 0.12$ and (c) $\gamma = 0.24$. The other parameters are given the following values: $\tilde{u} = 0.5$, $\alpha = 0.07$, $a = 0.5$, $\lambda = 0.75$, $s_\pi = 0.8$ and $w_0 = 0.6$ As an explicit form for the nonlinear component of the investment function we choose $\phi(u) = \beta_1 \arctan[\beta_2(u - \tilde{u})]$, where $\beta_1 = 0.015$ and $\beta_2 = 15$; and as an explicit form for the average labour productivity function we choose $b(\gamma) = b_0 + b_1 \arctan(b_2\gamma)$, where $b_0 = 1$, $b_1 = 0$ and $b_2 = 7.5$. Notice that the choice of this parameter constellation corresponds to the assumption that public expenditure does not affect the labour input coefficient $b' = 0$.
7. This is a typical result of the use of non-monotonic maps (see Alligood et al., 1997). A thorough analysis of the dynamical properties of map (6.17) is presented in Commendatore et al. (2007).
8. See previous footnote 6.
9. The technical details of this analysis and the corresponding diagrams are given in Commendatore et al. (2007).
10. To plot Figure 6.4, for the other parameters, we set the same configuration as Figure 6.1 and $u_0 = 0.51$ as initial condition.
11. To plot Figure 6.4 we used, for the other parameters, $\tilde{u} = 0.5$, $a = 0.5$, $s_\pi = 0.8$, $\beta_1 = 0.02$, $\beta_2 = 15$, $b_0 = 1$, $b_1 = 1.15$, $b_2 = 7.5$, $\lambda = 0.6$ and $w_0 = 0.72$. Moreover, we set as initial condition $u_0 = 0.51$.
12. To plot Figure 6.6, we used the following parameter constellation: $\tilde{u} = 0.5$, $a = 0.5$, $s_\pi = 0.8$, $\lambda = 0.75$, $w_0 = 0.6$, $\beta_1 = 0.02$, $\beta_2 = 7.5$, $b_0 = 1$, $b_1 = 0$, $b_2 = 7.5$, $\gamma = 0$ for panel (a) and $\gamma = 0.4$ for panel (b). As for Figure 6.1, this parameter configuration corresponds to the assumption $b' = 0$.
13. For a detailed description of this process, see Commendatore et al. (2007).
14. The diagram uses initial values (a) $u_0 = 0.49$ (belonging to the basin of attraction of the low equilibrium) and (b) $u_0 = 0.51$ (belonging to the basin of attraction of the high equilibrium) and the same parameter constellation as Figure 6.5(b).
15. To plot Figure 6.7(a) we used the following parameter constellation: $\tilde{u} = 0.5$, $a = 0.5$, $s_\pi = 0.8$, $\lambda = 0.75$, $w_0 = 0.72$, $\beta_1 = 0.02$, $\beta_2 = 7.5$, $b_0 = 1$, $b_1 = 0$, $b_2 = 7.5$. Moreover, we set $u_0 = 0.51$ as initial condition. To plot Figure 6.7(b) we used the following parameter constellation: $\tilde{u} = 0.5$, $a = 0.5$, $s_\pi = 0.8$, $\beta_1 = 0.02$, $\beta_2 = 7.5$, $b_0 = 0.5$, $b_1 = 1.12$, $b_2 = 7.5$, $\lambda = 0.7$ and $w_0 = 0.72$. Moreover, we set as initial condition $u_0 = 0.51$.

# REFERENCES


Alligood, K.T., T.D. Sauer and J.A. Yorke (1997), *Chaos: an Introduction to Dynamical Systems*, New York: Springer-Verlag.

Amadeo, E.J. (1986), 'The Role of Capacity Utilization in Long-period Analysis', *Political Economy*, **2**(2), 147–85.

Barro, R.J. (1990), 'Government Spending in a Simple Model of Endogenous Growth', *Journal of Political Economy*, **98**(5), S103–25.

Commendatore, P. (2006), 'Are Kaleckian Models Relevant for the Long Run?', in C. Panico and N. Salvadori (eds), *Classical, Neoclassical and Keynesian Views on Growth and Distribution*, Cheltenham, UK and Northampton, MA, USA: Edward Elgar.

Commendatore, P., S. D'Acunto, C. Panico and A. Pinto (2003), 'Keynesian theories of growth', in N. Salvadori (ed.), *The Theory of Economic Growth: a 'Classical Perspective*, Cheltenham, UK and Northampton, MA, USA: Edward Elgar.

Commendatore, P., C. Panico and A. Pinto (2005), 'Government Debt, Growth and Inequality in Income Distribution', in N. Salvadori and R. Balducci (eds), *Innovation, Unemployment and Policy in the Theories of Growth and Distribution*, Cheltenham, UK and Northampton, MA, USA: Edward Elgar.

Commendatore, P., C. Panico and A. Pinto (2007), 'Composition of Public Expenditure, Effective Demand, Distribution and Growth', Economic Growth: Institutional and Social Dynamics, PRIN 2005, *Working Paper WP-021*. http://growthgroup.ec.unipi.it/workingpapers.htm

Commendatore P., C. Panico and A. Pinto (2009), 'The Influence of Different Forms of Government Spending on Distribution and Growth', *Metroeconomica*, forthcoming.

Dutt, A.K. (1984), 'Stagnation, Income Distribution, and Monopoly Power', *Cambridge Journal of Economics*, **8**(1), 25–40.

Fleck, F.H. and C.M. Domenghino (1987), 'Government Activity *Does* Invalidate the "Cambridge Theorem of the Rate of Profit"', *Journal of Post Keynesian Economics*, **10**(1), pp. 22–36.

Harrod, R.F. (1951), *The Life of John Maynard Keynes*, London: Macmillan.

Hein, E., M. Lavoie and T. van Treeck (2008), 'Some Instability Puzzles in Kaleckian Models of Growth and Distribution: a Critical Survey', *IMK Working Paper*, no. 19/2008. http://www.boeckler.de/pdf/p_imk_wp_19_2008.pdf.

Kaldor, N. (1940), 'A Model of Trade Cycle', *The Economic Journal*, **50**(197), 79–82.

Kaldor, N. (1958), 'Monetary Policy, Economic Stability and Growth: a Memorandum Submitted to the Radcliffe Committee on the Working of the Monetary System', June 23, *Principal Memoranda of Evidence*, Cmnd 827, London HMSO (1960), 146–53. Reprinted in N. Kaldor (1964), *Essays on the Economic Policy I*, London: Duckworth, pp. 128–53.

Kaldor, N. (1966), *Causes of the Slow Rate of Growth of the United Kingdom: an Inaugural Lecture*, Cambridge: Cambridge University Press, reprinted in N. Kaldor (1978), *Further Essays on Economic Theory*, London: Duckworth.

Kaldor, N. (1967), *Strategic Factors in Economic Development*, Ithaca, New York: Cornell University.

Kaldor, N. (1971), 'Conflicts in National Economic Objectives', *Economic Journal*, **81**, 1–16, reprinted in N. Kaldor (1978), *Further Essays on Economic Theory*, London: Duckworth.

Kalecki, M. (1937), 'A Theory of the Business Cycle', *Review of Economic Studies*, **4**(2), 77–97.

Keynes J.M. (1924), 'Does Employment Need a Drastic Remedy?', *The Nation and Athenaeum*, May 24, in Moggridge, D. (ed.) (1981), 'Activities 1922–1929: the Return to Gold and Industrial Policy', Part I, *The Collective Writings of J.M. Keynes*, vol. XIX, London: Macmillan & Cambridge University Press for the Royal Economic Society, pp. 219–223.

Lavoie, M. (1992), *Foundations of Post-Keynesian Economic Analysis*, Aldershot, UK and Brookfield, US: Edward Elgar.

Lavoie, M. (1996), 'Traverse, Hysteresis, and Normal Rates of Capacity Utilization in Kaleckian Models of Growth and Distribution', *Review of Radical Political Economics*, **28**(4), 113–47.

Lavoie, M. (2000), 'Government Deficits in Simple Kaleckian Models', in H. Bougrine (ed.), *The Economics of Public Spending: Debts Deficits and Economic Performance*, Cheltenham, UK and Northampton, MA, USA: Edward Elgar.

Mastromatteo, G. (2009), 'The Role of the Public Sector in the Thought of Hyman Minsky', in N. Salvadori and A. Opocher (eds), *Long-run Growth, Social Institutions and Living Standards*, Cheltenham, UK and Northampton, MA, USA: Edward Elgar.

Panico, C. (1997), 'Government Deficits in Post Keynesian Theories of Growth and Distribution', *Contributions to Political Economy*, **4**, pp. 37–60.

Pasinetti, L.L. (1989), 'Government Deficit Spending is not Incompatible with the Cambridge Theorem of the Rate of Profit: a Reply to Fleck and Domenghino', *Journal of Post Keynesian Economics*, **11**(4), pp. 640–7.

Pressman, S. (1994), 'The Composition of Government Spending: Does it Make Any Difference?', *Review of Political Economy*, **6**(2), 221–39.

Rowthorn, R.E. (1981), 'Demand, Real Wages, and Economic Growth', *Thames Papers in Political Economy*, Autumn, 1–39.

Skott, P. (2008), 'Growth, Instability and Cycles: Harrodian and Kaleckian Models of Accumulation and Income Distribution', Department of Economics, University of Massachusetts Amherst, *Working Paper*, no. 2008–12. http://www.umass.edu/economics/publications/2008-12.pdf.

Shaikh, A. (2007), 'Economic Policy in a Growth Context: a Classical Synthesis of Keynes and Harrod', New York, New School University, mimeo, http://homepage.newschool.edu/~AShaikh/.

Steedman, I. (1972), 'The State and the Outcome of the Pasinetti Process', *Economic Journal*, **82**(328), pp. 1387–95.

You, J.I. and A.K. Dutt (1996), 'Government Debt, Income Distribution and Growth', *Cambridge Journal of Economics*, **20**(3), 335–51.

# 7. The role of human capital in economic growth: evidence from Greek regions*

**Nikos Benos and Stelios Karagiannis**

## 7.1. INTRODUCTION

Human capital theory argues that there are positive educational externalities: that is, benefits of individually-acquired education are not restricted to the individual but spill over to higher levels of aggregation in the same industry, city, region or the macroeconomy as a whole. These externalities provide the economic justification for public funding of education.[1]

In the recent literature, attempts have been made to empirically test the relationship between human capital and economic growth, usually employing cross-sectional country data. These studies use measures of formal education as proxies for human capital, since investment in education plays a central role in human capital accumulation. They provide contrasting results regarding the impact of human capital on growth: effects are found to be positive, statistically insignificant or even negative in some cases (Pritchett, 2001; Barro and Sala-i-Martin, 2004).

The main cause of these puzzling results is probably that most studies use international data sets, but incorrectly impose equal returns to schooling (single coefficients) among sample countries (Temple, 1999; Krueger and Lindahl, 2001; Di Liberto, 2007). This problem arises when education quality is affected by educational institutions, which often differ across countries. In this context, one explanation for the estimated low returns to education in international data sets is that national statistics are dissimilar. Moreover, returns to education tend to be higher in countries with a better-educated labour force, as predicted by some growth models (Azariadis and Drazen, 1990). Another issue appears to be that acquisition of educational skills is not linked with productivity in some cases – that is, education is not only an investment but also a consumption good for the individual. Finally, in many countries (especially those which are less developed), the public sector employs most of the skilled labour force: this creates distortions in the estimation of returns to schooling, owing to measurement problems of public sector output, inefficiency and lack of innovative activities in this sector (Griliches, 1997).

In this chapter, our objective is to estimate the impact of human capital on regional economic growth in Greece, and analyse the implications for economic policy. In order to control for the problems described above, we focus on a fairly homogeneous data set, which at the same time is relatively diverse in terms of human capital characteristics of the various regions. Furthermore, Greek regions are characterised by common institutions and, especially a homogeneous educational system.

Our approach features several important contributions. First, this study represents, to the best of our knowledge, the first attempt to provide a comprehensive set of estimates of the impact of human capital dynamics on growth of Greek regions (NUTS III level) for a fairly long period (1981–2003). Secondly, we define human capital more broadly than most of the literature, using various measures of education as well as healthcare. Thirdly, we investigate systematic growth differences between regions, which vary in terms of income level and location. Recent studies emphasise the presence of two income clubs in Greece based on: (a) access to the main transportation network (mostly the Athens–Thessaloniki highway), and (b) the highly developed tourist industry on the islands (Christopoulos, 2004; Prodromidis, 2006; Benos and Karagiannis, 2008). These two clubs are characterised by identical educational institutions together with significant differences in enrolment rates. This way, we allow for heterogeneity of the effect of human capital on growth across the two regional groups. Finally, we allow for human capital spillovers between neighbouring regions.

Our analysis is carried out using Random Effects (RE) and enhanced GMM (Arellano and Bond, 1991) estimators in order to handle endogeneity and unobserved heterogeneity problems. We find that the number of students in lower and upper secondary education levels affects growth positively. Additionally, a higher student/teacher ratio inhibits growth and the number of medical doctors fosters growth. Besides these, there is strong evidence of differential effects of the human capital variables between rich and poor regions. Finally, there are important human capital externalities across neighbouring regions.

The chapter is organised as follows. In Section 7.2, we present a review of the theoretical and empirical literature on human capital and growth. Section 7.3 describes the data, while Section 7.4 presents the econometric framework and methodology. In Section 7.5, estimation results are analysed, while Section 7.6 offers policy considerations and concluding comments. An Appendix contains detailed information on our data and empirical results.

## 7.2. LITERATURE REVIEW

The theoretical literature on the relationship between human capital and economic growth provides different models. In the first group of models, growth is sustained by human capital accumulation – that is, human capital is a factor of production and its accumulation influences the growth process. In this type of model, human capital is a flow variable (Lucas, 1988). In the second category, economic growth depends on the existing human capital stock, which generates new knowledge (Romer, 1990) or facilitates the imitation and adoption of foreign technologies (Nelson and Phelps, 1966). In the third class of models, human capital is a threshold variable – that is, the impact of human capital depends on the human capital stock accumulated within a given time period (Azariadis and Drazen, 1990). Thus human capital matters as a stock and flow variable, because its accumulation is necessary to achieve the stock level, above which the impact of human capital strengthens. One implication of these models is the existence of multiple equilibria in the growth path, since the growth path comprises various phases.

Regarding empirics, the investigation of the growth impact of human capital uses measures of formal education, such as adult literacy rates, school enrolment rates and average years of schooling, as proxies for human capital. This follows from the fact that investment in education is central to human capital accumulation and can be measured more easily than other elements, such as on-the-job training, experience and learning-by-doing.

In one of the early studies that examined the role of human capital on growth, Barro (1991) found that primary and secondary enrolment rates have a positive growth effect, but this was not always true for adult literacy rates. Mankiw et al. (1992) estimated an elasticity of output of about one-third with respect to the average percentage of the working-age population in secondary school. Benhabib and Spiegel (1994) found that the human capital flow did not have a statistically significant growth effect, while the average stock had a positive, though not always significant, growth impact. Durlauf and Johnson (1995) identified different growth regimes for groups of countries characterised by different initial GDP per capita and human capital levels supporting models with multiple equilibria.

More recently, De la Fuente and Domenech (2000) and Bassanini and Scarpetta (2001) estimated a positive effect of schooling years on growth. Bils and Klenow (2000) concluded that initial enrolment rates explain less than one third of the variation in growth rates and half of this is due to the fact that anticipated increases in growth raise schooling. Pritchett (2001) estimated a negative growth impact of human capital growth. However, Krueger and Lindahl (2001) showed that higher education attainment has a positive effect on economic growth once measurement errors are taken into account. Also, they showed that linearity and parameter homogeneity are rejected by the data. Kalaitzidakis et al. (2001) found non-linear effects of human capital on growth. Papageorgiou (2003) concluded that the role of human capital in the creation and adoption of technology increases with country income. In a review of the empirical literature, Sianesi and Van Reenen (2002) pointed out that education implies indirect growth benefits in terms of physical capital, technology transfer, fertility and other dimensions of human capital (for example, life expectancy, infant mortality).

Furthermore, some research has recently concentrated on the impact of human capital on regional growth. The idea is that knowledge produces spillovers: that is, firms learn from other firms and people get ideas from other people. Thus in regions with a high concentration of, and/or accessibility to, human capital, such as large cities, ideas disseminate quickly and human capital externalities are more likely to arise. Knowledge flows between different localities and regions imply spatial dependence among adjacent regions, which diminishes with distance (Grasjo, 2005; Andersson and Karlsson, 2007).

Finally, a number of recent papers examine the field of health as a human capital component, although several pioneering studies go back a few decades (Mushkin, 1962; Becker, 1964; Fuchs, 1966). In particular, health in the form of life expectancy has appeared in a number of cross-country empirics, which confirm the positive effect on the rate of growth (see Bloom and Canning, 2000, 2003). In addition, several papers include health indicators in growth regressions in an effort to incorporate direct or indirect effects on economic growth (see Barro and Lee, 1993; Barro, 1996; Caselli et al. 1996, Bloom and Sachs, 1998; Bloom and Williamson, 1998; Bloom et al., 1999; Barro and Sala-i-Martin, 2004).

## 7.3. DESCRIPTION OF THE DATA

We start our analysis with a brief description of the main regional educational and healthcare data used.[2] Our data include the number of students attending the two levels of secondary education[3] (upper and lower) together with the respective number of teachers at both levels.[4] Using these, we were able to construct the student/teacher ratio for the two levels of education. In addition, we include two healthcare indicators, namely the number of medical doctors and hospital beds available per region. All our variables span from 1981 through 2003 and cover the 51 regions of Greece (NUTS III level).

Figure 7.1 presents the division of the 51 NUTS III Greek regions into two sub-groups, according to whether their average GDP per capita for 1981–2003 lies above or below the median. Tables 7A.3 and 7A.4[5] provide the descriptive statistics of our variables based on the division of our sample into high- and low-income regions.

According to our calculations, there are numerous income, education and healthcare disparities among the Greek regions. High-income regions enjoy higher levels of per capita GDP when compared to low ones (the means are 10,835 and 7,968 Euros respectively, over the period studied). They are characterised by different numbers of students attending lower secondary education (the means are around 591 and 584 students per 1000 of the relevant age group, respectively). On the other hand, low-income regions exhibit a greater proportion of students attending the upper level of education than high-income regions. Overall, participation rates[6] in the two levels of secondary education in Greece differ substantially across regions as well as

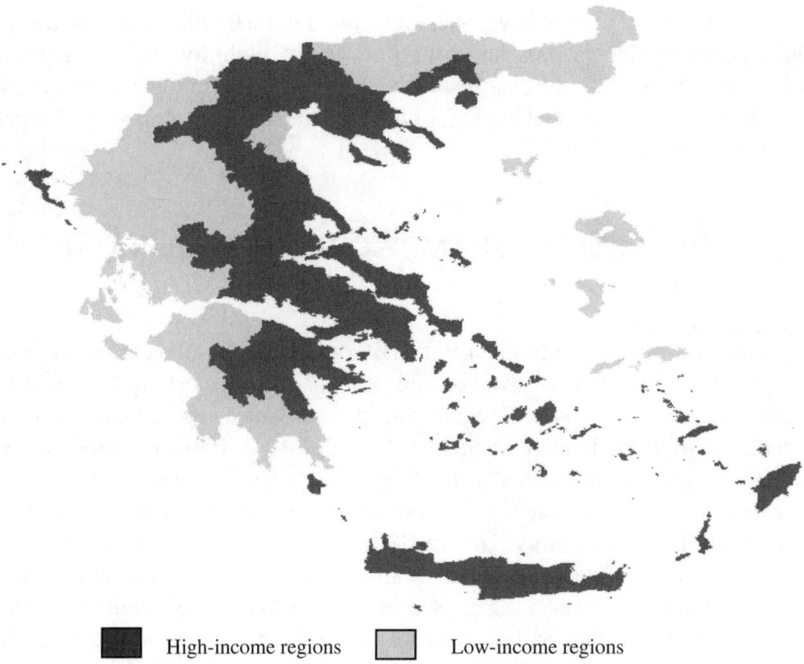


*Source*: Our elaborations based on sources mentioned in Table 7A.1.

*Figure 7.1. High- and low-income regions (NUTS III) in Greece (average GDP pc, 1981–2003)*

through time. Our data reveal that rural regions present lower enrolment rates compared with urban ones.[7] The above findings are in line with previous studies specialised in this field of work.[8] Also, participation rates improved during the period examined – especially in upper secondary education (from 35 per cent in 1981–94 to 60 per cent in the 1995–2003 period).

Healthcare variables reveal a greater inequality between the two sub-samples. The number of available hospital beds and, to a lesser extent, the number of medical doctors are greater in high-income than low-income regions (4.05 to 3.10 per 1000 people and 2.40 to 2.03 per 1000 people, respectively). Finally, public investment at the regional level is included in our regressions in order to disentangle the effect of physical capital from the effect of human capital on growth (see Krueger and Lindahl, 2001).[9] We believe this is a good proxy for total investment at the regional level. This is so, because public and private capital tend to behave similarly in Greek regions (Louri, 1989). Specifically, our proxy is based on the actual investment included in state budget expenditures at the regional level.[10] As evident from the descriptive statistics, the regional allocation of public investment in Greece presents disparities across high-/low-income regions (2.3 per cent and 2.5 per cent respectively) as well as throughout the period examined (2.2 per cent of regional GDP for the 1981–91 period to 2.5 per cent for 1992–2003).[11]

## 7.4. THEORETICAL FRAMEWORK AND EMPIRICAL MODEL

As human capital is multidimensional (Bloom et al., 2004), we need a model of growth that includes its major components. While most studies identify human capital narrowly with education, they do not consider health to be a crucial aspect of human capital, and therefore a critical ingredient of economic growth. In particular, the population's health impinges on growth through productive efficiency, life expectancy, learning capacity, creativity, coping skills and inequality (Howitt, 2005). Also, an increase in survivorship raises the returns from education because educational costs come at earlier ages and returns at later ages (see Becker, 1964, 1993; Meltzer, 1992; Ehrlich, 2000). In this chapter we consider both education and health in the formation of human capital as complementarities exist between its different forms (Becker, 2007).

We study the role of human capital in the growth process, using the framework suggested (among others) by Mankiw et al. (1992), de la Fuente (2002), Bloom et al. (2004), Barro and Sala-i-Martin (2004). Thus, we specify an empirical model by augmenting a standard aggregate production function with a technological progress function. In this framework, we allow for regional fixed effects.

We therefore assume a Cobb–Douglas aggregate production function

$$Y_{it} = K_{Git}^{\theta_{KG}} \left(A_{it} L_{it}\right)^{\theta_l} S_{it}^{\theta_s} H_{it}^{\theta_h} \tag{7.1}$$

where $Y_{it}$ denotes total output of region $i$ ($i = 1, \ldots, 51$) during period $t$ ($t = 1981, \ldots, 2003$), $K_{Git}$ the public stock of physical capital, $L_{it}$ is employment, $S_{it}$ the stock of educational human capital, $H_{it}$ is the stock of health human capital, and $A_{it}$ a (labour-augmenting) TFP indicator. Also, we assume $\theta_{KG} + \theta_l + \theta_s + \theta_h = 1$, so we have a Solow-type model. Thus, we take a broader view of human capital than most of the literature by including education and health in the production function of our economies. Both forms of human capital are seen as production factors, the accumulation of which affects growth, that is, human capital is a flow variable (Lucas, 1988). However, we allow for differential impact of the two components of human capital (education, heath) on output, hence on economic growth. Finally, incorporating $A_{it}$, we allow for permanent differences in the production functions of the various regions. The introduction of human capital in a broad sense, along with differential technical progress between regions, gives us the ability to obtain more accurate estimates of the model's parameters.

Now, equation (7.1) in per capita terms takes the form

$$\frac{Y_{it}}{L_{it}} = K_{Git}^{\theta_{KG}} A_{it}^{\theta_l} L_{it}^{\theta_l - 1} S_{it}^{\theta_s} H_{it}^{\theta_h} \tag{7.2}$$

Taking logs of (7.2)

$$\ln\left(\frac{Y_{it}}{L_{it}}\right) = \theta_{KG} \ln K_{Git} + \theta_l \ln A_{it} + \left(\theta_l - 1\right) \ln L_{it} + \theta_s \ln S_{it} + \theta_h \ln H_{it} \tag{7.3}$$

and then time differences, we get

$$\Delta\ln\left(\frac{Y_{it}}{L_{it}}\right) = \theta_{KG} \Delta\ln K_{Git} + \theta_l \Delta\ln A_{it} + \left(\theta_l - 1\right) \Delta\ln L_{it} + \theta_s \Delta\ln S_{it} + \theta_h \Delta\ln H_{it} \tag{7.4}$$

Before we estimate (7.4), we must specify the TFP growth term $\Delta\ln A_{it}$. We assume that the regional TFP variable (measured in logs) is the sum of two components:

$$\ln A_{it} = r_i + b_t \tag{7.5}$$

where $r_i$ is a regional fixed effect, which captures regional features that affect productivity and are constant over time (for example, location, climate etc.), and $b_t$ is nationwide technical progress, which evolves at a constant rate $g$:

$$\Delta b_t = g \tag{7.6}$$

Thus, human capital does not influence technical progress. Therefore, the rate of change of regional TFP is:

$$\Delta \ln A_{it} = \Delta r_i + g \tag{7.7}$$

and after substitution of (7.7) and some rearrangements, equation (7.4) becomes

$$\Delta \ln\left(\frac{Y_{it}}{L_{it}}\right) = \theta_s \Delta \ln S_{it} + \theta_h \Delta \ln H_{it} + \theta_{KG} \Delta \ln K_{Git} + (\theta_l - 1)\Delta \ln L_{it} + \theta_l \Delta r_i + \theta_l g \tag{7.8}$$

Since we estimate a Solow-type model, we include initial GDP per capita in the empirical counterpart of (7.8) in order to control for convergence effects on growth. We expect the education, health and public investment parameters to be positive, while the labour force parameter should be negative.

Real per capita growth is thus related to an array of control variables, region-specific effects and technological progress effects common to all regions. For the first two terms, we use several human capital indicators and since it is generally accepted that human capital affects growth with time lags, we use lagged values of these indicators (Di Liberto, 2004, 2007; Middendorf, 2006).[12]

These indicators include the following: a) students at lower secondary education level; b) students at higher secondary education level; c) medical doctors; d) hospital beds.[13] The first two variables measure schooling and the other two capture the impact of health on growth (Malik, 2006; Ricci and Zachariadis, 2007). Additionally, we use the student–teacher ratio in the two levels of education as a measure of the quality of education provision. We also employ public investment per region regarding the third term in (7.8). Furthermore, we proxy employment growth by population growth in (7.8), because there are no available data on the former. Finally, following Andersson and Karlsson (2007) and Grasjo (2005) we include two variables in order to explore the possibility of spatial externalities in terms of human capital (see Section 7.5.3).

Regarding estimation methodology, OLS assume that the error in each time period is uncorrelated with the explanatory variables in the same period. However, a primary motivation for using panel data is to solve the problem of omitted variables, which are effectively part of the error term and cause bias in the coefficient estimates. In light of that, in the first part of our estimations, we assume that there is a time-constant unobserved effect, which we treat as a random variable drawn from a population together with the observed dependent and explanatory variables. The unobserved effect may represent region-specific technology, tastes, historical and cultural factors. These characteristics are assumed to be correlated over time but uncorrelated with the observed explanatory variables, which is critical for the consistency of our estimates. We proceed with random effects estimation, which exploits the serial correlation in the error, due to the presence of the unobserved effect in every period. We apply GLS and compute robust standard errors of the coefficients.[14]

Furthermore, one of the most challenging problems in the empirical growth literature is the likely endogeneity of the right-hand-side variables. This is particularly true in the case of human capital variables, since education is highly income elastic and high-income economies dominated by the service sector require a well-educated workforce. In order to cope with this problem, in the second part of our estimations we use the GMM estimator of Arellano and Bond (1991), which calls for first differencing and using lags of the dependent and explanatory variables as instruments (Caselli et al., 1996). First differencing removes region-specific effects, which are a potential source of omitted variable bias (see above) and deals with series non-stationarity. Also, when choosing instruments, we allow the explanatory variables to be endogenous, which is the least restrictive assumption we can make. Thus, applying GMM we eliminate the inconsistency arising from the incorrect treatment of correlated region-specific effects and the endogeneity of explanatory variables. We are thus more confident about GMM compared with RE results and emphasise the former. At the same time, if the findings are similar, this is a signal of robustness.

## 7.5. EMPIRICAL RESULTS

### 7.5.1. Full Sample

Full sample estimations reveal that students at lower-secondary level and higher-secondary level exert a positive, albeit small, effect on growth in most cases (Table 7A.5, cols. 1–8). Furthermore, the student–teacher ratios in lower and upper secondary education, which are measures of education quality, exert a negative influence on growth in most cases as well – that is, the higher the number of students relative to teachers, the lower is human capital accumulation and growth. These findings accord with the fact that controlling for labour force quality reduces the impact of schooling on growth (Sianesi and Van Reenen, 2002). Overall, the results concur with our theoretical underpinnings and previous empirical evidence (Barro, 1991; Sianesi and Van Reenen, 2002).

Regarding healthcare indicators, we use the number of medical doctors, as it reflects the quality of health services. This is expected to boost productivity and growth.[15] The evidence confirms our intuition showing a positive impact on regional growth (Table 7A.5, cols. 2, 4, 6 and 8).[16, 17] Overall, the evidence supports the case for public funding of education and health care in Greece as a growth-enhancing policy.

Public investment does not have a statistically significant growth impact in most cases. This is possibly because it represents a small proportion of GDP in most regions and is inefficiently allocated in accordance with the electoral cycle theory (see Lambrinidis et al., 2005).

The estimated parameter of initial income indicates conditional convergence of Greek NUTS III regions at an annual rate of approximately 17 per cent (Table 7A.5, cols. 5–8).[18] This is in line with our Solow-type model, where an economy is in the process of transitional growth towards its steady state. The above convergence speed is similar in magnitude to those found by Caselli et al. (1996) and differs from results commonly found in work on convergence.[19, 20] Hence Greek regions are mostly near their steady states and differences in GDP per capita are due to differences in their steady-state levels. In this framework, areas with high growth are those which experienced repeated shifts in their steady state during the period covered by our sample. Finally, population growth exerts a negative influence on per capita income growth in accordance with theory and previous evidence (Eckey et al., 2006).[21]

### 7.5.2. Convergence Clubs

As mentioned in Section 7.2, there is a strong case, both theoretically and empirically, for different effects of human capital on growth among regions which vary in terms of income. Consequently, we split regions into low-income and high-income according to whether their average GDP per capita is below or above the median for our sample period (1981–2003).[22, 23] First, we estimate the same equations as before for the two sub-samples.

According to Tables 7A.6–7A.7, for the rich and poor regions respectively, we see that lower secondary education students have a positive impact on growth in the former (Table 7A.6, cols. 1, 5–6), while they are not statistically significant in the latter (Table 7A.7). Furthermore, there are positive growth returns to upper secondary education in the high-income regions (Table 7A.6, cols. 3–4, 7–8), while they are mostly insignificant in the low-income ones (Table 7A.7, cols. 3–4, 7–8). These differences among the income groups explain the very weak growth influence of both variables in the full sample estimation and agree with previous work (Durlauf and Johnson, 1995).

Also, we identify a strong negative effect on per capita growth of the student-teacher ratio at both the lower secondary and upper secondary education levels in the rich regions (Table 7A.6, cols. 1, 5–8). In poor regions, this impact appears mostly insignificant (Table 7A.7, cols. 1–8), implying a weak effect of this variable in the full sample. Besides these, the number of medical doctors boosts regional growth in both sub-samples (Tables 7A.6–7A.7, cols. 2, 4, 6, 8). However, it seems that the effect of healthcare on regional growth is stronger in low-income areas.

In addition, we estimate regressions, which include interaction terms for our education and health indicators in order to check the robustness of the previous results. In particular, we interact a binary variable that indicates rich and poor areas with the education and health variables. Our findings confirm the stronger impact of lower secondary education students and the student–teacher ratio in lower secondary education on growth in high-income regions relative to the poor areas (Table 7A.11, cols. 1–2, 5).

Thus, our evidence suggests parameter heterogeneity regarding the effect of human capital on growth – confirming previous studies. From a policy perspective the evidence presented above implies that it is optimal to direct public spending on education mostly towards rich regions if the aim is growth maximization.[24] Also, conditional convergence seems to hold in both sub-samples, as was the case for the whole sample. Finally, public investment does not have a growth impact and population growth affects per capita income growth negatively as before.

### 7.5.3. Spatial Externalities

Next, we proceed to examine whether there is dependence of regional growth on human capital in neighbouring regions – that is, human capital externalities among regions. We construct three types of variables to capture these effects. The first type includes students of both the region in question and its neighbouring regions (*Regional Students*). It replaces the students of the region in question in the regressions. The second type corresponds to the students of the neighbouring regions only (*Extra-Regional Students*). It is used in the equations in addition to the student variables used in the previous section. The third type refers to two variables: they add the number of university medical doctors and hospital beds, when direct access to a university hospital is available, to the medical doctors and hospital beds at the regional level used in the original estimations creating *University Medical Doctors* and *University Hospital Beds* respectively.

Looking at Table 7A.8, *Regional Students* of lower secondary (see cols. 9–10) and upper secondary education (see cols. 11–12) have a much stronger impact on growth than the original student variables (Table 7A.5). This is in line with the evidence which shows that students of neighbouring regions (*Extra-Regional Students*) have a positive effect on growth (Table 7A.8, cols. 13–14). Lower and upper secondary school students continue to affect growth positively (Table 7A.8, cols. 2, 6, 10, 12–13). Regarding healthcare variables, *University Medical Doctors* affect growth positively and *University Hospital Beds* do not influence the growth process as before (Table 7A.8, cols. 7–8, 15–16). Thus, there is quite strong evidence of spatial externalities, in the sense that regions seem to be affected by the performance of their neighbours in terms of education and health status. This is in accordance with recent findings for Sweden (Andersson et al., 2007). The results do not change when we incorporate public investment in the regressions, which continues to be statistically insignificant (Table 7A.11, cols. 5–7).

When estimating the same equations in the two sub-samples of rich and poor regions, the findings are somewhat different. We observe that the positive impact of *Regional Students* (both lower and upper secondary levels) on growth is stronger in the wealthy regions compared to the lagging ones (Tables 7A.9–7A.10, cols. 9–12). The same pattern is true for the *Extra-Regional Students* at both education levels (Tables 7A.9–7A.10, cols. 13–14). Besides these, students of lower and upper secondary level education continue to exert a positive growth influence in all but one case in rich regions (Table 7A.9, cols. 2, 6, 10, 12–13), while their effect is not statistically significant in poor regions in most cases (Table 7A.10, cols. 2, 4–6, 10, 12–14). Furthermore, *University Medical Doctors* and *University Hospital Beds* do not affect growth in the affluent regions, contrary to the results for the former variable in the full sample, while they have a positive growth impact in poor regions (Tables 7A.9–7A.10, cols. 7–8, 15–16). At this point we should note that *Medical Doctors* are significant in high-income regions (see Table 7A.6, cols. 2, 4, 6 and 8) but *University Medical Doctors* are not. This seemingly awkward result can be explained by the fact that since university hospitals are mainly hosted in rich regions, their effect is captured by *Medical Doctors*. Consequently, there is no additional impact of *University Medical Doctors* to be estimated in these regions.

These findings are consistent with the evidence obtained when we use interaction terms to estimate the differential impact of *Regional Students, Extra-Regional Students and University Medical Doctors* on growth between high- and low-income areas (Table 7A.11, cols. 5–7). For example, *Regional Students* in upper secondary education boost growth in rich regions more strongly than in poor ones. Also, *University Medical Doctors* have a larger growth impact in poor areas compared to rich ones. Thus, we continue to find evidence of parameter heterogeneity regarding human capital variables in Greek regions when we take into account spatial externalities. Also, in both sub-samples conditional convergence holds and population growth is detrimental to per capita output growth, as is true for the whole sample.

As a result, evidence presented in this section emphasizes the need for larger public funding of education and health in both high- and low-income regions in order to realize the benefits arising from spatial externalities of human capital accumulation on regional growth. Additionally, the results underline that healthcare is a more important growth determinant in poor than in rich regions. On the contrary, education seems to matter more for growth in wealthy than lagging regions. In light of these findings, policy makers should direct a larger share of the funding for human capital accumulation towards healthcare in poor regions and education in rich ones.[25]

## 7.6. CONCLUSIONS

This chapter examined the social returns to human capital at regional level in Greece using education and healthcare indicators. We estimated the effect of these variables for all regions and separately for poor and rich ones, allowing for spatial heterogeneity of rates of return to human capital. Overall, we found that there are differences between the two regional clubs. In particular, our results show a positive impact of education on growth in high-income regions, while the evidence is much weaker for low-income regions. On the contrary, health is more important for growth in poor than rich regions. Also, there are important human capital externalities across neighbouring regions. Thus, the findings imply the need for larger public spending on education and healthcare in all areas as a growth-enhancing policy. However, the policy makers should direct a larger share of human capital expenditure on education in wealthy regions and health in lagging regions.

To conclude with some possible research extensions, we could employ alternative estimation methods as a check for the robustness of the results (that is, spatial econometrics). We might also use other measures of human capital, taking more comprehensive account of its quality, additional stages of education (higher education) and other forms of education (job training) when data become available. These are left for future work.

# APPENDIX

*Table 7A.1. Description of variables*

| Dependent variable | Description | Source |
|---|---|---|
| GDP per capita | in Euros, at 2000 constant prices; | National Statistical Service of Greece, Quarterly Regional and Satellite Accounts Section |
| *Explanatory variable* | | |
| Public investment | Investment of the state budget at regional level (NUTS 3) as a % of regional GDP. The variable is constructed by extracting payments for services rendered from total regional state budget expenditures. | National Statistical Service of Greece, Public Sector Survey Section |
| Students; Lower secondary level | Number of students attending the lower secondary level of education at regional level (NUTS 3). The variable is denoted per 1000 children aged 10 to 14 years of age. | National Statistical Service of Greece, Social Accounts Section |
| Students; Upper secondary level | Number of students attending the upper secondary level of education at regional level (NUTS 3). The variable is denoted per 1000 children aged 15 to 19 years of age. | National Statistical Service of Greece, Social Accounts Section |
| Student–teacher ratio; Lower secondary level | The number of students divided by the number of teachers at the lower secondary level of education at regional level (NUTS 3). Teachers are denoted per 1000 inhabitants at regional level. | National Statistical Service of Greece, Social Accounts Section |
| Student–teacher ratio; Upper secondary level | The number of students divided by the number of teachers at the upper secondary level of education at regional level (NUTS 3). Teachers are denoted per 1000 at regional level. | National Statistical Service of Greece, Social Accounts Section |

| | | |
|---|---|---|
| Medical doctors | Number of medical doctors per 1000 inhabitants at regional level (NUTS 3). | National Statistical Service of Greece, Social Accounts Section |
| Hospital beds | Number of hospital beds per 1000 inhabitants at regional level (NUTS 3). | National Statistical Service of Greece, Social Accounts Section |
| Regional students; Lower secondary level | Number of students attending the lower secondary level of education at regional level (NUTS 3), including students at the same level of education from neighbouring regions. | National Statistical Service of Greece, Social Accounts Section |
| Regional students; Upper secondary level | Number of students attending the upper secondary level of education at regional level (NUTS 3), including students at the same level of education from neighbouring regions. | National Statistical Service of Greece, Social Accounts Section |
| Extra-regional students; Lower secondary level | Number of students attending the lower secondary level of education from neighbouring regions only (NUTS 3). | National Statistical Service of Greece, Social Accounts Section |
| Extra-regional students; Upper secondary level | Number of students attending the upper secondary level of education from neighbouring regions only (NUTS 3). | National Statistical Service of Greece, Social Accounts Section |
| University medical doctors | Number of university medical doctors per 1000 inhabitants at regional level (NUTS 3). The number of university medical doctors (when direct access to the respective university hospital is available) is added to medical doctors at regional level (NUTS 3). | National Statistical Service of Greece, Social Accounts Section |
| University hospital beds | Number of university hospital beds per 1000 inhabitants at regional level (NUTS 3). The number of university hospital beds (when direct access to the respective university hospital is available) is added to hospital beds at regional level (NUTS 3). | National Statistical Service of Greece, Social Accounts Section |

*Table 7A.2. Descriptive statistics: Greek regions, 1981–2003 (NUTS III)*

| | Obs. | Mean | St. dev. | Min | Max |
|---|---|---|---|---|---|
| GDP per capita | 1173 | 9373.0 | 2796.8 | 5272.6 | 33490.7 |
| GDP pc growth | 1173 | 0.016 | 0.069 | –0.349 | 0.521 |
| Population growth | 1173 | 0.003 | 0.010 | –0.121 | 0.060 |
| Public investment | 1169 | 0.024 | 0.015 | 0.001 | 0.123 |
| Students; Lower secondary level | 1168 | 587.2 | 71.8 | 300.8 | 995.8 |
| Student; Upper secondary level | 1168 | 393.0 | 124.9 | 140.2 | 775.9 |
| Student– teacher ratio; Lower secondary level | 1168 | 1168 | 207.8 | 41.7 | 80.0 |
| Student–teacher ratio; Upper secondary level | 1168 | 1170 | 180.2 | 32.2 | 87.5 |
| Medical doctors | 1173 | 1173 | 2.211 | 1.152 | 0.47 |
| Hospital beds | 1173 | 1173 | 3.569 | 1.964 | 0.51 |

*Table 7A.3. Descriptive statistics: low-income regions, 1981–2003 (NUTS III)*

| | Obs. | Mean | St. dev. | Min | Max |
|---|---|---|---|---|---|
| GDP per capita | 598 | 7967.7 | 1435.9 | 5272.6 | 16509.5 |
| GDP pc growth | 572 | 0.016 | 0.071 | –0.256 | 0.400 |
| Population growth | 572 | 0.003 | 0.009 | –0.072 | 0.060 |
| Public investment | 597 | 0.025 | 0.012 | 0.001 | 0.104 |
| Students; Lower secondary level | 595 | 583.8 | 80.7 | 300.8 | 995.8 |
| Student; Upper secondary level | 596 | 394.8 | 123.7 | 151.1 | 700.1 |
| Student–teacher ratio; Lower secondary level | 595 | 205.8 | 40.7 | 95.4 | 365.7 |
| Student–teacher ratio; Upper secondary level | 596 | 177.1 | 28.6 | 107.9 | 271.9 |
| Medical doctors | 598 | 2.03 | 1.04 | 0.47 | 7.11 |
| Hospital beds | 598 | 3.10 | 1.25 | 1.03 | 8.12 |

*Table 7A.4. Descriptive statistics: high-income regions, 1981–2003 (NUTS III)*

| | Obs. | Mean | St. dev. | Min | Max |
|---|---|---|---|---|---|
| GDP per capita | 575 | 10834.6 | 3103.1 | 6377.4 | 33490.7 |
| GDP pc growth | 550 | 0.016 | 0.067 | –0.349 | 0.521 |
| Population growth | 550 | 0.004 | 0.012 | –0.121 | 0.040 |
| Public investment | 572 | 0.023 | 0.018 | 0.001 | 0.123 |
| Students; Lower secondary level | 573 | 590.7 | 61.2 | 380.9 | 755.2 |
| Student; Upper secondary level | 574 | 391.2 | 126.2 | 140.2 | 775.9 |
| Student–teacher ratio; Lower secondary level | 573 | 209.9 | 42.7 | 80.0 | 342.7 |
| Student–teacher ratio; Upper secondary level | 574 | 183.6 | 35.3 | 87.5 | 505.1 |
| Medical doctors | 575 | 2.40 | 1.23 | 0.75 | 6.83 |
| Hospital beds | 575 | 4.05 | 2.41 | 0.51 | 15.88 |

*Table 7A.5. Panel data estimates: education and healthcare variables (all regions)*

| | Random effect estimates | | | | Arellano-Bond estimates | | | |
|---|---|---|---|---|---|---|---|---|
| Explanatory Variables [4] | (1) | (2) | (3) | (4) | (5) | (6) | (7) | (8) |
| Students; Lower secondary level | 0.001 ** (2.51) | 0.148 ** (2.24) | – | – | 0.001 *** (3.55) | 0.001 (1.41) | – | – |
| Student–teacher ratio; Lower secondary level | –0.062 *** (–5.75) | –0.024 ** (–2.14) | – | – | –0.018 (–0.64) | –0.003 (0.13) | – | – |
| Student; Upper secondary level | – | – | 0.001 *** (5.80) | 0.001 ** (1.51) | – | – | 0.001 *** (3.12) | 0.001 *** (3.88) |
| Student–teacher ratio; Upper secondary level | – | – | –0.033 *** (–2.66) | –0.018 ** (–1.49) | – | – | –0.020 (–0.85) | –0.011 *** (–0.50) |
| Medical doctors | – | 0.024 *** (4.59) | – | 0.010 *** (2.97) | – | 0.092 *** (4.52) | – | 0.092 *** (4.61) |
| *GDP initial* [1] | –0.005 (–0.06) | –0.016 (–1.52) | –0.004 (–0.45) | –0.016 (–1.51) | –0.185 *** (–6.31) | –0.166 *** (–5.81) | –0.182 *** (–6.23) | –0.158 *** (–5.58) |
| *Public investment* | 0.002 (0.69) | –0.007 * (–1.73) | 0.001 (0.49) | –0.005 (–1.33) | 0.005 (0.78) | 0.002 (0.31) | –0.007 (1.16) | 0.003 (0.51) |
| *Population growth* | –1.147 *** (–5.77) | –1.303 *** (–6.73) | –1.124 *** (–5.69) | –1.297 *** (–6.66) | –1.411 *** (–5.68) | –1.545 *** (–6.56) | –1.421 *** (–5.78) | –1.555 *** (–6.68) |
| Obs. | 1070 | 1019 | 1070 | 1020 | 1019 | 968 | 1019 | 968 |
| $R^2$ | 0.066 | 0.075 | 0.084 | 0.079 | – | – | – | – |
| Sargan test (p-value) [2] | – | – | – | – | 0.104 | 0.116 | 0.121 | 0.138 |
| Autocovariance test of order 2 (p-value) [3] | – | – | – | – | 0.302 | 0.128 | 0.670 | 0.312 |

*Notes*:

Dependent variable GDP per capita growth in region $i$ ($i = 1, \ldots, 51$) in period $t$ ($t = 1981, \ldots, 2003$). $z$-statistics in parentheses; *, **, *** denote 10%, 5% and 1% significance respectively.

[1] Initial per capita GDP in region $i$ in period $t - 1$.

[2] The null hypothesis is that the instruments used are not correlated with the residuals.

[3] The null hypothesis is that the errors in the first-differenced regression exhibit no second order serial correlation.

[4] See Table 7A.1 for the definition of the variables used. Explanatory variables lagged 2 periods and Medical Doctors lagged 3 periods. All the explanatory variables were used as instruments.

*Table 7A.6. Panel data estimates: education and healthcare variables (high-income regions)*

| | Random effect estimates | | | | Arellano-Bond estimates | | | |
|---|---|---|---|---|---|---|---|---|
| Explanatory Variables [4] | (1) | (2) | (3) | (4) | (5) | (6) | (7) | (8) |
| Students; Lower secondary level | 0.001** | 0.001 | – | – | 0.001*** | 0.001 ** | – | – |
| | (2.33) | (0.46) | | | (3.47) | (2.36) | | |
| Student–teacher ratio; Lower secondary level | –0.051*** | –0.021 | – | – | –0.003** | –0.018 ** | – | – |
| | (–3.59) | (–1.41) | | | (–0.09) | (–2.11) | | |
| Student; Upper secondary level | – | – | 0.001 *** | 0.001 ** | – | – | 0.001 *** | 0.001 *** |
| | | | (4.30) | (2.04) | | | (3.45) | (3.93) |
| Student–teacher ratio; Upper secondary level | – | – | –0.021 ** | –0.012 ** | – | – | –0.055 ** | –0.049 ** |
| | | | (–1.25) | (–0.73) | | | (–2.05) | (–1.88) |
| Medical doctors | – | 0.018** | – | 0.005 ** | – | 0.058 ** | – | 0.055 ** |
| | | (2.45) | | (0.53) | | (2.05) | | (0.50) |
| *GDP initial* [1] | –0.001 | –0.012 | –0.018 | –0.022 | –0.133*** | –0.128 *** | –0.133 *** | –0.118 *** |
| | (–0.00) | (0–.74) | (–1.12) | (–1.37) | (–3.20) | (–3.03) | (–3.21) | (–2.82) |
| *Public investment* | –0.001 | –0.009 | –0.002 | –0.007 | 0.008 | 0.002 | 0.008 | 0.001 |
| | (–0.29) | (–2.45) | (–0.48) | (–1.20) | (0.95) | (0.24) | (1.08) | (0.06) |
| *Population growth* | –1.066*** | –1.143*** | –1.085 *** | –1.125 *** | –1.413*** | –1.474 *** | –1.366 *** | –1.409 *** |
| | (–4.31) | (–4.64) | (–4.50) | (–4.64) | (–4.83) | (–5.12) | (–4.70) | (–4.94) |
| Obs. | 524 | 499 | 524 | 499 | 499 | 474 | 499 | 474 |
| $R^2$ | 0.067 | 0.068 | 0.086 | 0.068 | – | – | – | – |
| Sargan test (p-value) [2] | – | – | – | – | 0.062 | 0.074 | 0.099 | 0.106 |
| Autocovariance test of order 2 (p-value) [3] | – | – | – | – | 0.176 | 0.122 | 0.146 | 0.144 |

*Notes*:
Dependent variable GDP per capita growth in region $i$ ($i$ = 1, …, 25) for high-income regions and $i$ ($i$ =1, …, 26) for low-income regions; in period $t$ ($t$ =1981, …, 2003). $z$-statistics in parentheses; *, **, *** denote 10%, 5% and 1% significance respectively.
[1] Initial per capita GDP in region $i$ in period $t – 1$.
[2] The null hypothesis is that the instruments used are not correlated with the residuals.
[3] The null hypothesis is that the errors in the first-differenced regression exhibit no second order serial correlation.
[4] See Table 7A.1 for the definition of the variables used. Explanatory variables lagged 2 periods and Medical Doctors lagged 3 periods. All the explanatory variables were used as instruments.

*Table 7A.7. Panel data estimates: education and healthcare variables (low-income regions)*

| | Random effect estimates | | | | Arellano-Bond estimates | | | |
|---|---|---|---|---|---|---|---|---|
| Explanatory Variables [4] | (1) | (2) | (3) | (4) | (5) | (6) | (7) | (8) |
| Students; Lower secondary level | 0.001<br>(1.51) | –0.001<br>(–0.83) | – | – | 0.001<br>(0.97) | –0.001<br>(–0.81) | – | – |
| Student–teacher ratio; Lower secondary level | –0.080 ***<br>(–4.64) | –0.023<br>(–1.24) | – | – | –0.046<br>(–1.19) | –0.003<br>(–0.10) | – | – |
| Student; Upper secondary level | – | – | 0.001 ***<br>(4.08) | 0.001<br>(0.82) | – | – | 0.001<br>(1.27) | 0.029<br>(0.72) |
| Student–teacher ratio; Upper secondary level | – | – | –0.042 **<br>(–2.14) | –0.014<br>(–0.76) | – | – | –0.039<br>(–1.11) | –0.020<br>(–0.63) |
| Medical doctors | – | 0.028 ***<br>(3.66) | – | 0.026 ***<br>(2.92) | – | 0.089 ***<br>(3.71) | – | 0.087 ***<br>(3.64) |
| *GDP initial* [1] | –0.032<br>(–1.21) | –0.047**<br>(–1.87) | –0.031<br>(–1.21) | –0.049 **<br>(–1.96) | –0.245 ***<br>(–6.07) | –0.215 ***<br>(–5.65) | –0.244 ***<br>(–6.05) | –0.211 ***<br>(–5.55) |
| *Public investment* | –0.001<br>(–0.25) | –0.001<br>(–0.19) | 0.007<br>(1.02) | –0.001<br>(–0.19) | –0.001<br>(–0.04) | 0.001<br>(0.06) | 0.003<br>(0.36) | 0.003<br>(0.39) |
| *Population growth* | –1.367 ***<br>(–4.02) | –1.547 ***<br>(–4.78) | –1.210 ***<br>(–3.51) | –1.502 ***<br>(–4.52) | –1.548 ***<br>(–3.77) | –1.702 ***<br>(–4.49) | –1.560 ***<br>(–3.80) | –1.632 ***<br>(–4.32) |
| Obs. | 546 | 520 | 546 | 520 | 520 | 494 | 520 | 494 |
| $R^2$ | 0.070 | 0.092 | 0.084 | 0.095 | – | – | – | – |
| Sargan test (p-value) [2] | – | – | – | – | 0.129 | 0.280 | 0.123 | 0.330 |
| Autocovariance test of order 2 (p-value) [3] | – | – | – | – | 0.302 | 0.314 | 0.620 | 0.524 |

*Notes*:
Dependent variable GDP per capita growth in region $i$ ($i$ = 1, …, 25) for high-income regions and $i$ ($i$ =1, …, 26) for low-income regions; in period $t$ ($t$ =1981, …, 2003). $z$-statistics in parentheses; *, **, *** denote 10%, 5% and 1% significance respectively.

[1] Initial per capita GDP in region $i$ in period $t$ – 1.

[2] The null hypothesis is that the instruments used are not correlated with the residuals.

[3] The null hypothesis is that the errors in the first-differenced regression exhibit no second order serial correlation.

[4] See Table 7A.1 for the definition of the variables used. Explanatory variables lagged 2 periods and Medical Doctors lagged 3 periods. All the explanatory variables were used as instruments.

*Table 7A.8. Panel data estimates: regional and extra-regional education and healthcare variables (all regions)*

| | Random effect estimates | | | | | | | |
|---|---|---|---|---|---|---|---|---|
| Explanatory Variables [4] | (1) | (2) | (3) | (4) | (5) | (6) | (7) | (8) |
| Regional students; Lower secondary level | –0.005<br>(–1.61) | –0.011 ***<br>(–3.32) | – | – | – | – | – | – |
| Regional students; Upper secondary level | – | – | 0.003<br>(1.07) | 0.002<br>(0.79) | – | – | – | – |
| Extra-regional students; Lower secondary level | – | – | – | – | –0.003<br>(–0.83) | – | – | – |
| Extra-regional students; Upper secondary level | – | – | – | – | – | –0.003<br>(–0.85) | – | – |
| Students; Lower secondary level | – | – | – | 0.000<br>(1.24) | –0.026<br>(–1.51) | – | – | – |
| Students; Upper secondary level | – | 0.000 ***<br>(7.16) | – | – | – | 0.045 ***<br>(5.66) | – | – |
| University medical doctors | – | – | – | – | – | – | 0.016<br>(3.19) | – |
| University hospital beds | – | – | – | – | – | – | – | 0.002<br>(0.45) |
| *GDP Initial* [1] | –0.003<br>(–0.39) | –0.003<br>(–0.35) | –0.009<br>(–0.95) | –0.010<br>(–0.99) | –0.003<br>(–0.29) | –0.004<br>(–0.45) | –0.015<br>(–1.62) | –0.011<br>(–1.17) |
| *Population Growth* | –1.168 ***<br>(–5.73) | –1.231 ***<br>(–6.17) | –1.045 ***<br>(–5.12) | –1.075 ***<br>(–5.24) | –1.220 ***<br>(–5.39) | –1.123 ***<br>(–5.56) | –1.233 ***<br>(–6.43) | –1.210 ***<br>(–6.29) |
| Obs. | 1071 | 1071 | 1071 | 1071 | 903 | 903 | 1020 | 1020 |
| $R^2$ | 0.031 | 0.080 | 0.051 | 0.040 | 0.035 | 0.079 | 0.064 | 0.043 |
| Sargan test (p-value) [2] | – | – | – | – | – | – | – | – |
| Autocovariance test of order 2 (p-value) [3] | – | – | – | – | – | – | – | – |

*Table 7A.8. Continued*

| | Arellano-Bond estimates | | | | | | | |
|---|---|---|---|---|---|---|---|---|
| Explanatory Variables [4] | (9) | (10) | (11) | (12) | (13) | (14) | (15) | (16) |
| Regional students; Lower secondary level | 0.253 ***<br>(4.79) | 0.236 ***<br>(4.41) | – | – | – | – | – | – |
| Regional students; Upper secondary level | – | – | 0.092 ***<br>(4.03) | 0.783 ***<br>(3.37) | – | | – | – |
| Extra-regional students; Lower secondary level | – | – | – | – | 0.295 ***<br>(3.88) | – | – | – |
| Extra-regional students; Upper secondary level | – | – | – | – | – | 0.086 **<br>(2.27) | – | – |
| Students; Lower secondary level | – | – | – | 0.155 ***<br>(3.43) | 0.086 **<br>(1.39) | | – | – |
| Students; Upper secondary level | – | 0.047 **<br>(2.34) | – | – | – | 0.001 **<br>(0.02) | – | – |
| University medical doctors | – | – | – | – | – | – | 0.106***<br>(3.99) | – |
| University hospital beds | – | – | – | – | – | – | – | 0.038<br>(1.26) |
| *GDP Initial* [1] | –0.186 ***<br>(–6.40) | –0.182 ***<br>(–6.28) | –0.174 ***<br>(–6.01) | –0.176 ***<br>(–6.10) | –0.187 ***<br>(–5.92) | –0.167 ***<br>(–5.29) | –0.168 ***<br>(–5.93) | –0.163 ***<br>(–1.26) |
| *Population Growth* | –1.37 ***<br>(–5.60) | –1.369 ***<br>(–5.60) | –1.389 **<br>(–5.70) | –1.350 ***<br>(–5.53) | –1.482 ***<br>(–5.56) | –1.493 ***<br>(–5.60) | –1.629 ***<br>(–6.96) | –1.147 ***<br>(–6.35) |
| Obs. | 1020 | 1020 | 1020 | 1020 | 860 | 860 | 969 | 969 |
| $R^2$ | – | – | – | – | – | – | – | – |
| Sargan test (p-value) [2] | 0.656 | 0.722 | 0.632 | 0.740 | 0.629 | 0.832 | 0.680 | 0.741 |
| Autocovariance test of order 2 (p-value) [3] | 0.530 | 0.563 | 0.788 | 0.707 | 0.621 | 0.813 | 0.941 | 0.799 |

*Notes*:
Dependent variable GDP per capita growth in region $i$ ($i = 1, \ldots, 51$) in period $t$ ($t = 1981, \ldots, 2003$). $z$-statistics in parentheses; *, **, *** denote 10%, 5% and 1% significance respectively.
[1] Initial per capita GDP in region $i$ in period $t - 1$.
[2] The null hypothesis is that the instruments used are not correlated with the residuals.
[3] The null hypothesis is that the errors in the first-differenced regression exhibit no second order serial correlation.
[4] See Table 7A.1 for the definition of the variables used. Explanatory variables lagged 2 periods and Medical Doctors lagged 3 periods. All the explanatory variables were used as instruments.

*Table 7A.9. Panel data estimates: regional and extra-regional education and healthcare variables (high-income regions)*

| | Random effect estimates | | | | | | | |
|---|---|---|---|---|---|---|---|---|
| Explanatory Variables [4] | (1) | (2) | (3) | (4) | (5) | (6) | (7) | (8) |
| Regional students; Lower secondary level | –0.004<br>(–0.89) | –0.010 **<br>(–2.08) | – | – | – | – | – | – |
| Regional students; Upper secondary level | – | – | 0.004<br>(1.08) | 0.003<br>(0.85) | – | – | – | – |
| Extra-regional students; Lower secondary level | – | – | – | – | –0.001<br>(–0.32) | – | – | – |
| Extra-regional students; Upper secondary level | – | – | – | – | – | –0.002<br>(–0.50) | – | – |
| Students; Lower secondary level | – | – | – | 0.037<br>(1.35) | –0.039<br>(–1.28) | – | – | – |
| Students; Upper secondary level | – | 0.045 ***<br>(5.04) | – | – | – | 0.048 ***<br>(4.35) | – | – |
| University medical doctors | – | – | – | – | – | – | 0.008<br>(1.11) | – |
| University hospital beds | – | – | – | – | – | – | – | 0.004<br>(0.54) |
| *GDP Initial* [1] | –0.007<br>(–0.49) | –0.009<br>(–0.66) | –0.014<br>(–0.98) | –0.013<br>(–0.87) | –0.005<br>–0.32 | –0.011<br>(–0.72) | –0.018<br>(–1.18) | –0.011<br>(–0.77) |
| *Population Growth* | –1.08 ***<br>(–4.36) | –1.254 ***<br>(–5.10) | –0.984 ***<br>(–3.96) | –1.064 ***<br>(–4.17) | –1.117 ***<br>–4.33 | –1.125 ***<br>(–4.73) | –1.125 ***<br>(–4.66) | –1.082 ***<br>(–4.50) |
| Obs. | 525 | 525 | 525 | 525 | 462 | 462 | 500 | 500 |
| $R^2$ | 0.039 | 0.087 | 0.051 | 0.055 | 0.039 | 0.089 | 0.054 | 0.047 |
| Sargan test (p-value) [2] | – | – | – | – | – | – | – | – |
| Autocovariance test of order 2 (p-value) [3] | – | – | – | – | – | – | – | – |

*Table 7A.9. Continued*

| | Arellano-Bond estimates | | | | | | | |
|---|---|---|---|---|---|---|---|---|
| Explanatory Variables [4] | (9) | (10) | (11) | (12) | (13) | (14) | (15) | (16) |
| Regional students; Lower secondary level | 0.345 ***<br>(4.19) | 0.293 ***<br>(3.45) | – | – | – | – | – | – |
| Regional students; Upper secondary level | – | – | 0.113 ***<br>(3.71) | 0.089 ***<br>(2.83) | – | | – | – |
| Extra-regional students; Lower secondary level | – | – | – | – | 0.309 ***<br>(2.81) | – | – | – |
| Extra-regional students; Upper secondary level | – | – | – | – | – | 0.475 **<br>(2.43) | – | – |
| Students; Lower secondary level | – | – | – | 0.184 ***<br>(2.65) | 0.007 **<br>(1.19) | | – | – |
| Students; Upper secondary level | – | 0.068 **<br>(2.44) | – | – | – | –0.086 **<br>(2.27) | – | – |
| University medical doctors | – | – | – | – | – | – | 0.052<br>(1.42) | – |
| University hospital beds | – | – | – | – | – | – | – | 0.004<br>(0.11) |
| *GDP Initial* [1] | –0.130 ***<br>(–3.15) | –0.122 ***<br>(–2.96) | –0.114 ***<br>(–2.77) | –0.119 ***<br>(–2.89) | –0.150 ***<br>(–3.43) | –0.127 ***<br>(–2.91) | –0.116 ***<br>(–2.79) | –0.117 ***<br>(–2.81) |
| *Population Growth* | –1.35 ***<br>(–4.69) | –1.393 ***<br>(–4.82) | –1.348 ***<br>(–4.69) | –1.385 ***<br>(–4.81) | –1.368 ***<br>(–4.52) | –1.369 ***<br>(–4.52) | –1.428 ***<br>(–4.98) | –1.349 ***<br>(–4.79) |
| Obs. | 500 | 500 | 500 | 500 | 440 | 440 | 475 | 475 |
| $R^2$ | – | – | – | – | – | – | – | – |
| Sargan test (p-value) [2] | 0.872 | 0.541 | 0.911 | 0.852 | 0.853 | 0.832 | 0.734 | 0.741 |
| Autocovariance test of order 2 (p-value) [3] | 0.946 | 0.827 | 0.761 | 0.2808 | 0.762 | 0.813 | 0.638 | 0.622 |

*Notes*:
Dependent variable GDP per capita growth in region $i$ ($i = 1, \ldots, 25$) in period $t$ ($t = 1981, \ldots, 2003$). $z$-statistics in parentheses; *, **, *** denote 10%, 5% and 1% significance respectively.
[1] Initial per capita GDP in region $i$ in period $t-1$.
[2] The null hypothesis is that the instruments used are not correlated with the residuals.
[3] The null hypothesis is that the errors in the first-differenced regression exhibit no second order serial correlation.
[4] See Table 7A.1 for the definition of the variables used. Explanatory variables lagged 2 periods and Doctors University & Beds University lagged 3 periods. All the explanatory variables were used as instruments.

*Table 7A.10. Panel data estimates: regional and extra-regional education and healthcare variables (low-income regions)*

| | Random effect estimates | | | | | | | |
|---|---|---|---|---|---|---|---|---|
| Explanatory Variables [4] | (1) | (2) | (3) | (4) | (5) | (6) | (7) | (8) |
| Regional students; Lower secondary level | 0.005 (1.27) | 0.011 (2.51) | – | – | – | – | – | – |
| Regional students; Upper secondary level | – | – | 0.002 (0.61) | 0.015 (0.37) | – | – | – | – |
| Extra-regional students; Lower secondary level | – | – | – | – | –0.004 (–0.79) | – | – | – |
| Extra-regional students; Upper secondary level | – | – | – | – | – | –0.003 (–0.59) | – | – |
| Students; Lower secondary level | – | – | – | 0.019 (0.95) | 0.026 (1.18) | – | – | – |
| Students; Upper secondary level | – | 0.051*** (5.25) | – | – | – | 0.045*** (3.79) | – | – |
| University medical doctors | – | – | – | – | – | – | 0.025*** (3.43) | – |
| University hospital beds | – | – | – | – | – | – | – | 0.001 (0.15) |
| *GDP Initial* [1] | –0.299 (–1.14) | –0.039 (–1.52) | –0.382 (–1.46) | –0.043 (–1.62) | –0.040 (–1.20) | –0.047 (–1.48) | –0.022 (–0.87) | –0.035 (–1.34) |
| *Population Growth* | –1.26*** (–3.61) | –1.171*** (–3.42) | –1.102*** (–3.14) | –1.094 (–3.12) | –1.32 (–3.18) | –1.199*** (–2.92) | –1.153*** (–3.43) | –1.154*** (–3.40) |
| Obs. | 546 | 546 | 546 | 546 | 441 | 441 | 546 | 546 |
| $R^2$ | 0.025 | 0.080 | 0.032 | 0.032 | 0.029 | 0.070 | 0.072 | 0.026 |
| Sargan test (p-value) [2] | – | – | – | – | – | – | – | – |
| Autocovariance test of order 2 (p-value) [3] | – | – | – | – | – | – | – | – |

*Table 7A.10. Continued*

| | Arellano-Bond estimates | | | | | | | |
|---|---|---|---|---|---|---|---|---|
| Explanatory Variables [4] | (9) | (10) | (11) | (12) | (13) | (14) | (15) | (16) |
| Regional students; Lower secondary level | 0.150 ** (2.38) | 0.148 ** (2.32) | – | – | – | – | – | – |
| Regional students; Upper secondary level | – | – | 0.057 * (1.77) | 0.054 * (1.67) | – | | – | – |
| Extra-regional students; Lower secondary level | – | – | – | – | 0.266 *** (2.98) | – | – | – |
| Extra-regional students; Upper secondary level | – | – | – | – | – | 0.080 * (1.67) | – | – |
| Students; Lower secondary level | – | – | – | 0.042 (0.81) | 0.020 (0.30) | | – | – |
| Students; Upper secondary level | – | 0.014 (0.53) | – | – | – | –0.033 (–0.84) | – | – |
| University medical doctors | – | – | – | – | – | – | 0.094 *** (3.00) | – |
| University hospital beds | – | – | – | – | – | – | – | 0.071 *** (0.01) |
| *GDP Initial* [1] | –0.024 *** (–6.20) | –0.248 *** (–6.17) | –0241 *** (–6.04) | –0.241 *** (–6.05) | –0.237 *** (–5.30) | –0.022 *** (–4.99) | –0.224 *** (–5.92) | –0.219 *** (–5.69) |
| *Population Growth* | –1.443 *** (3.58) | –1.419 *** (–3.50) | –1.456 *** (–3.62) | –1.416 *** (–3.50) | –1.861 *** (3.85) | –1.898 *** (–3.92) | –1.771 *** (–4.75) | –1.657 *** (–4.40) |
| Obs. | 520 | 520 | 520 | 520 | 420 | 420 | 494 | 494 |
| $R^2$ | – | – | – | | – | – | – | – |
| Sargan test (p-value) [2] | 0.810 | 0.781 | 0.881 | 0.970 | 0.997 | 0.747 | 0.897 | 0.789 |
| Autocovariance test of order 2 (p-value) [3] | 0.982 | 0.954 | 0.854 | 0.910 | 0.781 | 0.968 | 0.741 | 0.822 |

*Notes*:
Dependent variable GDP per capita growth in region $i$ ($i$ = 1, …, 26) in period $t$ ($t$ = 1981, …, 2003). $z$-statistics in parentheses; *, **, *** denote 10%, 5% and 1% significance respectively.
[1] Initial per capita GDP in region $i$ in period $t - 1$.
[2] The null hypothesis is that the instruments used are not correlated with the residuals.
[3] The null hypothesis is that the errors in the first-differenced regression exhibit no second order serial correlation.
[4] See Table 7A.1 for the definition of the variables used. Explanatory variables lagged 2 periods and Doctors University & Beds University lagged 3 periods. All the explanatory variables were used as instruments.

*Table 7A.11. Panel data estimates: robustness analysis (Arellano-Bond estimates)*

| Explanatory Variables [4] | (1) | (2) | (3) | (4) | (5) | (6) | (7) |
|---|---|---|---|---|---|---|---|
| Students; Lower secondary level | 0.001<br>(1.33) | –0.001<br>(–1.28) | – | – | –0.013<br>(–0.45) | 0.036<br>(1.07) | – |
| Students; Upper secondary level | – | – | 0.001 *<br>(1.84) | 0.001 **<br>(1.92) | – | – | – |
| Student–teacher ratio; Lower secondary level | –0.022<br>(–0.56) | 0.222<br>(1.29) | – | – | – | – | – |
| Student–teacher ratio; Upper secondary level | – | – | –0.017<br>(–0.49) | 0.003<br>(0.10) | – | – | – |
| Medical doctors | – | 0.085 ***<br>(4.59) | – | 0.114 ***<br>(4.83) | – | – | – |
| Students; Lower secondary level * Income | 0.250 **<br>(2.55) | 0.229 **<br>(6.14) | – | – | 0.100 **<br>(1.82) | 0.159 ***<br>(3.71) | – |
| Students; Upper secondary level * Income | – | – | 0.027<br>(0.89) | 0.049<br>(1.38) | – | – | – |
| Student–teacher ratio; Lower secondary level * Income | 0.016<br>(0.28) | –0.072 ***<br>(–2.77) | – | – | – | – | – |
| Student–teacher ratio; Upper secondary level * Income | – | – | –0.004<br>(–0.11) | –0.022<br>(–0.51) | – | – | – |
| Medical doctors * Income | – | –0.012<br>(–0.67) | – | 0.057 *<br>(1.77) | – | – | – |
| Regional students; Upper secondary level | – | – | – | – | 0.113 **<br>(14.94) | – | – |
| Extra-regional students; Lower secondary level | – | – | – | – | – | 0.190 **<br>(2.59) | – |
| University medical doctors | – | – | – | – | – | – | 0.094 ***<br>(10.37) |
| Regional students; Upper secondary level * Income | – | – | – | – | 0.046 ***<br>(3.76) | – | – |
| Extra-regional students; Lower level * Income | – | – | – | – | – | 0.017<br>(0.18) | – |
| University medical doctors * Income | – | – | – | – | – | – | –0.030 ***<br>(–3.85) |
| *GDP Initial* [1] | –0.187 ***<br>(–6.34) | –0.144 ***<br>(–11.36) | –0.180 ***<br>(–6.13) | –0.158 ***<br>(–5.56) | –0.071 ***<br>(–6.42) | –0.191 ***<br>(–6.00) | –0.161 ***<br>(–5.80) |
| *Public Investment* | 0.006<br>(0.87) | 0.001<br>(0.11) | –0.007<br>(–1.06) | –0.003<br>(–0.54) | 0.004<br>(1.00) | 0.003<br>(–0.79) | –0.004<br>(–1.28) |
| *Population Growth* | –1.445 ***<br>(–5.81) | –1.506 ***<br>(–6.01) | –1.419 ***<br>(–5.73) | –1.516 ***<br>(–6.45) | –1.372 ***<br>(–21.2) | –1.504 ***<br>(–5.70) | –1.559 ***<br>(–6.84) |
| Obs. | 1019 | 968 | 1019 | 968 | 968 | 859 | 968 |
| Sargan test (p-value) [2] | 0.610 | 0.115 | 0.712 | 0.773 | 0.804 | 1.000 | 1.000 |
| Autocovariance test of order 2 (p-value) [3] | 0.807 | 0.509 | 0.720 | 0.244 | 0.941 | 0.608 | 0.540 |

*Notes*:

Dependent variable GDP per capita growth in region $i$ ($i$ = 1, ..., 26) in period $t$ ($t$ = 1981, ..., 2003). $z$-statistics in parentheses; *, **, *** denote 10%, 5% and 1% significance respectively.

[1] Initial per capita GDP in region $i$ in period $t - 1$.

[2] The null hypothesis is that the instruments used are not correlated with the residuals.

[3] The null hypothesis is that the errors in the first-differenced regression exhibit no second order serial correlation.

[4] See Table 7A.1 for the definition of the variables used. Explanatory variables lagged 2 periods and Doctors University & Beds University lagged 3 periods. All the explanatory variables were used as instruments.

Income is a binary variable taking the value of 1 if observation belongs to high-income regions.

# NOTES

* The authors would like to thank the two anonymous referees for comments and constructive remarks. They also thank K. Angelopoulos, P. Kammas, C. Karpetis and P.-I. Prodromidis for constructive and helpful suggestions. They would also like to thank participants in the Conference on Institutional and Social Dynamics of Growth and Distribution in Lucca, Italy (2007), the 15th World Congress of the International Economic Association, Istanbul (2008) and the 7th Conference on Research on Economic Theory and Econometrics in Naxos, Greece (2008), for their fruitful comments.

1. A commonly used definition of human capital includes the set of knowledge, skills, competencies and abilities embodied in individuals and acquired through education, training and experience (Bassetti, 2007).
2. Detailed definitions of the variables are available in the Appendix (Table 7A.1).
3. We do not include data on the number of primary education students since there is no significant variation across regions, thus we would not be able to identify a distinct growth impact of such variables on regional growth.
4. The use of enrolment rates as a human capital variable is justified by the notion that current investment in human capital will be reflected in the future stock of human capital (Bassetti, 2007). We would have been keen to use human capital stock in our estimations (that is, average years of schooling) but unfortunately it is not available for Greek regions (NUTS 3 level). In addition, such data depend on arbitrary assumptions about depreciation and rely on inaccurate measures of benchmark stocks and investment flows (Barro and Sala-i-Martin, 2004). Studies that consider school enrolment rates include Barro (1991), Levine and Renelt (1992) and Mankiw et al. (1992).
5. Tables 7A.2–7A.4 provide all descriptive statistics (see Appendix).
6. Nine years of education (primary and lower secondary) has been compulsory in Greece since 1976 (Hellenic Constitution, Article 16, Paragraph 3).
7. Rural regions present enrolment rates of approximately 60–65 per cent over the whole period in lower secondary education and include prefectures such as Rodopi, Xanthi, Grevena, Euritania and Rethimno. The same regions exhibit enrolment rates around 30–40 per cent at the beginning of our sample period. In contrast, urban regions such as Athens, Thessaloniki and Achaia present enrolment rates of around 90–95 per cent.
8. See Kanelopoulos (1994), Paleocrassas (1996), Paleocrassas et al. (1997) and Kanelopoulos et al. (2003).
9. Here we should note that data on regional private investment (NUTS 3 level) are not available for Greece.
10. Please note that this is the second attempt for the computation of such a variable in the relevant literature on Greek regions; the initial one was by Lambrinidis et al. (2005).
11. According to Lambrinidis et al. (2005) regional public investment disparities in Greece are positively associated with the national elections and the infrastructure capital stock, and negatively associated with population size and regional product per capita.
12. The unavailability of average years of schooling as a measure of human capital, combined with the relatively short time span, led us to use 2-year lags in our estimations. We tried longer lags (3–5 years) and the results were essentially the same. Our final choice was dictated by the need to maintain a sufficient number of observations.
13. For detailed definitions of the variables see Table 7A.1.
14. Spatial autocorrelation might be an issue in this context. However, island prefectures constitute almost 30 per cent of Greek regions and mainland Greece is dominated by a mountain range (Pindos). As a result, labour and capital mobility between Greek regions are

quite limited, and the location of economic activity is mostly stable over time, which limits spatial autocorrelation. Nevertheless, spatial externalities are partially taken into account in Section 7.5.3.

15. The correlations between students (lower and upper secondary level) and medical doctors are 0.13 and 0.57 respectively and thus do not influence our results.
16. We also tried using hospital beds per 1000 population, but it was not significant. We think this is because it is a measure of the quantity of health services, in contrast with doctors who measure better the quality of services provided.
17. We do not use variables employed in cross-country studies, like life expectancy and infant mortality, since there are no such data at regional level in Greece.
18. The relevant specification tests provided no evidence of misspecification of our models.
19. Caselli et al. (1996) showed that their estimation methodology, which is very similar to ours, implies consistent estimates of convergence in contrast with most empirical growth literature.
20. The presence of business cycles possibly induces upward bias in the convergence coefficient. However, in our case regional business cycles are likely to be correlated, so this effect is rather weak. Also, previous work with the same dataset with 5-year averages indicated that findings are not sensitive to the time span employed in the estimation (Benos and Karagiannis, 2008).
21. Furthermore, we include in our model a number of geographical dummies (North/South, East/West, and islands/mainland) in order to capture spatial effects across groups of Greek regions. Our estimations exhibit a positive sign regarding mainland regions, meaning that these regions enjoy a positive growth differential with respect to islands. This might be explained by the insufficient public infrastructure and problematic connection of the islands with the mainland, especially during the non-tourist period of the year.
22. See Figure 7.1 (Section 7.3) for the spatial allocation of the two income groups. The *high-income group* includes: (a) the mainland regions with access to the main transportation network (from Athens to Thessaloniki), and (b) the island regions with highly developed tourist industry (Crete, Corfu, Cyclades, Dodecanese). The *low-income group* includes most regions of Thrace, Western Macedonia, Epirus, Peloponnese, North Aegean and Eptanisa.
23. Our spatial division of Greek regions concurs with the findings of recent studies. Christopoulos (2004) reports similar evidence on the spatial segregation of Greek regions and states that such regional divergence exists due to employment and output differentials. Prodromidis (2006) traces the same effects at NUTS 4 (post code) level and argues that access to the Athens–Thessaloniki transportation network acts as an income corridor between Greek regions. Finally, Benos and Karagiannis (2008) present similar findings arguing that two convergence clubs exist in the Greek economy.
24. However, one must always keep in mind that economic growth is only one of the government objectives along with, for example, stabilization, income equality, and external balance. In light of that, higher funding on education in rich regions relative to poor ones may not be desirable, because it will increase spatial income inequality.
25. However, we should point out here that policy makers should also take into account the overall characteristics of every region, such as geographic location, when designing specific growth-promoting policies.

## REFERENCES

Andersson, M. and C. Karlsson (2007), 'Knowledge in Regional Economic Growth – the Role of Knowledge Accessibility', *Industry and Innovation*, **14**(2), 129–49.

Andersson, M., U. Grasjo and C. Karlsson (2007), 'Human Capital and Productivity in a Spatial Economic System – Relating the Extent of Spatial Dependence to Localities Position', *Annales d' Economie et de Statistique,* 87–88, 125–44.

Arellano, A. and T.M. Fullerton Jr. (2005), 'Educational Attainment and Regional Economic Performance in Mexico', *International Advances in Economic Research*, **11**(2), 231–42.

Arellano, M. and S. Bond (1991), 'Some Tests of Specification for Panel Data: Monte Carlo Evidence and an Application to Employment Equations', *The Review of Economic Studies*, **58**(2), 277–97.

Azariadis, C. and A. Drazen (1990), 'Threshold Externalities in Economic Development', *Quarterly Journal of Economics*, **105**, 501–26.

Barro, R.J. (1991), 'Economic Growth in a Cross Section of Countries', *Quarterly Journal of Economics*, **106**(425), 407–43.

Barro, R.J. (1996), 'Determinants of Economic Growth: a Cross Country Empirical Study', *NBER Working Paper*, no. 5698.

Barro, R.J. and J.-W. Lee (1993), 'International Comparisons of Educational Attainment', *Journal of Monetary Economics*, **32**(3), 363–94.

Barro, R.J and X. Sala-i-Martin (2004), *Economic Growth*, Cambridge, MA: MIT Press.

Bassanini, A. and S. Scarpetta S. (2001), 'The Driving Forces of Economic Growth: Panel Data Evidence for the OECD Countries', *OECD Economic Studies*, **33**, 9–56.

Bassetti, T. (2007), 'Human Capital and Economic Growth: a Selective Survey', *PRIN 2005 Working Paper*, no. 018.

Becker, G.S. (1964), *Human Capital: a Theoretical and Empirical Analysis with Special Reference to Education*, New York: National Bureau of Economic Research.

Becker, G.S. (1993), *Human Capital: a Theoretical and Empirical Analysis with Special Reference to Education*, Chicago: University of Chicago Press.

Becker, G.S. (2007), 'Health as Human Capital: Synthesis and Extensions', *Oxford Economic Papers*, **59**(3), 379–410.

Benhabib, J. and M. Spiegel (1994), 'The Role of Human Capital in Economic Development: Evidence from Aggregate Cross-country Data', *Journal of Monetary Economics*, **34**, 143–74.

Benos, N. and S. Karagiannis (2008), 'Convergence and Economic Performance in Greece: Evidence at Regional and Prefecture Level', *Review of Urban and Regional Development Studies*, **20**(1), 52–69.

Bils, M. and P.J. Klenow (2000), 'Does Schooling Cause Growth?', *American Economic Review*, **90**(5), 1160–83.

Bloom, D.E. and D. Canning (2000), 'Health as Human Capital and its Impact on Economic Performance', *The Geneva Papers on Risk and Insurance*, **28**(2), 304–15.

Bloom, D.E. and D. Canning (2003), 'Health and the Wealth of Nations', *Science*, **287**(5456), 1207–9.

Bloom, D.E. and J. Sachs (1998), 'Geography, Demography, and Economic Growth in Africa', *Brookings Papers on Economic Activity*, **2**, 207–95.

Bloom, D.E. and J. Williamson (1998), 'Demographic Transitions and Economic Miracles in Emerging Asia', *World Bank Economic Review*, **12**(3), 419–55.

Bloom, D.E., B. Bloom, J. Cohen and J. Sachs (1999), 'Investing in the World Health Organization', *Science*, **284**, 911.

Bloom, D.E., D. Canning and J. Sevilla (2004), 'The Effect of Health on Economic Growth: a Production Function Approach', *World Development*, **32**(1), 1–13.

Caselli, F., G. Esquivel and F. Lefort (1996), 'Reopening the Convergence Debate: a New Look at Cross-country Growth Empirics', *Journal of Economic Growth*, **1**(3), 363–89.

Christopoulos, D. (2004), 'The Relationship Between Output and Unemployment: Evidence From Greek Regions', *Papers in Regional Science*, **83**(3), 611–20.

De la Fuente, A. (2002), 'On the Sources of Convergence: a Close Look at the Spanish Regions', *European Economic Review*, **46**(3), 569–99.

De la Fuente, A. and R. Domenech (2000), *Human Capital in Growth Regressions: How Much Difference Does Data Quality Make?*, Universidad Autonoma de Barcelona, mimeo.

Di Liberto, A. (2004), 'Convergence Clubs, and the Role of Human Capital in Spanish Regional Growth', in H. Folmer and J. Surinach (eds), *Knowledge and Regional Economic Development*, Cheltenham, UK and Northampton, MA, USA: Edward Elgar.

Di Liberto, A. (2007), 'Education and Italian Regional Development', *Economics of Education Review*, **27**(1), 94–107.

Durlauf, S.N and P.A. Johnson (1995), 'Multiple Regimes and Cross-country Growth Behaviour', *Journal of Applied Econometrics*, **10**(4), 365–84.

Eckey, H.-F., C. Dreger and M. Turck (2006), 'European Regional Convergence in a Human Capital Augmented Solow Model', *University of Kassel Working Paper*, no. 88.

Ehrlich, I. (2000), 'Uncertain Lifetime, Life Protection, and the Value of Life Saving', *Journal of Health Economics*, **19**(3), 341–67.

Fuchs, J. (1966), 'The Contribution of Health Services to the American Economy', *Milbank Memorial Fund Quarterly*, **44**(4), 65–102.

Grasjo, U. (2005), 'Human Capital, Rand and Regional Exports', *Working Paper Series in Economics and Institutions of Innovation*, no. 50, Royal Institute of Technology, CESIS.

Griliches, Z. (1997), 'Education, Human Capital and Growth: a Personal Perspective', *Journal of Labour Economics*, **5**(1), 330–44.

Howitt, P. (2005), 'Health, Human Capital, and Economic Growth: a Schumpeterian Perspective', in G. López-Casasnovas, B. Rivera and L. Currais (eds), *Health and Economic Growth: Findings and Policy Implications,* Cambridge, MA: MIT Press, pp. 19–40.

Kalaitzidakis, P., T. Mamuneas, A. Savvides and T. Stengos (2001), 'Measures of Human Capital and Nonlinearities in Economic Growth', *Journal of Economic Growth*, **6**(3), 229–54.

Kanelopoulos, K., (1994), *Greek Education in the 2000 Horizon*, Reports No. 10, KEPE, Athens [in Greek].

Kanelopoulos, K., K. Mauromaras and Th. Mitrakos (2003), *Education and the Labour Market*, Studies No. 50, KEPE, Athens [in Greek].

Krueger, A.B. and M. Lindahl (2001), 'Education for Growth: Why and For Whom?', *Journal of Economic Literature*, **39**(4), 1101–36.

Lambrinidis, M., Y. Psycharris and A. Rovolis (2005), 'Regional Allocation of Public Infrastructure Investment: the Case of Greece', *Regional Studies*, **39**(9), 1231–44.

Levine R. and D. Renelt (1992), 'A Sensitivity Analysis of Cross-country Growth Regressions', *American Economic Review*, **82**(4), 942–63.

Louri, H. (1989), 'Regional Policy and Investment Behaviour: the Case of Greece, 1971–1982', *Regional Studies*, **23**(3), 231–9.

Lucas, R.E. (1988), 'On The Mechanics of Economic Development', *Journal of Monetary Economics*, **22**(1), 3–42.

Malik, G. (2006), 'An Examination of the Relationship Between Health and Economic Growth', *ICRIER Working Paper.*

Mankiw, N., D. Romer and D. Weil (1992), 'A Contribution to the Empirics of Economic Growth', *Quarterly Journal of Economics*, **107**(2), 407–37.

Meltzer, D.O. (1992), *Mortality Decline, the Demographic Transition, and Economic Growth*, Dissertation, Chicago: University of Chicago, December.

Middendorf, T., (2006), 'Human Capital and Economic Growth in OECD Countries', *Jahrbucher Fur Nationalokonomie Und Statistik*, **226**(6), 670–86.

Mushkin, S.J. (1962), 'Health as an Investment', *Journal of Political Economy*, **70**, supplement, 129–57.

Nelson, R.R. and S.E. Phelps (1966), 'Investment in Humans, Technological Diffusion, and Economic Growth', *American Economic Review*, **56**(1–2), 69–75.

Paleocrassas, S. (1996), *Student Dropouts in Gymnasium and Their Needs for Professional Education and Training*, Pedagogical Institute, OEEK [in Greek].

Paleocrassas, S., P. Rousseas and V. Vretakou (1997), 'Greek Lower Secondary School Dropouts: Results from a National Survey', *European Educational Research Association Bulletin*, **3**(1), 12–18.

Papageorgiou, C. (2003), 'Distinguishing Between the Effects of Primary and Post-Primary Education on Economic Growth', *Review of Development Economics*, **7**(4), 622–35.

Pritchett, L. (2001), 'Where Has all the Education Gone?', *World Bank Economic Review*, **15**(3), 367–91.

Prodromidis, P.I. (2006), *A Regional Analysis of Declared Incomes in Greece*, Studies No. 63, KEPE, Athens.

Ricci, F. and M. Zachariadis (2007), 'Determinants of Public Health Outcomes: A Macroeconomic Perspective', *Computing in Economics and Finance Working Papers.*

Romer, P.M. (1990), 'Endogenous Technological Change', *Journal of Political Economy*, **98**(5), 71–102.

Sianesi, B. and J. Van Reenen (2002), 'The Returns to Education: a Review of the Empirical Macroeconomic Literature', *IFS Working Paper*, no. 02/05.

Temple, J. (1999), 'The New Growth Evidence', *Journal of Economic Literature*, **37**(1), 112–56.

# 8. Adult longevity and economic take-off from Malthus to Ben-Porath*

**David de la Croix**

## 8.1. INTRODUCTION

Adult longevity, as measured for example by the conditional life expectancy at age 10, is undoubtedly positively correlated with income per person. This is true both over time and across countries. Figure 8.1 plots this relationship for Sweden from 1751 until today. The dotted line represents life expectancy at age 10 and is measured in years on the right axis,[1] while the solid line represents the logarithm of income per capita in constant dollars and is measured on the left axis.[2] The trends in the two series are amazingly similar. Up to the 1820s we have stagnation in both series, then a slight upward trend after the Napoleonic wars is discernible, but at a very modest level (averaging around half a percent a year for income per capita). There is an increasing growth trend though and, after 1850, average growth rates in income per capita start to exceed the 1 percent level.

This positive relation between adult longevity and growth is also found is a cross-section of countries. Figure 8.2 plots this relationship for the year 2000. Life expectancy at age 10 is taken from the life tables provided by the World Health Organization (and results from model life tables for certain countries), while GDP per capita is measured using the World Development Indicators. The relation between the two variables is also very strong; the countries lying much below the regression line are those which are strongly hit by the AIDS epidemics.

This strong relationship is obviously very important to understand the processes that led the various countries through the transition from stagnation to sustained growth (industrial revolution), but is also key to improving the design of today's development policy. Unfortunately, the correlations highlighted above do not say anything on the direction of causality. Did improvements in longevity simply follow better living conditions, and, at best, reinforce the growth process, or, on the contrary,

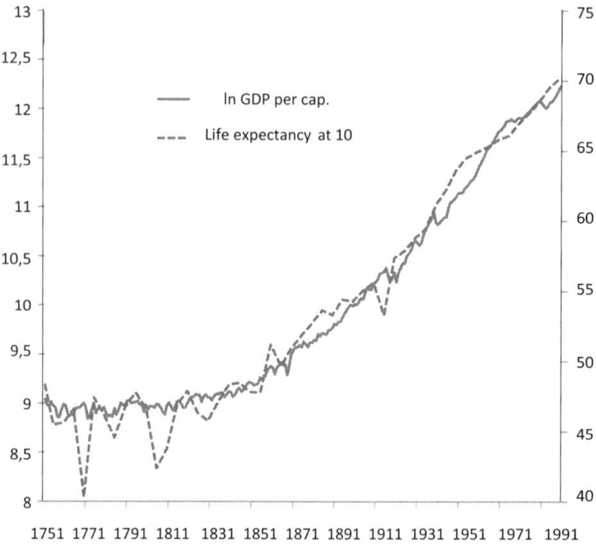


*Figure 8.1. Life expectancy at age 10 and income per capita in Sweden*

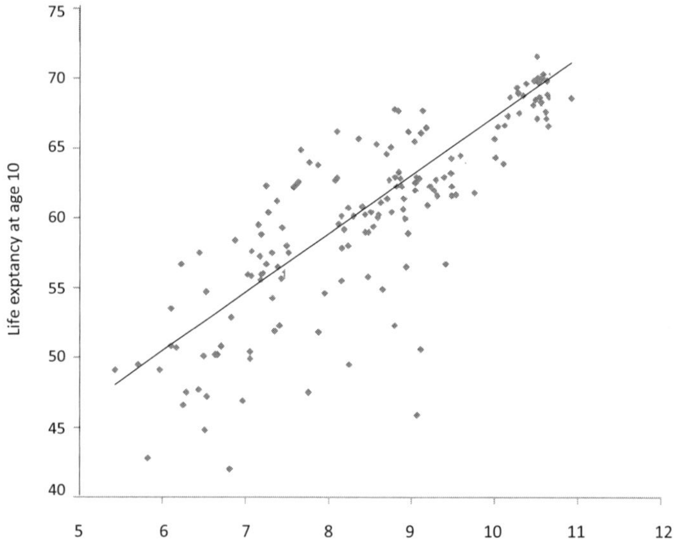


*Figure 8.2. Life expectancy at age 10 and income per capita across countries (year 2000)*

did adult longevity rise before the industrial revolution and play a crucial role in its release?

It is undisputed that longevity was positively influenced by standard of living. However, the question on whether longevity played a key role in the industrial revolution is disputed. The two views mentioned above are present in the literature. The view according to which longevity improvements reinforce growth but were not key is illustrated by the following citation:

> It appears that the industrial demand for human capital (...) provided the inducement for investment in education and the associated reduction in fertility rates, whereas the prolongation of life may have re-enforced and complemented this process (Galor, 2005).

The alternative according to which longevity played a key role was earlier defended by the same author:

> Changes in mortality can serve as the basis for a unified model that describes the complete transition from the Malthusian Regime to the Modern Growth Regime. Consider the effect of an initial reduction in mortality (due to an exogenous shock to health technology or to standards of living). The effect of lower mortality in raising the expected rate of return to human capital investments will nonetheless be present, leading to more schooling and eventually to a higher rate of technological progress. This will in turn raise income and further lower mortality... (Galor and Weil, 1999).

In this chapter we defend the idea that longevity is a key factor. For this purpose we will provide four arguments using various data sets: Geneva and Venice longevity data before the Industrial Revolution (Section 8.3), mortality data of English aristocrats (Section 8.4), evidence on the rise in medical knowledge (Section 8.5), and height of Swedish soldiers (Section 8.6). Before going into these details we briefly survey various theories which formally examine mechanisms through which longevity affects growth (Section 8.2).

## 8.2. THEORIES

Theories accounting for a positive effect of adult longevity on income per capita can be classified into four categories.

We label the first theory the Ben-Porath mechanism, following Ben-Porath (1967)'s seminal contribution. According to this theory, the return to investment in education depends on the length of time during which education will be productive, that is, a longer active life makes initial investment in human capital more profitable. Longer education makes future income higher. Provided that human capital is an engine of growth, this may in turn sustain permanent income growth. The first authors to put this argument to work in an endogenous growth model are de la Croix and Licandro (1999). Further contributions are in Boucekkine et al. (2002), Soares (2005) and Cervellati and Sunde (2005). Quantifications of the effect can be found in de la Croix et al. (2008) and Cordoba and Ripoll (2008).

A second mechanism argues that longer lives give stronger incentives to save and invest. Let us label this the life-cycle hypothesis. Following the intuition of the life-cycle hypothesis, Nicolini (2004) claims that the increase in adult life expectancy must have implied less farmer impatience and could have caused more investment in nitrogen stock and land fertility, the increase in agricultural land, and higher production per acre in eighteenth-century England.

Beyond the 'horizon' effect caused by longer lives, there might also be a healthiness effect. Healthier children have an increased capacity to absorb human capital (Hazan and Zoabi, 2006).

The last mechanism is based on the fact that, keeping given fertility and migration, lower mortality increases the size of the population. Increased population density fosters the efficiency of the transmission of human capital (Lagerloef, 2003). Increased population growth may also improve the advancement of skill-biased technologies (Weisdorf, 2004).

Beyond these theoretical approaches to the interaction between longevity trends and long-run income growth prospects, there is another tradition which has an agnostic view of the mechanisms actually in place; it is the demographic dividend literature which analyzes the empirical relationships between demographic variables and growth in income per capita in recent data (see Bloom and Williamson, 1998). Following this line, de la Croix et al. (2009) consider a demographically-based statistical growth model estimated on global post-war growth data to study whether it can account for the long-term growth process that can be observed in the Swedish data. The global model estimates show a drift in the most productive activity period with life expectancy. The peak productivity shifts from around 30 years of age when life expectancy is low to an age around 50 for actual life expectancies in developed and emerging economies. The model is used to backcast Swedish economic growth back to 1750. The backcast shows that the statistical model can account not only for recent changes in per capita income but also for the long-term process of Swedish economic development since the mid nineteenth century.

## 8.3. GENEVA AND VENICE DATA[3]

To assess the role of the decline in mortality in the economic take-off of Western Europe, it is necessary to distinguish the fluctuations of infant mortality from the reduction in the mortality of adults. Infant mortality fluctuates strongly as a function of economic and sanitary conditions, as children will be the first to suffer from bad crops and diseases. Child mortality has a major influence on the estimation of life expectancy at birth. Since improvements in infant mortality have arisen very late in the nineteenth century, it is not surprising that life expectancy at birth shows little trend before that time. Using the data built by Wrigley and Schofield (1989) for England, life expectancy at birth peaks in England at 39.5 years around the year 1575, then drops to 33 years in the period 1670–1750, and rises again and reaches its 1575 level in 1820. Then, it remains steady at 40 years until 1850. However, this absence of large improvement before 1850, due to a high and volatile infant mortality, hides more subtle improvements on the front of adult mortality. We shall eliminate the effects of this volatility on life expectancy estimations to get a much better picture of the evolution of adult mortality.

To study how adult mortality evolved over time, we need cohort life tables at different periods. We have found two data sets adapted to our purposes. The first one is from Perrenoud (1978) who constructed life tables from 1625 to 1825 on the basis of a wide nominative study in Geneva (Switzerland). The second set was built by Beltrami (1951). He uses parish registers to reconstitute the age-group dynamics of the Venetian population over the period 1600–1790. Complete life tables are available for the cohorts born between 1600 and 1700; for the cohorts born after 1700 we only have partial tables, since the study ends in 1790. Survival laws are normalized to 1000 at age 10. By doing so, we eliminate the shifts generated by changes in infant mortality and concentrate on the mortality of adults. Figures 8.3 and 8.4 display the survival laws of selected cohorts. These data sets are available from the author upon request.

Geneva's picture, in Figure 8.3, displays upward shifts in the curve from one generation to the next. The drop in the death rates essentially concerns ages 40 to 65. Notice that the end of the curve does not move much, reflecting that the gains in longevity do not translate into a rise in the maximum attainable age. Very few persons live longer than 85.

In Figure 8.4 we find the same trend in Venice's data, that have been built from different sources. The lower curve represents the survival law for the generation born in 1600–1610. The dip in the curve at the age of 30 reflects the dramatic plague experienced by the city in 1630. The data from this

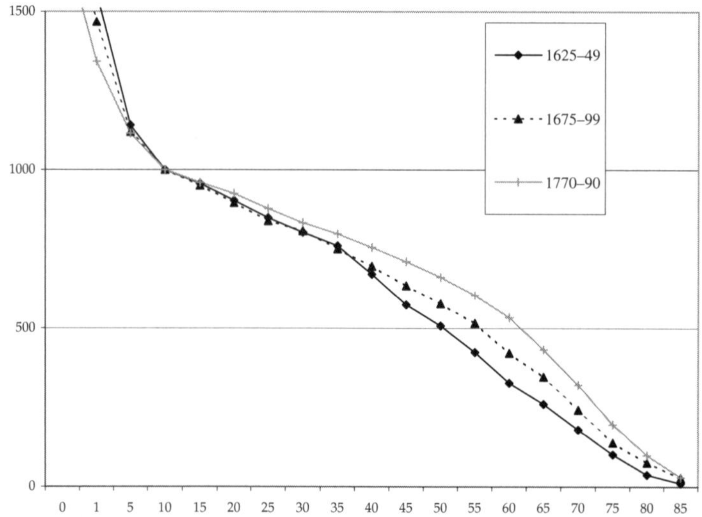


*Figure 8.3. Survival probabilities – Geneva*

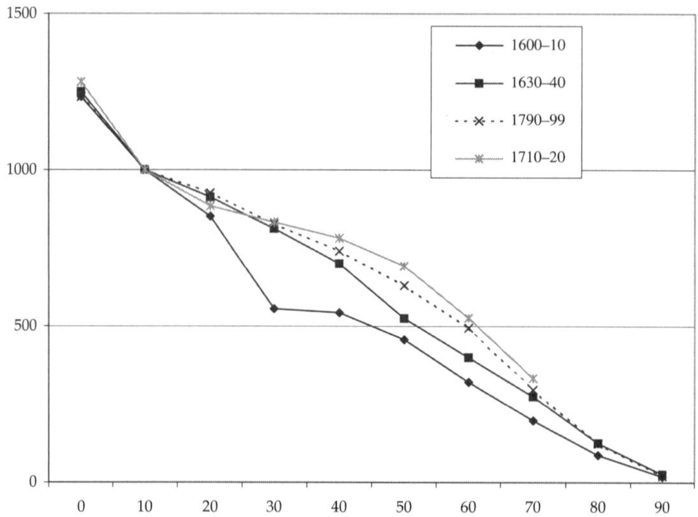


*Figure 8.4. Survival probabilities – Venice*

period are thus rather pessimistic about longevity, as they take into account the damage caused by these particularly vigorous epidemics. To have a more prudent view of the improvement in longevity, we can compare the generation born in 1630–40 to the one born in 1710–20. There is no plague during this century in Venice (except the one of 1630 that only affects infant mortality of the generation 1630–40). Here again, the gains in longevity are concentrated on the working ages, and life expectancy at 10 increases significantly over the period.

The main finding of Boucekkine et al. (2003) that the observed changes in adult mortality from the last quarter of the seventeenth century to the first quarter of the eighteenth century described in Figures 8.3 and 8.4 played a fundamental role in launching modern growth. The decline in adult mortality induced an increase in the growth rate of around 70 per cent of the increase estimated by Maddison. This study thus promotes the view that the early decline in adult mortality is responsible for a large part of the acceleration of growth at the dawn of the modern age.

The debate concerning the causes of the initial decline in mortality is not settled yet. The classical view is that pre-industrial mortality was reduced when nutritional standards were improved. Perrenoud (1985) and Fridlizius (1985) claim that human factors (nutrition, medicine, sanitary conditions and economy) did not play a prominent role in the first phase of the process. Instead, the decline in mortality should be found elsewhere; it can be connected to changes in immunology and/or improvement in the climate.

Could the shifts of the survival curve witnessed in Geneva and Venice be generalized to the whole of Europe? We do not know, but at least not probably to England. In Boucekkine et al. (2007), we estimate that mortality improvements account for only one sixth of the rise in literacy and growth in England over the period 1530–1860. This is small especially compared to the important role it was supposed to play in Nicolini (2004) and Boucekkine et al. (2003).

Looking first at the raw data, Figure 8.5 compares the survival function in England as estimated by Wrigley et al. (1997) with the one for Geneva from Figure 8.3. Again we have normalized the series to 1000 at the age of 10 to concentrate on the mortality of adults. During the early seventeenth century (data for 1625–49), surviving was more likely in England than in Geneva, specially for the ages 35–65. English longevity was remarkably high for this period. Fifty years later, mortality in Geneva had dropped substantially, becoming lower compared to England. More surprisingly, English mortality had in fact increased over this period. This different evolution in mortality is probably due to the sharp rise in urbanization in England. At that time, big cities were unhealthy places. According to Bairoch et al. (1988), the population of London went from 50 thousand in 1500 to 948 thousand in 1800, while it grew only from 12 thousand to 25 thousand in Geneva over the whole period. In the eighteenth century, finally, survival probabilities increased at all ages in both England and Geneva. Over the two centuries, the

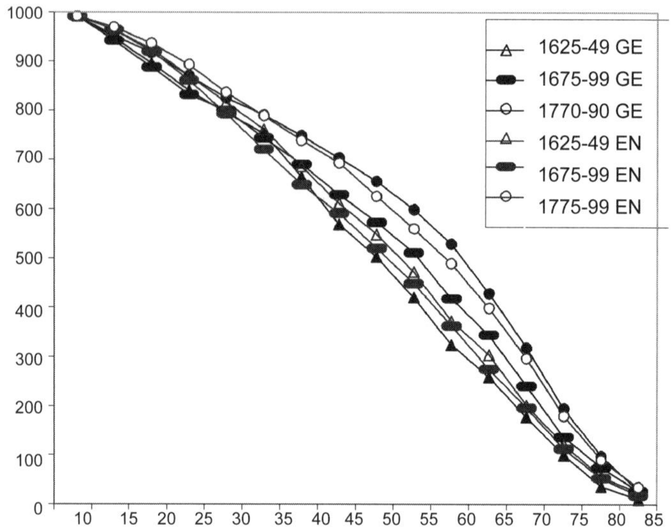


*Figure 8.5. Estimated survival probabilities – England*

improvements in longevity were steady in Geneva, while they came quite late in England probably because of the fast urbanization process. This is why, in the quantitative exercise of Boucekkine et al. (2007), mortality reductions play a role only in the eighteenth century.

## 8.4. ENGLISH ARISTOCRATS[4]

Another way to search for changes in mortality that could have preceded the Industrial Revolution is to look for forerunners in mortality decline. Even if little is visible at the aggregate level, longevity improvements benefiting specific groups could have sparked a modification in their behavior along the lines proposed in Section 8.2.

It is difficult to find data on mortality rates or life expectancy by income groups for the pre-industrial period. We gather here some evidence for England as a whole, combining sources from Hollingsworth (1977) and Wrigley et al. (1997), and for two cities in continental Europe, based on surveys by Perrenoud (1975) and Bardet (1983).

Starting with England, Figure 8.6 compares life expectancy at birth of the average person (from parish records (Wrigley et al., 1997)) with that of the English aristocracy (from genealogical data (Hollingsworth 1977)). Before 1700, there is not much difference in adult mortality across social classes.

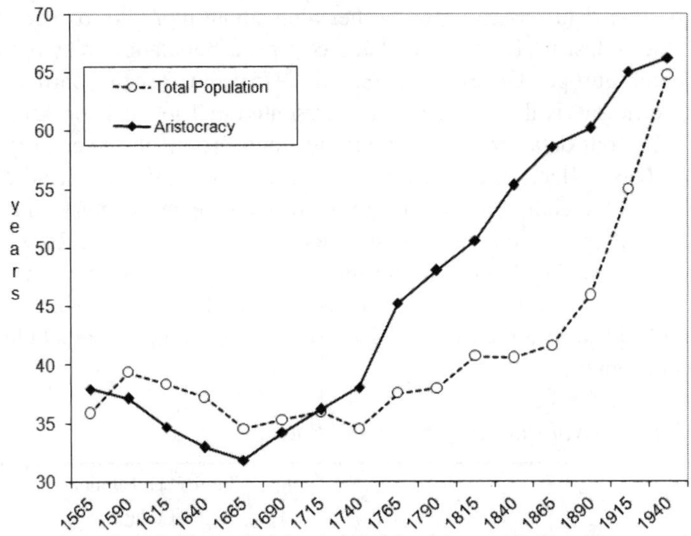


*Figure 8.6. Life expectancy at birth in England*

Surprisingly the elites have lower life expectancy; this unexpected result is attributed by Johansson (1999) to an urban penalty paid by the aristocracy for the pleasures and opportunities of city life. The quasi-egalitarian mortality regime began to change by 1700. Life expectancy rose for all groups but faster and further for the elite.

In de la Croix and Sommacal (2009) we argue that this picture could be consistent with a decomposition of the evolution of medical knowledge and life expectancy into three periods. Before the seventeenth century the effectiveness of medicine was very low. In fact, medicine was probably not effective at all. Given the low effectiveness of medical services, doctors hardly managed to increase the life expectancy of their patients. As a consequence, differential mortality between the rich (who could afford the services of a doctor) and the common people was very low, or even non-existent: income was of little importance in determining life expectancy. Next came a time when medicine became more effective. The rich were the first to benefit from these improvements, and their life expectancy rose. Differential mortality started to increase, because the improvements in longevity still did not benefit the whole population. In the third period there was a global improvement in health. Medicine became more and more effective, and the advantage of the upper classes in terms of longevity declined. Differential mortality decreased. We will look further into the evolution of medical knowledge over time in the next section.

Two other data sets can give further hints about mortality by social class before the Industrial Revolution. They cover the population of two cities in continental Europe, Geneva (Perrenoud 1975) and Rouen (Bardet 1983). Age-specific survival probabilities are presented in Table 8.1 for three social classes. In both data sets, infant mortality rates are much lower in the elite groups. This reflects their better living conditions. We also find that in Geneva (seventeenth century) and in Rouen (eighteenth century) there was not much difference in adult mortality across social classes. In Rouen, there was no significant difference in the survival probabilities from age 15 to age 30 or from age 30 to age 45 of notables and simple workers. This is in line with the English data presented above. In Geneva, the upper social class had a slight advantage.

*Table 8.1. Survival rates in Geneva and Rouen*

| | Social class | Survival probabilities | | |
|---|---|---|---|---|
| | | 0–15 | 15–30 | 30–45 |
| | workers | 0.34 | 0.80 | 0.70 |
| Geneva 17th | merchants | 0.45 | 0.84 | 0.74 |
| | nobility | 0.61 | 0.89 | 0.81 |
| | workers | 0.33 | 0.85 | 0.87 |
| Rouen 18th | merchants | 0.49 | 0.87 | 0.86 |
| | nobility | 0.47 | 0.86 | 0.84 |

## 8.5. RISE IN MEDICAL KNOWLEDGE[5]

We have seen in the previous sections that adult longevity started to improve before the increase in income per capita related to the Industrial Revolution. The determinants of the evolution of life expectancy during these centuries have been the subject of lively discussions in medical history and mortality history. One of the issues concerns the role of medical science. Remember the Galor and Weil citation provided in the introduction: 'Consider the effect of an initial reduction in mortality (due to an exogenous shock to health technology or to standards of living)'. We are precisely looking for this exogenous shock.

As a matter of medical knowledge, it is certain that ancient ideas persisted for a long time in modern Europe and the confidence of consumers in medicine was low. Popular proverbs endorsed this distrust: one doctor makes work for another.[6] As a consequence some authors claim that the rise of life expectancy in early modern Europe relied more on changes in immunology and/or improvement in the climate than on human factors such as medical advances.

Johansson (1999) argues against the traditional therapeutic nihilism that tends to deny that medicine had any effectiveness before the end of the nineteenth century, and suggested an increase in medical effectiveness as a possible explanation for the change, documented in Figure 8.6, from an egalitarian mortality regime to a regime characterized by a mortality differential between rich and poor people.

Indeed in the period 1500–1800, medicine showed an increasingly experimental attitude: no improvement was effected on the grounds of the disease theory (which was still mainly based on traditional ideas), but significant advances were made based on practice and empirical observations. For example, although the theoretical understanding of how drugs work only came progressively in the nineteenth century with the development of chemistry (Weatherall 1996), the effectiveness of the treatment of some important diseases was improved thanks to the practical use of new drugs coming from the New World.[7] Advances in the treatment of syphilis were made due to improvements in the development of condoms. For a long period, mainly due to their high cost, these new medical advances were only available to rich people.[8]

Moreover Table 8.2, which shows the number of books containing lifestyle advice written in the period 1600–1800 by sub-periods, provides some indirect evidence of the fact that lifestyle advice (concerning, for example, personal and domestic cleanliness) became popular among upper class readers. This trend is also supported by the evidence provided by on book production in early modern Europe from 1450 to 1799.

As suggested by Baten and van Zanden (2008) the cumulative effects of these improvements could have produced a net increase in the efficacy of medicine in the eighteenth century.

*Table 8.2. Number of books on health published in England, 1600–1800*

| Period | Number of books |
|---|---|
| 1600–24 | 9 |
| 1625–49 | 16 |
| 1650–74 | 17 |
| 1675–99 | 25 |
| 1700–24 | 28 |
| 1725–49 | 34 |
| 1750–74 | 53 |
| 1775–1800 | 81 |

> As early as 1829 Dr. F.B. Hawkins wrote a book entitled Elements of Medical Statistics, in which lie described what could be called an early modern epidemiological transition. Several centuries before his own time leprosy, plague, sweating sickness, ague, typhus, smallpox, syphilis and scurvy had been leading causes of death. Now all of these diseases had disappeared, could be cured, or treated effectively. At the present scarlet fever, consumption, gout, dropsy, palsy, apoplexy (including heart attacks and strokes), mania, and diseases of the brain were the most prevalent causes of death. The last six of the eight diseases listed were not contagious; they were chronic diseases most likely to strike older adults (Johansson, 1999, p. 48).

We conclude this section with an important remark. Even if advances in medical knowledge and practice (as above, we use this term in a broad sense, to include lifestyle advice) could be responsible for early improvements in the length of life, this does not mean that the increase in life expectancy can be explained only by advances in medical science. Many factors may have contributed to the reduction in mortality since the eighteenth century (nutrition, medicine, immunology, etc.) and attributing a specific weight to each of them is very difficult (Fogel 2004). Medical effectiveness could still be key to explain the differential mortality between social classes before the Industrial Revolution.

## 8.6. HEIGHT OF SWEDISH SOLDIERS[9]

Let us now go deeper into one mechanism through which adult longevity could have increased. From the epidemiology literature we know that providing children with appropriate health care and nutrition and promoting good attitudes towards health ensure them a longer life when adults (see a survey in Harris (2001)). Starting with Kermack et al. (1934), who showed that the first fifteen years of life were central in determining the longevity of the adult, the relationship between early development and late mortality within cohorts has been well-established. Another important contribution in the field is that of Barker and Osmond (1986) who related lower childhood health status to higher incidence of heart disease in later life. This idea also had an echo in the literary tradition as witnessed by the aphorism ‘The Child is Father of the Man’ (Wordsworth 1809), meaning that the way a child is brought up determines what he or she will become in the future.

Height is a simple measure of childhood development, since both better nutrition and lower exposure to infections leads to increased height.[10] Height is constant after, say, the age of 18, but is still a good predictor of life expectancy and mortality in old age. According to Waaler (1984), the trend towards greater height found in the data means that younger cohorts, which have grown up with better nutrition, will have better health and live longer as adults.

Height is a frequently used indicator in microeconomic studies of the relationship between health and income. Weil (2007) finds that the effect on wages of an additional centimeter of height ranges between 3.3 per cent and 9.4 per cent, depending on the data set used. In a second step, he exploits the correlation between height and direct measures of health such as the adult survival rate to evaluate health's role in accounting for income differences among countries; he finds that eliminating health variations would reduce world income variance by a third.

The height of conscripts has been systematically recorded by the Swedish army since 1820, which provides time-series information on changes in height throughout the demographic transition. Figure 8.7 presents data[11] for the cohorts born between 1760 and 1960. The left panel shows that the height of soldiers (measured at approximately age 20) is highly correlated with the life expectancy of the same generation.[12] The right panel of Figure 8.7 shows that body height and years of schooling are positively correlated and, more importantly, that changes in height precede changes in education.

In de la Croix and Licandro (2007) we propose a new theory of the demographic transition based on the evidence reported above that body development during childhood is an important predictor of life expectancy. The key and novel mechanism we propose is that parents face a trade-off between the quantity of children they have and the amount they can afford to spend on each of them during childhood. Parents like to have children, but they also care about their longevity. By ensuring an appropriate physical development for their children and protecting them from infections, parents provide them with greater health capital and a longer life. Such provision is costly though, and its cost is proportional to the number of children. As a consequence, having many children prevents parents of spending much on their health capital. The proposed quality/quantity trade-off makes longevity and fertility negatively related.

In our chapter, the mechanism relating demographics and growth is the Ben-Porath hypothesis that longevity positively affects education and human capital accumulation, by extending an individual active life. We assume that adults decide about their own optimal amount of education, and we take basic education, even if provided by parents, as being exogenously given. In addition to the trade-off between the number and development of children stressed above, adults face a trade-off between having children and improving their own education, which makes the number of children and schooling negatively related. This is similar to the trade-off faced by parents in a Beckerian world, where they care about the quantity and quality (education) of their offsprings.

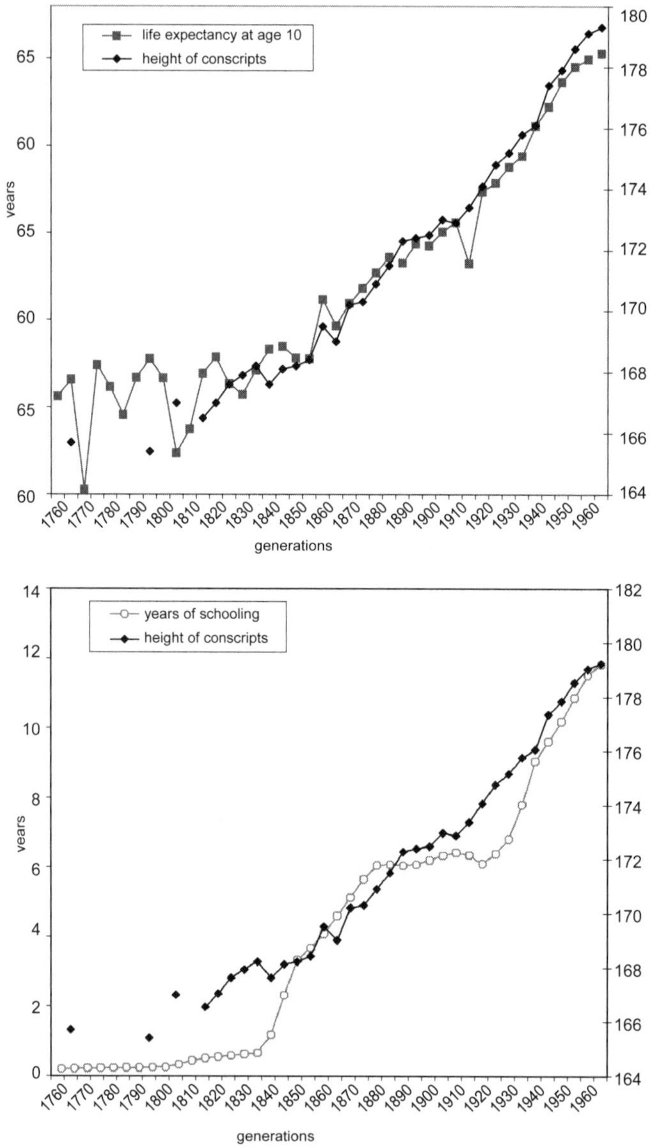


*Figure 8.7. Height, life expectancy and education in Sweden*

The dynamics of de la Croix and Licandro (2007)'s model displays the key features of the demographic transition, including the hump in total net fertility rate and in population growth. In particular, it is able to replicate the observed rise in life expectancy and educational attainment, as well as the initial increase and then decline in fertility. If the mechanisms we describe predominate, the logic of the demographic transition could well be the reverse of that which is usually assumed: the key trade-off is not between fertility and education, with effects on longevity as a byproduct, but between fertility and healthier and longer living children, with a subsequent effect on education. This timing is evident in the data presented above.

## 8.7. CONCLUDING REMARK

The transition from a world of low economic growth with high mortality and high fertility to one with low mortality and fertility but sustained growth has been the subject of intensive research in recent years. In this literature, the relation between growth and fertility results from the quantity/quality trade-off faced by parents between the number of children and their education. Indeed, the gradual increase in the observed level of for human capital during the nineteenth century 'has led researchers to argue that the increasing role of human capital in the production process induced households to increase investment in the human capital of their offspring, ultimately leading to the onset of the demographic transition' (Galor 2005). If the rise is education was indeed driven by a stronger demand for skills from the industrial sector, one should have observed a rise in the skill premium during and following the industrial revolution.

Looking for such evidence, Clark (2005) computes a skill premium over the period 1220–1990 in two different ways. First by measuring the relative wage of all skilled building workers relative to all laborers and, second, by using only those observations in which there is a matched pair for the same place and year of wages for craftsmen and laborers. The two methods lead to the same conclusion: the skill premium did not rise during the Industrial Revolution. And Clark concludes that 'The market premium for skills, does not explain the increased investment in human skills evident after 1600'. Hence, we might wonder whether the human capital interpretations of the Industrial Revolution are based on the right trade-off.

The evidence provided in this chapter points to an alternative mechanism which does not require any increase in the skill premium (and hence would not be dismissed by Clark's data) because it is based on a supply side argument. Rather than grounding the rise in education on the growing demand for skilled workers from the industry, we argue that households may have wanted to increase their investment in human skills as a response to longer lives.

The whole story line could then be as evoked by Galor and Weil (1999): following a positive shock to health technology, the environment during childhood improved and adult mortality consequently decreased. This occurred at least for a sub-group of the population: the upper class, and those living in cities. This raised the expected rate of return to human capital investments for them, leading to more education, a faster accumulation of skills, and eventually to a higher rate of productivity growth. This in turn initiated the transition from Malthusian stagnation to sustained growth.

## NOTES

* I acknowledge the financial support of the Belgian French speaking community (Grant ARC 03/08-235 'New Macroeconomic Approaches to the Development Problem') and the Belgian Federal Government (Grant PAI P6/07 'Economic Policy and Finance in the Global Economy: Equilibrium Analysis and Social Evaluation').

1. Already in 1749, Sweden had established a public agency with a responsibility for producing population statistics. These statistics were based on population records kept by the parish priests of the Swedish Lutheran church. Thanks to this effort we have access to detailed data of high quality on how mortality and fertility changed as Sweden developed from a poor agricultural country in the eighteenth century into a rich, highly industrialized country in the twentieth century (Hofsten and Lundström 1976).
2. Historical estimates of GDP per capita in Sweden are available from several sources. Back to 1861 they all build on work done by Lindahl et al. (1937) but lately these estimates have been extended backwards by Edvinsson (2005) all the way back to 1720.
3. This section borrows some material from Boucekkine et al. (2003).
4. This section borrows some material from de la Croix and Sommacal (2009).
5. This section borrows some material from de la Croix and Sommacal (2009).
6. For further details of the history of medicine: Siraisi (1990) and Porter (1995).
7. Ipecacuanha was used for severe dysentery, guaiacum for syphilis, and the bark of the cinchona tree for malaria. Citrus fruits started to be used in the prevention and treatment of scurvy.
8. In the eighteenth century bubonic plague also disappeared from England. The reasons for this are still hotly debated and some authors explain it in exogenous terms. In any case, independently of this debate, it should be noticed that by the seventeenth century a 'warning system' had been developed in London. Weekly bills of mortality, containing the cause of death, were published: when the number of plague deaths reached a worrying value, foreshadowing the outbreak of an epidemic, people with enough money to move left the city. This system, though not effective in the treatment of the plague itself, can be interpreted as a public health measure, that had an effect on the health of rich people.
9. This section borrows some material from de la Croix and Licandro (2007).
10. According to Silventoinen (2003), height is a good indicator of childhood living conditions (mostly family background), not only in developing countries but also in modern Western societies. In poor societies, the proportion of cross-sectional variation in body height explained by living conditions is larger than in developed countries, with lower heritability of height as well as larger socioeconomic differences in height.

11. Sources: Sandberg and Steckel (1997) for height data from 1820; Floud (1984) for height data before 1820 from Denmark. The 'Human Mortality Database' for life expectancy data; and de la Croix et al. (2008) for education data.
12. Notice that this strong correlation over time can also be established in a cross-section of countries: Baten and Komlos (1998) regressed life expectancy at birth on adult height and explained 68 per cent of the variance for a sample of 17 countries in 1860.

## REFERENCES

Bairoch, P., J. Batou and P. Chèvre (1988), *The Population of European Cities from 800 to 1850*, Genève: CIEH.

Bardet, J.-P. (1983), *Rouen au XVII$^{e}$ et XVIII$^{e}$ siècles*, Paris: SEDES.

Barker, D. and C. Osmond (1986), 'Infant Mortality, Childhood Nutrition, and Ischaemic Heart Disease in England and Wales', *Lancet*, **10**(1), 1077–81.

Baten, J. and J. Komlos (1998), 'Review: Height and the Standard of Living', *The Journal of Economic History*, **58**(3), 866–70.

Baten, J. and J.L. van Zanden (2008), 'Book Production and the Onset of Modern Economic Growth', *Journal of Economic Growth*, **13**(3), 217–35.

Beltrami, D. (1951), 'Lineamenti di storia della popolazione di Venezia nei secoli XVI, XVII e XVIII', *Atti dell'Istituto Veneto di Scienze, Lettere ed Arti*, vol. 109.

Ben-Porath, Y. (1967), 'The Production of Human Capital and the Life-cycle of Earnings', *Journal of Political Economy*, **75**(4), 352–65.

Bloom, D.E. and J.G. Williamson (1998), 'Demographic Transitions and Economic Miracles in Emerging Asia', *World Bank Economic Review*, **12**(3), 419–55.

Boucekkine, R., D. de la Croix and O. Licandro (2002), 'Vintage Human Capital, Demographic Trends and Endogenous Growth', *Journal of Economic Theory*, **104**, 340–75.

Boucekkine, R., D. de la Croix and O. Licandro (2003), 'Early Mortality Declines at the Dawn of Modern Growth', *Scandinavian Journal of Economics*, **105**(3), 401–18.

Boucekkine, R., D. de la Croix and D. Peeters (2007), 'Early Literacy Achievements, Population Density, and the Transition to Modern Growth', *Journal of the European Economic Association*, **5**(1), 183–226.

Cervellati, M. and U. Sunde (2005), 'Human Capital Formation, Life Expectancy and the Process of Development', *American Economic Review*, **95**(5), 1653–72.

Clark, G. (2005), 'The Condition of the Working Class in England, 1209–2004', *Journal of Political Economy*, **113**(6), 1307–40.

Cordoba, J.C. and M. Ripoll (2008), 'Life Expectancy and the Wealth of Nations', paper presented at SED 2008, Boston.

de la Croix, D. and O. Licandro (1999), 'Life Expectancy and Endogenous Growth', *Economics Letters*, **65**(2), 255–63.

de la Croix, D. and O. Licandro (2007), 'The Child is Father of the Man: Implications for the Demographic Transition', *CEPR Discussion Paper 6493*.

de la Croix, D. and A. Sommacal (2009), 'A Theory of Medical Effectiveness, Differential Mortality, Income Inequality and Growth for Pre-industrial England', *Mathematical Population Studies*, **16**, 1–34.

de la Croix, D., T. Lindh and B. Malmberg (2008), 'Swedish Economic Growth and Education Since 1800', *Canadian Journal of Economics*, **41**, 166–85.

de la Croix, D., T. Lindh and B. Malmberg (2009), 'Demographic Change and Economic Growth in Sweden: 1750–2050', *Journal of Macroeconomics*, **31**, 132–48.

Edvinsson, R. (2005), 'Growth, Accumulation, Crisis', Volume 41 of *Stockholm Studies in Economic History*, Stockholm: Almqvist & Wiksell International. PhD thesis.

Floud, R. (1984), 'The Heights of Europeans Since 1750: a New Source For European Economic History', *NBER Working Paper 1318*.

Fogel, R. (2004), *The Escape from Hunger and Premature Death, 1700–2100*, Cambridge: Cambridge University Press.

Fridlizius, G. (1985), 'The Mortality Decline in the First Phase of the Demographic Transition: Swedish Experiences', in T. Bengtsson, G. Fridlizius and R. Ohlsson (eds), *Pre-industrial Population Change*, Stockholm: Almquist and Wiksell International, pp. 71–114.

Galor, O. (2005), 'From Stagnation to Growth: Unified Growth Theory', in P. Aghion and S. Durlauf (eds), *Handbook of Economic Growth*, Vol. 1, Ch. 4, pp. 171–293, Amsterdam: Elsevier.

Galor, O. and D. Weil (1999), 'From Malthusian Stagnation to Modern Growth', *American Economic Review*, **89**(2), 150–54.

Harris, B. (2001), '"The Child is Father of Man", the Relationship Between Child Health and Adult Mortality in the 19th and 20th Centuries', *International Journal of Epidemiology*, **35**(3), 658–63.

Hazan, M. and H. Zoabi (2006), 'Does Longevity Cause Growth? A Theoretical Critique', *Journal of Economic Growth*, **11**(4), 363–376.

Hofsten, E. and H. Lundström (1976), *Swedish Population History: Main Trends from 1750 to 1970*, Stockholm: LiberFörlag.

Hollingsworth, T. (1977), 'Mortality in the British Peerage Families since 1600', *Population*, **32**, 323–52.

Johansson, R. (1999), 'Death and the Doctors: Medicine and Elite Mortality in Britain from 1500 to 1800', *Cambridge Group for the History of Population and Social Structure Working Paper Series*. No. 7.

Kermack, W., A. McKendrick and P. McKinlay (1934), 'Death Rates in Great Britain and Sweden: Some General Regularities and their Significance', *Lancet*, **1**, 698–703.

Lagerloef, N.-P. (2003), 'From Malthus to Modern Growth: Can Epidemics Explain the Three Regimes?', *International Economic Review*, **44**(2), 755–77.

Lindahl, E., E. Dahlgren and K. Kock (1937), 'National Income of Sweden 1861–1930', Part One and Two, Volume III of *Wages, Cost of Living and National Income of Sweden, 1860–1930*, London: P.S. King & Son, Ltd.

Nicolini, E. (2004), 'Mortality, Interest Rates, Investment, and Agricultural Production in 18th century England', *Explorations in Economic History*, **41**(2), 130–55.

Perrenoud, A. (1975), 'L'inégalité sociale devant la mort à Genève au XVII$^{e}$ siècle', *Population*, **30**, 221–43.

Perrenoud, A. (1978), 'La mortalité à Genève de 1625 à 1825', *Annales de Démographie Historique*, **15**, 209–33.

Perrenoud, A. (1985), 'Mortalty Decline in its Secular Setting', in T. Bengtsson, G. Fridlizius and R. Ohlsson (eds), *Pre-industrial Population Change*, Stockholm: Almquist and Wiksell International, pp. 41–69.

Porter, R. (1995), *Disease, Medicine, and Society in England, 1550–1860. New Studies in Economic and Social History*, Cambridge: Cambridge University Press.

Sandberg, L. and R. Steckel (1997), 'Was Industrialization Hazardous to your Health? Not in Sweden', in R. Steckel and R. Floud (eds), *Health and Welfare during Industrialization*, Chicago: University of Chicago Press.

Silventoinen, K. (2003), 'Determinants of Variation in Adult Body Height', *Journal of Biosocial Science*, **35**, 263–85.

Siraisi, N. (1990), *Medieval and Early Renaissance Medicine: an Introduction to Knowledge and Practice*, Chicago: University of Chicago Press.

Soares, R.R. (2005), 'Mortality Reductions, Educational Attainment, and Fertility Choice', *American Economic Review*, **95**(3), 580–601.

Waaler, H. (1984), 'Height, Weight and Mortality: the Norwegian Experience', *Acta Medica Scandinavica*, Supplementum 679, 1–56.

Weatherall, M. (1996). 'Drug Treatment and the Rise of Pharmacology', in *Cambridge Illustrated History: Medicine*, Cambridge: Cambridge University Press.

Weil, D. (2007), 'Accounting for the Effect of Health on Economic Growth', *Quarterly Journal of Economics*, **122**(3), 1265–306.

Weisdorf, J.L. (2004), 'From Stagnation to Growth: Revisiting Three Historical Regimes', *Journal of Population Economics*, **17**(3), 455–72.

Wordsworth, W. (1809), 'My Heart Leaps Up', *Poems in Two Volumes*, London: Longman, Hurst, Rees and Orme.

Wrigley, E. and R. Schofield (1989), *The Population History of England, 1541–1871: a Reconstruction*, Cambridge, MA: Cambridge University Press.

Wrigley, E., R. Davies, J. Oeppen and R. Schofield (1997), *English Population History from Family Reconstitution: 1580–1837*, Cambridge: Cambridge University Press.

# 9. Endogenous age structure in descriptive macroeconomic growth models: a general framework and some steady state analysis*

**Luciano Fanti, Mimmo Iannelli and Piero Manfredi**

## 9.1. INTRODUCTION

Since Solow's (1956) contribution, continuous time descriptive macroeconomic growth models have proved to be not only cornerstone contributions to economic growth theory but also, once amended to include realistic refinements such as human capital, very useful tools for the empirical analysis of growth (Barro and Sala-i-Martin, 1995; Mankiw et al., 1992 and subsequent contributions). Another fundamental descriptive model is Goodwin's (1967) growth-cycle, which represents the paradigm of non-linear dynamics in economics.

In descriptive macroeconomic growth models population plays an important role – through the growth of the labour supply it triggers the growth of absolute output – yet it is taken as fully exogenous to the economic system. Despite the large number of papers aiming to endogenise population in macroeconomic growth models, the main feature of the demographic system, that is, age structure, has, with few exceptions, been neglected or dealt with in an oversimplified manner, as for instance in Overlapping Generation Models. This is a somewhat odd fact given that, at least from Malthus ([1798]1992) onwards, the role of age structure as the 'conveyor belt' linking economic shocks, their demographic response, for instance in terms of fertility, and their ultimate feedback on the economic system, was well present to classical economists. For instance, McCulloch (1854, p. 34) stated 'the supply of labourers in the market can neither be speedily increased when wages rise, nor speedily diminished when they fall. When wages rise a period of eighteen or twenty years must elapse before the stimulus, given the principle of population, can be felt in the market'. McCulloch's description provides the first definition of the causal factor underlying the fundamental demo-economic concept of Malthusian cycles, which are the consequence: 'of the lags between the response of fertility to current labour market conditions and the time when the resulting births actually enter the labour force' (Lee 1997, p. 1097). Malthusian cycles are a major example of demo-economic oscillations and a well documented fact in population economics. See for instance the oscillations of birth, death and wage rates in UK history (Lee and Anderson, 2002, p. 201), the Swedish cycles 1700–1914, and the post-transitional fertility fluctuations, such as the baby-booms observed in the Western world in the 1960s, sometimes explained by Easterlin's effect (Easterlin, 1961).

There are some exceptions to the paucity of theoretical studies of the dynamic interplay between the population age structure and macro-dynamics. Several papers have been devoted to the search for Easterlinian mechanisms leading to sustained Malthusian oscillations (Lee, 1974; Samuelson, 1976; Frauenthal and Swick, 1983; Feichtinger and Sorger, 1989, 1990; Feichtinger and Dockner, 1990; Chu and Lu, 1995). Most such works, however, are simplistic in that they include the economic system only implicitly through some non-linear demographic relationship. Manfredi and Fanti (2006a, 2006b) made a more genuine attempt to integrate the age structure of the population and the macroeconomic structure, within Goodwin's model. In order to end up with a tractable model (that is, described by ordinary differential equations, ODEs) they used a simplified representation of age structure by considering three additional differential equations modelling the main phases of the individual life cycle, namely youth, adulthood, and retirement. The ensuing model shows a clear-cut dynamic effect of age structure on growth, particularly as regards the generation of stable or chaotic Malthusian oscillations around the path of balanced growth of the economy.

In a different vein Arthur and McNicoll (1977) considered the issue of the optimal control of the economy in a fully age-structured population from a central planner's perspective. The same authors (1978) also initiated the study of the implications of the dynamics of age structure on the performance of the economy. Their approach has become the standard route to investigate the implication of demographic change, such as the onset of below replacement fertility and ageing in industrialised countries, on economic profiles (Lee, 1994; Lindh and Malmberg, 1999; Miles, 1999; Prskawetz and Fent, 2007). More recently the role of age structure has also been considered within micro-founded growth models, for instance in the 'vintage human capital approach' (Boucekkine et al., 2002), which shows that (exogenous) mortality decline in history could have been a factor of sustained endogenous growth.

This chapter explores the implications of age structure for macroeconomic growth. As a first step we build a general framework embedding the age structure of the population in descriptive growth models in a fully realistic manner. We do this by (1) considering a generic model of descriptive macroeconomic growth and the fundamental equation for the dynamics of a closed, age structured, population, that is, the Von Foerster partial differential equation (PDE), and (2) integrating them by appropriately modelling the main link function between the economic and demographic systems, that is, the rate of change of the labour supply. Compared to other works in the literature our approach is fully general. Second, we seek a mathematically convenient reformulation of our model and start to investigate its main dynamic implications, looking at the existence of stationary states, that is, joint population–economy balanced growth paths, in selected examples. In particular, we consider a basic case of no feedback from the economic system on demographic behaviour, useful to state the demographic assumptions underlying classical exogenous growth models, and a Solow-type model with endogenous fertility modelled as a declining function of per-capita income, as observed during the demographic transition. The model shows the possibility of many equilibria, some of which appear as a consequence of correctly taking age structure into account, that is, the fact that equilibrium per-capita income is the outcome of both capital dilution and intergenerational transfer effects (Arthur and MacNicoll, 1978). This gives an insight on issues such as the optimum population growth rate, and the overall structure of balanced growth equilibria. Some remarks on the potential of our model for studying the role of age structure for growth are also added.

The chapter is organised as follows. Section 9.2 introduces our general framework. In Section 9.3 we seek a mathematically convenient formulation. In Section 9.4 we consider some selected case studies. Some conclusions are drawn in Section 9.5.

## 9.2. A GENERAL FRAMEWORK FOR DESCRIPTIVE MACROECONOMIC GROWTH WITH AGE STRUCTURE

### 9.2.1. Descriptive Models of Macroeconomic Growth

The most influential descriptive growth schemes are the neoclassical model of Solow (1956) and the growth cycle (Goodwin, 1967). Descriptive models are described by systems of non-linear ODEs of the form

$$\dot{X} = H(X;Z) \qquad (9.1)$$

where $X = (x_1, x_2, ..., x_n)$ is the vector of key economic variables (capital per worker, employment, wage share, etc.), $H$ a suitable map, and $Z$ a constant vector reflecting the steady input provided by the constant exogenous growth of labour supply and technology. In this paper we assume for simplicity that $Z$ just includes population growth.

Descriptive models show exogenous growth, that is, growth is promoted by variables such as the total labour supply and the level of technology, which are exogenously defined (exponentially growing over time). In other words, such models explain the mechanics of economic growth provided there is a steady, unexplained, input of population and technology.

**Example 1** (Solow's 1956 model without technical progress). In this case $X$ is one-dimensional and is given by the amount of capital per worker $K/L = k$ and $H$ is the map:

$$H(k;Z) = sf(k) - (Z + d)k \qquad (9.2)$$

where $f$ is a constant returns to scale neoclassical production function (in intensive form), $s$ the saving ratio, $Z = n$ the growth rate of the labour supply, and $d$ the rate of capital depreciation.

**Example 2** (Goodwin's 1967 growth cycle model). $X$ is the 2-dimensional vector $(E, V)$, where $E$ is the employment rate at time $t$, defined as the ratio between the labour actually employed $L$ and the supply of labour $N_s$, while $V = w/A$ is the labour share, where $w$ is the real wage and $A$ average labour productivity. The model is

$$\dot{E} = E\left[m(1-V) - \alpha - n_S\right]$$

$$\dot{V} = V\left[-(\alpha+\gamma) + \rho E\right]$$

where $0 < \gamma < \rho$ are the parameters of the 'real wage' Phillips' curve: $w'/w = -(\alpha+\gamma) + \rho E$ governing the relationship between the growth rate of the wage and the employment rate, $m > 0$ is the output–capital ratio, and $\alpha > 0$, $n_s > 0$ respectively denote the rate of change of labour productivity and the labour supply. In this case $Z = (Z_1, Z_2) = (\alpha, n_S)$.

Solow's and Goodwin's model can be integrated to obtain flexible families of growth models: for instance replacing Goodwin's assumption of a Leontief technology with a neoclassical CES production function (Van der Ploeg, 1988) one obtains a family of descriptive neoclassical models with unemployment (Fanti and Manfredi, 2003).

### 9.2.2. Endogenisation of Age Structure

We start from the fact that under our assumptions the rate of change $Z$ of the labour supply $Q$:

$$Z = \frac{\dot{Q}(t)}{Q(t)} \tag{9.3}$$

is the only direct 'link function' between the economic sub-system and the demographic one. The labour supply is defined as:

$$Q(t) = \int_{A(X)}^{B(X)} \gamma(a, X) n(a, t) da \tag{9.4}$$

where $a$ denotes an individual's age, $n(a,t)$ is the age density of the population at time $t$, $\gamma(a, X)$ the participation rate (that is, the fraction supplying labour at each age), and the interval $(A(X), B(X))$ defines the work age span. The latter is, at least in principle, endogenously determined, as a consequence of workers' choice. The population is assumed to be closed to migration such that its *age density obeys Von Foerster's PDE* (Keyfitz, 1985):

$$\frac{\partial n(a,t)}{\partial a} + \frac{\partial n(a,t)}{\partial t} = -\mu(a,X,N) n(a,t) \tag{9.5}$$

where $\mu(a,X,N)$ is the age-specific mortality rate, which is taken as a function of the economic variables, and of some summary measure of the population state, for instance the total population $N(t) = \int_0^\infty n(a,t) da$. The PDE (9.5) describes the dynamics of the age density $n(a,t)$ following the ageing process of individuals along their birth cohort over time. Intuitively during each time interval $(t, t+h)$ the individual of age $a$ at the beginning of the interval will have age $a+h$ at the end of the interval. In other words, the life course of a given individual is represented in the time–age plane by the 45-degree segments originating on the $a$-axis at the time of birth of the individual (and obviously ending at his/her death). This means that the natural way to consider the evolution of the age density $n(a,t)$ during $(t, t+h)$ is by looking at the variation $\Delta n = n(a+h, t+h) - n(a,t)$. In the absence of migration this variation will only be due to mortality. If the function $n(a,t)$ is regular, $\Delta n$ can be expanded, for a small enough $h$, as $(\partial n / \partial a)h + (\partial n / \partial t)h$. During the same interval some individuals will be removed by mortality, at a rate given by $\mu(a,X,N)n(a,t)h$. Letting $h$ go to zero finally explains equation (9.5). The PDE (9.5) needs to be completed by a boundary condition, which specifies the rate at which new individuals enter the system at age zero, through births. This is given by the *birth equation*

$$n(0,t)=B(t)=\int_0^{\infty}\beta(a,X,N)n(a,t)da \qquad (9.6)$$

where $B(t)$ is the birth function at time $t$, and $\beta(a,X,N)$ the age-specific fertility rate. Equations (9.1), (9.3), (9.4), (9.5) and (9.6) define the general form of a descriptive macroeconomic growth model with a fully endogenous age structure, summarised below:

$$\dot{X}=H\left[X(t),Z(t)\right] \qquad (9.7a)$$

$$Z(t)=\frac{\dot{Q}(t)}{Q(t)} \qquad (9.7b)$$

$$Q(t)=\int_{A(X)}^{B(X)}\gamma(a,X)n(a,t)da \qquad (9.7c)$$

$$\left(\frac{\partial}{\partial a}+\frac{\partial}{\partial t}\right)n(a,t)=-\mu(a,X,N)n(a,t) \qquad (9.7d)$$

$$n(0,t)=B(t)=\int_0^{\infty}\beta(a,X,N)n(a,t)da \qquad (9.7e)$$

Some remarks are useful to clarify the point. Equations (9.7) show the main ingredients of the problem: (a) the dynamics of the economy, given by equation (9.7a), which depend on the 'link' function $Z(t)$; (b) a definition for the link function, as the rate of change of the labour supply (eq. (9.7b)); (c) a definition for the labour supply (eq. 9.7c); (d) the dynamics of the population (eqs (9.7d)–(9.7e)). In (9.7) the demographic rates $\beta(.),\mu(.)$ and the participation rate $\gamma(.)$ are endogenously determined through possibly non-linear dependencies on their economic inputs. From the viewpoint of non-linear population mathematics, (9.7) is an extension of the classical non-linear age-dependent model first considered by Gurtin and MacCamy (1974). The main difference is that (9.7) includes the external control factors, only implicitly included by Gurtin and MacCamy, in an explicit manner according to an underlying theory of demo-economic interaction. However, Gurtin and MacCamy (1974) were mainly interested in the conditions under which density-dependent conditions were responsible for the onset of a (locally) stable equilibrium age distribution. Here we are mainly interested in the conditions yielding joint persistent solutions of the demographic and economic sub-system (called *stable solutions* in demographic jargon, and 'balanced growth' solutions in the economic jargon), and of course on whether other types of solutions, such as steady demo-economic oscillations, are possible. The dependency of vital rates on the total population $N$

summarises the possible presence of economic feedbacks not captured by $X$, or of density-dependent effects (see Gurtin and MacCamy, 1974 for the age-structured extension of the logistic equation of classical population mathematics). We further note that the adopted demographic equation is a one-sex equation, as in standard population mathematics. This means that (9.7d) and (9.7e) may be inadequate when differential patterns by gender are assumed.

Initial value problems for (9.7) require initial conditions for the economic variables $X$, and the specification of an initial (that is, at time $t = 0$) age distribution for the population, of the form $n(a,0) = \psi(a)$, specifying the density of individuals in age group $a$ at the initial time.

## 9.3. A CONVENIENT FORMULATION FOR THE DEMOGRAPHIC COMPONENT

We first look for a convenient formulation of the demographic part of (9.7). The purpose is to simplify the problem by removing components which are unnecessary to understanding the dynamics. We do this in several steps. First we assume that the mortality rate can be written as:

$$\mu(a,X,N) = \mu_1(a) + \mu_2(a,X,N)$$

that is, as the sum of a 'normal' or baseline component, which is only age-dependent, and of a component also reflecting the action of the economic system. This implies that the overall survival function $\pi(a,t)$, representing the probability of surviving up to any age $a$ at time $t$, can be factored as

$$\pi(a,t) = \exp\left[-\int_0^a \mu_1(s)ds\right] \exp\left(-\int_0^a \mu_2\{s, X[t-(a-s)], N[t-(a-s)]\}ds\right) =$$

$$= \pi_1(a)\pi_2(a,t)$$

where $\pi_1(a)$ defines survival to 'normal mortality'. Let us now introduce the following change of variable:

$$u(a,t) = \frac{n(a,t)}{\pi_1(a)} \tag{9.8a}$$

$$q(a,t) = \frac{u(a,t)}{Q(t)} \tag{9.8b}$$

Both $u(a,t)$ and $q(a,t)$ are useful auxiliary quantities to deal with our general framework. The first is defined by the ratio between the absolute (non-normalised) population density and the survival probability to baseline mortality $\pi_1(a)$. Therefore when $\pi_1(a)=\pi(a)$,, that is, when the overall mortality is only age-dependent, since $n(a,t)=B(t-a)\pi(a)$ holds, then $u(a,t)=B(t-a)$, that is, it coincides with past births occurring $a$ years ago. In general, $u(a,t)$ represents a population density for which the pure age-dependent component of the risk of mortality has been removed, and only exposure to the economic-dependent component $\mu_2(a,X,N)$ remains, as is clear from the first of subsequent equation (9.9).

On the other hand, $q(a,t)$ is obtained by dividing $u(a,t)$ by the total labour supply $Q(t)$. Therefore if we only focus on the work age span (still on the assumption that $\pi_1(a)=\pi(a)$), $q(a,t)$ may be considered the component of the *current total labour force* $Q(t)$ coming from births occurring $a$ years ago, a quantity of strong interest from the demo-economic point of view. Note that $q(a,t)$ is an improper density function.

A partial differentiation shows that $u(a,t)$ and $q(a,t)$ satisfy the following Von Foerster PDEs

$$u_a+u_t=-\mu_2(a,X,N)u(a,t) \tag{9.9a}$$

$$q_a+q_t=-\left[\mu(a,X,N)+Z(t)\right]q(a,t) \tag{9.9b}$$

with boundary conditions:

$$u(0,t)=\int_0^\infty m_1(a,X,N)u(a,t)da$$

$$q(0,t)=\int_0^\infty m_1(a,X,N)q(a,t)da$$

where:

$$m_1(a,X,N)=\beta(a,X,N)\pi_1(a)$$

In addition, using (9.8a) the overall labour supply can be rewritten as:

$$Q(t)=\int_{A(X)}^{B(X)} \delta_1(a,X)u(a,t)da$$

where:

$$\delta_1(a,X)=\gamma(a,X)\pi_1(a) \tag{9.10}$$

Moreover, by (9.8b) one gets the constraint:

$$\int_0^\infty \delta_1(a,X)q(a,t)da=1 \tag{9.11}$$

Finally, let us seek an expression for the growth rate of the labour supply Z. For simplicity we take $A(X)=0, B(X)=\infty$. Indeed, though the ages of entry/exit into/from the labour market are choice variables from the individual's point of view, perhaps bounded by some minimal and maximal 'institutional' age, by suitably endogenising the participation rate at each age $\gamma(a,X)$, essentially any pattern of work participation by age can be described.

By a time differentiation of (9.15), and treating for simplicity *X* as a scalar variable, one finds:

$$\dot{Q}(t)=\dot{X}\int_0^\infty u(a,t)\frac{\partial\delta_1(a,X)}{\partial X}da-\int_0^\infty \delta_1(a,X)u_a(a,t)da-\int_0^\infty \mu_2(a,X,N)\delta_1(a,X)u(a,t)da \tag{9.12}$$

The last expression implies that $Z=\dot{Q}/Q$ can be written as:

$$Z=Z_1+Z_2+Z_3$$

where:

$$Z_1=\dot{X}\int_0^\infty\frac{\partial\delta_1(a,X)}{\partial Y}q(a,t)da$$

$$Z_2=-Q^{-1}\int_0^\infty \delta_1(a,X)u_a(a,t)da$$

$$Z_3=-\int_0^\infty \mu_2(a,X,N)\delta_1(a,X)q(a,t)da$$

Examples can be of help in interpreting the quantities $Z_i$. The term $Z_3$ is the (average) component of the mortality rate which is affected by economic inputs. This becomes clear by taking $\upsilon_2$ independent of age: $\mu_2(a,X,N)=\mu_2(X,N)$. In this case, thanks to (9.11), the following simply holds:

$$Z_3=\int_0^\infty \mu_2(a,X,N)\delta_1(a,X)q(a,t)da=\mu_2(X,N)\int_0^\infty \delta_1(a,X)q(a,t)da=\mu_2(X,N)$$

The term $Z_2$ depends on the assumptions actually made on the rate of participation to the labour force $\gamma$. For instance, if $\gamma$ is compactly supported over (*A*,*B*) and discontinuous at *A*,*B* (for example, when there are minimal/maximal 'institutional' ages of entry and exit into/out of the labour force), we get by a parts integration over age

$$Z_2 = \int_A^B \left[ \frac{\partial}{\partial a} \delta_1(a,X) \right] q(a,t)da + \delta_1(A,X)q(A,t) - \delta_1(B,X)u(B,t) \quad (9.13)$$

The latter expression is the balance of the entries in the labour force at the minimal legal age (*A*), the exits at the maximal age (*B*), and the relative changes occurring in the participation rate over age. The latter term reflects the compositional effect that arises as the participation rate is not constant over time. If the participation rate is only age-dependent (9.13) reduces to:

$$Z_2(t) = \int_0^\infty \left[ \frac{\delta'(a)}{\delta(a)} \right] \delta(a)q(a,t)da + \delta(A)q(A,t) - \delta(B)q(B,t)$$

where the first term is easily seen to be the average of the rate of change of the participation rate over age. Finally the $Z_1$ term is the component of the overall growth rate of the labour supply due to time changes in its economic determinants *X*.

To sum up we have written the dynamics of the demographic component in the following manner

$$q_a + q_t = -[\mu_2(a,X,N) + Z(t)]q(a,t) \quad (9.14a)$$

$$q(0,t) = \int_0^\infty m_1(a,X,N)q(a,t)da \quad (9.14b)$$

$$Z = \frac{\dot{Q}}{Q} = \dot{X} \int_0^\infty \frac{\partial \delta_1(a,X)}{\partial X} q(a,t)da - Q^{-1} \int_0^\infty \delta_1(a,X)u_a(a,t)da +$$

$$- \int_0^\infty \mu_2(a,X,N)\delta_1(a,X)q(a,t)da \quad (9.14c)$$

plus the constraint (9.11).

The reformulation (9.14) has some advantages. First it uses the 'profile' variable *q* instead of the absolute age density *n(a,t)*. This has some implications for the search of *stable* (or persistent, or 'balanced') *solutions* for the population. In terms of the absolute profile these are separable solutions of the form $n(a,t) = G(a)e^{rt}$ implying the exponential growth (or decay) of absolute variables (for example, overall population, labour supply, total births, population in each age group) but unchanging age profiles. In fact, if we look for instance at the profile of the overall population, that is, the normalised population density $c(a,t) = n(a,t)/N(t)$,[1] the previous position implies $c(a,t) = G(a)/\int_0^\infty G(a)da$. This means that the profile is unchanging over time, that is, the exponential growth is 'balanced'. Clearly, under (9.14a) such type of solutions correspond to steady states of the profile $q$. Second, a comparison of (9.14a) with the PDE for the normalised population density $c(a,t) = n(a,t)/N(t)$, given by:

$$c_a + c_t = -\left[\mu_2(a,X,N) + \frac{\dot{N}}{N}\right]c(a,t)$$

indicates that the growth rate of the overall population in the balanced growth state, $r = \dot{N}/N$, must always equal the growth rate $Z$ of the labour supply. Last, 'stable' balanced growth solutions are the only form of stationary solutions of (9.14).

## 9.4. SOME EXAMPLES

### 9.4.1. The Case of no Economic Feedback on the Demographic System: Asymptotic Balanced Growth of the Economy Forced by Balanced Population Growth

Under constant coefficients

$$\mu(a,X,N) = \mu(a), \beta(a,X,N) = \beta(a), \gamma(a,X) = \gamma(a)$$

no feedback from the economic system is assumed, that is, vital (mortality and fertility) and participation rates are unaffected by the economic conditions. This case is not economically trivial, as it shows the proper demographic background underlying the standard formulations of descriptive models of economic growth. Moreover, on the applied side, it represents the theoretical framework underlying the common investigations of the impact of changes in the age composition of the population on economic performance under the so-called 'constant vital rates scenario' which are usually supplied by all agencies providing demographic projection (Miles, 1999; Prskawetz and Fent, 2007).

In this case the demographic component is independent of the economic one. Thus we may first characterise the evolution of the demographic component, and then take its output $Z^*(t)$ to characterise the economic sub-system as follows:

$$\dot{X} = F\left[X(t), Z^*(t)\right]$$

The corresponding long-term dynamics obeys:

$$\dot{X} = F\left[X(t), Z^*_\infty\right]$$

In particular, denoting for brevity $\delta_1(a)=\delta(a)$, the rate of change of the labour supply simplifies to:

$$Z(t)=\int_0^\infty\left[\frac{\delta'(a)}{\delta(a)}\right]\delta(a)q(a,t)da+\delta(A)q(A,t)-\delta(B)q(B,t)$$

The final form for the demographic system is:

$$q_a+q_t+Zq(a,t)=0 \tag{9.15a}$$

$$q(0,t)=\int_0^\infty m_1(a)q(a,t)da \tag{9.15b}$$

$$Z(t)=\int_0^\infty\left[\frac{\delta'(a)}{\delta(a)}\right]\delta(a)q(a,t)da+\delta(A)q(A,t)-\delta(B)q(B,t) \tag{9.15c}$$

plus the constraint (9.12). We now look for stable solutions for the demographic component. As already pointed out, such solutions have the form:

$$n(a,t)=G(a)e^{rt}$$

This implies the following relationships:

$$u(a,t)=\frac{G(a)e^{rt}}{\pi(a)}$$

$$Q(t)=\int_0^\infty\delta_1(a)\frac{G(a)e^{rt}}{\pi(a)}da=Q^*e^{rt}$$

$$Q'(t)=rQ^*e^{rt}$$

$$q(a,t)=\Psi(a)$$

$$q_a+q_t=\Psi'(a)$$

$$Z(t)=Z^*$$

where $\Psi(a)$ is a function of age such that

$$Z^*=\int_0^\infty\left[\frac{\delta'(a)}{\delta(a)}\right]\delta(a)\Psi(a)da+\delta(A)\Psi(A)-\delta(B)\Psi(B)$$

Note in particular that from the definition of $Z$ it follows that its stable form is given by

$$Z^* = \frac{\dot{Q}(t)}{Q(t)} = r$$

which confirms that if the population is stably evolving at rate $r$ then the overall labour supply must evolve at the same rate. In particular, (9.15a) and (9.15b) can be written, using the equality $Z^* = r$, as

$$\Psi'(a) + r\Psi(a) = 0$$

$$\Psi(0) = \int_0^\infty m_1(a)\Psi(a)da$$

This gives:

$$\Psi(a) = \Psi(0)e^{-ra}$$

and therefore

$$\Psi(0) = \int_0^\infty m_1(a)\Psi(0)e^{-ra}da$$

which yields

$$1 = \int_0^\infty m_1(a)e^{-ra}da$$

Recalling that $m_1(a) = \beta(a)\pi_1(a)$ we obtain

$$1 = \int_0^\infty \beta(a)\pi(a)e^{-ra}da$$

The previous expression is a standard Lotka intrinsic equation defining the asymptotic, or 'intrinsic', growth rate of the population in its stable state. Therefore the population eventually achieves a state of stable balanced growth where absolute variables (population size by age group and total, births, overall labour supply, and so on) grow asymptotically at rate $r = Z^*$, keeping an unchanging age profile.

The previous discussion has provided the proof of the following result:

**Proposition 1** (case of constant coefficients). If $\mu_2(a,Y) = \mu_2(a)$, $m(a,Y) = m(a)$, $\gamma(a,Y) = \gamma(a)$, then the demographic sub-system decouples. In this case:

All equilibrium solutions of the demographic system are stable solutions, that is, the demographic system eventually approaches a stable growth path with a speed of growth given by Lotka's intrinsic growth rate *r*. In particular $Z_{\infty}^{*} = r$.

The solution of the economic subsystem, described by the non-autonomous equation: $\dot{X} = H[X, Z(t)]$ converges asymptotically to the solution of the asymptotically autonomous system:

$$\dot{X} = H(X, r)$$

Thus, for instance in the case of Solow's model, the classical Solow's dynamics would arise only asymptotically as a consequence of the stabilisation of the dynamics of the population about its stable state, and it is driven by the following asymptotically autonomous map

$$H_r(k) = sf(k) - (d + r)k$$

On the other hand, the transient phase would be disturbed by the adjustment oscillations of the age distribution, the classical 'stable echoes'.

### 9.4.2. A Solow-type Model with Endogenous Fertility: Joint Balanced Growth Solutions of the Economy and Population

We now consider an economy governed by the standard Solow equation (9.2) under a constant returns to scale (CRS) Cobb–Douglas production function. As regards the demographic component, we assume that fertility is endogenously related to per capita income $y = Y/N$, where *Y* is absolute output, as largely justified on empirical grounds. Though we will simply take the relation between fertility and income as given, since our interest is in its dynamic implications and not in its microfoundations, it can nonetheless be microfounded both in a traditional, namely Malthusian, perspective, yielding an increasing relation between the fertility rate and income, and in a modern, say Beckerian perspective (Becker and Barro, 1988; Becker et al., 1990), where it yields a decreasing relation between fertility and income. Jones (2001) microfounded a humped relation between the fertility rate and per-capita income which explains the increase in fertility sometimes seen at the onset of the demographic transition (Dyson and Murphy 1985).

Here we consider the special but important case: $\beta(a, y) = \beta_1(a)\beta_2(y)$, that is, changes in per capita income only affect the scale of fertility, represented by the gross reproduction rate $GRR(y) = \beta_2(y)\int_0^{\infty}\beta_1(a)da$ (GRR), but not the age density at childbearing. This is a simplification as we know from empirical studies, in that timing of fertility is related to economic conditions as well. In addition we take only age-dependent mortality and participation. The final form of the system is

$$\dot{k} = sk^{\alpha} - (Z(t) + \delta)k \tag{9.16a}$$

$$q_a(a,t)+q_t(a,t)=-Z(t)q(a,t) \quad (9.16b)$$

$$q(0,t)=\beta_2(y)\int_0^\infty \beta_1(a)\pi(a)q(a,t)da \quad (9.16c)$$

$$Z(t)=\frac{\dot{Q}}{Q}=\delta_1(A)q(A,t)-\delta_1(B)q(B,t)+\int_0^\infty \delta_1'(a)q(a,t)da \quad (9.16d)$$

where

$$y=\frac{Y}{N}=\frac{Y}{L}\frac{L}{N}=y_w\frac{\int_A^B \gamma(a)n(a,t)da}{\int_0^\infty n(a,t)da}=y_wE=k^\alpha E \quad (9.16e)$$

where $L$ is labour demand, taken as identically equal to labour supply, $y_w$ the output per worker, and $E$ the ratio between the population actually employed and the total population.

Model (9.16) encompasses many theoretical and simulations models used in the descriptive demo-economic literature. For instance, Solow-type models with endogenous fertility but without age have been used to represent the demographic transition (Strulik, 1997, 1999, 2000; Prskawetz et al., 2000; Fanti and Manfredi, 2003). The above model includes age in such frameworks. On the other hand, model (9.16)–(9.17) represents the full dynamic system underlying the macro-simulative approaches used in the literature on the impact of age structure on macroeconomic performance (Arthur and MacNicoll, 1978; Blanchet, 1988; Miles, 1999; Prskawetz and Fent, 2007).

Let us look at *joint balanced growth solutions of the economy and the population*. By this description we mean solutions characterised by (a) stable exponential growth of all absolute variables (that is, both demographic, as in the previous example, and economic), and (b) unchanging age profiles of the demographic variable, as a consequence of the position $n(a,t)=G(a)e^{rt}$, and steady state growth of the per-worker economic variable. In particular, since we are considering a Solow model without technical progress, a balanced growth solution of the economy is simply a steady state of the fundamental equation corresponding to a stationary value of $Z$ allowed by an underlying exponential growth of the overall labour supply. From equation (9.16a)

$$sk^\alpha-(Z+d)k=0$$

as $y_w=k^\alpha$, we find

$$y_w = \left(\frac{s}{d+Z}\right)^{\frac{\alpha}{1-\alpha}} \tag{9.17}$$

In addition Z must be defined as the intrinsic growth rate of a stably growing population, that is, $Z = r$ must hold. Setting as before $n(a,t) = G(a)e^{rt}$ we get:

$$y = \left(\frac{s}{r+d}\right)^{\frac{\alpha}{1-\alpha}} E^* \tag{9.18a}$$

$$E^* = \frac{\int_A^B \gamma(a)e^{-ra}\pi(a)da}{\int_0^\infty e^{-ra}\pi(a)da} \tag{9.18b}$$

$$\Psi'(a) = -r\Psi(a) \tag{9.18c}$$

$$\Psi(0) = \beta_2(y)\int_0^\infty \beta_1(a)\pi(a)\Psi(a)da \tag{9.18d}$$

Joint balanced growth solutions, if any, arise from system (9.18), where there is the additional complication that the equilibrium value $E^*$ of $E$ is itself a function of the population growth rate in the balanced growth state. From the two latter equations one finds:

$$1 = \beta_2(y)\int_0^\infty \beta_1(a)\pi(a)e^{-ra}da \tag{9.19}$$

which, using (9.18a) and (9.18b), yields the following 'expanded' intrinsic equation:

$$1 = \beta_2(y(r))\int_0^\infty \beta_1(a)\pi(a)e^{-ra}da \tag{9.20a}$$

$$y(r) = \left(\frac{s}{r+d}\right)^{\frac{\alpha}{1-\alpha}} E^*(r) = \left(\frac{s}{r+d}\right)^{\frac{\alpha}{1-\alpha}} \frac{\int_A^B \gamma(a)e^{-ra}\pi(a)da}{\int_0^\infty e^{-ra}\pi(a)da} \tag{9.20b}$$

A careful discussion of (9.20) requires that we distinguish among the various possibilities as regards the shape of the $\beta_2(.)$ function, describing how fertility rates by age are scaled by changing levels of income per capita.

If $\beta_2(.)$ is taken to be a monotonic function of income, a simpler discussion of (9.20) can be obtained by setting

$$g(r) = \int_0^\infty \beta_1(a)\pi(a)e^{-ra}da$$

and solving for income per capita:

$$y(r) = \beta_2^{-1}\left(\frac{1}{g(r)}\right) \tag{9.21}$$

In this case the lhs of the previous expression relates possible equilibrium levels of per-capita income to the population growth rate in a stable population. Such a relation has a noteworthy shape due to the interaction between so-called capital dilution (CD) and intergeneration transfer (IT) effects (Arthur and MacNicoll, 1978; Blanchet, 1988; Fanti and Manfredi, 2005). This relation can take, even in the simplistic case of a flat participation rate over (*A*,*B*), the shape in Figure 9.1, with very high levels of income per capita when *r* approaches its lower bound (–*d*), that is, when the CD effect certainly dominates, then as *r* increases *y(r)* approaches a Worst Population Growth Rate (WPGR), an Optimum Population Growth Rate (WPGR), and finally steadily declines and approaches zero for very large *r*.

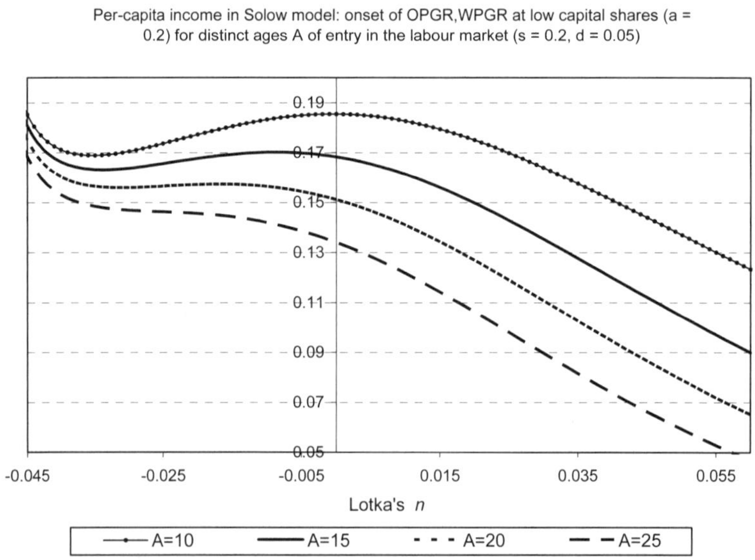


*Figure 9.1. Income per capita as a function of the equilibrium population growth rate in a stable population*

On the other hand, since $g(r)$ is monotonically decreasing in $r$, the rhs will be a decreasing function of $r$ when $\beta_2(.)$ is decreasing in income per capita, while it will be increasing in $r$ when $\beta_2(.)$ is increasing. Though computations of the solutions of (9.21) are still to be carried out under realistic parameter values, potentially interesting demo-economic findings are suggested. For instance, consider the case of the decreasing S-shaped $\beta_2(.)$ function, starting from high fertility levels at very low levels of per capita income, then decreasing initially rapidly as income increases, and subsequently slowing down and plateauing at a lower level for very high levels of income per capita. Such a form broadly corresponds to the conventional demographers' description of the demographic transition (Keyfitz, 1985; Chesnais, 1987), and has been used in descriptive economic models of the demographic transition (Strulik, 1997, 1999; Prskawetz et al., 2000). In this case equation (9A.1) may have multiple solutions, each corresponding to a possible state of joint balanced growth of the population and the economy. For example, a frequent case shows five solutions (Figure 9.2). Though no formal stability analysis was carried out it is tempting to interpret the equilibrium with a high rate of population growth ($E_1$) as a (locally stable?) Malthusian trap, the one with the intermediate rate of population change ($E_3$) as a (locally stable?) post-transitional equilibrium with population growth not too far from stationarity, and finally the equilibrium with very low, largely negative, growth rate ($E_5$), as a (locally stable?) 'super-modern' equilibrium, a sort of 'richness trap' characterised by sustained below-replacement fertility, as currently spreading in much of the industrialised world (Billari and Kohler, 2004).

The previous results raise interesting considerations as regards the debate on multiple equilibria of the population-economy system in history, the existence and escape from the Malthusian trap, and modern growth regimes.

The possibility of three equilibria (a locally stable Malthusian trap, an intermediate unstable equilibrium and a stable regime of modern growth) is a common result in Solow-type models of the demographic transition (Strulik 1997, 1999, 2000; Fanti and Manfredi 2003). Here it is suggested that the incorporation of age structure might lead to the appearance of two further equilibria, one of which might be interpreted as a 'richness trap' with sustained below-replacement fertility. This phenomenon is the consequence of correctly taking into account the dependence of fertility on per-capita income, as a consequence of the peculiar relation between equilibrium levels of income per capita and regimes of population growth.

The discussion also indicates that once one takes properly into account the overall dynamic interaction between the economic system and the demographic one then: a) the curve $y(r)$ will not anymore to be interpreted, as traditionally done, as a locus of equilibria; b) the WPGR and OPGR will not be equilibrium solutions, unless by chance.

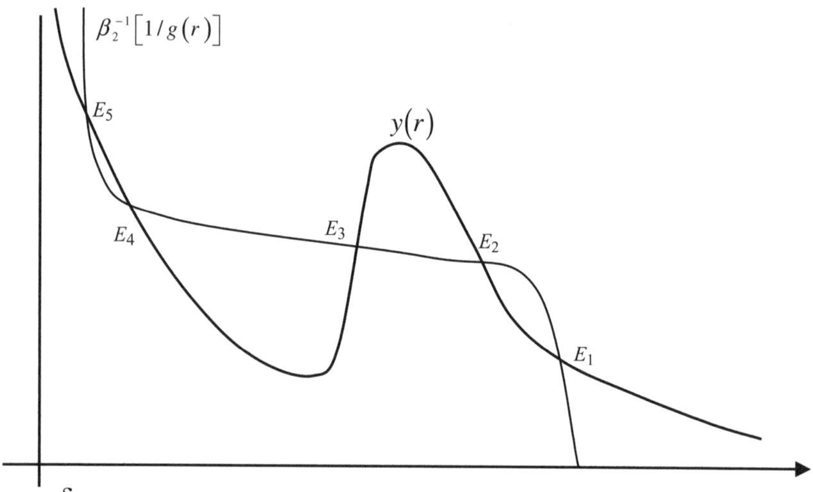


*Figure 9.2. From the 'Malthusian' to the 'Richness' trap. Multiple balanced growth equilibria when fertility is a decreasing function of per-capita income according to a 'Demographic Transition' pattern*

The Malthusian case can be discussed similarly. In this case at most three equilibria are possible. The case of a humped $\beta_2(.)$ function (Jones, 1999) is of course more complicated and leads potentially to a more complex equilibrium structure.

### 9.4.3. Remarks on Age Structure and Technical Progress

An interesting issue regards our current omission of technological progress. Besides the simple case of exogenous labour-augmenting technical progress, given that our framework focuses on the dynamic role of the population and the labour force, a 'natural' and consistent way to include technical progress would be to endogenise the rate of technical progress $\dot{A}/A$ according to Jones's (1992, 1995) 'idea-based' technical progress, or according to the Boserupian assumption used by Kremer (1993), and extended in many subsequent studies (for example, Klasen and Nestmann, 2006). These efforts typically postulate: $\dot{A}/A = f_\kappa(P,y)$ where $P$ is the total population, $y$ income per capita, and $\kappa$ the research productivity per person. Our framework allows us – at least in principle – to go into greater depth in that it models more finely the relation between technological progress and population including age structure. For instance, there are studies documenting that the productivity of researchers is strongly related to the individual's age (Skirbeck, 2003). This implies that if, as commonly taken, the number of innovations per unit time obeys, for example, a Poisson process at each age, then the expected number of innovations in a small interval of time *dt* might be described as $dt\left[P_1(t)\int_0^\infty g_1(a,t)\xi(a,t)da\right]$ where $P_1(t)$ is the absolute number of individuals working in the research sector at time *t*, $g_1(a,t)$ is the age density of individuals working in the research sector of the economy, and $\xi(a,t)$ the probability that the single researcher aged *a* years gives rise to an innovation. If we assume that $P_1(t)=\sigma(t)P(t)$ where $\sigma(t)$ is the fraction of the total population working in the research sector we are led to the equation $\dot{A}/A=P_1(t)\left[\sigma(t)\int_0^\infty g_1(a,t)\xi(a,t)da\right]$, which can be considered an extension of Kremer's (1993) basic equation with a fine specification of the innovation process with respect to age. Many further refinements are of course possible, such as (a) adopting more general specifications, such as Jones's (1992, 1995) idea that the growth rate of technology is also a non-linear function of the level of technology, or that population acts non-linearly on the rate of technological change (Grossman and Helpman, 1991; Aghion and Howitt, 1992), or (b) endogenising the main quantities, for example, assuming that $\xi=\xi(a,y),\sigma=\sigma(y)$, that is, that they are endogenously related to income per-capita.

Obviously the neoclassical descriptive growth perspective considered here – which offers a widely used framework (Grimm and Harttgen, 2008) for investigating the macroeconomic effects of changes in the age structure with the advantage of being well-tailored on classical population mathematics – represents just part of the economic growth story. If our aim is a better understanding of the possible impact of macro-demographic phenomena, such as mortality changes, fertility transitions or population ageing, on the economy, we cannot really neglect the micro level. Demographic change affects macroeconomic variables, and macroeconomic variables in turn affect individuals' choices, in terms for instance of education, investment in human capital, savings and so on which will ultimately feed back on individuals' demographic choices, and so on. Therefore the reliance on macroeconomic descriptive models is a key limitation of this chapter, which it is our aim to remove in future work.

## 9.5. DISCUSSION

The chapter reports progress in developing a framework fully integrating age structure within descriptive macrodynamic growth models. The ensuing model can be considered the appropriate dynamic framework underlying macro-demographic–macro-simulation models used to investigate the implications of changes in the population's age distribution upon macroeconomic performance. Preliminary analysis of selected subcases, that is, a Solow model descriptively embedding a fertility transition according to the conventional demographic viewpoint, indicates that the model can provide useful insight on the possible dynamic interaction between population and economic growth. Further mathematical steps will be devoted to a thorough investigation of the steady state structure under realistic parameter constellation, investigation of the stability of balanced growth paths and related oscillation issues. For instance, the inclusion of age structure makes the appearance of sustained Malthusian oscillations around the possible paths of balanced growth a fairly plausible possibility.

From a prospective point of view many other demo-economic problems can be investigated by the present framework such as the inclusion of: a) further endogenous demographic and economic parameters; b) 'not-only scale' effects of the economy on demographic patterns, such as the shift in childbearing age recently observed in very low-fertility countries (Billari and Kohler, 2004); (c) population and labour force immigration (Manfredi and Valentini, 2000 and references therein) or the marriage process (Billari et al., 2000); (d) other macroeconomic growth environments, such as Goodwin and AK models; (e) further age-related heterogeneity in economic profiles, as the labour productivity across age (Miles, 1999); (f) further issues beyond the growth problem, namely how age structure affects income distribution along growth paths, according to Fanti and Manfredi (2005). This suggests that the present framework is a flexible one deserving further investigation.

# APPENDIX

We report some details on the derivation of our framework in an intermediate case in which the vital rates are fully endogenised whereas the parameters of labour supply remain exogenous. In particular, we assume that the participation rate $\gamma$ is compactly supported on ($A$, $B$). Restart from the basic equations

$$Z(t)=\frac{\dot{Q}(t)}{Q(t)} \tag{9A.1a}$$

$$Q(t)=\int_A^B \gamma(a)n(a,t)da \tag{9A.1b}$$

$$\left(\frac{\partial}{\partial a}+\frac{\partial}{\partial t}\right)n(a,t)=-\mu(a,X,P)n(a,t) \tag{9A.1c}$$

$$n(0,t)=B(t)=\int_0^\infty \beta(a,X,P)n(a,t)da \tag{9A.1d}$$

We assume that the mortality rate can be written as:

$$\mu(a,Y)=\mu_1(a)+\mu_2(a,X,P) \tag{9A.2}$$

which amounts to stating that mortality is the sum of a 'normal' or baseline component, which is only age-dependent, and of a component which also reflects the action of the inputs from the economic sub-system. This implies that the survival function can be written as

$$\pi(a)=\exp\left[-\int_0^a \mu_1(s)ds\right]\exp\left\{-\int_0^a \mu_2\left[s,X(t-a-s),P(t-a-)\right]ds\right\}=\pi_1(a)\pi_2(a,t)$$

where $\pi_1(a)$ defines survival to 'normal mortality'. Let us introduce the change of variable:

$$u(a,t)=\frac{n(a,t)}{\pi_1(a)}$$

and derive a MacKendrick–Von Foerster PDE for $u(a, t)$. We have:

$$u_a+u_t=\frac{1}{\pi_1(a)}\left[n_a+n_t-n(a,t)\frac{\pi_1'(a)}{\pi_1(a)}\right]$$

that is,

$$u_a + u_t = \frac{1}{\pi_1(a)}\left[-\mu_1(a) - \mu_2(a,X,P) - \frac{\pi_1^{'}(a)}{\pi_1(a)}\right]n(a,t)$$

Since:

$$\frac{\pi_1^{'}(a)}{\pi_1(a)} = -\mu_1(a)$$

Then

$$u_a + u_t = -\mu_2(a,X,P)u(a,t)$$

and

$$u(0,t) = \frac{n(0,t)}{\pi_1(0)} = B(t) = \int_0^\infty \beta(a,X,P)\pi_1(a)u(a,t)da$$

In addition:

$$Q(t) = \int_0^\infty \gamma(a)\pi_1(a)u(a,t)da$$

Let us now define:

$$m_1(a,X,P) = \beta(a,X,P)\pi_1(a)$$

$$\delta_1(a,X) = \gamma(a,X)\pi_1(a)$$

Then (9A.1) can be reformulated as

$$Z(t) = \frac{\dot{Q}(t)}{Q(t)}$$

$$Q(t) = \int_0^\infty \delta_1(a)u(a,t)da$$

$$u_a + u_t = -\mu_2(a,Y,P)u(a,t)$$

$$u(0,t) = \int_0^\infty m_1(a,Y,P)u(a,t)da$$

Next let us consider the change of variable:

$$q(a,t) = \frac{u(a,t)}{Q(t)}$$

and let us derive a MacKendrick–Von Foerster PDE for $q(a, t)$. We have:

$$q_a + q_t = \frac{1}{Q(t)}\left[u_a + u_t - u(a,t)\frac{\dot{Q}(t)}{Q(t)}\right]$$

and therefore

$$q_a + q_t = -\left[\mu(a,Y,P) + Z(t)\right]q(a,t)$$

The corresponding boundary condition is:

$$q(0,t) = \frac{u(0,t)}{Q(t)} = \int_0^\infty m_1(a,X,P)\frac{u(a,t)}{Q(t)}da = \int_0^\infty m_1(a,X,P)q(a,t)da$$

Let us finally seek an equation for $Z(t)$. The following holds:

$$\dot{Q}(t) = \int_A^B \left\{\delta_1(a)\left[-u_a - \mu_2(a,X,P)u(a,t)\right]\right\}da =$$

$$= (-1)\left[\int_A^B \delta_1(a)u_a da + \int_A^B \mu_2(a,X,P)\delta_1(a)u(a,t)da\right]$$

If $\mu_2(a,X,P)$ is independent of age the previous expression reduces to

$$\dot{Q}(t) = (-1)\left[\int_0^\infty \delta_1(a)u_a da + \mu_2(X,P)Q(t)\right]$$

By a parts integration

$$\int_A^B \delta_1(a)u_a da = \left[\delta_1(a)u(a,t)\right]_A^B - \int_A^B \delta_1'(a)u(a,t)da =$$

$$= \left[\delta_1(B)u(B,t) - \delta_1(A)u(A,t)\right] - Q(t)\int_A^B \delta_1'(a)q(a,t)da$$

We thus obtain

$$\dot{Q}(t) = \delta_1(A)Q(t)q(A,t) - \delta_1(B)Q(t)q(B,t) + Q(t)\int_A^B \delta_1'(a)q(a,t)da - \mu_2(X,P)Q(t)$$

and therefore

$$Z(t) = \delta_1(A)q(A,t) - \delta_1(B)q(B,t) - \int_0^\infty \delta_1'(a)q(a,t)da - \mu_2(Y,P)$$

which is a general form for the rate of change of the overall labour supply. The final form for the demographic system therefore is:

$$Z(t)=\frac{\dot{Q}}{Q}=\delta_1(A)q(A,t)-\delta_1(B)q(B,t)+\int_0^\infty \delta_1'(a)q(a,t)da-\mu_2(Y,P)$$

$$q_a+q_t=-\left[\mu_2(a,Y,P)+Z(t)\right]q(a,t)$$

$$q(0,t)=\int_0^\infty m_1(a,Y,P)q(a,t)da$$

plus the restraint

$$\int_A^B \delta_1(a)q(a,t)da=1.$$

## NOTES

* We warmly thank Anna Variato for her deep discussion of the first draft of this chapter at the Conference. We also thank two anonymous referees whose suggestions contributed to greatly improve the exposition of the paper. Usual disclaimers apply.

1. We apologise for the use of the notation *c* ubiquitously used in economics to denote the *consumption* level: unfortunately *c* is also ubiquitously used in mathematical demography to denote population *composition*. Fortunately no risk of confusion occurs in this chapter since we do not consider consumption.

## REFERENCES

Aghion, P. and P. Howitt (1992). 'A Model of Growth Through Creative Destruction', *Econometrica*, **60**, 323–51.

Arthur, WB and G. McNicoll (1977), 'Optimal Time Paths with Age Dependence', *Review of Economic Studies*, **44**(1), 111–23.

Arthur, WB and G. McNicoll (1978), 'Samuelson, Population and Intergenerational Transfers', *International Economic Review*, **19**(1), 241–6.

Barro, R.J. and X. Sala-i-Martin (1995), *Economic Growth*, New York: McGraw Hill.

Becker, G.S. and R.J. Barro (1988), 'A Reformulation of the Economic Theory of Fertility', *Quarterly Journal of Economics*, **103**(1), 1–25.

Becker, G.S., K.M. Murphy and R. Tamura (1990), 'Human Capital, Fertility, and Economic Growth', *Journal of Political Economy*, **98**(5), S12–S37.

Billari, F. and H.P. Kohler (2004), 'Patterns of Lowest Low Fertility in the Western World', *Population Studies*, **58**(2), 161–76.

Billari, F.C., P. Manfredi and A. Valentini (2000), 'Macro-demographic Effects of the Transition to Adulthood: Multistate Stable Population Theory and an Application to Italy', *Mathematical Population Studies*, **9**(1), 33–63.

Blanchet, D. (1988), 'Age Structure and Capital Dilution Effects in Neo-classical Growth Models', *Journal of Population Economics*, **1**(3),183–94.

Boucekkine, R., D. De la Croix and O. Licandro (2002), 'Vintage Human Capital, Demographic Trends, and Endogenous Growth', *Journal of Economic Theory*, **104**, 340–75.

Chesnais, J.C. (1987), *The Demographic Transition*, Oxford: Oxford University Press.

Chu, C.Y. and H. Lu (1995), 'Toward a General Analysis of Endogenous Easterlin Cycles', *Journal of Population Economics*, **8**(1), 35–57.

Dyson, T. and M. Murphy (1985), 'The Onset of Fertility Transition', *Population and Development Review*, **11**(3), 399–440.

Easterlin, R.A. (1961), 'The American Baby-boom in Historical Perspective', *American Economic Review*, **51**(5), 869–911.

Fanti, L. and P. Manfredi (2003), Population, Unemployment and Growth Cycles: a Further Explanatory Perspective', *Metroeconomica*, **54**(2–3), 179–207.

Fanti, L. and P. Manfredi (2005), 'Age Distribution and Age Heterogeneity in Economic Profiles as Sources of Conflict Between Dynamic Efficiency and Equity in the Solow–Stigliz Framework', in N. Salvadori and C. Panico (eds), *Classical, Neo Classical and Keynesian Views on Growth and Distribution*, Cheltenham, UK and Northampton, MA, USA: Edward Elgar.

Feichtinger, G. and H. Dockner (1990), 'Capital Accumulation, Endogenous Population Growth and Easterlin Cycles', *Journal of Population Economics*, **4**(2), 73–87.

Feichtinger, G. and G. Sorger (1989), 'Self-generating Fertility Waves in a Nonlinear Continuous Overlapping Generations Model', *Journal of Population Economics*, **3**(2), 267–80.

Feichtinger, G. and G. Sorger (1990), 'Capital Adjustment, Aspiration Adjustment, and Population Growth: Limit Cycles in an Easterlin-type Model', *Mathematical Population Studies*, **2**(2), 93–103.

Frauenthal, J. and K. Swick (1983), 'Limit Cycle Oscillations of the Human Population', *Demography*, **20**(3), 285–98.

Goodwin, R.M. (1967), 'A Growth Cycle', in C.H. Feinstein (ed.), *Socialism, Capitalism and Growth*, Cambridge: Cambridge University Press.

Grimm, M. and K. Harttgen K. (2008), 'Longer Life, Higher Welfare?', *Oxford Economic Papers*, 60(2), 193–211.

Grossman, G.M. and E. Helpman (1991), *Innovation and Growth in the Global Economy*, Cambridge, MA: MIT Press:

Gurtin, M. and R. MacCamy (1974), 'Nonlinear Age-dependent Population Dynamics, *Archive for Rational Mechanics and Analysis*, **54**, 281–300.

Jones, C.I. (1992), 'R&D Based Models of Economic Growth', unpublished, MIT.

Jones, C.I. (1995), 'R&D Based Models of Economic Growth', *Journal of Political Economy*, **103**(4), 759–84.

Jones, C.I. (1999), 'Was an Industrial Revolution Inevitable? Economic Growth Over the Very Long Run', *NBER Working Paper*, no. 7375.

Jones, C. (2001), 'Was an Industrial Revolution Inevitable? Economic Growth Over the Very Long Run', *Advances in Macroeconomics*, **1**(2), 1–45.

Keyfitz, N. (1985), *Applied Mathematical Demography*, New York: Wiley & Son.

Klasen S. and T. Nestmann (2006), 'Population, Population Density and Technological Change', *Journal of Population Economics*, **19**(3), 611–26.

Kremer, M. (1993), 'Population Growth and Technological Change One Million B.C. to 1990', *Quarterly Journal of Economics*, **108**(3), 681–716.

Lee, R.D. (1974), 'The Formal Dynamics of Controlled Populations, and the Echo, the Boom, and the Bust', *Demography*, **11**(4), 563–85.

Lee, R.D. (1994), 'The Formal Demography of Population Aging, Transfers, and the Economic Life Cycle', in L. Martin and S.H. Preston (eds), *The Demography of Aging*, Washington: National Academy Press, pp. 8–49.

Lee, R.D. (1997), 'Population Dynamics: Equilibrium, Disequilibrium, and Consequences of Fluctuations', in M.R. Rosenzweig and O. Stark (eds), *Handbook of Population and Family Economics*, Amsterdam: North Holland.

Lee, R.D. and M. Anderson (2002), 'Malthus in State Space: Macro Economic–Demographic Relations in English History, 1540–1870', *Journal of Population Economics*, **15**(2), 195–220.

Lindh T. and B. Malmberg (1999), 'Age Structure Effects and Growth in the OECD 1950–1990', *Journal of Population Economics*, **12**(3), 431–49.

Malthus, T.R. (1992), *An Essay on the Principle of Population*, first edn, 1798, Cambridge: Cambridge University Press.

Manfredi, P. and A. Valentini (2000), 'Populations with Below Replacement Fertility and Immigration: Theoretical Considerations and Scenarios from the Italian Laboratory', *Rivista Internazionale di Scienze Sociali*, **108**(1), 61–91.

Manfredi, P. and L. Fanti (2006a), 'The Complex Effects of the Interaction Between the Economy and Population', *Structural Change and Economic Dynamics*, **17**(2), 148–73.

Manfredi, P. and L. Fanti (2006b), 'Demography in Macroeconomic Models: When Labour Supply Matters for Economic Cycles', *Metroeconomica*, **57**(4), 536–63.

Mankiw, N.G., D. Romer and D.N. Weil (1992), 'A Contribution to the Empirics of Economic Growth', *Quarterly Journal of Economics*, **107**(2), 407–37.

McCulloch, J.R. (1854), *A Treatise on the Circumstances which Determine the Rate of Wage and the Condition of the Labouring Classes*, London: Heinemann.

Miles, D. (1999), 'Modelling the Impact of Demographic Change upon the Economy', *Economic Journal*, **109**(452), 1–36.

Prskawetz, A. and T. Fent (2007), 'Workforce Ageing and the Substitution of Labour. The Role of Supply and Demand of Labour in Austria', *Metroeconomica*, **58**(1), 95–126.

Prskawetz, A., G. Steinmann and G. Feichtinger (2000), 'Human Capital, Technological Progress and the Demographic Transition', *Mathematical Population Studies*, **7**(4), 343–63.

Samuelson, P.A. (1976), 'An Economist's Nonlinear Model of Self-generated Fertility Waves', *Population Studies*, **30**(2), 243–7.

Skirbeck, V. (2003), 'Age and Individual Productivity: a Literature Survey', *MPIDR Working Paper*, no. 2003-028.

Solow, R.M. (1956), 'A Contribution to the Theory of Economic Growth', *Quarterly Journal of Economics*, **70**(1), 65–94.

Strulik, H. (1997), 'Learning by Doing, Population Pressure, and the Theory of Demographic Transition', *Journal of Population Economics*, **10**(3), 285–98.

Strulik, H. (1999), 'Demographic Transition, Stagnation, and Demoeconomic Cycles in a Model for the Less Developed Economy', *Journal of Macroeconomics*, **21**(2), 397–413.

Van der Ploeg, F. (1987), 'Growth Cycles, Induced Technical Change and Perpetual Conflict over the Distribution of Income', *Journal of Macroeconomics*, **9**(1), 1–12.

# 10. Bright and wealthy: exploring assortative mating*

**Valerio Filoso**

## 10.1. INTRODUCTION

In his first work on marriage markets, Becker (1973) noted that sorting between traits of married couples is not a random phenomenon, since people prefer to match according to personal characteristics, like age, beauty, labour productivity and education. He coined the term assortative mating for the pattern of trait pairings between partners in a monogamous marriage market.

In a given marriage market, assortative mating can either be negative or positive. For example, assume that in a marriage market the only relevant trait in pairing is labour productivity: under positive assortative mating couples are formed by individuals endowed with similar levels of productivity, whereas under negative assortative mating they are formed by spouses whose productivity in labour activities tends to be different.[1] If positive assortative mating prevails, the correlation between the spouses' productivity displays a positive sign and testifies to a tendency of likes to marry likes.

The issue of marital sorting is relevant to empirical research in economics since a high degree of assortative mating between partners in a given society reinforces income inequalities across families, impacts negatively on the returns of education, and on the probability of the children engaging in criminal activities (Ermisch et al., 2006; Fernández et. al., 2005; Ermisch and Francesconi, 2002; Fernández and Rogerson, 2001).

When it comes to matching on more than one variable – so-called *multidimensional sorting* – the interpretation of cross correlations becomes much more tricky. For example, a positive empirical relationship is usually observed between spousal education and one's earnings (Benham, 1974; Boulier and Rosenzweig, 1984) and identifying the exact nature of these cross effects can be highly problematic. On the one hand, game theorists (Roth and Sotomayor, 1990; Gale and Shapley, 1962) maintain that the outcome of the marriage market competition is such that the more educated members of one sex tend to marry the more educated members of the other: the observed cross correlations are simply a by-product of mating on education. On the other hand, spousal education may well help partners to accumulate human capital and increase earnings, since couples with high levels of education are more likely to share ideas, values and tastes within the family, and this homogeneity may impact positively also upon market productive traits (Huang et al., 2006). In a simple OLS regression context, the two models are observationally equivalent. The identification problems are similar to those found in the human capital literature with regard to alternative explanations for the positive correlation between schooling and earnings, that is, a problem of mutual causation. Higher education could either signal high-skilled individuals, as in Spence (1973), or a deliberate attempt to increase the level of human capital, as in Becker (1964): when multiple causality exists, devising a test to disentangle the relative importance of selectivity from that of cross-productivity is an open issue, since finding genuinely exogenous instrumental variables is far from simple.

This chapter is an empirical study of multidimensional mating in the marriage market and its contribution is twofold. First, we point out that the marriage market jointly determines assortative mating on schooling *and* on wages, that is, market and household productivity, because schooling and wages are only partly substitutable in the marriage market, as emphasized by the theory of compensating differentials (Grossbard-Shechtman and Neuman, 1988).

Secondly, we estimate a simultaneous equations model for the Italian marriage market in which schooling and market productivity are the main traits which jointly determine the pattern of marital sorting, along with a Mincer-like wage equation. To our knowledge, this estimation has not been attempted elsewhere. Assuming that prospective partners have rational expectations and private information on each other's traits that are revealed only gradually across time, we estimate a structural equation system which shows how marriage and labour markets interact. The data are extracted from the Bank of Italy's Survey on Household Income and Wealth (SHIW), with families tracked longitudinally from 1989 to 2006. The temporal structure of the dataset allows for an estimation of long-run performance in the job market and in the educational system which cannot be fully disclosed at the beginning of marriage, but whose expected value is relevant to spouse selection. Unfortunately, the SHIW dataset does not include information on family background and age at marriage: this precludes the possibility of systematically disentangling the effect of marital sorting at the time of marriage and intervening change along the life-cycle. To mitigate this identification problem, we compare a subsample of young couples to the whole sample: interestingly, we find that marital life does not radically change the pattern of mating as observed in the first years of marriage. This corroborates our initial hypothesis that the marriage market plays a significant role in determining social stratification.

Our key finding indicates that wage has predictive power in forecasting educational mating and that education also helps predict wage sorting. The inclusion of these cross variables significantly decreases the level of the observed univariate correlations in the data. Furthermore, we also investigate the issue of substitutability in depth using a non-linear model: we find that wage and schooling are substitutable inputs in men's search process, whereas the same inputs are complementary in women's search.

The chapter is organized as follows. The next section surveys the current literature on cross effects of wage and schooling between partners. Then we introduce a stylized model of the marriage market which can account for multidimensional sorting. Various estimates for the model are provided and the resulting evidence is discussed, along with possible directions for further research.

## 10.2. BACKGROUND LITERATURE

The study of spousal matching over personal traits has long been a topic of research in the fields of biology, economics and sociology. Epstein and Guttman (1984), in one of the most extensive studies to date on unidimensional sorting, observe positive assortative mating for ages, wages, education, religion, heights, IQ scores and ethnicity measured by robust statistical association. The applied economic literature on multidimensional sorting dates back to the work of Benham (1974) on the cross effects of education: he finds that wife's education increases husband's wage by 3 per cent in the US. According to Tiefenthaler (1997), wife's education increases husband's wage by 5–7 per cent in Brazil, while husband's education increases wife's wage by roughly 5 per cent, though his estimation does not explicitly control for sample selection due to assortative mating. Also, significant benefits are found to arise from role specialization in the family and job association, that is, working in the same market sector. In their study on Chinese twins, controlling for selectivity in the marriage market and for family background, Huang et al. (2006) find that husband's education boosts wife's earnings by 3.5 per cent, but cannot find any effect running in the opposite direction. They provide evidence that the increase in wife's earnings is explained by a positive effect on hourly wages.

Empirical results invariably show a positive sign for the crude correlation between spouses' wages. In their study of assortative mating, Zhang and Liu (2003), correcting for sample selection and cross-productivity effects, find that the correlation between spouses' potential wages is not statistically significant, such that the main gains from marriage seem to derive from role specialization, as in Becker (1991[1981]). This evidence is partly consistent with the work of Smith (1979) who comes across low correlations between wage residuals once the estimation procedure takes into account sample selection. To date, the only result of negative assortative mating on wages has been obtained by Zimmer (1996) with a negative coefficient for North-American whites and a positive coefficient for blacks, even though Becker (1991[1981], pp. 118–19) cites unpublished negative coefficients obtained by Gregg Lewis. Grossbard-Shechtman and Neuman (1991), using the 20 per cent sample from the 1983 census of Israel, find evidence of reciprocal influence of spouses' levels of schooling and significant complementarities in earnings-related measures. Hours of work have also received interest within this research field: Pencavel (1998) tests whether market work hours of husbands and wives are correlated with their spouses' schooling levels. Using the 1990 census for the US, he finds that husbands' labour supply is weakly influenced by their wives' schooling, while women married to a college-educated man work 4 per cent fewer market hours than women married to high-school dropouts, and the effect is almost doubled when the couple have children aged less than six years. This suggests that college-educated husbands substitute some of their own hours of work with their wives' hours in the market.

According to another stream of literature, the process of mating involves variables which the researcher can with difficulty fully control for. In this perspective, unobserved components of educational and income mating are employed to make inferences about the systematic patterns of marriage. Rupert and Cornwell (1997) find weak evidence of cross-productive effects in marriage: according to their estimation based on the National Longitudinal Survey of Young Men, the marriage premium – the observed positive difference in the wage level between married and unmarried men – is attributable to unobservable individual effects that are correlated with marital status and wages. Nakosteen and Zimmer (2001), using unobservable components of hourly wages observed immediately after marriage, find evidence of positive assortative mating on the basis of earnings for the subjects observed in the Panel Study of Income Dynamics (PSID). Mating equations are also employed to estimate components of the human capital which do not fall into the category of formal schooling. Behrman et al. (1995) use an educational mating equation to estimate unobservable skills which are found to impact significantly on the wage of Indian husbands. In their recent contribution, Brynin and Francesconi (2004) extended the same econometric methodology to wives and found several measures of market success associated with unobservable components of human capital.

When datasets contain observations on the same people before and after marriage, it is also possible to test selectivity against cross-productivity, especially with regard to wages: to date, the only study in this fashion has been that of Nakosteen et al. (2004) who take advantage of a one-of-a-kind Swedish archive recording data for the entire workforce. They find evidence of positive correlations between wages before marriage, a result supporting the presence of positive assortative mating net of any cross-productivity effects. The authors also find that the strength of the correlation declines after marriage, possibly due to diminished specialization within the family.

In contrast to previous literature, this chapter argues that marital sorting operates not only along the educational dimension but also on the income dimension. However, since education and labour income are not perfectly correlated, both correlations need to be taken into account when studying marital sorting. In this perspective, we contribute to clarify a missing link in the applied literature between the job market and the marriage market, a point which recently received attention in a theoretical contribution by Chiappori et al. (2006). Up to now, joint estimation of market productivity and educational sorting for married couples has not been attempted. It will be the theme of the next sections.

## 10.3. THE MARRIAGE MARKET

The model of the marriage market presented here is based on the assumption that schooling produces monetary effects because more educated people usually have better jobs, obtain higher salaries on the job market, and have greater chances of moving upward socially (Kalmijn, 1994). Non-monetary effects also follow from schooling, since education generally provides broader perspectives on world visions and relaxes strictness from inherited cultural values. Married individuals can gain from their spouses' higher level of education because of the monetary and non-monetary benefits from schooling: couples in which both spouses share the same background values enjoy higher utility streaming from the production of household public goods. In an ideal setting in which schooling and wages were perfectly correlated with no significant heterogeneity between people, the same pattern of marital sorting would prevail with regard to education and wages since the choice variable of matching would really make no difference.

In contrast, the real world is characterized by imperfect correlations between schooling and wages: this impacts the labour market as well as the marriage market. Explanations for the imperfect correlation in the labour market are not particularly relevant to our intent, since here we focus on what happens in the marriage market and on the heterogeneity observed inside and among couples, but it must be taken into account when estimating a model for the marriage market. This heterogeneity in sorting patterns is mainly due to: (1) different personal tastes toward the monetary and the non-monetary benefits flowing from education, and (2) unobservable individual factors which the social scientist can with difficulty control for.

Assuming that utility is transferable between partners, as in the classical Becker model, partners can make themselves attractive by compensating a low level of a personal trait with a high level of another valuable personal trait. After marriage, this compensation can take the form of monetary transfers, like in the model of Grossbard-Shechtman and Neuman (1988), but to a certain extent this compensation of traits can also take place in the marriage market: for example, a prospective husband endowed with low market productivity could make himself more attractive when endowed with relatively higher education. If this holds true, schooling and income are partly substitutable in women's eyes. As a result, marital sorting happens not only along the educational dimension, but partly also on the income dimension. Multidimensional matching – with regard to education and job prospects – and simultaneity are the cornerstones of the present model. We also assume that, when people meet in the marriage market, they tend to form rational expectations on each other's chances to obtain education and wage. Obviously, any family can benefit from high levels of wage and from high levels of education, but imperfect correlation and personal tastes introduce the possibility of substitution between the two inputs of household production.

Formally, actual household production for a generic family can be written as

$$F = F(\mathbf{v}) \tag{10.1}$$

where $F$ is the total value of household-produced goods,

$$\mathbf{v} \equiv [e_w \quad e_h \quad s_w \quad s_h]' \tag{10.2}$$

is a vector containing the levels of education $(e)$ and levels of wages $(s)$ of the wife $(w)$ and husband $(h)$. $F$ is assumed to be increasing in the level of each observable independent variable. Further, assuming competition among women and among men to marry the best partners, the marriage market mechanism maximizes the sum of the expected value of (10.1) across all possible matches (Becker, 1973, pp. 82–4).

Competition in the marriage market is based on the assumptions that matching is not completely random and that potential partners are at least partially substitutable. Thus the possibility of marrying a man of a given educational level depends, among other things, upon a person's educational and wage levels. This systematic relation between one's traits and his/her partner's is termed mating function (or mating equation) and has been introduced in the context of family economics by Boulier and Rosenzweig (1984): basically, it represents a reduced form equation summarizing the outcome of the marital search process as a function of the searcher's personal traits. While the current literature on human capital (Brynin and Francesconi, 2004; Behrman et al., 1995) estimates mating functions only with regard to schooling, we allow for simultaneous determination of educational and income sorting. With all the assumptions previously stated, equilibrium in the marriage market can be represented by the following system of mating equations:

$$\mathbf{Dv}+\mathbf{X}'\beta+\mathbf{\Omega}=\mathbf{0} \tag{10.3}$$

where

$$\mathbf{D}\equiv\begin{bmatrix} 1 & -d_1 & 0 & -d_2 \\ -d_3 & 1 & d_4 & 0 \\ 0 & -d_5 & 1 & -d_6 \\ -d_7 & 0 & -d_8 & 1 \end{bmatrix} \tag{10.4}$$

is the matrix of coefficients for the endogenous variables, **X** is a matrix of exogenous variables, $\boldsymbol{\beta}$ is a vector of estimated parameters for the exogenous variables, and

$$\mathbf{\Omega}\equiv\begin{bmatrix}\omega_w^e & \omega_h^e & \omega_w^s & \omega_h^s\end{bmatrix}' \tag{10.5}$$

is a vector of i.i.d. error terms.

To make things clearer, let us consider only the first two mating equations for wife's education and wage. These equations can be written as:

$$e_w = d_1 e_h + d_2 s_h + \mathbf{x}_h^e \beta_h^e + \omega_w^e \tag{10.6}$$

$$s_w = d_5 e_h + d_6 s_h + \mathbf{x}_h^s \beta_h^s + \omega_w^s \tag{10.7}$$

where the $\beta$ coefficients for the exogenous characteristics **x** are allowed to vary across equations. As shown previously, the hypotheses that

$$d_1 > 0 \tag{10.8}$$

$$d_6 > 0 \tag{10.9}$$

have been tested in the literature under the implicit assumption that $d_2 = d_5 = 0$ and found true. Instead, we are interested in testing whether

$$d_1, d_2 > 0 \tag{10.10}$$

$$d_6, d_5 > 0 \tag{10.11}$$

i.e., if there is any possibility of trade between schooling and market productivity. To sum up, this structure for marital mating is based on four equations: two for schooling of husbands and wives and two more for wages of the same spouses. Each mating equation implies that a man's wage and schooling jointly determine the expected levels of schooling and wage of his prospective wife, and the same causal relation holds true also for women. This implies the possibility that education and wage can impact differently upon the prospective spouse's wage and schooling.

This linear marriage market is exactly identified, since it is made up of four variables and four equations. However, wages and schooling levels are linked not only through the marriage market, but also through the labour market, for higher education implies higher wages. This is a potential source of collinearity which must be taken into account, due to its economic and statistical relevance. Accordingly, for both partners $i \in \{h, w\}$ of the $j$-th couple we must add a wage equation of the type

$$s_{i,j} = r_i e_{i,j} + \mathbf{y}_{i,j} \beta_i + \theta_{i,j} \tag{10.12}$$

where $r$ is the return from education, $\mathbf{y}$ is a vector of controls, $\theta$ is an i.i.d. error term, and $j$ represents the $j$-th observation. This wage equation is estimated jointly with the mating equation for wage and the mating equation for education, separately for each gender: accordingly, the estimated effects of schooling and wages on marital sorting are net of direct labour market effects from schooling to wages. Estimation of this equation system will be the subject of the next section.

## 10.4. ESTIMATION AND DATA

### 10.4.1. The Dataset

The data used for estimation originate from the Bank of Italy's Survey on Household Income and Wealth (SHIW) sample, containing observations on families and individual components tracked longitudinally from 1989 to 2006. Though SHIW's data collection actually dates back to 1977, it is only since 1989 that data on education have also been collected for non-working individuals. Apart from observations from 1977 to 1987, other groups were dropped: (1) couples for which education is missing, (2) couples for which job status is missing, (3) couples in which one or both spouses are retired, (4) couples in which husbands are older than 65 and wives are older than 60. All income and wealth measures are adjusted to 2006-equivalent euros. Education and wages are in logarithms, with the censoring point for wage (originally set equal to zero) being shifted by one euro to obtain non-missing values for predicted wages also in the case of non-working individuals. In our sample, 47 per cent of wives work and receive a salary, and 95 per cent of husbands.

### 10.4.2. Estimation Procedure and Technique

The estimation procedure designed to test for cross effects of schooling and income is structured as follows:

1. The first problem to tackle when estimating the effects of sorting on observed labour behaviour is to obtain reasonable estimates of the expectations of $e_i$ and $s_i$ as they enter the evaluation that prospective partners make while dating. We assume that prospective partners have rational expectations on each other's achievements, both in the educational system and in the job market, that is,

$$E_{t-1}\left[e_{i,t} \mid I_{t-1}\right]=e_{i,t} \tag{10.13}$$

$$E_{t-1}\left[s_{i,t} \mid I_{t-1}\right]=s_{i,t} \tag{10.14}$$

   where $E$ is the expectation operator and $I$ is the set of relevant information. This implies that the observed values in the data for $e_i$ and $s_i$ can be used to recover their expected levels, provided that some sort of temporal smoothing is operated to obtain the expected values as computed before marriage. Since the data in SHIW have a panel structure, i.e., repeated observations across the years for the same couples, we can exploit this feature to obtain estimates of the variables relevant to the mating system. For computing expected education, we use the maximum level of schooling actually observed in the data. For computing expected salary, we use the median salary, given the notorious asymmetry of this variable.
2. Since salary is not observed for people permanently unemployed or outside the workforce and using only observations for working partners would introduce sample selection bias, we use Heckman's model (Heckman, 1979) to account for censoring and estimate the potential logarithm of wage for non-working wives and husbands. Accordingly,

we set up a selection probit equation, whose dependent variable is a dummy for participation in the labour market, along with a wage equation which includes the inverse Mills ratio derived from the selection equation. Both equations are jointly estimated using Full Maximum Likelihood. The selection equation for wives includes age, age squared, dummies for maximum schooling level achieved, number of children and husband's wage. The squared terms account for the non-linearities in wives' behaviour.[2] The regressors for wives' wages include dummies for maximum schooling level achieved, expertise, expertise squared, dummies for main professional qualification, and dummies for the productive sector. The equations for husbands parallel those for wives, except for spouse's wage and main professional qualification which are not included in the selection equation.

3. Exploratory analysis of the variables and their interactions is performed using conventional parametric and non-parametric statistics.
4. Using predicted wages, we perform a three-stage least squares (3SLS) procedure for a system of three equations: one mating equation for schooling, another mating equation for schooling, and a Mincer-like wage equation. This procedure is run separately for wives and for husbands. The 3SLS estimator iterates over the estimated disturbance covariance matrix and parameter estimates until the parameter estimates converge. As a comparison, we also re-estimate the system using a seemingly unrelated regression (SUR) technique to check whether simultaneity is an issue. Along with direct and cross effects, mating equations contain controls for personal wealth (approximated by home ownership and income from capital), the inverse Mills ratio to account for censoring, and job qualification.
5. Finally, we check the relationship in the educational mating equations between schooling and salary using a flexible functional form. This allows us to distinguish between complementarity and substitutability between the inputs used in the process of marital sorting.

## 10.5. RESULTS

### 10.5.1. Selection Model

The pattern of labour participation of wives is displayed in Table 10A.1. Participation in the labour market rises monotonically with schooling. Using the *no schooling* modality as the baseline, we find that obtaining a bachelor's degree increases the probability of participation by 16.8 – 0.6 = 16.2 per cent, while wives who finished high school register an increase of

46.8 – 0.6 = 46.2 per cent in the probability of participation compared to wives with no education at all. This information may help explain the pattern of participation of wives in the labour market when used jointly with data about wages.

The results from the Heckman model for sample selection, obtained by Maximum Likelihood Estimation and displayed in Table 10A.7, highlight the concave effect of age on the probability of entering the job market.[3] While the model estimated for men is not particularly interesting given the small fraction of men outside the workforce, some insights can be derived from the model estimated for wives. For this sample we find a significantly negative impact of children on labour market participation. Interestingly, higher husband's wages tend to favour the wife's entry on the job market. While Becker (1991[1981]) argues that the higher the husband's wage, the lower must be wives' hazard in participation, Lam (1988) has proved that this only holds when household production does not include public goods. The positive estimated coefficient in the present model supports the hypothesis that labour participation decisions of Italian wives are mainly driven by public goods considerations. Education also has explanatory power in the participation equation. Compared to the omitted modality (no schooling at all), earning a BA increases the likelihood of participation by a factor of 1.7. By contrast, women endowed with low levels of schooling tend not to work outside the house: in any case, however, more education tends to increase participation in the labour market. Two factors can be used to explain this tendency: first, at low levels of schooling, women find it more profitable to specialize in household production; secondly, women with higher education may have a stronger preference toward working outside the home, since they may attach value to working *per se*.

Compared to husbands, the wives' wage equation shows that expertise exerts a somewhat weaker influence: this is testified by smaller linear and quadratic coefficients; both husbands and wives show the usual U-reversed pattern. This evidence is consistent with two main explanations: (1) women tend to retire earlier than men, thus leaving their jobs when their human capital is still relatively productive; (2) women's human capital depreciates at a slower pace than men's. If proved robust by more detailed analysis, not to be conducted here for reasons of overall consistency, this last insight may help redesign the current laws about mandatory retirement. Moreover, job qualification is also important for explaining wages. Here the omitted modality is worker. Compared to this baseline, wives gain 38.9 per cent more by becoming freelancers, 81.2 per cent more by becoming entrepreneurs, and 29 per cent more by becoming executives. Using the same omitted variable for husbands, husbands gain the same as women by becoming executives, while the payoff from entrepreneurial and freelance activities is higher.

### 10.5.2. Exploratory Analysis

To check the basic relations between wages and schooling, pairwise unconditional correlations on the censored sample are listed in Table 10A.5 and contrasted with the coefficients calculated over the uncensored sample, reported in Table 10A.6. In the uncensored sample, the notional wages for women and men permanently out of work are estimated using Heckman's selection model.

In the censored sample, the correlation between spouses' schooling is around 63 per cent, a value somewhat higher than the average 50 per cent reported by Lam (1988) for the US, while the correlation between wages is 41 per cent. Correlations between education and wages are both remarkably similar across gender, amounting to 38 per cent. Inspecting correlations for the uncensored sample reveals some interesting facts. As expected, the linear relation between schooling levels remains constant, since the small discrepancy is due to missing data excluded from calculations. The returns from education for wives drop by 15.7 per cent, while husbands lose 3.6 per cent. The main result here is that wage correlation between spouses drops by 12.8 per cent.[4] This suggests that the very choice of wives to enter the job market is highly dependent upon agreements made in the family and upon potential returns from schooling, which seem markedly low for non-working wives.

From inspection of mating patterns a question about causality naturally arises: to what extent is educational sorting determined by the marriage market or by cross-productive effects? To investigate the issue, Table 10A.4 collects figures for those who experienced a transition toward a higher level of schooling in the years under study. The tabulations reveal that educational levels remain almost completely stable for married people, with less than 1 per cent of the sample achieving higher education while married. In other words, couples tend to form only after the educational path ends. Obviously, the estimates do not account for censoring, since young couples face a positive probability of increasing education during their lifetime; however, the small numbers of transitions observed suggest that assortative mating is mainly determined in the marriage market and subsequent adjustments play a negligible role. A natural implication is that changes in the level of assortative mating observed during the life cycle are almost exclusively attributable to variations in wages and in returns from schooling.

Since we are interested not only in the strength of the linear relation between the variables, but also in whether and how this relation changes as we move toward the tails of the distributions, we employ the method of quantile regressions, as described in Koenker (2005). Figure 10.1 displays the relation between the logs of husband's wage and wife's wage, provided that both work in the marketplace, according to the relation

$$s_{w,i} = g\left(s_{h,i}\right) + \delta_i. \tag{10.15}$$

On the $x$-axis we have the quantiles of the dependent variable and on the $y$-axis the values of the corresponding estimated coefficient. The straight line is the value of the OLS estimator, being used as a benchmark, surrounded by confidence bands at 90 per cent. The kinked line, surrounded by grey-shaded confidence bands, shows the values of quantile regression coefficients obtained at different points of the distribution of the dependent variable.

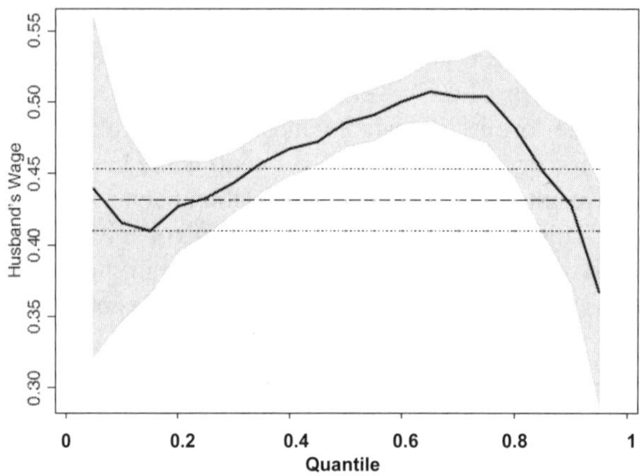


*Figure 10.1. Correlation between spouses' wages (censored sample)*

Conditioning on wives' wage quantiles, the strength of the relation between the two variables displays a non-linear trend across the distribution, with steadily decreasing values until the last quantiles, where the relation jumps back to the same values observed for the low-wage wives. Point estimates of elasticities are always significantly greater than zero and range from 51 per cent at the third quartile to 37 per cent at the top quantiles and to 41 per cent at the lowest quantiles. The couples in which both partners work find that significant gains can be found in the central section of the distribution, even though the data do not allow the cross-productivity effects from assortative mating to be disentangled. However, the fact that the relation becomes weaker at higher quantiles suggests that both motivations become less important as wages go up. Most probably, when husband's wage goes up, the income effect induces substitution between partners' work efforts, resulting in higher levels of leisure enjoyed by women and decreased participation in the labour market.

Correcting for selectivity displays a relation between spouses' wages of increasing strength as we move upward to the distribution of the wife's wage, as is evident from Figure 10.2. The strength of this link becomes markedly lower at the first quantiles, dropping to 5 per cent. This is an interesting insight into the nature of matching, since it provides a new perspective on the age-old discussion of sorting between wages which cannot be obtained through OLS. Using a simple OLS estimator we would have incorrectly concluded that the coefficient is around 20 per cent, while this relation grows monotonically from 5 per cent at the lowest quantiles to 50 per cent at the top quantiles.

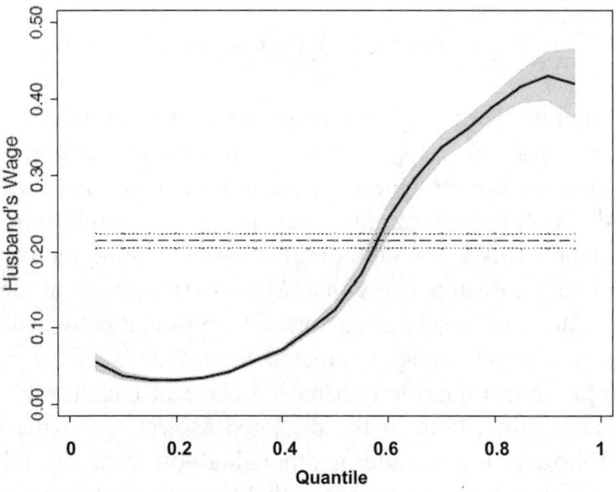


*Figure 10.2. Correlation between spouses' wages (uncensored sample)*

**Finding 1** (Wage Sorting). *Focusing on the whole distribution of wages, Becker's conjecture that negative assortative mating is optimal looks partly confirmed.*

At low levels of wages Figure 10.2 shows that people tend to match according to the traditional model of labour division, such that the resulting sorting is very weak. Within these families, most of the gains from marriage derive from labour allocation between market and household production. By contrast, shifting to higher wages increases the possibility of enjoying higher levels of public goods, like child quality and leisure: accordingly, the level of positive assortative mating tends to increase. Comparison between Figures 10.1 and 10.2 reveals major differences due to the behaviour of non-working wives. Most likely, women tend not to work both when their husband's wage is very low and when it is very high: at very low wage levels, traditional roles may prevail, while at high wage levels women enjoy more leisure since they receive high monetary transfers from their husbands. At both tails of the distribution the same labour participation pattern of wives prevails, but for very different reasons.

### 10.5.3. Mating Equations

To develop some intuition about the interaction between schooling and wages, we start regressing the years of schooling of a partner $i$ on the years of schooling of his/her partner $j$. Also, the same level of schooling is interacted with the quartiles of income of the $j$ partner, according to the following equation

$$e_i = \sigma e_j + \sum_{q \in Q} \psi_{q,j} e_j s_{q,j} + \varepsilon_i. \tag{10.16}$$

If no interaction between wage and education is present, then we should find that $E[\psi_{q,j}]=0$ for any $q \in Q$, where $q$ are dummy variables for the $q$-th quartile of income. We estimate the equation for wives and husbands, using the full and the censored sample alternately. The results are reported in Tables 10A.8 and 10A.9, with the omitted variable being the first quartile of income from wage. Results show that $E[\psi_{q,j}]>0$ in most of the estimates.[5] In particular, husband's schooling interacts systematically with income in determining wife's schooling: compared to husbands in the first quartile, husbands in the fourth quartile register a 3 per cent increase in the elasticity of educational mating, both in the censored as well as in the full sample. Wives also follow a similar pattern, although at lower quartiles the estimated parameters of interaction are noisy, probably due to a higher proportion of notional wages. Our results suggest that educational mating interacts systematically with income and that people in the upper wage quartiles tend to display higher levels of educational homogamy.

Tables 10A.10, 10A.12 and 10A.14 show the results for the estimation of the complete structural model, for both husbands and wives of all ages, while Tables 10A.11, 10A.13 and 10A.15 contain estimation results for the subsample of husbands aged 16–35 and wives aged 16–33. The observations for non-working husbands were omitted from this estimation because of the very small fraction of men permanently out of work. Given the possible non-linearities between levels of education, we also estimated an alternative specification with quadratic terms for the years of schooling. Moreover, both these specifications – the linear and the quadratic – are carried out over the censored sample and over the uncensored sample. This was done since non-participation in the labour market is pervasive for wives and a significant fraction of their wages is notional. Consequently, estimates for wives should be considered with care and our comments will mainly focus on the estimates for husbands.

**Finding 2** (Overall Fitting). *Estimation results of the full structural model show that the relation between spousal wages is modest, while the relation between spousal schooling levels is strong. This evidence weakly supports the Beckerian analysis which implies a low level of predictive power of wages for matching.*

The results show overall significance for both structural models. The $R^2$s statistics display acceptable values for the fitting of the educational mating equations (around 40 per cent) and low values for the wage equation.

**Finding 3** (Returns to Schooling). *Own schooling impacts husbands' wages, while wives' schooling has a much noisier effect on their own wages.*

Most probably, women's choice of participation in the job market and carrier choice do not closely follow the educational background and are much more family-dependent, when compared to men's choices.

**Finding 4** (Direct Effects). *The strongest effects of years of schooling and wage are direct ones: schooling of one partner helps predict the schooling of the other partner and wage of one partner helps predict the wage of the other.*

According to the schooling mating equation displayed in Table 10A.10, considered in its linear specification, the elasticity of an additional year of schooling, calculated around the mean, increases the prospective partner's schooling by 0.56–0.63. In the quadratic specification, the quadratic term and the linear term for schooling are found positive, such that we can conclude that the strength of educational sorting increases with the level of own schooling. According to the wage mating equation, the elasticity of an additional euro of own wage increases the prospective partner's wage by 0.52–0.63 in the uncensored sample and by 1.1 in the censored sample. This difference can be rationalized as follows: since the uncensored sample contains a large fraction of wives who choose not to work because of their low reservation wage and then prefer specialization in household production while their husbands do not, the impact of labour market productivity, approximated by the wage, is lower for the whole sample.

**Finding 5** (Cross-Effect of Wage). *In the mating equation for wife's schooling, the elasticity of the impact of husband's wage is positive, ranging from 0.06 to 0.13. This is evidence that prospective husbands can partially compensate low schooling with high wages.*

The value of cross-elasticity signals that wage and schooling are at least partially substitutable in determining the prospective partner's education: this validates our initial intuition about the functioning of the marriage market. Interestingly, the effect of wife's wage on husband's schooling is stronger, as is evident from Table 10A.12 which shows that women with high wages tend to marry highly educated men. In a sense, with marriage, women's wage buys more education than men's. Compared to men, women are likely to be more interested in sharing values, tastes, and intellectual background because they attach less weight to traditional divisions of labour inside the household and more weight to the production of household public goods, like children's education; moreover, the strength of this effect grows stronger as the wife's wage goes up.

**Finding 6** (Cross-Effect of Schooling). *While the effect of husband's schooling on his prospective bride's wage is noisy in the linear specification, in the quadratic specification, the quadratic term is positive while the linear term is negative. In contrast, wife's schooling shows an elasticity of 0.103–0.362 in predicting husband's wage* (see Table 10A.17).

This means that the effect of schooling is positive only after a given threshold which is equal to $e^{0.431/2\times 0.107} \approx 7.5$ years of schooling for the censored sample and to $e^{0.378/2\times 0.092} \approx 7.8$ years of schooling for the uncensored sample. These figures suggest that, apart from people who did not finish secondary school, a higher level of completed education is able to buy partners with a higher level of wage.

The issue of simultaneity is also relevant to our results: using as a benchmark a companion model of the same three equations obtained through the seemingly unrelated regression (SUR) technique reported in Table 10A.14, assuming only links between error terms and not between variables, the 3SLS-estimated equations display non-trivial differences between estimated coefficients, especially with regard to cross effects. This also supports our initial conjecture that wages and education jointly impact the sorting between spouses and that simultaneity does matter because (1) the marriage market has margins for substitution between wage and schooling, and (2) the marriage market and the labour market are closely linked.

Tables 10A.16 and 10A.17 compare several estimates over the whole sample to the same estimates over the sample of young couples: the exercise is interesting since young couples' traits in terms of schooling and wage are closer to the original traits found in the marriage market. Some interesting patterns emerge. Since all the variability in assortative mating during life is due to changing job conditions and not to changes in schooling and men experience more variability than women, the effect of wife's schooling on husband's schooling is stable around 0.550–0.609, while the husband's estimated effect lies between 0.484 and 0.653.

**Finding 7** (Matching on Wages Across Lifetimes). *The degree of assortative mating on wages varies across lifetimes. The difference between the whole sample and the young sample degree of assortative mating on wage is around +0.268. For husbands, the change is around +0.131.*

### 10.5.4. More on Substitutability

Linear specification of the model, while permitting an appreciation of the process of marital sorting, cannot be used to investigate the issue of substitutability in depth. In the linear model, as the cross derivatives of the mating function with regard to the partner's education or wage are always zero, it is impossible to test whether schooling and wage are substitutable or complementary inputs in the matching process.

To deal with this issue, non-linear specification is needed to allow for more flexible determination of cross derivatives. With this intent, we picked the constant elasticity of substitution (CES) function. Within this scheme, the mating equation can be written as:

$$e_j = \lambda\left[\theta e_i^{\eta} + (1-\theta)s_i^{\eta}\right]^{1/\eta} \tag{10.17}$$

with $i,j \in \{h,w\}$ and $i \neq j$. Parameter $\theta$ is a distribution factor, while the elasticity of substitution $\sigma$ between $e_j$ and $s_j$ can be derived according to the formula $\sigma = 1/(1-\eta)$. When $\sigma = 0$, that is $\eta \to -\infty$, the factors are perfect complements, while when $\sigma \to \infty$, which corresponds to $\eta = 1$, the factors are perfect substitutes. The case $\sigma = 1$ corresponds to the Cobb–Douglas function.

We estimate the schooling mating equation for husbands and wives in two different specifications. In the first, we estimate only the CES function through the non-linear least squares (NLS); in the second, we add a linear equation explaining wages with the level of schooling and estimate the system of equations using the non-linear seemingly unrelated method (NLSUR). The results are displayed in Tables 10A.18–10A.21. The first two columns contain the estimates for wives' schooling, the second two for husbands'. The first and third columns report the estimates for the NLS model, while the second and fourth do likewise for the NLSUR model. Estimation is performed both for schooling and wage mating.

**Finding 8** (Complementarity and Substitutability). *Non-linear estimation shows that schooling and wage are substitutes for wives, while the same variables are (weak) complements for husbands.*

The search technology of husbands for their wives' schooling exhibits an elasticity of substitution of 0.62–0.76; similar figures are found for the wage mating equation. This can be taken as evidence of a tendency toward complementarity. The search technology of wives for their husbands' schooling lies between 1.36 and 3.33, while in the wage mating equation the elasticity varies between 1.53 and 5.25, which testifies a tendency toward substitutability. Most likely, family organization is important for matching and helps explain this asymmetric evidence. Women who do not participate in the job market are more interested in their husbands' wage than women working outside the household. Consequently, men who are interested in these women perceive that income from labour and schooling must complement each other to obtain a good match. By contrast, as women are not generally expected to be the main earner in the household, they can trade education and wage more easily. Quite interestingly, the NLSUR model provides higher values when compared to the NLS model.

## 10.6. FINAL REMARKS

In this chapter we tackled the role of education and wages in determining the level of assortative mating between partners. Since correlation between wages and education is far from perfect, we explicitly took both of them into account, along with the conventional wage equation commonly employed in the labour economics literature. Using data from Italian couples, we did find evidence that wages and education simultaneously determine how people match. We also found evidence of non-trivial differences in the mating behaviour between men and women.

It is also instructive to compare our results with those obtained by Behrman et al. (1995) and Brynin and Francesconi (2004), who apply the following mating equation:

$$e_w = d_1 e_h + \mathbf{x}_h^e \beta_h^e + \phi + \omega_w^e \qquad (10.18)$$

where $\phi$ is an unobservable component of human capital to be estimated consistently from the post-regression residuals $\hat{e}_w - e_w$. They find that $\phi$ impacts positively on wages. Our results show that part of this unobservable variable depends upon wage, since marital sorting is multidimensional and education is not the only variable that prospective spouses may consider. If our interpretation holds true, then the expected return of unobservable human capital to wages should be lower than Behrman's estimates.

Lastly, an obvious way to enhance the present econometric exercise to take into account how mating coefficients change across the distribution of personal traits would be to employ a technique of simultaneous quantile regressions, as indicated by Chernozhukov and Hansen (2006) and Kim and Muller (2004): although still in its infancy, this approach looks extremely promising for modelling complex non-linear links like those observed in the marriage market.

# 10A. APPENDIX

## 10A.1. Statistical

### 10A.1.1. Descriptive statistics

*Table 10A.1. Wife's education and job status*

| | Wife's working status | | | | | |
|---|---|---|---|---|---|---|
| | Working | | Not working | | Total | |
| Wife's education | Row % | Col % | Row % | Col % | Row % | Col % |
| No schooling | 9.8 | 0.6 | 90.2 | 3.5 | 100.0 | 2.4 |
| Elementary | 17.3 | 9.9 | 82.7 | 30.2 | 100.0 | 22.3 |
| Secondary | 30.4 | 25.9 | 69.6 | 37.9 | 100.0 | 33.2 |
| High school | 54.8 | 46.8 | 45.2 | 24.7 | 100.0 | 33.3 |
| BA/Postgrad. | 74.0 | 16.8 | 26.0 | 3.8 | 100.0 | 8.9 |
| Total | 39.0 | 100.0 | 61.0 | 100.0 | 100.0 | 100.0 |

*Table 10A.2. Husband's characteristics and wife's job status*

| | Wife's working status | | | | | |
|---|---|---|---|---|---|---|
| | Working | | Not working | | Total | |
| | Row % | Col % | Row % | Col % | Row % | Col % |
| **Husband's education** | | | | | | |
| No schooling | 15.6 | 0.7 | 84.4 | 2.4 | 100.0 | 1.7 |
| Elementary | 20.5 | 10.2 | 79.5 | 25.3 | 100.0 | 19.4 |
| Secondary | 35.0 | 31.6 | 65.0 | 37.4 | 100.0 | 35.2 |
| High school | 48.7 | 42.2 | 51.3 | 28.4 | 100.0 | 33.8 |
| BA/Postgrad. | 60.1 | 15.3 | 39.9 | 6.5 | 100.0 | 9.9 |
| Total | 39.0 | 100.0 | 61.0 | 100.0 | 100.0 | 100.0 |
| **Quartiles of husband's wage** | | | | | | |
| No schooling | 36.2 | 23.2 | 63.8 | 26.1 | 100.0 | 25.0 |
| Elementary | 41.8 | 26.8 | 58.2 | 23.9 | 100.0 | 25.0 |
| Secondary | 34.6 | 22.3 | 65.4 | 26.9 | 100.0 | 25.1 |
| High school | 43.3 | 27.7 | 56.7 | 23.1 | 100.0 | 24.9 |
| BA/Postgrad. | 39.0 | 100.0 | 61.0 | 100.0 | 100.0 | 100.0 |
| Total | 39.0 | 100.0 | 61.0 | 100.0 | 100.0 | 100.0 |

*Note*: The table contains (1) percent distribution of job status of wives according to the level of completed education of their husband and (2) percent distribution of job status of wives according to the quantiles of their husband's income. All values are calculated over the working life cycle.

*Table 10A.3. Husband's and wife's educational sorting*

| | Husband's education | | | | | | |
|---|---|---|---|---|---|---|---|
| | No Schooling | Elementary | Secondary | High school | BA/Post-grad. | Total | **N** |
| **Wife's education** | | | | | | | |
| No schooling | 32.3 | 48.5 | 16.0 | 3.0 | 0.2 | 100.0 | 468 |
| Elementary | 3.2 | 57.7 | 30.5 | 8.2 | 0.4 | 100.0 | 4,430 |
| Secondary | 0.7 | 12.9 | 56.4 | 28.2 | 1.9 | 100.0 | 6,602 |
| High school | 0.0 | 3.3 | 26.2 | 57.3 | 13.1 | 100.0 | 6,627 |
| BA/Postgrad. | 0.0 | 0.3 | 6.0 | 39.2 | 54.5 | 100.0 | 1,762 |
| **N** | 339 | 3,861 | 6,994 | 6,724 | 1,971 | 19,889 | |

*Note*: The cells of the table represent the fraction of the married couple sharing a given combination of schooling. Along the main diagonal is the percent of married couples sharing the same schooling level, that is, those which are perfectly matched.

*Table 10A.4. Schooling transitions over the lifetime*

| | **Husbands** | | | |
|---|---|---|---|---|
| **Wives** | None | One | Two | Total |
| None | 97.66 | 0.95 | 0.00 | 98.61 |
| One | 0.87 | 0.49 | 0.01 | 1.37 |
| Two | 0.01 | 0.01 | 0.00 | 0.02 |
| **Total** | 98.54 | 1.45 | 0.01 | 100.00 |

*Note*: Every cell of the table contains the total percentage of lifetime transitions toward higher levels of schooling. The percentage of people who experienced schooling transition when married is extremely low.

## 10A.1.2. Correlations

*Table 10A.5. Correlations – censored sample*

| Variables | Wife's schooling | Husband's schooling | Wife's wage | Husband's wage |
|---|---|---|---|---|
| Wife's schooling | 1.000 | | | |
| Husband's schooling | 0.645 | 1.000 | | |
| Wife's wage | 0.382 | 0.306 | 1.000 | |
| Husband's wage | 0.306 | 0.388 | 0.412 | 1.000 |

*Table 10A.6. Correlations – uncensored sample*

| Variables | Wife's schooling | Husband's schooling | Wife's wage | Husband's wage |
|---|---|---|---|---|
| Wife's schooling | 1.000 | | | |
| Husband's schooling | 0.630 | 1.000 | | |
| Wife's wage | 0.225 | 0.178 | 1.000 | |
| Husband's wage | 0.270 | 0.361 | 0.281 | 1.000 |

## 10A.2. Estimation Results

### 10A.2.1. Heckman selection model

*Table 10A.7. Wives*

| | Coefficients | | | Stats | |
|---|---|---|---|---|---|
| Variables | $\beta$ | s.e. | Sig. | Mean | $\sigma$ |
| **Dependent variable: wife's wage** | | | | | |
| Elementary | 0.004 | 0.074 | | 0.217 | 0.412 |
| Secondary | 0.004 | 0.075 | | 0.332 | 0.471 |
| High school | –0.060 | 0.078 | | 0.338 | 0.473 |
| Bachelor | 0.109 | 0.080 | | 0.089 | 0.284 |
| Postgraduate | 0.068 | 0.134 | | 0.002 | 0.044 |
| Expertise | 0.017 | 0.003 | *** | 24.392 | 10.825 |
| Expertise (Square)/100 | –0.014 | 0.005 | ** | 7.121 | 5.629 |
| White collar/Teacher | 0.227 | 0.015 | *** | 0.230 | 0.421 |
| Executive | 0.290 | 0.029 | *** | 0.016 | 0.125 |
| Freelancer | 0.388 | 0.050 | *** | 0.005 | 0.073 |
| Entrepreneur | 0.812 | 0.139 | *** | 0.014 | 0.119 |
| Self-employed | 0.114 | 0.094 | | 0.080 | 0.272 |
| Manufacturing | 0.519 | 0.029 | *** | 0.099 | 0.298 |
| Marketing/Catering | 0.476 | 0.031 | *** | 0.088 | 0.283 |
| Transportation/Communications | 0.542 | 0.047 | *** | 0.008 | 0.088 |
| Finance | 0.652 | 0.039 | *** | 0.016 | 0.125 |
| Public administration/Service | 0.580 | 0.029 | *** | 0.243 | 0.429 |
| Outside workforce | 0.021 | 0.041 | | 0.524 | 0.499 |
| Constant | 5.361 | 0.084 | *** | | |
| **Selection Equation** | | | | | |
| Age | 0.110 | 0.009 | *** | 40.671 | 8.982 |
| Age (Square)/100 | –0.135 | 0.011 | *** | 17.348 | 7.341 |
| Elementary | 0.246 | 0.084 | ** | 0.217 | 0.412 |
| Secondary | 0.598 | 0.083 | *** | 0.332 | 0.471 |
| High school | 1.173 | 0.083 | *** | 0.338 | 0.473 |
| Bachelor | 1.693 | 0.088 | *** | 0.089 | 0.284 |
| Postgraduate | 1.576 | 0.224 | *** | 0.002 | 0.044 |
| Number of children | –0.116 | 0.009 | *** | 1.679 | 1.079 |
| Husband's wage | 0.051 | 0.003 | *** | 4.323 | 2.767 |
| Constant | –3.274 | 0.188 | *** | | |
| tanh($\rho$) Constant | –1.184 | 0.035 | *** | | |
| ln($\sigma$) Constant | –0.520 | 0.014 | *** | | |
| **Statistics** | | | | | |
| Subjects | 19,888 | | | | |

*Notes*:
$p$-value thresholds: * < 5%, ** < 1%, *** < 0.1%.
Omitted modality for education: no schooling.
Omitted modality for professional qualification: worker.
Omitted modality for sector: agriculture.

## 10A.2.2. Interaction wage–schooling

*Table 10A.8. Husbands: interaction schooling–wage*

| | Coefficients | | | Stats | | |
|---|---|---|---|---|---|---|
| Variables | $\beta$ | s.e. | Sig. | $\beta$ | s.e. | Sig. |
| Wife's schooling | 0.560 | 0.011 | *** | 0.613 | 0.021 | *** |
| Schooling * 2nd income quartile | 0.002 | 0.003 | | –0.003 | 0.005 | |
| Schooling * 3rd income quartile | –0.011 | 0.003 | *** | 0.004 | 0.004 | |
| Schooling * 4th income quartile | 0.030 | 0.002 | *** | 0.029 | 0.004 | *** |
| Constant | 1.022 | 0.026 | *** | 0.892 | 0.050 | *** |
| **Statistics** | | | | | | |
| Subjects | 19,888 | | | 7,754 | | |
| $R^2$ | 0.403 | | | 0.427 | | |

*Notes*:
$p$-value thresholds: * < 5%, ** < 1%, *** < 0.1%.
Dependent variable: Husbands' years of completed schooling.
Years of schooling are in log units.

*Table 10A.9. Wives: interaction schooling–wage*

| | Coefficients | | | Stats | | |
|---|---|---|---|---|---|---|
| Variables | $\beta$ | s.e. | Sig. | $\beta$ | s.e. | Sig. |
| Husbands' schooling | 0.636 | 0.013 | *** | 0.589 | 0.021 | *** |
| Schooling * 2nd income quartile | 0.023 | 0.004 | *** | 0.016 | 0.004 | *** |
| Schooling * 3rd income quartile | 0.034 | 0.003 | *** | 0.029 | 0.004 | *** |
| Schooling * 4th income quartile | 0.036 | 0.004 | *** | 0.033 | 0.005 | *** |
| Constant | 0.749 | 0.028 | *** | 0.990 | 0.048 | *** |
| **Statistics** | | | | | | |
| Subjects | 19,888 | | | 7,754 | | |
| $R^2$ | 0.401 | | | 0.426 | | |

*Notes*:
$p$-value thresholds: * < 5%, ** < 1%, *** < 0.1%.
Dependent variable: Wives' years of completed schooling.
Years of schooling are in log units.

*Table 10A.10. Full structural estimation for husbands – 3SLS estimator*

| | Linear specification | | | | | | Quadratic specification | | | | | |
|---|---|---|---|---|---|---|---|---|---|---|---|---|
| | Cens. sample | | | Uncens. sample | | | Cens. sample | | | Uncens. sample | | |
| | $\beta$ | s.e. | Sig. | $\beta$ | s.e. | Sig. | $\beta$ | s.e. | Sig. | $\beta$ | s.e. | Sig. |
| **Mating equation for schooling** | | | | | | | | | | | | |
| Dependent variable: wife's schooling | | | | | | | | | | | | |
| Husband's schooling | 0.556 | 0.014 | *** | 0.633 | 0.010 | *** | 0.408 | 0.042 | *** | 0.371 | 0.026 | *** |
| Husband's wage | 0.155 | 0.019 | *** | 0.131 | 0.015 | *** | 0.134 | 0.020 | *** | 0.071 | 0.016 | *** |
| Husband's schooling (square) | | | | | | | 0.037 | 0.010 | *** | 0.075 | 0.007 | *** |
| Constant | 0.172 | 0.095 | | 0.024 | 0.076 | | 0.430 | 0.122 | *** | 0.572 | 0.093 | *** |
| **Mating equation for wage** | | | | | | | | | | | | |
| Dependent variable: wife's wage | | | | | | | | | | | | |
| Husband's wage | 1.050 | 0.073 | *** | 0.525 | 0.038 | *** | 1.125 | 0.070 | *** | 0.632 | 0.036 | *** |
| Husband's schooling | 0.027 | 0.030 | | –0.028 | 0.012 | * | –0.431 | 0.074 | *** | –0.378 | 0.027 | *** |
| Husband's schooling (square) | | | | | | | 0.107 | 0.018 | *** | 0.092 | 0.008 | *** |
| Constant | 0.178 | 0.320 | | 3.089 | 0.171 | *** | 0.308 | 0.338 | | 2.877 | 0.173 | *** |
| **Wage equation** | | | | | | | | | | | | |
| Dependent variable: husband's wage | | | | | | | | | | | | |
| Husband's schooling | 0.313 | 0.017 | *** | 0.246 | 0.010 | *** | 0.318 | 0.017 | *** | 0.262 | 0.010 | *** |
| Constant | 4.588 | 0.053 | *** | 4.777 | 0.033 | *** | 4.568 | 0.053 | *** | 4.734 | 0.033 | *** |
| Control for qualification | Yes | | | Yes | | | Yes | | | Yes | | |
| Control for job sector | Yes | | | Yes | | | Yes | | | Yes | | |
| Control for expertise | Yes | | | Yes | | | Yes | | | Yes | | |
| Control for wealth | Yes | | | Yes | | | Yes | | | Yes | | |
| Control for non-labour income | Yes | | | Yes | | | Yes | | | Yes | | |
| **Statistics** | | | | | | | | | | | | |
| Subjects | 6,093 | | | 13,915 | | | 6,093 | | | 13,915 | | |
| $R^2$ 1st equation | 0.418 | | | 0.400 | | | 0.422 | | | 0.409 | | |
| $R^2$ 2nd equation | 0.064 | | | –0.012 | | | 0.019 | | | –0.092 | | |
| $R^2$ 3rd equation | 0.376 | | | 0.363 | | | 0.376 | | | 0.362 | | |

*Note*: *p*-value thresholds: * <5%, ** < 1%, *** < 0.1%.

*Table 10A.11. Full structural estimation for young husbands – 3SLS estimator*

| | Linear specification | | | | | | Quadratic Specification | | | | | |
|---|---|---|---|---|---|---|---|---|---|---|---|---|
| | Cens. sample | | | Uncens. sample | | | Cens. sample | | | Uncens. sample | | |
| | $\beta$ | s.e. | Sig. | $\beta$ | s.e. | Sig. | $\beta$ | s.e. | Sig. | $\beta$ | s.e. | Sig. |
| **Mating equation for schooling** | | | | | | | | | | | | |
| Dependent variable: wife's schooling | | | | | | | | | | | | |
| Husband's schooling | 0.521 | 0.028 | *** | 0.472 | 0.019 | *** | 1.165 | 0.167 | *** | 0.261 | 0.051 | *** |
| Husband's wage | 0.073 | 0.039 | | 0.218 | 0.030 | *** | 0.078 | 0.039 | * | 0.185 | 0.032 | *** |
| Husband's schooling (square) | –0.136 | 0.036 | *** | 0.059 | 0.013 | *** | | | | | | |
| Constant | 0.786 | 0.196 | *** | –0.030 | 0.157 | | 0.007 | 0.310 | | 0.332 | 0.182 | |
| **Mating equation for wage** | | | | | | | | | | | | |
| Dependent variable: wife's wage | | | | | | | | | | | | |
| Husband's wage | 1.127 | 0.214 | *** | 0.166 | 0.108 | | 1.209 | 0.206 | *** | 0.243 | 0.102 | * |
| Husband's schooling | 0.113 | 0.080 | | 0.020 | 0.030 | | –0.935 | 0.394 | * | –0.435 | 0.074 | *** |
| Husband's schooling (square) | | | | | | | 0.221 | 0.086 | ** | 0.123 | 0.020 | *** |
| Constant | –0.863 | 0.886 | | 4.666 | 0.488 | *** | –0.000 | 1.095 | | 4.660 | 0.481 | *** |
| **Wage equation** | | | | | | | | | | | | |
| Dependent variable: husband's wage | | | | | | | | | | | | |
| Husband's schooling | 0.290 | 0.048 | *** | 0.224 | 0.029 | *** | 0.293 | 0.048 | *** | 0.230 | 0.029 | *** |
| Constant | 4.679 | 0.159 | *** | 5.037 | 0.092 | *** | 4.659 | 0.159 | *** | 4.990 | 0.093 | *** |
| Control for qualification | Yes | | | Yes | | | Yes | | | Yes | | |
| Control for job sector | Yes | | | Yes | | | Yes | | | Yes | | |
| Control for expertise | Yes | | | Yes | | | Yes | | | Yes | | |
| Control for wealth | Yes | | | Yes | | | Yes | | | Yes | | |
| Control for non-labour income | Yes | | | Yes | | | Yes | | | Yes | | |
| **Statistics** | | | | | | | | | | | | |
| Subjects | 1,278 | | | 2,852 | | | 1,278 | | | 2,852 | | |
| $R^2$ 1st equation | 0.337 | | | 0.314 | | | 0.345 | | | 0.328 | | |
| $R^2$ 2nd equation | –0.014 | | | 0.033 | | | –0.058 | | | 0.031 | | |
| $R^2$ 3rd equation | 0.275 | | | 0.269 | | | 0.275 | | | 0.269 | | |

*Note*: $p$-value thresholds: * <5%, ** < 1%, *** < 0.1%.

*Table 10A.12. Full structural estimation for wives – 3SLS estimator*

| | **Linear specification** | | | | | | **Quadratic Specification** | | | | | |
|---|---|---|---|---|---|---|---|---|---|---|---|---|
| | Cens. sample | | | Uncens. sample | | | Cens. sample | | | Uncens. sample | | |
| | $\beta$ | s.e. | Sig. | $\beta$ | s.e. | Sig. | $\beta$ | s.e. | Sig. | $\beta$ | s.e. | Sig. |
| **Mating equation for schooling** | | | | | | | | | | | | |
| Dependent variable: husband's schooling | | | | | | | | | | | | |
| Wife's schooling | 0.565 | 0.014 | *** | 0.550 | 0.006 | *** | 0.417 | 0.044 | *** | 0.248 | 0.020 | *** |
| Wife's wage | 0.149 | 0.015 | *** | 0.164 | 0.011 | *** | 0.133 | 0.016 | *** | 0.107 | 0.011 | *** |
| Wife's schooling (square) | | | | | | | 0.037 | 0.010 | *** | 0.086 | 0.005 | *** |
| Constant | 0.174 | 0.070 | * | 0.125 | 0.061 | * | 0.402 | 0.094 | *** | 0.673 | 0.070 | *** |
| **Mating equation for wage** | | | | | | | | | | | | |
| Dependent variable: husband's wage | | | | | | | | | | | | |
| Wife's wage | 0.642 | 0.032 | *** | 0.786 | 0.029 | *** | 0.606 | 0.032 | *** | 0.718 | 0.028 | *** |
| Wife's schooling | 0.103 | 0.021 | *** | 0.304 | 0.009 | *** | –0.068 | 0.062 | | 0.006 | 0.027 | |
| Wife's schooling (square) | | | | | | | 0.044 | 0.015 | ** | 0.087 | 0.007 | *** |
| Constant | 2.169 | 0.146 | *** | 0.884 | 0.166 | *** | 2.508 | 0.165 | *** | 1.489 | 0.167 | *** |
| **Wage equation** | | | | | | | | | | | | |
| Dependent variable: wife's wage | | | | | | | | | | | | |
| Wife's schooling | –0.034 | 0.036 | | –0.090 | 0.010 | *** | –0.001 | 0.038 | | –0.056 | 0.011 | *** |
| Constant | 5.399 | 0.127 | *** | 5.239 | 0.043 | *** | 5.250 | 0.134 | *** | 5.072 | 0.045 | *** |
| Control for inverse Mills ratio | Yes | | | Yes | | | Yes | | | Yes | | |
| Control for qualification | Yes | | | Yes | | | Yes | | | Yes | | |
| Control for job sector | Yes | | | Yes | | | Yes | | | Yes | | |
| Control for expertise | Yes | | | Yes | | | Yes | | | Yes | | |
| Control for wealth | Yes | | | Yes | | | Yes | | | Yes | | |
| Control for non-labour income | Yes | | | Yes | | | Yes | | | Yes | | |
| **Statistics** | | | | | | | | | | | | |
| Subjects | 6,216 | | | 14,173 | | | 6,216 | | | 14,173 | | |
| $R^2$ 1st equation | 0.412 | | | 0.400 | | | 0.418 | | | 0.417 | | |
| $R^2$ 2nd equation | 0.079 | | | 0.034 | | | 0.110 | | | 0.073 | | |
| $R^2$ 3rd equation | 0.367 | | | 0.436 | | | 0.368 | | | 0.438 | | |

*Note*: $p$-value thresholds: * <5%, ** < 1%, *** < 0.1%.

*Table 10A.13. Full structural estimation for young wives – 3SLS estimator*

| | **Linear specification** | | | | | | **Quadratic Specification** | | | | | |
|---|---|---|---|---|---|---|---|---|---|---|---|---|
| | Cens. sample | | | Uncens. sample | | | Cens. sample | | | Uncens. sample | | |
| | $\beta$ | s.e. | Sig. | $\beta$ | s.e. | Sig. | $\beta$ | s.e. | Sig. | $\beta$ | s.e. | Sig. |
| **Mating equation for schooling** | | | | | | | | | | | | |
| Dependent variable: husband's schooling | | | | | | | | | | | | |
| Wife's schooling | 0.527 | 0.029 | *** | 0.578 | 0.016 | *** | 0.892 | 0.179 | *** | 0.402 | 0.059 | *** |
| Wife's wage | 0.126 | 0.027 | *** | 0.119 | 0.020 | *** | 0.124 | 0.027 | *** | 0.099 | 0.021 | *** |
| Wife's schooling (square) | | | | | | | –0.076 | 0.038 | * | 0.045 | 0.015 | ** |
| Constant | 0.423 | 0.130 | ** | 0.318 | 0.117 | ** | 0.002 | 0.264 | | 0.592 | 0.146 | *** |
| **Mating equation for wage** | | | | | | | | | | | | |
| Dependent variable: husband's wage | | | | | | | | | | | | |
| Wife's wage | 0.297 | 0.060 | *** | 0.228 | 0.070 | ** | 0.305 | 0.060 | *** | 0.173 | 0.069 | * |
| Wife's schooling | 0.137 | 0.046 | ** | 0.342 | 0.028 | *** | –0.189 | 0.258 | | 0.049 | 0.086 | |
| Wife's schooling (square) | | | | | | | 0.069 | 0.054 | | 0.074 | 0.020 | *** |
| Constant | 3.736 | 0.275 | *** | 3.845 | 0.421 | *** | 4.080 | 0.433 | *** | 4.419 | 0.440 | *** |
| **Wage Equation** | | | | | | | | | | | | |
| Dependent variable: husband's wage | | | | | | | | | | | | |
| Wife's schooling | 0.055 | 0.126 | | –0.291 | 0.043 | *** | 0.049 | 0.126 | | –0.275 | 0.043 | *** |
| Constant | 4.695 | 0.447 | *** | 5.420 | 0.158 | *** | 4.717 | 0.448 | *** | 5.355 | 0.159 | *** |
| Control for inverse Mills ratio | Yes | | | Yes | | | Yes | | | Yes | | |
| Control for qualification | Yes | | | Yes | | | Yes | | | Yes | | |
| Control for job sector | Yes | | | Yes | | | Yes | | | Yes | | |
| Control for expertise | Yes | | | Yes | | | Yes | | | Yes | | |
| Control for wealth | Yes | | | Yes | | | Yes | | | Yes | | |
| Control for non-labour income | Yes | | | Yes | | | Yes | | | Yes | | |
| **Statistics** | | | | | | | | | | | | |
| Subjects | 1,325 | | | 2,940 | | | 1,325 | | | 2,940 | | |
| $R^2$ 1st equation | 0.306 | | | 0.322 | | | 0.310 | | | 0.327 | | |
| $R^2$ 2nd equation | 0.151 | | | 0.102 | | | 0.147 | | | 0.109 | | |
| $R^2$ 3rd equation | 0.284 | | | 0.431 | | | 0.284 | | | 0.431 | | |

*Note*: $p$-value thresholds: * <5%, ** < 1%, *** < 0.1%.

*Table 10A.14. Full structural estimation for husbands – SUR estimator*

| | Linear specification | | | | | | Quadratic Specification | | | | | |
|---|---|---|---|---|---|---|---|---|---|---|---|---|
| | Cens. sample | | | Uncens. sample | | | Cens. sample | | | Uncens. sample | | |
| | $\beta$ | s.e. | Sig. | $\beta$ | s.e. | Sig. | $\beta$ | s.e. | Sig. | $\beta$ | s.e. | Sig. |
| **Mating equation for schooling** | | | | | | | | | | | | |
| Dependent variable: wife's schooling | | | | | | | | | | | | |
| Husband's schooling | 0.585 | 0.011 | *** | 0.653 | 0.008 | *** | 0.422 | 0.042 | *** | 0.374 | 0.025 | *** |
| Husband's wage | 0.099 | 0.009 | *** | 0.086 | 0.007 | *** | 0.091 | 0.009 | *** | 0.062 | 0.007 | *** |
| Husband's schooling (square) | | | | | | | 0.039 | 0.010 | *** | 0.076 | 0.006 | *** |
| Constant | 0.436 | 0.049 | *** | 0.249 | 0.040 | *** | 0.646 | 0.070 | *** | 0.618 | 0.049 | *** |
| **Mating equation for wage** | | | | | | | | | | | | |
| Dependent variable: wife's wage | | | | | | | | | | | | |
| Husband's wage | 0.459 | 0.017 | *** | 0.189 | 0.008 | *** | 0.453 | 0.017 | *** | 0.184 | 0.008 | *** |
| Husband's schooling | 0.191 | 0.021 | *** | 0.042 | 0.009 | *** | –0.193 | 0.073 | ** | –0.245 | 0.027 | *** |
| Husband's schooling (square) | | | | | | | 0.094 | 0.017 | *** | 0.080 | 0.007 | *** |
| Constant | 2.705 | 0.123 | *** | 4.609 | 0.055 | *** | 3.113 | 0.144 | *** | 4.864 | 0.059 | *** |
| **Wage equation** | | | | | | | | | | | | |
| Dependent variable: husband's wage | | | | | | | | | | | | |
| Husband's schooling | 0.311 | 0.017 | *** | 0.233 | 0.010 | *** | 0.312 | 0.017 | *** | 0.235 | 0.010 | *** |
| Constant | 4.605 | 0.054 | *** | 4.806 | 0.034 | *** | 4.600 | 0.054 | *** | 4.797 | 0.034 | *** |
| Control for qualification | Yes | | | Yes | | | Yes | | | Yes | | |
| Control for job sector | Yes | | | Yes | | | Yes | | | Yes | | |
| Control for expertise | Yes | | | Yes | | | Yes | | | Yes | | |
| Control for wealth | Yes | | | Yes | | | Yes | | | Yes | | |
| Control for non-labour income | Yes | | | Yes | | | Yes | | | Yes | | |
| **Statistics** | | | | | | | | | | | | |
| Subjects | 6,093 | | | 13,915 | | | 6,093 | | | 13,915 | | |
| $R^2$ 1st equation | 0.424 | | | 0.403 | | | 0.426 | | | 0.409 | | |
| $R^2$ 2nd equation | 0.235 | | | 0.104 | | | 0.238 | | | 0.111 | | |
| $R^2$ 3rd equation | 0.377 | | | 0.363 | | | 0.377 | | | 0.363 | | |

*Note*: *p*-value thresholds: * <5%, ** < 1%, *** < 0.1%.

*Table 10A.15. Full structural estimation for young husbands – SUR estimator*

| | Linear specification | | | | | | Quadratic Specification | | | | | |
|---|---|---|---|---|---|---|---|---|---|---|---|---|
| | Cens. sample | | | Uncens. sample | | | Cens. sample | | | Uncens. sample | | |
| | $\beta$ | s.e. | Sig. | $\beta$ | s.e. | Sig. | $\beta$ | s.e. | Sig. | $\beta$ | s.e. | Sig. |
| **Mating equation for schooling** | | | | | | | | | | | | |
| Dependent variable: wife's schooling | | | | | | | | | | | | |
| Husband's schooling | 0.536 | 0.023 | *** | 0.515 | 0.016 | *** | 1.175 | 0.166 | *** | 0.270 | 0.050 | *** |
| Husband's wage | 0.040 | 0.017 | * | 0.106 | 0.013 | *** | 0.048 | 0.017 | ** | 0.091 | 0.013 | *** |
| Husband's schooling (square) | | | | | | | –0.135 | 0.035 | *** | 0.066 | 0.013 | *** |
| Constant | 0.946 | 0.100 | *** | 0.536 | 0.076 | *** | 0.156 | 0.225 | | 0.828 | 0.092 | *** |
| **Mating equation for wage** | | | | | | | | | | | | |
| Dependent variable: wife's wage | | | | | | | | | | | | |
| Husband's wage | 0.438 | 0.043 | *** | 0.097 | 0.021 | *** | 0.434 | 0.043 | *** | 0.090 | 0.021 | *** |
| Husband's schooling | 0.272 | 0.061 | *** | 0.031 | 0.025 | | –0.744 | 0.382 | | –0.408 | 0.074 | *** |
| Husband's schooling (square) | | | | | | | 0.218 | 0.081 | ** | 0.122 | 0.019 | *** |
| Constant | 1.870 | 0.336 | *** | 4.972 | 0.130 | *** | 3.056 | 0.561 | *** | 5.343 | 0.142 | *** |
| **Wage equation** | | | | | | | | | | | | |
| Dependent variable: husband's wage | | | | | | | | | | | | |
| Husband's schooling | 0.306 | 0.049 | *** | 0.235 | 0.030 | *** | 0.305 | 0.049 | *** | 0.237 | 0.030 | *** |
| Constant | 4.653 | 0.164 | *** | 5.004 | 0.094 | *** | 4.655 | 0.164 | *** | 4.996 | 0.094 | *** |
| Control for qualification | Yes | | | Yes | | | Yes | | | Yes | | |
| Control for job sector | Yes | | | Yes | | | Yes | | | Yes | | |
| Control for expertise | Yes | | | Yes | | | Yes | | | Yes | | |
| Control for wealth | Yes | | | Yes | | | Yes | | | Yes | | |
| Control for non-labour income | Yes | | | Yes | | | Yes | | | Yes | | |
| **Statistics** | | | | | | | | | | | | |
| Subjects | 1,278 | | | 2,852 | | | 1,278 | | | 2,852 | | |
| $R^2$ 1st equation | 0.340 | | | 0.338 | | | 0.348 | | | 0.344 | | |
| $R^2$ 2nd equation | 0.166 | | | 0.036 | | | 0.170 | | | 0.050 | | |
| $R^2$ 3rd equation | 0.276 | | | 0.270 | | | 0.276 | | | 0.270 | | |

*Note*: *p*-value thresholds: * <5%, ** < 1%, *** < 0.1%.

## 10A.3. Estimate Comparison

*Table 10A.16. Husbands*

| Estimator | 3SLS | | | | SUR | | | |
|---|---|---|---|---|---|---|---|---|
| Sample | Censored | | Uncensored | | Censored | | Uncensored | |
| Selection | (C) | (Y) | (C) | (Y) | (C) | (Y) | (C) | (Y) |
| **Mating equation for schooling** | | | | | | | | |
| Husband's schooling | 0.590 | 0.480 | 0.665 | 0.494 | 0.608 | 0.492 | 0.663 | 0.537 |
| Husband's wage | 0.106 | 0.073 | 0.033 | 0.165 | 0.076 | 0.049 | 0.037 | 0.084 |
| **Mating equation for wage** | | | | | | | | |
| Dependent variable: wife's wage | | | | | | | | |
| Husband's wage | 1.027 | 0.844 | 0.645 | 0.135 | 0.424 | 0.397 | 0.190 | 0.086 |
| Husband's schooling | 0.045 | 0.148 | –0.016 | 0.046 | 0.231 | 0.258 | 0.105 | 0.057 |
| **Wage equation** | | | | | | | | |
| Dependent variable: husband's wage | | | | | | | | |
| Husband's schooling | 0.400 | 0.307 | 0.404 | 0.349 | 0.383 | 0.315 | 0.361 | 0.364 |

*Notes*: C = complete sample, Y = young couples sample.

*Table 10A.17. Wives*

| | 3SLS | | | | SUR | | | |
|---|---|---|---|---|---|---|---|---|
| | Censored | | Uncensored | | Censored | | Uncensored | |
| | (C) | (Y) | (C) | (Y) | (C) | (Y) | (C) | (Y) |
| **Mating equation for schooling** | | | | | | | | |
| Wife's schooling | 0.562 | 0.499 | 0.611 | 0.560 | 0.603 | 0.538 | 0.618 | 0.564 |
| Wife's wage | 0.145 | 0.145 | 0.111 | 0.136 | 0.083 | 0.076 | 0.086 | 0.087 |
| **Mating equation for wage** | | | | | | | | |
| Dependent variable: wife's wage | | | | | | | | |
| Wife's wage | 0.681 | 0.353 | 0.838 | 0.191 | 0.327 | 0.199 | 0.402 | 0.166 |
| Wife's schooling | 0.114 | 0.146 | 0.410 | 0.437 | 0.241 | 0.191 | 0.397 | 0.437 |
| **Wage equation** | | | | | | | | |
| Dependent variable: husband's wage | | | | | | | | |
| Wife's schooling | –0.013 | 0.205 | –0.136 | –0.130 | 0.125 | 0.287 | –0.035 | –0.114 |

*Notes*: C = complete sample, Y = young couples sample.

## 10A.4. Elasticity of Substitution

*Table 10A.18. Schooling: complete sample*

| Variables | Wives | | Husbands | |
|---|---|---|---|---|
| | (1) | (2) | (1) | (2) |
| $\lambda$ | 0.529 *** | 0.536 *** | 0.749 *** | 0.702 *** |
| | 0.081) | (0.067) | (0.038) | (0.026) |
| $\theta$ | 0.668 *** | 0.727 *** | 0.963 *** | 0.968 *** |
| | (0.121) | (0.092) | (0.019) | (0.010) |
| $\eta$ | –0.617 *** | –0.444 *** | 0.423 ** | 0.602 *** |
| | (0.157) | (0.128) | (0.160) | (0.097) |
| **Elasticity $\sigma$** | | | | |
| Coefficient | 0.619 | 0.693 | 1.734 | 2.514 |
| Upper bound | 0.685 | 0.760 | 2.399 | 3.331 |
| Lower bound | 0.564 | 0.636 | 1.357 | 2.019 |
| $p$-value for $H_0 : \eta < 0$ | 1.000 | 1.000 | 0.004 | 0.000 |
| $N$ | 19,887 | 19,887 | 19,887 | 19,887 |
| $R^2$ | 0.917 | 0.917 | 0.921 | 0.920 |

*Notes*:
Dependent variable: Years of completed schooling. Standard errors in parentheses.
$p$-value thresholds: * < 5%, ** < 1%, *** < 0:1%.
(1) Non-linear Least Squares (NLS).
(2) Non-linear Seemingly Unrelated Estimate (NLSUR).

*Table 10A.19. Schooling: young couple sample*

| Variables | Wives | | Husbands | |
|---|---|---|---|---|
| | (1) | (2) | (1) | (2) |
| $\lambda$ | 0.664 *** | 0.658 *** | 0.759 *** | 0.727 *** |
| | (0.098) | (0.075) | (0.049) | (0.035) |
| $\theta$ | 0.858 *** | 0.886 *** | 0.968 *** | 0.973 *** |
| | (0.096) | (0.063) | (0.025) | (0.014) |
| $\eta$ | –0.155 | 0.002 | 0.448 | 0.630 *** |
| | (0.227) | (0.170) | (0.255) | (0.163) |
| **Elasticity $\sigma$** | | | | |
| Coefficient | 0.866 | 1.002 | 1.810 | 2.700 |
| Upper bound | 1.077 | 1.208 | 3.367 | 4.816 |
| Lower bound | 0.724 | 0.856 | 1.238 | 1.876 |
| $p$-value for $H_0 : \eta < 0$ | 0.753 | 0.496 | 0.040 | 0.000 |
| $N$ | 3,966 | 3,966 | 3,966 | 3,966 |
| $R^2$ | 0.931 | 0.931 | 0.933 | 0.932 |

*Notes*:
Dependent variable: Years of completed schooling. Standard errors in parentheses.
$p$-value thresholds: * < 5%, ** < 1%, *** < 0:1%.
(1) Non-linear Least Squares (NLS).
(2) Non-linear Seemingly Unrelated Estimate (NLSUR).

*Table 10A.20. Wage: complete sample*

| Variables | Wives (1) | Wives (2) | Husbands (1) | Husbands (2) |
|---|---|---|---|---|
| $\lambda$ | 6.120 *** | 6.152 *** | 27.350 *** | 24.830 *** |
| | (1.524) | (1.430) | (3.882) | (3.608) |
| $\theta$ | 0.331 ** | 0.372 ** | 0.939 *** | 0.930 *** |
| | (0.126) | (0.120) | (0.046) | (0.047) |
| $\eta$ | –0.515 *** | –0.421 ** | 0.577 * | 0.604 ** |
| | (0.155) | (0.138) | (0.230) | (0.205) |
| **Elasticity $\sigma$** | | | | |
| Coefficient | 0.660 | 0.704 | 2.364 | 2.528 |
| Upper bound | 0.735 | 0.780 | 5.181 | 5.253 |
| Lower bound | 0.599 | 0.641 | 1.532 | 1.665 |
| $p$-value for $H_0 : \eta < 0$ | 1.000 | 0.999 | 0.006 | 0.002 |
| $N$ | 19,887 | 19,887 | 19,887 | 19,887 |
| $R^2$ | 0.762 | 0.761 | 0.654 | 0.653 |

*Notes*:
Dependent variable: Years of completed schooling. Standard errors in parentheses.
$p$-value thresholds: * < 5%, ** < 1%, *** < 0:1%.
(1) Non-linear Least Squares (NLS).
(2) Non-linear Seemingly Unrelated Estimate (NLSUR).

*Table 10A.21. Wage: young couple sample*

| Variables | Wives (1) | Wives (2) | Husbands (1) | Husbands (2) |
|---|---|---|---|---|
| $\lambda$ | 26.627 *** | 26.525 *** | 28.884 *** | 27.251 *** |
| | (0.291) | (0.256) | (3.961) | (3.472) |
| $\theta$ | 0.993 | 0.775 | 0.969 *** | 0.966 *** |
| | – | – | (0.043) | (0.035) |
| $\eta$ | –44.061 | –63.913 | 0.573 | 0.644 * |
| | – | – | (0.414) | (0.317) |
| **Elasticity $\sigma$** | | | | |
| Coefficient | 0.022 | 0.015 | 2.342 | 2.807 |
| Upper bound | 0.022 | 0.015 | 75.463 | 25.647 |
| Lower bound | 0.022 | 0.015 | 1.190 | 1.485 |
| $p$-value for $H_0 : \eta < 0$ | – | – | 0.083 | 0.021 |
| $N$ | 3,966 | 3,966 | 3,966 | 3,966 |
| $R^2$ | 0.748 | 0.748 | 0.714 | 0.714 |

*Notes*:
Dependent variable: Years of completed schooling. Standard errors in parentheses.
$p$-value thresholds: * < 5%, ** < 1%, *** < 0:1%.
(1) Non-linear Least Squares (NLS).
(2) Non-linear Seemingly Unrelated Estimate (NLSUR).

## NOTES

* I would like to thank Neri Salvadori, Carlo Panico, Pasquale Commendatore, Salvatore Capasso, Simone D'Alessandro, Tamara Fioroni, the COFIN 2005 Research Group, Mark Walters, and the participants at the conference on The Institutional and Social Dynamics of Growth and Distribution held in Lucca, Italy, 2007: during the panel on Gender and Marriage, Graziella Bertocchi provided sound advice and detailed discussion of the paper. I also thank Shoshana Grossbard, José Alberto Molina, Nacho Giménez and the participants at the Third Workshop on the Economics of the Family, held in Zaragoza, Spain, 2008. I have benefited from long discussions on estimation issues with Erasmo Papagni, Thomas Bassetti and Peter Katuscak. My special thanks also go to an anonymous referee who delivered great insights which substantially broadened the scope and enhanced the methodology of this research. Last but not least, my gratitude goes to Stefania for showing me how an optimal marriage can be implemented in our everyday life. All remaining errors are mine.

1. The observed degree of assortative mating also depends on the marginal distribution of traits in the two sides of the market, since a given degree of assortative mating is always observed in the data because of random matching. Using marriage-market-level data, it is possible to decompose sorting between random and systematic factors. See Sundaram (2004) and Liu and Lu (2006).
2. These nonlinearities will be discussed in more detail in Section 10.5.2.
3. Estimation results for husbands are not displayed here, but are available upon demand.
4. For other details on the structure of mating in Italy see Filoso (2008).
5. I thank Graziella Bertocchi for bringing this to my attention.

## REFERENCES

Becker, G.S. (1964), *Human Capital*, New York: Columbia University Press.

Becker, G.S. (1973), 'A Theory of Marriage: Part I', *Journal of Political Economy*, **81**(4), 813–46.

Becker, G.S. (1991 [1981]), *A Treatise on the Family* (Enlarged Edition), Cambridge and London: Harvard University Press.

Behrman, J., N. Birdsall and A. Deolalikar (1995): 'Marriage Markets, Labor Markets, and Unobserved Human Capital: an Empirical Exploration for South-Central India', *Economic Development and Cultural Change*, **43**(3), 585–601.

Benham, L. (1974), 'Benefits of Women's Education within Marriage', *The Journal of Political Economy*, **82**(2), 57–71.

Boulier, B.L. and Rosenzweig, M.R. (1984), 'Schooling, Search, and Spouse Selection: Testing Economic Theories of Marriage and Household Behavior', *The Journal of Political Economy*, **92**(4), 712–32.

Brynin, M. and M. Francesconi (2004), 'The Material Returns to Partnership: the Effects of Educational Matching on Labour Market Outcomes and Gender Equality', *European Sociological Review*, **20**(4), 363–77.

Chernozhukov, V. and C. Hansen (2006), 'Instrumental Quantile Regression Inference for Structural and Treatment Effect Models', *Journal of Econometrics*, **132**(2), 491–525.

Chiappori, P., M. Iyigun and Y. Weiss (2006), 'Investment in Schooling and the Marriage Market', *IZA Discussion Papers*, no. 2454.

Epstein, E. and R. Guttman (1984), 'Mate Selection in Man: Evidence, Theory, and Outcome', *Social Biology*, **31**(3–4), 243–78.

Ermisch, J. and M. Francesconi (2002), 'Intergenerational Social Mobility and Assortative Mating in Britain', *IZA Discussion Paper*, no. 465.

Ermisch, J.F., M. Francesconi and T. Siedler (2006), 'Intergenerational Mobility and Marital Sorting', *The Economic Journal*, **116**(513), 659–79.

Fernández, R. and R. Rogerson (2001), 'Sorting and Long-run Inequality', *The Quarterly Journal of Economics*, **116**(4), 1305–41.

Fernández, R., N. Guner and J. Knowles (2005), 'Love and Money: a Theoretical and Empirical Analysis of Household Sorting and Inequality, *The Quarterly Journal of Economics*, **120**(1), 273–344.

Filoso, V. (2008). 'Capitale umano, salari e instabilità coniugale in Italia', in S. Vinci, M.R. Carillo and E. Papagni (eds), *Dualismo, nuove torie della crescita e sviluppo del Mezzogiorno*, Bologna: Il Mulino, pp. 199–226.

Gale, D. and L. Shapley (1962), 'College Admissions and the Stability of Marriage', *American Mathematical Monthly*, **69**, 9–15.

Grossbard-Shechtman, S.A. and S. Neuman (1988), 'Women's Labor Supply and Marital Choice', *The Journal of Political Economy*, **96**(69), 1294–302.

Grossbard-Shechtman, S.A. and S. Neuman (1991), 'Cross Productivity Effects of Education and Origin on Earnings: Are They Really Reflecting Productivity?', in R. Frantz, H. Singh and J. Gerber (eds), *Handbook of Behavioral Economics*, vol. 2A, Greenwich: JAI Press, pp. 125–45.

Heckman, J.J. (1979), 'Sample Selection as a Specification Error', *Econometrica*, **47**(1), 153–61.

Huang, C., H. Li, P.W. Liu and J. Zhang (2006), 'Why Does Spousal Education Matter for Earnings? Assortative Mating or Cross-productivity', *The Chinese University of Hong Kong Working Paper*.

Kalmijn, M. (1994), 'Assortative Mating by Cultural and Economic Occupational Status', *The American Journal of Sociology*, **100**(2), 422–52.

Kim, T. and C. Muller (2004), 'Two-stage Quantile Regression when the First Stage is Based on Quantile Regression', *The Econometrics Journal*, **7**(1), 218–31.

Koenker, R. (2005), *Quantile Regression*, New York, NY: Cambridge University Press.

Lam, D. (1988), 'Marriage Markets and Assortative Mating with Household Public Goods', *Journal of Human Resources*, **23**(4), 462–87.

Liu, H. and J. Lu (2006), 'Measuring the Degree of Assortative Mating', *Economics Letters*, **92**(3), 317–22.

Nakosteen, R.A. and M.A. Zimmer (2001), 'Spouse Selection and Earnings: Evidence of Marital Sorting', *Economic Inquiry*, **39**(2), 201–13.

Nakosteen, R.A., O. Westerlund and M.A. Zimmer (2004), 'Marital Matching and Earnings: Evidence from the Unmarried Population in Sweden', *The Journal of Human Resources*, **39**(4), 1033–44.

Pencavel, J. (1998), 'Assortative Mating by Schooling and the Work Behavior of Wives and Husbands', *The American Economic Review*, **88**(2), 326–9.

Roth, A.E. and M.A.O. Sotomayor (1990), *Two-Sided Matching: a Study in Game-Theoretic Modeling and Analysis*, Cambridge: Cambridge University Press.

Rupert, P. and C. Cornwell (1997), 'Unobservable Individual Effects, Marriage and the Earnings of Young Men', *Economic Inquiry*, **35**(2), 285–94.

Smith, J. (1979), 'The Distribution of Family Earnings', *The Journal of Political Economy*, **87**(5), 163–92.

Spence, M. (1973), 'Job Market Signaling', *The Quarterly Journal of Economics*, **87**(3), 355–74.

Sundaram, R. (2004), 'Correlation of Traits in Married Couples: Assortative Matching or Just Who You Meet?', *Society for Economic Dynamics 2004 Meeting Papers*, no. 797, available at http://ideas.repec.org/p/red/sed004/797.html.

Tiefenthaler, J. (1997), 'The Productivity Gains of Marriage: Effects of Spousal Education on Own Productivity across Market Sectors in Brazil', *Economic Development and Cultural Change*, **45**(3), 633–50.

Zhang, J. and P.-W. Liu (2003), 'Testing Becker's Prediction on Assortative Mating on Spouses' Wages', *Journal of Human Resources*, **38**(1), 99–110.

Zimmer, M.A. (1996), 'Assortative Mating and Ethnicity in the Low Wage Population: an Examination of Spouses' Earnings', *Applied Economics Letters*, **3**(5), 311–15.

# 11. Information networks and knowledge spillovers: simulations in an agent-based model framework

**Christian Henning and Volker Saggau**

## 11.1. INTRODUCTION

Starting from the seminal work of Arrow (1962), new models of endogenous growth theory stress the importance of knowledge spillovers between firms, that is, the fact that the technological know-how of one firm may positively effect the technological know-how of another firm without full compensation (Romer, 1986; Grossman and Helpman, 1991). In particular, spatial diffusion of knowledge is considered as one of the key factors explaining different regional economic growth. For example, Romer stresses in two seminal papers (1992, 1993) that access to the ideas available in leading industrialized countries is critical for many poor countries (or regions).

However, although these new models of endogenous growth theory certainly contribute a great deal to our understanding of the role of knowledge spillovers in economic growth, they still leave some points unsolved.

First, existing studies on knowledge spillovers and regional economic growth focus on knowledge spillovers between a lead and a follower region, while they generally neglect diffusion of knowledge within the follower region. This fact has been nicely pointed out by Rogers (2003).

Second, most existing studies in new economic growth theory consider knowledge spillovers as a black box and do not explicitly model the process of knowledge spillovers between firms. In contrast, many empirical studies emphasize the importance of interaction patterns between firms for knowledge accumulations and economic growth, for example, communication, information flows, staff exchange, or interlocking directory. Technically, these interaction patterns can be best captured by a network concept. For example, Antonelli (1996) states 'The development of knowledge within industries is strongly influenced by the network structure of relations among firms'. Analogously, Knack and Keefer (1997) stress the importance of social capital, defined as norms and networks that allow collective action, for economic growth.[1]

In general, firms' capacity to absorb new knowledge from external sources can be subdivided into two dimensions: firms' access to external knowledge and firms' capacity to process new external knowledge.

Most studies focus on the latter. For example, one of the first studies focusing on firms' absorption capacity and economic growth is Nelson and Phelps (1966), who assume that firms' capacity to adopt exogenous technological innovation generated in the science sector is determined by human capital of the firm.

Later, other neoclassical studies focus explicitly on knowledge diffusion between firms, but analogously to Nelson and Phelps (1966) understand absorption capacity as the firms' capability to process external technological knowledge. Meanwhile, they implicitly assume perfect access to external knowledge of other firms (Spence, 1984; D'Aspremont and Jacquemin, 1988).

As a critique of simple neoclassical models evolutionary models of innovation diffusion and technological progress have been developed (Dawid, 2006). In contrast to neoclassic, evolutionary economics focuses on an explicit procedural way of representing decision-making rather than relying on abstract optimizing calculus (Dopfer, 2001; Dosi and Winter, 2002; Fagerberg and Verspagen, 2002; Nelson, 1995; Nelson and Winter, 2002). Pioneering work in evolutionary economics in this field apply agent-based models, for example, Nelson and Winter (1982). Inspired by the work of Nelson and Winter (1982) a large body of literature applying agent based computational economics (ACE) modeling approaches to explain innovation and technological change have been developed, which commonly understand innovation and technological progress as a result of a dynamic process among interacting heterogenous agents. Moreover, this literature highlights in particular the special nature of knowledge as the most important factor for the production of innovation (Dawid, 2006). ACE models contributed significantly to the understanding of the complex process of innovation and technological progress. In particular, Cantner and Pyka (1998) model endogenous strategy to invest in absorbing capacity in the presence of knowledge spillovers in an evolutionary economic framework. However, they also interpret absorption capacity as the firms' ability to process external knowledge, while access to external knowledge is not explicitly considered.

In contrast, research into industrial networks, geography, and innovation clearly underline the importance of network structures of relations among firms for the development of knowledge within industries (Antonelli, 1996; Feldman and Audretsch, 1999; Sako, 1999; Paci and Usai, 2000).

The impact of networks on economic behavior is an innovative and emerging field in economics that also profited tremendously from agent-based computational economics (ACE)-modeling (Jackson, 2005; Wilhite, 2006). However, economic research on networks is still in its infancy and studies on the impact of network structures on innovation diffusion and technological progress do not yet exist. Nevertheless, some notable exceptions exist that focus explicitly on network structures and knowledge spillovers.

An interesting study of the emergence of cooperation networks within a game-theoretical model has been provided by by Goyal and Joshi (2003). In particular, they analyze in an oligopoly setting the formation of pair-wise collaboration links among firms, where the set of all links among a fixed set of firms is defined as a collaborative network. An important assumption driving the results of Goyal and Joshi is how network structures influence firms' profits. Here, Goyal and Joshi (2003) simply assume that marginal costs decrease increasingly with network ties. This specific impact of network structures is only exogenously assumed and is not derived from any detailed mechanism of knowledge transfer between firms. Basically, it corresponds to microeconomic models of knowledge spillovers (Spence, 1984); hence, it would be interesting to analyze the extend to which these assumptions correspond to an explicit model of knowledge diffusion and accumulation in networks.

Another very interesting study considering global network structure is provided by Pyka and Saviotti (2001), who analyze the emergence of collaboration networks in the biotech industry within a complex agent-based model approach. However, while they study the emergence of cooperation network structures in depth they do not explicitly analyze how global network structures influence knowledge diffusion and its impact on overall technological progress in the industry.

In this context our chapter offers an agent-based modeling approach to model the process of knowledge spillovers and knowledge accumulation. Technically, we derive a rather simple model that particularly focuses on the role of global network structures as determinants of knowledge diffusion and its implied impact on knowledge accumulation in a network of firms. Applying our simple agent-based model we simulate the impact of different network typologies on knowledge diffusion. In particular, we simulate three different network types, that is, random, small-world, and scale-free networks, by varying global network structures, which are clustering and centralization.

The rest of the chapter is organized as follows. In the next section we provide a brief background and motivation of our approach. In particular, we relate our approach to relevant existing studies in the literature.

In Section 11.3 we present our formal model. Moreover, we give a brief overview on the network concepts and indicators that we used as we consider these concepts as non-standard to mainstream economists.

In Section 11.4 we discuss the central results of our simulation analyses. Moreover, we identify specific framework conditions which amplify or attenuate the impact of network structures on the speed of knowledge accumulation. Finally, in Section 11.5 we conclude and relate our main results to existing theories of knowledge spillovers and regional growth.

## 11.2. BACKGROUND AND MOTIVATION

Following recent approaches on knowledge spillovers we consider that knowledge spillovers between firms are imperfect. Thus, if we denote the knowledge of firm $j$ by $k_j$, firm $i$ has only limited access to this knowledge:

$$\theta_{ij} * k_j, \quad \text{with } 0 \leq \theta_{ij} \leq 1$$

$\theta_{ij}$ is the absorption capacity of firm $i$ regarding knowledge of firm $j$.

The absorption capacity of firm $i$ regarding firm $j$ can be subdivided into two aspects: the capability of firm $i$ to observe technological knowledge of firm $j$ and the capability to process the observed information. We denote $\pi_{ij}$ as a measurement of the first and $\lambda_{ij}$ as a measurement for the second capability; then absorption capability results as:

$$\theta_{ij} = \lambda_{ij}\pi_{ij}$$

We cover the first aspect via an information network $\Pi = [\pi_{ij}]$, where $\pi_{ij}$ denotes the information exchange frequency between firm $i$ and $j$.

Thus, firm $i$ can only observe the knowledge of firm $j$ if $i$ and $j$ have established an information network tie where $\pi_{ij}$ denotes the strength of this tie. Following quantitative network theory (Burt, 1982) as well as recent approaches on networks in economics, for example, Jackson (2005), conclude that establishing and maintaining a network tie is costly, i.e., requires resources. Accordingly, firms do not establish information ties with all other firms, but only with a share of firms. Empirical network studies show that information networks among firms are sparse, for example, the average number of information ties observed for a firm rather exceeds 10 (Henning et al., 2008). This is very low for a larger set of firms, compared to the maximal possible number of ties.

What is the impact of the structure of information networks on the absorption capacity of firms and thus on knowledge spillovers and accumulation? The answer to these questions crucially depends on how the process of knowledge transfers and processing is designed.

These questions also highlight a common observation, that knowledge spillovers between firms cannot be the only source of knowledge. Accordingly, studies generally consider an external source of knowledge. Let $k_o$ denote the external source of knowledge. Following the seminal paper of Nelson and Phelps (1966) we interpret this external source of knowledge as the knowledge sector, for example, universities, research labs, etc. Accordingly, $k_o$ is the maximal stock of knowledge or techniques available to firms, while $k_i$ denotes the best practice technology realized by firm $i$.[2]

Analogous to firm spillovers, the capacity to absorb knowledge of the external source is also limited. For example, Nelson and Phelps (1966) analyzed firms' limited capacities to absorb knowledge of the science sector, while other scholars study firms' limited capacities to generate new knowledge via learning-by-doing or R&D-activities (see Cantner and Pyka, 1998). In general, we define:

$$\theta_{io} * k_o, \quad \text{with } 0 \leq \theta_{io} \leq 1$$

Neoclassical studies such as Spence (1984) focus only on firms' limited processing capacity, $\lambda$, assuming perfect access, $\pi_{ij} = 1 \ \forall i, j$.

Moreover, as Spence (1984) presumes that all firms have the same limited processing capacity, it follows:

$$\theta_{ij} = \lambda = \theta$$

Furthermore, as Spence (1984) implicitly assumes that only newly generated knowledge (denoted by $\Delta k_{io}$ in the following) can be transmitted among firms. Knowledge is generated proportionally to resources allocated to R&D activities. Let $m_i$ denote the amount of resources firm $i$ allocated to R&D, then as Spence (1984) assumes: $\Delta k_{io} = m_i$ . Now, firms have access to newly generated knowledge of other firms, where $\theta$ denotes the share of new knowledge of firm $i$ that is available to all other firms $j$ (this follows since $\pi_{ij} = 1 \ \forall j$). Thus it holds:

$$\Delta k_i = \Delta k_{io} + \theta \sum_j \Delta k_{jo} = m_i + \theta \sum_j m_j$$

Accordingly, the only network impact on technological diffusion that as Spence (1984) identifies is a simple size effect, for example, the larger the total set of firms, the larger is, ceteris paribus, the knowledge generation induced by knowledge spillovers between firms. However, as Spence (1984) did not intend to analyze network effects. Instead he focused on the decision to invest in R&D ($m_i$) in the presence of spillover effects. Obviously, in the presence of knowledge spillovers, an increase of firms' absorption capacity of external knowledge implies external effects, as this also increases the knowledge of other firms, that is, it follows directly $d\Delta k_j / dm_i = \theta \geq 0$. Spence (1984) nicely demonstrated that firms' incentives to invest in their own R&D crucially depends on market structures.

Analogously to Spence (1984), Cantner and Pyka (1998) also analyze firms' incentives to invest in R&D in comparison to investing in absorption capacity. However, while Cantner and Pyka (1998) in contrast to Spence (1984) undertake their analyses in an evolutionary economic framework, their study also focuses on firms' restricted capacity to process knowledge, that is, a restriction of $\lambda$, while they do not consider network effects, this means firms' restricted access to knowledge.

A simple way to introduce imperfect access in the model set-up of Spence (1984) or Cantner and Pyka (1998) would be to assume that firms establish network ties only to a subset of other firms, for example, we define the neighbourhood of firm $i$, $N_i$: $N_i = \{j \in N | \pi_{ij} > 0\}$.

Moreover, considering network structures as endogenous variables, it also follows quite plainly that firms have incentives to invest in their networks, where $\theta \cdot m_k$ would be the additional knowledge spillovers resulting from a tie to a firm $k$.

This is basically the approach of Goyal and Joshi (2003), who studied firms' incentives to establish cooperation ties with other firms, so that cooperation among firms induces knowledge spillovers and thus has an impact on firms' profits. However, Goyal and Joshi (2003) did not explicitly analyze how network structures influence knowledge spillovers and thus firm profits. Instead, they simply assumed that the firms' marginal production costs decrease with the number of ties.

Based on this ad hoc assumption, they could derive stable and efficient network structures. Of course, firms preferences over network ties result from the anticipated impact of those ties on firm profits. It follows quite plainly that the impact of an additional network tie on firms' profit can be quite different depending on the concrete process of knowledge diffusion. In particular, we demonstrate that central assumptions of Goyal and Joshi (2003), regarding the impact of network structures on firms' profit would have to be revised in the framework of our model.

A very interesting study considering global network structures is provided by by Pyka and Saviotti (2001), who analyze the emergence of collaboration networks in the biotech industry within a complex agent-based model approach. In contrast to Goyal and Joshi (2003), Pyka and Saviotti (2001) apply an evolutionary economic approach that explicitly takes into account the fundamental uncertainty and complexity characterizing firms' decisions to establish networks ties. In particular, the evolutionary economic approach of Pyka and Saviotti (2001) emphasizes – in contrast to Goyal and Joshi (2003) – that strategic investment in network ties is often a very complex process characterized by fundamental uncertainty. Accordingly, often it is not straightforward to derive rational strategies regarding how firms should invest in network ties, and therefore firms apply more simple – though certainly not always optimal – heuristic rules of thumb.

Overall, it is still fair to conclude that although empirical studies have clearly recognized the importance of established informal and formal interfirm network structures for knowledge accumulation and its role in innovation processes, only a few (though very interesting) theoretical studies on the impact of networks on knowledge spillovers exist. Accordingly, many issues have not been fully addressed. For example, the impact of information network structures on knowledge diffusion between firms and its impact on the speed of knowledge accumulation has not been comprehensively analyzed.

That gap is addressed in this chapter. Therefore, in the next subsection we derive a simple agent-based model to study how knowledge diffuses and is accumulated in a set of firms, explicitly including the structure of information network channels in which knowledge flows between firms.

## 11.3. THE MODEL

### 11.3.1. Basic Assumptions

The aim is to model the impact of global and local network structures on aggregate knowledge accumulation within a set of firm. We consider a set of business firms $N$, with $i=1,...,n$ denoting an individual firm.

Moreover, accumulation of knowledge involves several mechanisms, for example, in-house R&D, informal transfer of knowledge between companies (spillovers), or learning-by-doing. In this chapter we focus on the diffusion of knowledge between firms rather than on the process of generation of new knowledge by firms. Accordingly, we assume that new technological knowledge is constantly generated outside of the firm network, for example, in an external science sector or in an external leading region. Firms can directly absorb external knowledge generated outside the network or absorb knowledge from other firms in the network.[3]

Modeling knowledge accumulation, we incorporate fundamental results of previous studies on technological spillovers. First, the firms' capacity to absorb external knowledge is generally limited and can be subdivided into two aspects: the firms' ability to observe external knowledge and their capacity to process observed knowledge, respectively.

Regarding the latter aspect, we follow Cantner and Pyka (1998) and assume that the firms' ability to process received information crucially depends on their current stock of knowledge. As will be elaborated upon below, we formally incorporate the impact of the firms' current knowledge on knowledge accumulation. We do this by assuming that new technological knowledge can only be processed if the firms' current knowledge is already above a specific threshold. Moreover, we assume that information processing is a stochastic process in which firms' limited ability to process external knowledge is measured as the expected amount of knowledge a firm is able to process.

An essential characteristic highlighted in previous studies (Nelson and Phelps, 1966; Cantner and Pyka, 1998) is that knowledge from other firms in the network is generally easier to process than new knowledge from an external source, for example, the science sector or a leading region or generating it via learning-by-doing processes. Basically, this feature makes knowledge accumulation within a network of firms a collective process (see Cantner and Pyka, 1998). In our model we take this essential characteristic into account by assuming that, ceteris paribus, firms observe a much higher capacity to process knowledge from other firms in their network when compared to processing knowledge from an external source outside the network.

Moreover, previous studies suggest that firms' can invest in their capacity to process knowledge Cantner and Pyka (1998).[4] However, at this stage we try to keep our model simple and therefore we assume that the firms' capacity to process knowledge from other firms is constant and exogenously determined.

Regarding the first aspect – firms' capacity to observe knowledge – we have already established that diffusion of knowledge between firms is not trivial, this means it requires the existence of an established information network channel between firms (Cohen and Levinthal, 1989; Rosenberg, 1990). Transmission of new technological knowledge between firms can only occur if staff members of two firms communicate with each other. Obviously, communication between firms requires specific opportunities to interact, for example, doing business or meeting within a business organization or even meeting at social events such as dinner parties, playing golf, and so on. Of course, depending on the specific business, organizational and social opportunities for interactions vary significantly across firms. Accordingly, the frequency of information transmission varies significantly across pairs of firms. As will be shown in detail below, the firms' opportunities to communicate can be captured by defining firm specific information network ties, where the structure of information networks has a crucial impact on knowledge accumulation.

To facilitate our analyses we focus our studies on a binary information network $Z$, where the latter is defined as a graph of $N^2$, for example, the information network is a subset of pairs $(i,j) \in N^2$, where $i,j \in N$ are usually called vertices and a pair $(i,j)$ is called an edge. Let $z_{ij} = 1$ indicate a tie between firms $i$ and $j$ implying that firms $i$ and firm $j$ have an established information channel. Then the binary information network $Z$ can be defined as follows:

$$Z = \left\{ (i,j) \in N^2 \middle| z_{ij} = 1 \right\} \tag{11.1}$$

Information flows, $\pi_{ij}$, between firm $i$ and $j$ can only occur in established information channels. Thus, let $\pi$ denote the common conditional probability that information flows within an established information channel: then a valued information network, $\Pi$, results from our binary information network $Z$ via multiplying with the scalar $\pi$: $\Pi = \pi Z$.

In detail, networks can have different structures and different graphs have different topologies. Quantitative network theory developed a set of local and global network indicators to describe specific network structures and typologies (Wasserman and Faust, 1994).

Before we present our agent-based model (ABM) and simulation analyses we will briefly define relevant global and local network indicators. Although these network indicators are described in standard textbooks of quantitative network analysis (Wasserman and Faust, 1994), they are not standard in the economic literature.

#### 11.3.1.1. Network indicators

Given the fact that we are mainly interested in the impact of social network structures on information and innovation diffusion beyond global network size, $n$, the following global and local indicators are of interest:

*Local network size*

If we denote the number of ties an individual firm $i$ forms by $z_i$, then local network size, $\overline{z}$, is defined as the average number of ties of firms:

$$\overline{z} = \frac{\sum_{i \in N} z_i}{n} \tag{11.2}$$

*Network density*

Network density is defined as the number of realized ties divided by the number of theoretically possible ties.

$$\phi = \frac{\sum_{i \in N} z_i}{n^2} = \frac{\overline{z}}{n} \tag{11.3}$$

To simulate density we keep total network size $n$ constant and simulate an average number of network ties, $\overline{z}$.

*Global centralization*

Global centralization of a network measures the difference in individual network ties (degrees). Accordingly, the larger the variance of individual degrees of actors, the larger is, ceteris paribus, the centralization. Let $\sigma^2$ denote the variance of degrees in a network, then it holds:

$$\sigma^2 = \frac{1}{n} \sum_{i \in N} \left( z_i - \overline{z} \right)^2 \tag{11.4}$$

Thus, by definition, centralization is measured by the variance or standard deviation of network degrees, $\sigma^2$ or $\sigma$, respectively.

*Clustering/transitivity*

Network clustering or transitivity is defined as the average density of the actor's neighborhood network. A neighborhood network $N_i$ of an actor $i \in N$ is defined as the subset of actors $j \in N$ which have a tie to $i$:

$$N_i = \left\{ j \in N \middle| z_{ij} = 1 \right\} \tag{11.5}$$

Now, given $z_i$ neighbors of an actor $i$, the density of the neighborhood network $N_i$ is defined as:

$$\gamma_i = \frac{\sum_{k \in N_i} \sum_{j \in N_i} z_{kj}}{z_i (z_i - 1)} \tag{11.6}$$

Finally, the global clustering is defined as the average density of all neighborhood networks:

$$\gamma = \frac{1}{n} \sum_{i \in N} \gamma_i \tag{11.7}$$

*Characteristic path length*

We define $g_{ij}$ as the minimum path length connecting an actor $i$ with an actor $j$. To define $g_{ij}$ formally we define $Z_{ij}^r$ as the $ij$-component of the matrix $Z^r$, with $Z = [Z_{ij}]$. Then $g_{ij}$ is defined as follows:

$$g_{ij} = \underset{r}{Min} \left\{ r \middle| Z_{ij}^r > 0 \right\} \tag{11.8}$$

Further, we define $g_i$ as the mean of all $g_{ij}$. Then the characteristic path length ($L$) is defined as the median of all means $g_i$. A problem arises if a network is not a strong component, that is, some actors are isolated. The path length to isolated actors becomes infinitely. In this case the characteristic path length can not be calculated. A solution to this problem would be to calculate the characteristic path length only for the strong component of the network, that is, the largest subset of actors that are connected with each other via a finite path.

#### 11.3.1.2. Random, small-world and scale-free networks

In the emerging literature on 'networks and economics' different types of networks characterized by specific network indicators have become very popular, that is, random networks, small-world networks, and scale-free networks (Jackson, 2005). Therefore, we briefly define these specific network types based on characteristic values for global network indicators. Hence it is helpful to identify the range of network types and their implications for measuring performance by network indicators.

*Random graphs*

A random graph is a graph in which the edges between the vertices are generated randomly. $Z(n,p)$ with a natural number $n \geq 1$ and a probability $p$ denotes the class of all graphs where, for every tuple $(i,j)$ of vertices, the probability $p$ determines if they are connected, that is, $z_{ij} = 1$ with probability $p$ for all $i,j \in N$. This takes place independently of the other edges. In particular, random models of network formation include Bernoulli random graphs (Erdös and Renyi, 1959; Bollobás, 2001) and Markov graphs or $p^*$-networks (Frank and Strauss, 1986; Wasserman and Pattison, 1996).

*Small-world graphs*

An algorithm for building links that differs from a pure Bernoulli random graph, has been suggested by Watts and Strogatz (1998) and Watts (1999). In particular, Watts and Strogatz (1998) wanted to generate a network that exhibits both relatively low diameter and nondegenerate clustering. They called this specific network structure they generated small-world networks. Small-world graphs have become very popular since the pathbreaking work of Watts (1999). In particular, small-world networks combine two characteristic properties: a relatively high clustering and a relatively low average characteristic path length. In contrast to small-world networks, random networks exhibit a relatively low characteristic path length, but clustering is also low for these network types. Deffuant et al. (2002) investigated small-world networks (SWN) with respect to opinion formation and convergence.

*Scale-free graphs*

However, the way Watts (1999) generated small-world networks implies that the degree distribution of generated networks has a great deal more regularity and less variance than observed for real social networks.

To generate networks that exhibit degree distributions as observed in many social networks, one needs a process of link formation that differs from the pure Bernoulli type process, as observed distributions often exhibit fatter tails. The idea behind generating distributions with such fat tails dates back to Pareto (1896), for which the standard power law distribution is named. Accordingly, generated networks are called power law or scale-free networks. The characteristic property of scale-free networks is a high global centralization, where some nodes have an extremely high number of ties (these are called hubs). The distribution of vertices and the number of edges follows a power law: $P \sim z^{-\xi}$. A prominent example of a scale-free network is the Internet. Accordingly, if a computer virus reaches a hub it can spread and diffuse rapidly through the network. Analogously epidemiology and disease spreading via infection also take place rapidly within scale-free networks.

*Hybrid networks*

Finally, hybrid models to generate networks have been developed since purely random graph models do not exhibit the clustering or degree distribution that match many observed networks, while generated small-world networks do not exhibit observed degree distribution and power law or scale free networks do not exhibit observed clustering (Pennock et al., 2002; Kleinberg et al., 1999; Levene et al., 2002; Kumar et al., 2000; Cooper and Frieze, 2003).

To construct information networks a modified $\alpha$-model of Watts (1999) is applied, which can generate hybrid networks combining properties of scale-free, small-world, and random networks. The model is described in detail in Henning and Saggau (2009).

A specific property of a social network is clustering, this means the fact that the likelihood of a connection among two firms is correlated with the existing connections among firms. In detail, the higher the number of overlapping connections between a pair of firms, the higher the probability that these two will form a connection as well. How exactly clustering occurs is a very interesting topic in itself. In the Watt's $\alpha$-model clustering is basically determined by a single parameter, $\alpha$, which can vary between 0 and infinity. The lower the values for $\alpha$ the more a network is clustered.

Our modified $\alpha$-algorithm includes the existence of stars, keeping the idea of clustering. In detail, we assume that only one star exists, and we vary the number of ties this star forms (for the detailed network generation mechanism see Henning and Saggau, 2009).

### 11.3.2. Agent-based Model of Knowledge Accumulation in an Information Network

Given the information network, $Z$, we assume the following simple three-stage procedure of knowledge accumulation in a network of firms, $N$:

1. **Generation and transmission of new knowledge**
New knowledge is constantly generated in an external science sector or a leading region and randomly transmitted to a firm $i \in N$ of the network. In particular, we denote $k_t$ as the new knowledge signal generated in period $t$ and $K_T = \sum_{t=1}^{T} k_t$ the maximal accumulated knowledge available in the science sector. For simplicity, we assume that each knowledge signal equals 1: $k_t = 1 \ \forall t$.
A firm can absorb knowledge from the external source in each time period. Knowledge absorption is stochastic. In particular, we assume that in each time period, $T$, a firm can maximally learn one additional knowledge signal, where $p_i(m_i)$ denotes the probability that a firm $i$ actually learns an additional signal. Formally, we assume that a firm will learn new knowledge if its effective invested resources, $m_i^e$, are above a threshold. Firms invest resources $m_i$ to learn new knowledge from the external source. However, the transformation of invested $(m_i)$ into effective resources $(m_i^e)$ is a stochastic process. Technically, we assume that the threshold for each firm equals 1 and that effective resources are uniformly distributed over the interval $(0, m_i)$. Under this assumptions $p_i$ results as: $p_i = (1/m_i)(m_i - 1)$.
Further, let $K_{iT}$ denote the stock of knowledge accumulated by firm $i$ at time period $T$ and let $\Delta K_{iT}^o$ denote the additional knowledge a firm absorbs form the external source then it holds:
$$K_{i1} = 0$$
$$\Delta K_{iT}^o = \begin{cases} 1, & \text{if } m_i^e \geq 1 \\ 0, & \text{if } m_i^e < 1 \end{cases} \tag{11.9}$$

2. **Diffusion of knowledge between regional firms**
Firms communicate their accumulated knowledge to other firms within information network channels in each time period. Formally, let $\pi$ denote the common conditional probability that firm $i$ transmits its accumulated knowledge, $K_{it}$, to another firm $j$, if both firms have an established information tie, $z_{ij} = 1$. Then for each firm $i$ we can define the set of received information in period $T$: $M_{iT} = \{K_{jT} + \Delta K_{jT}^o | d_{ijT} z_{ij} = 1\}$, where $d_{ijT}$ is a random variable which is 1 with probability $\pi$ and zero

with probability $1-\pi$. To accumulate observed knowledge a firm has to process received knowledge. Again, the firms' processing capacity is limited. In particular, we assume that in each time period, $T$, a firm can maximally learn one additional knowledge signal. However, a firm is only able to learn from other firms if knowledge observed from another firm is new compared to the existing knowledge stock. Therefore, let $\Delta K_{iT}^{N}$ denote the additional knowledge a firm absorbs from knowledge spillovers then it holds:

$$\Delta K_{iT}^{N} = \begin{cases} 1, & \text{if } K_{iT} + \Delta K_{iT}^{o} \;<\; MaxM_{iT} \\ 0, & \text{if otherwise} \end{cases} \tag{11.10}$$

where $MaxM_{iT}$ is the maximum of the set of received information, $M_{iT}$.

3. **Knowledge accumulation**
Depending on the technological information received from knowledge spillovers within the network, as well as on the new knowledge absorbed outside the network, each firm accumulates its new knowledge, for example, the new knowledge stock available in the next time period $T+1$, $K_{iT+1}$, results as:

$$K_{iT+1} = K_{iT} + \Delta K_{iT}^{o} + \Delta K_{iT}^{N} \tag{11.11}$$

### 11.3.3. An Intuitive Approach to our Model of Knowledge Accumulation

To get an intuitive understanding of the process of knowledge accumulation our simple model defines, consider stage 1 in our model. At stage 1 the knowledge stock of each firm in the network is 0 and the external source has generated the first knowledge signal $k_1$.

According to our defined process, the probability that a firm $i$ will absorb this knowledge from the external source equals $p_i$. For simplicity we assume every firm has invested the same amount into its absorbtion capacity, for example, for any firm $i$ the probability to learn the new external information equals $p$. Accordingly, the probability that the network collectively will learn the new signal results as:

$$1-(1-p)^n \tag{11.12}$$

Obviously, as long as $p$ is small and the number of firms $(n)$ is sufficiently large collective knowledge accumulation is much faster when compared to isolated accumulation of an individual firm. However, the long-term speed of collective learning crucially depends on the speed of knowledge diffusion through the network, that is on the number of firms that learn a new information signal via knowledge spillovers in a given period of time. For example, assume that the firms have no established network ties, i.e., $z_{ij} = 0 \ \forall i, j \in N$. Then, obviously, the speed of knowledge accumulation just equals the speed observed for an isolated firm, that is $p$. On the contrary, considering a perfect connected network, that is, $z_{ij} = 1 \ \forall i, j \in N$ implies that the average speed of learning equals $1-(1-p)^n$. What will be the average speed of learning if we assume an imperfect communication network, that is, $z_{ij} = 1$ for some $i, j \in N$?

Consider a firm $i$ has received the information signal in period $t=1$. Then this signal is communicated in the same period to all other firms $j$ to which firm $i$ has an established network tie. We define the subset of firms to which firm $i$ has a direct network tie as his 1-path neighborhood, $N_i(1)$. Accordingly, we can define the 2-path neighborhood of a firm $i$ as the subset of firms $j$ to which firm $i$ has indirect contact via one other intermediate. In general, we can define the $r$-path neighborhood as the following subset:

$$N_i(r) = \{ j \in N \mid g(i,j) \leq r \} \tag{11.13}$$

where $g(i,j)$ is defined as the minimum path length between $i$ and $j$ (see above).

Now we define $A_{ir} = |N_i(r)|$ as the size of the $r$-path neighborhood of firm $i$. Further, let $A_r$ denote the average size of the $r$-neighborhoods of all firms in the network. Then we can calculate the probability that the $r$-neighborhood of a firm $i$ will receive the next new knowledge signal, $P^r$, as:

$$P^r = 1-(1-p)^{A_r} \tag{11.14}$$

Obviously, the higher $A_r$ for every communication round $r$ the greater is the speed of knowledge diffusion.

The average size of $r$-neighborhoods depends on the average number of ties a firm has, that is, on the average local network size, $\overline{z}$. At a first glance one could assume that the size of $r$-path-neighborhoods just equals $\overline{z}^r$, since every firm knows $\overline{z}$ other firms. However, it is easy to see that this approximation is too simple. First, our information network is symmetric. Therefore, every firm in the neighborhood of a 'parent' firm $i$ has one tie with this parent firm. Therefore, the size of an $r$-neighborhood reduces to: $\overline{z} * (\overline{z}-1)^{r-1}$. Moreover, it is also clear that the total size of any $r$-neighborhood cannot be larger than the size of the total network. Furthermore, clustering has an impact on size of $r$-neighborhoods. This impact corresponds to the fact that the newly contacted firms and the other $\overline{z}-1$ firms contacted by its 'parent' firm form triadic configurations.

Technically, the average cluster coefficient, $\gamma$, measures the share of triadic configurations occurring within a direct neighborhood.

Accordingly, it follows for the approximation of the average size of an $r$-neighborhood:

$$A_r = Min\left\{\overline{z} * \left[(\overline{z}-1)*(1-\gamma)\right]^{r-1}, n\right\} \tag{11.15}$$

Finally, the total network size also has an impact on the size of $r$-neighborhoods that are lower than the total network size. This follows from the fact that the smaller the total number of firms in a network the higher the probability that two firms in an $r$-neighborhood of a 'parent' firm form a tie to the same firm. However, it is tentative to find an analytical form correcting for this additional bias so it is omitted here.[5]

Analogously, introducing stars into the network implies that the average size of $r$-neighborhoods, $A_r$, increases. For example, assuming that a central star that has a direct tie to every other firm implies that for every firm every $r$-path neighborhood with $r>1$ already includes the complete network. Accordingly, for networks with large stars knowledge diffusion will be much faster when compared to corresponding SWNs.

So far, we have only analyzed knowledge diffusion through the network. Next we combine diffusion with knowledge accumulation. To this end we first assume that knowledge accumulation can only take place in an $r$-neighborhood, that is, only every $r$-time period firms have the opportunity to learn new knowledge from the external source, while knowledge spillovers occur every time period. Hence, firm maximal speed of knowledge accumulation corresponds to $1/r$. Moreover, firms learn in $r$-neighborhoods, thus the realized speed of knowledge accumulation results as:

$$\frac{1}{r}P^r \tag{11.16}$$

Accordingly, speed of knowledge accumulation in the $r$-neighborhoods crucially depends on knowledge diffusion in $r$-neighborhoods, that is the size of the $r$-neighborhood $A_r$. Finally, according to our model, firms do simultaneously learn in all $r$-neighborhoods. Thus, although we do not present a complete analytical solution approximating the speed of knowledge accumulation within our agent-based model, it is intuitively clear that overall knowledge accumulation will proceed faster the higher the speed of knowledge accumulation in all $r$-neighborhoods. Therefore, it follows directly from our expositions above that, ceteris paribus, the speed of knowledge accumulation increases the lower the clustering coefficient ($\gamma$) as well as the higher the global and the local network size, $n$ and $\overline{z}$, respectively. Moreover, the speed should be significantly higher for star networks when compared to SWNs.

## 11.4. RESULTS

### 11.4.1. Simulated Information Networks

To be able to analyze the impact of network structures on speed of knowledge accumulation we have systematically simulated information accumulation in various SW- and hybrid networks. Networks have been generated using the modified $\alpha$-model of Watts (1999).[6] A central parameter of this network generation algorithm is $\alpha$ which determines global network characteristics, that is, clustering and characteristic path length (see Table 11A.1 in the appendix).

In particular, starting from a basic network comprising $n=1000$ firms, who on average have $\overline{z}=10$ direct contacts, we generated different SW-networks assuming $\alpha$-values ranging from 0 to 10. Furthermore, we also generated different hybrid networks assuming one star with direct contacts in the range of 100, 250, 500 and 1000. Moreover, to analyze the impact of global network size, $n$, as well as the impact of the local network size, $\overline{z}$, we also ran simulations for $n=3000$ and $n=5000$, as well as for $\overline{z}=15$ and $\overline{z}=20$.

Overall, each specific network parameter constellation can be characterized by global and local network sizes ($n=1000, 3000, 5000$; $\overline{z}=10, 15, 20$), existences of a star (star = yes or star = no), the number of ties of the star (star-density = 100, 250, 500, 1000) and the $\alpha$-parameter ($\alpha=0,...,10$). Accordingly, we simulated knowledge accumulation in 180 different SW-networks and 720 different hybrid networks. Further, due to the random nature of our model we repeated each simulation run for each network parameter constellation 100 times, which means that all reported variable values generally correspond to the mean over 100 simulation runs.

Moreover, we set $\pi=1$ for all simulation runs, thus we assumed that knowledge is transferred with certainty whenever firms have established an information tie, that is, $z_{ij}=1$. In essence, the main results regarding the impact of network structure on knowledge accumulation will not change if we assume different values for $\pi$, although the absolute speed of knowledge accumulation would significantly change.

Finally, the standard setting for $p$ is 0.001 for all simulation runs. However, to analyze the impact of networks on speed of knowledge accumulation under different innovation intensities we also ran simulations assuming $p=0.01$ and $p=0.1$.

To get a better understanding of our main results, central network indicators have been calculated for all simulated networks. The mean values over the 100 simulation runs are reported in Table 11A.1 in the appendix.

### 11.4.2. Network Typology and Knowledge Accumulation

The key question of our simulation analysis is how different network typologies influence the accumulation of knowledge in a given network of firms. Accordingly, a relevant indicator is the average knowledge accumulated by an individual firm in the network.[7]

Let $\bar{K}_t$ denote the average accumulated knowledge in period $t$, while $w_t = \bar{K}_t / t$ denotes the average accumulated knowledge per time period.

#### 11.4.2.1. Impact of network types

Figure 11.1 presents average accumulated knowledge per time period for the different network types, namely a random network, a small-world network, and a 1000-star network (that is, the star has 1000 ties), where the last two networks are both generated setting $\alpha = 7$.

As can be seen from Figure 11.1, for all network types knowledge accumulation follows a linear trend, where simulations normally approach

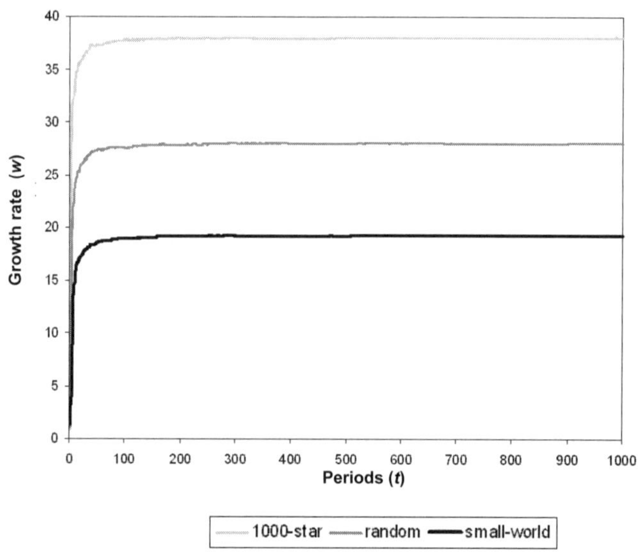


*Source*: Own calculations

*Figure 11.1. Average growth rates ($w_t = \bar{K}_t / t$) of accumulated knowledge for different networks*

stable linear growth rates after 100 time periods, while each simulation run includes 1000 time periods. Accordingly, we focus our further analyses on long-term linear growth rates, which we denote by $w$. Technically, in the following analyses reported values of $w$ correspond to the linear growth rate calculated after 100 time periods.[8]

In particular, linear growth rates vary significantly over network types. In absolute terms the growth rate is the highest for the 1000-star network followed by the random network, while growth rate is the lowest for the SWN. Furthermore, as can bee seen from reported standard errors in Table 11.1, these differences in growth rates are statistically significant.

To see how knowledge accumulation is determined by global network structures beyond different network types, we next analyze how speed of knowledge accumulation varies for different $\alpha$-values and different star sizes.

### 11.4.2.2. Clustering

By construction Watt's $\alpha$-algorithm implies that the lower the $\alpha$-value the more networks are locally clustered. As can be seen in Table 11.1 and as illustrated in Figure 11.2, clustering has a significant impact on knowledge accumulation.

In particular, within SW-networks growth rates increase by a factor of almost 8 from 3.4 to 27 percent for $\alpha$-values ranging from 0 to 10, while for $\alpha$-values above 10 simulated growth rates do not further increase significantly (see Table 11.1).

Please note that unconnected networks correspond to an extreme form of clustering. Accordingly, one can observe that growth rates steeply increase between $\alpha=6$ and $\alpha=7$, that is, between unconnected and connected networks. However, please note further that also local clustering generally decreases with $\alpha$. As explained above, this fact is not perfectly reflected by corresponding global cluster coefficient ($\gamma$). Thus, for disconnected networks the effective network size is much lower than $n$ depending on the size of the connected components. Accordingly, following our intuitive explanation above, observed low growth rates of knowledge stocks technically result from the low effective global network size in disconnected networks.

Clustering also has a significant impact on speed of knowledge accumulation within connected networks as growth rates increase by 35 percent from 20 to 27 percent, ranging $\alpha$ from 7 to 10. Note that simulated differences between different clustering structures are statistically significant given the extremely low standard errors for average growth rates reported in Table 11.1.

*Table 11.1. Simulation results of knowledge accumulation assuming different network structures*

| Alpha | | 0 | 1 | 2 | 3 | 4 | 5 | 6 | 7 | 8 | 9 | 10 |
|---|---|---|---|---|---|---|---|---|---|---|---|---|
| Network type | Growth | | | | | | | | | | | |
| SWN-1000 | $w$ | 3.39 | 3.26 | 3.45 | 3.35 | 3.79 | 3.84 | 8.68 | 20.00 | 24.66 | 26.64 | 27.03 |
| $z = 10$ | $\sigma^2_w$ | 5.62 | 4.24 | 5.34 | 3.72 | 5.24 | 7.24 | 18.19 | 0.14 | 0.11 | 0.10 | 0.10 |
| | error | **0.07** | **0.07** | **0.07** | **0.06** | **0.07** | **0.09** | **0.13** | **0.01** | **0.01** | **0.01** | **0.01** |
| | $w^m$ | 8.35 | 7.73 | 8.52 | 7.72 | 8.52 | 9.22 | 12.95 | 20.77 | 25.31 | 27.24 | 27.59 |
| SWN-1000 | $w$ | 3.76 | 4.14 | 4.84 | 4.26 | 5.46 | 7.53 | 22.73 | 27.99 | 29.78 | 30.26 | 30.48 |
| $z = 15$ | $\sigma^2_w$ | 5.05 | 6.13 | 6.33 | 4.68 | 8.23 | 12.55 | 0.14 | 0.09 | 0.09 | 0.08 | 0.07 |
| | error | **0.07** | **0.08** | **0.08** | **0.07** | **0.09** | **0.11** | **0.01** | **0.01** | **0.01** | **0.01** | **0.01** |
| | $w^m$ | 8.62 | 9.01 | 9.62 | 8.71 | 10.52 | 12.59 | 23.45 | 28.62 | 30.42 | 30.75 | 31.07 |
| SWN-1000 | $w$ | 4.70 | 6.88 | 6.38 | 6.58 | 6.86 | 19.23 | 28.87 | 31.22 | 32.07 | 32.44 | 32.60 |
| $z=20$ | $\sigma^2_w$ | 5.78 | 13.20 | 12.06 | 7.70 | 7.93 | 9.67 | 0.10 | 0.07 | 0.09 | 0.09 | 0.08 |
| | error | **0.08** | **0.11** | **0.11** | **0.09** | **0.09** | **0.10** | **0.01** | **0.01** | **0.01** | **0.01** | **0.01** |
| | $w^m$ | 9.55 | 12.87 | 12.29 | 11.18 | 11.68 | 20.75 | 29.52 | 31.86 | 32.61 | 32.97 | 33.14 |
| SWN-3000 | $w$ | 3.05 | 2.96 | 3.41 | 3.57 | 3.70 | 4.00 | 15.48 | 25.52 | 29.77 | 30.93 | 31.12 |
| | $\sigma^2_w$ | 4.32 | 3.93 | 4.61 | 5.44 | 5.58 | 6.42 | 16.75 | 0.13 | 0.11 | 0.09 | 0.11 |
| | error | **0.04** | **0.04** | **0.04** | **0.04** | **0.04** | **0.05** | **0.07** | **0.01** | **0.01** | **0.01** | **0.01** |
| | $w^m$ | 8.90 | 8.56 | 9.20 | 9.69 | 9.86 | 10.09 | 18.08 | 26.52 | 30.61 | 31.81 | 31.97 |
| SWN-5000 | $w$ | 2.79 | 3.22 | 3.35 | 3.53 | 3.47 | 4.72 | 20.37 | 27.59 | 31.09 | 31.79 | 31.96 |
| | $\sigma^2_w$ | 3.66 | 4.54 | 4.55 | 4.84 | 4.37 | 9.43 | 1.42 | 0.12 | 0.12 | 0.12 | 0.12 |
| | error | **0.03** | **0.03** | **0.03** | **0.03** | **0.03** | **0.04** | **0.02** | **0.00** | **0.00** | **0.00** | **0.00** |
| | $w^m$ | 8.80 | 9.75 | 9.46 | 9.95 | 9.59 | 12.46 | 21.84 | 28.66 | 32.07 | 32.71 | 32.85 |
| 100-star | $w$ | 11.08 | 14.47 | 15.18 | 13.39 | 12.38 | 10.98 | 20.58 | 23.48 | 25.53 | 28.41 | 29.63 |
| | $\sigma^2_w$ | 94.19 | 94.96 | 95.58 | 88.89 | 89.87 | 85.64 | 38.07 | 0.15 | 0.11 | 0.11 | 0.09 |
| | error | **0.31** | **0.31** | **0.31** | **0.30** | **0.30** | **0.29** | **0.20** | **0.01** | **0.01** | **0.01** | **0.01** |
| | $w^m$ | 21.82 | 22.98 | 23.14 | 22.10 | 22.04 | 21.90 | 23.45 | 24.23 | 26.18 | 29.08 | 30.21 |
| 500-star | $w$ | 33.03 | 33.68 | 34.97 | 34.54 | 34.87 | 35.05 | 35.48 | 35.48 | 36.55 | 37.02 | 37.45 |
| | $\sigma^2_w$ | 11.42 | 0.11 | 0.07 | 17.72 | 15.95 | 0.10 | 0.09 | 0.11 | 0.07 | 0.05 | 0.03 |
| | error | **0.11** | **0.01** | **0.01** | **0.13** | **0.13** | **0.01** | **0.01** | **0.01** | **0.01** | **0.01** | **0.01** |
| | $w^m$ | 33.90 | 34.13 | 35.49 | 35.58 | 35.81 | 35.50 | 35.92 | 35.93 | 36.95 | 37.40 | 37.92 |
| 1000-star | $w$ | 38.74 | 38.71 | 38.56 | 38.38 | 38.85 | 38.78 | 38.88 | 38.68 | 38.76 | 38.54 | 38.87 |
| | $\sigma^2_w$ | 0.00 | 0.00 | 0.01 | 0.00 | 0.00 | 0.00 | 0.01 | 0.00 | 0.00 | 0.01 | 0.00 |
| | error | **0.00** | **0.00** | **0.00** | **0.00** | **0.00** | **0.00** | **0.00** | **0.00** | **0.00** | **0.00** | **0.00** |
| | $w^m$ | 39.09 | 39.07 | 39.01 | 38.71 | 39.22 | 39.15 | 39.32 | 39.05 | 39.18 | 39.00 | 39.23 |
| 1000-star | $w$ | 39.74 | 40.94 | 39.60 | 41.94 | 43.61 | 41.13 | 45.47 | 45.91 | 46.83 | 47.65 | 47.67 |
| $n = 3000$ | $\sigma^2_w$ | 118.11 | 96.97 | 156.33 | 132.70 | 69.51 | 164.83 | 0.22 | 0.15 | 0.11 | 0.09 | 0.08 |
| | error | **0.20** | **0.18** | **0.23** | **0.21** | **0.15** | **0.23** | **0.01** | **0.01** | **0.01** | **0.01** | **0.01** |
| | $w^m$ | 43.51 | 44.13 | 44.53 | 45.89 | 45.94 | 46.01 | 46.25 | 46.68 | 47.41 | 48.26 | 48.31 |
| 1000-star | $w$ | 33.46 | 35.47 | 34.59 | 35.64 | 36.08 | 40.31 | 45.29 | 46.16 | 48.22 | 48.33 | 48.41 |
| $n = 5000$ | $\sigma^2_w$ | 319.43 | 292.27 | 340.93 | 342.98 | 344.17 | 230.05 | 6.24 | 0.21 | 0.15 | 0.13 | 0.12 |
| | error | **0.25** | **0.24** | **0.26** | **0.26** | **0.26** | **0.21** | **0.04** | **0.01** | **0.01** | **0.01** | **0.00** |
| | $w^m$ | 44.45 | 45.03 | 45.98 | 46.82 | 47.22 | 47.25 | 46.48 | 47.09 | 48.95 | 49.02 | 49.16 |
| 3000-star | $w$ | 48.97 | 49.18 | 49.05 | 49.28 | 49.02 | 49.11 | 49.06 | 49.13 | 49.16 | 48.97 | 49.07 |
| | $\sigma^2_w$ | 0.00 | 0.00 | 0.00 | 0.00 | 0.00 | 0.00 | 0.00 | 0.00 | 0.00 | 0.00 | 0.00 |
| | error | **0.00** | **0.00** | **0.00** | **0.00** | **0.00** | **0.00** | **0.00** | **0.00** | **0.00** | **0.00** | **0.00** |
| | $w^m$ | 49.52 | 49.65 | 49.54 | 49.73 | 49.46 | 49.58 | 49.62 | 49.66 | 49.61 | 49.51 | 49.63 |
| 5000-star | $w$ | 50.50 | 50.49 | 50.50 | 50.45 | 50.47 | 50.29 | 50.39 | 50.50 | 50.42 | 50.42 | 50.53 |
| | $\sigma^2_w$ | 0.00 | 0.00 | 0.00 | 0.00 | 0.00 | 0.00 | 0.00 | 0.00 | 0.00 | 0.00 | 0.00 |
| | error | **0.00** | **0.00** | **0.00** | **0.00** | **0.00** | **0.00** | **0.00** | **0.00** | **0.00** | **0.00** | **0.00** |
| | $w^m$ | 51.05 | 50.97 | 50.97 | 50.92 | 50.93 | 50.88 | 50.91 | 50.92 | 50.95 | 50.93 | 51.04 |

*Note*:
$w$ = average knowledge accumulation; $\sigma^2_w$ = variance of average knowledge accumulation; $w^m$ = highest information; error = standard error

*Source*: Own calculations

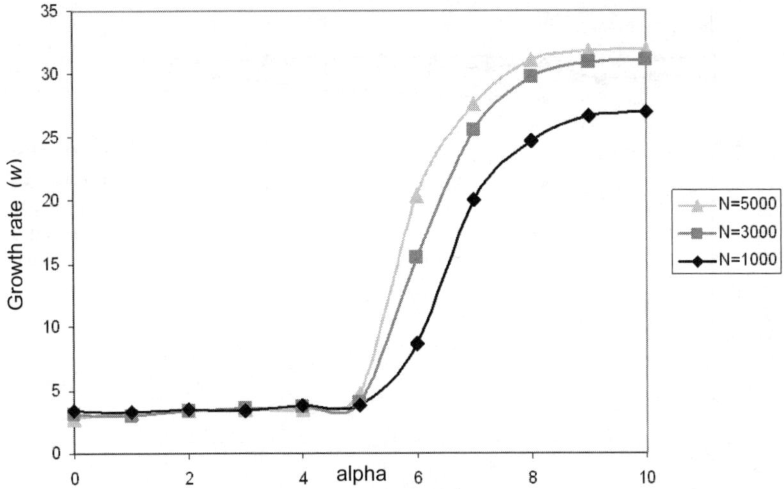


*Figure 11.2. Clustering and growth rates ($w$ in percent) of accumulated knowledge in SWNs*

The impact of clustering is clearly attenuated in hybrid networks including a star (see Figure 11.3).

For example, for a 100-star network, that is, a star with 100 ties, increasing clustering from ($\alpha=10$) to ($\alpha=7$) implies only a decrease of the growth rate ($w$) by a factor of 1.26 from 23.5 to 29.5 percent. Moreover, the larger the star the more the impact of clustering vanishes, for example, for a central star connected to every other firm (star-1000), clustering has almost no impact on knowledge accumulation (see Figure 11.3). Further, star networks are generally completely connected (see Table 11.1). Only the star-100 and -250 networks are not fully connected for $\alpha$-values below 7, and here we also observe that knowledge accumulation is significantly slower for unconnected networks.

Finally, comparing Figures 11.2 and 11.3, one can clearly see that although clustering generally reduces the speed of knowledge accumulation in both network types, in quantitative terms the impact is much higher for SWNs.

Again, all simulated differences between different clustering structures are statistically significant given the extremely low standard errors for average growth rates reported in Table 11.1.

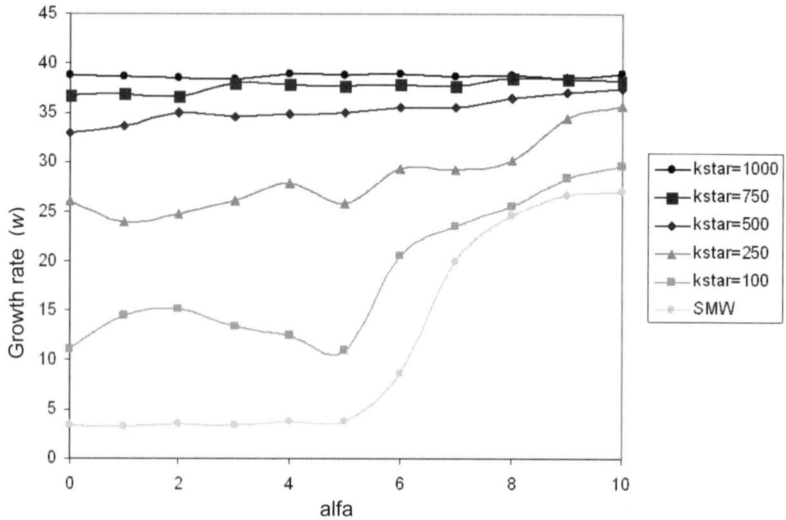


*Figure 11.3. Clustering and growth rates (w) of accumulated knowledge in star networks*

**11.4.2.3. Size of the star**

Further, Figure 11.3 clearly shows that the larger the size of the star the higher the speed of knowledge accumulation. This clearly results from our intuitive interpretation of our agent-based model, since the higher the number of ties of the star the larger are ceteris paribus the *r*-neighborhoods and thus the faster knowledge diffuses through the network accelerating knowledge accumulation. Obviously, the existence of a central star being connected to every node in the network (1000-star in Figure 11.3) implies that the 2-path neighborhood already includes the complete network. In this case the growth rate of knowledge accumulation approximates 0.5 as the network learns a new signal approximatively every second time period. An important question is how central stars are conceivable in real firm networks. One idea might be that large firms which are technological leaders become central stars in firm information networks. However, alternative candidates for central stars could be consulting companies or business associations. Empirically, it appears more conceivable for the latter to maintain many network ties than a large firm (Henning et al., 2008).

**11.4.2.4. Global network size**

As can bee seen in Figure 11.2, the global network size for the SW-network significantly increases the speed of knowledge. However, there is a significant negative interaction effect among clustering and network size, where impact of increasing network size almost vanishes when clustering is sufficiently high. For example, for $\alpha=10$, indicating a cluster coefficient of $\gamma=0.115$, an increase of global network size from 1000 to 5000 implies an increase of the speed of knowledge accumulation from 0.27 to 0.32, while for $\alpha=0$ almost no increase can be observed.

A similar increase of knowledge growth induced by a higher global network size can be observed for star networks (see Table 11.1). Note that only $n$ is increased, while the local network size, that is, the average number of network ties, $\bar{z}$, is held constant, which means the global network density decreases. Moreover, the global cluster coefficient, $\gamma$, decreases, while the characteristic path length $L$ increases with global network size (see Table 11A.1 in the appendix). Accordingly, the impact of increased global network size on knowledge accumulation can be separated into two different effects. A direct effect results, holding clustering constant. The explanation for the direct effect of global network size results from the fact that a larger network size implies ceteris paribus that the size of all $k$-path neighborhoods increases, since the probability of redundant network ties decreases with $n$.

Beyond the direct effect, shifting global network size also has an indirect effect, since an increased global network size implies less clustering for any given $\alpha$-value (see Table 11A.1 in the appendix). This indirect effect on knowledge accumulation via reduced clustering is also positive.

A similar effect of network size can be observed for star-networks (see Table 11.1), although we do not present this effect graphically to save space. However, especially for large stars, the effect of network size on knowledge accumulation is attenuated (see Table 11.1).

#### 11.4.2.5. Local network size

Finally, obviously the diffusion of knowledge through the network is the faster the higher the average number of direct ties, that is the larger average local network size, $\bar{z}$. As Table 11.1 shows, local network size has a significant impact on average knowledge growth rates. Again, a strong negative interaction effect with clustering can be observed, where the positive impact of a higher average local network size increases with $\alpha$. Hence, technically, the optimal speed of knowledge would result in a perfectly connected network, where every firm is connected to every other firm. In contrast, economically the cost of establishing network ties must be taken into consideration, implying that completely connected networks are not necessarily most efficient.

So far, we have only analyzed how an increase of the average local network size affects average knowledge accumulation in the network. Another interesting question is how individual local network size, $z_i$, affects the speed of knowledge accumulation of individual firms. Here, the exogenous assumption of Goyal and Joshi (2003) would clearly imply that firms with a higher local network size should also observe a higher speed of knowledge accumulation. However, our simulation results clearly contradict this implication. As Table 11.5 shows, the difference between the maximal accumulated knowledge in the network and the average accumulated knowledge is lower than or equal to 1 for all connected networks. Moreover, in the long run this difference is constant over time, which implies that all firms in a connected network accumulate knowledge at the same speed.

Interestingly, the same results can be observed for star-networks (see average and maximal knowledge stocks in Table 11.1). Even the star with a much larger local network size cannot accumulate faster knowledge when compared to the average firm in the network. Moreover, note that the variance of total information accumulated after 100 time periods across all firms in the network as reported in Table 11.1 ($\sigma_w^2$) is extremely low. Accordingly, this variance indicates that firms in a connected network hardly differ in their accumulated knowledge stocks, that is, the firms' accumulated knowledge differs less than 1 unit from the average accumulated knowledge. It is only in disconnected networks that firms differ in their accumulated knowledge stocks as well as speed of knowledge accumulation in the long run (see Table 11.1). Further, reported standard errors of the variance of accumulated knowledge in the network are extremely low, indicating that a low variance of knowledge stocks across firms and a constant growth rate of knowledge within connected networks is a stable finding of our simulation analyses. Finally, we also calculated correlation coefficients between firm's local network size ($z_i$) and firm's accumulated knowledge stock in each time period $t = 1, ..., 100$.[9] Calculated correlation coefficients are extremely low for all SWN as well as for star networks. For example, for our baseline SWN ($n = 1000$, $\alpha = 7$) calculated correlation coefficients range between 0.018 and 0.09, while for a 1000-star network calculated correlation coefficients range from 0.29 to 0.35. Thus, to give a more intuitive interpretation of these correlation coefficients, we have also calculated the estimated parameter of local network size resulting form a simple linear regression of accumulated knowledge on local network size. This parameter corresponds to the relation of the covariance of local network size with accumulated knowledge divided by the variance of local network size. Thus, our results imply a regression parameter around 0.001 for the star networks and around 0.025 for the SWN indicating a neglectable marginal effect of local network size on accumulated knowledge.

These results clearly contradict the assumption of Goyal and Joshi (2003) and seem surprising at first glance. However, given our assumed mechanism of knowledge accumulation it follows quite plainly that knowledge accumulation as defined by our model is basically a collective process. The probability that an individual firm adopts new knowledge from the external source is extremely low ($p = 0.001$); thus, speed of knowledge accumulation can be accelerated only if the network collectively learns.

Even a central star can only accumulate knowledge at a higher rate than 0.001 if his neighborhood accumulates at the same rate as the star. Moreover, note that in general the speed of knowledge accumulation is the same in the long run for all firms in a connected network. Moreover, assuming all firms have no knowledge (or the same amount of knowledge) at the beginning, the maximal difference of accumulated knowledge between firms is always limited to the maximal path length in the network. For the networks considered in our simulation analyses this differences hardly exceeds 1 as can be seen from Table 11.1. How can we intuitively understand this result? Basically, two different processes can be distinguished in a connected network. On the one hand the probability that the complete network learns a new signal. Obviously, this probability crucially depends on the number of firms that hold the maximal knowledge stock in the network. On the other hand the number of firms that hold the maximal knowledge in the network in each time period crucially depends on the speed of diffusion of knowledge through the network. In essence the diffusion process can be described by a recursive formula (see Rapoport, 1953), which approximatively corresponds to equation (11.15) above. However, as long as the second process is faster than the first, it follows that every new knowledge learned by the network completely diffused through the network before the network learns the next new signal. For example, for networks between 1000 and 5000 with a local network size of 10 and clustering coefficient lower than 0.45 a signal completely diffuses through the network within 3 time periods. Accordingly, as long as the maximal speed of knowledge accumulation is not above 1/3 (which basically implies that a firm learns every 3 time periods a new signal), the expected maximal difference of knowledge stocks between firms would be 1. For example, take a 1000-star network, where every firm is connected to the firm in the center of the star. In this case any new knowledge signal received by any firm except the star diffused through the complete network within two time periods, while the maximal growth rate is 31 percent (see Table 11.1). Therefore also for the 1000-star the maximal difference of the accumulated knowledge between any pair of firms is 1.

Of course, we must admit that our results are specific inasmuch as we are assuming a specific process of knowledge accumulation. However, we argue that the assumed process, especially the feature that individual learning is much harder than imitating other firms, corresponds sufficiently to many processes of knowledge accumulation that can be found in reality.

### 11.4.3. The Impact of Networks Under Different Innovation Intensities

So far we have analyzed to what extent network structures have an impact on knowledge spillovers and thus on knowledge accumulation, assuming a specific innovation intensity, that is, the probability that an individual firm acquires new knowledge in a given time period was set to $p=0.001$. However, the impact of network structures obviously depends on the innovation intensity, that is, the firms' investment into absorption capacity, $m_i$. For example, it is obvious that if the innovation intensity is extremely low, for example, $p$ approximates 0, individual firms quasi never learn. Accordingly, knowledge spillovers and thus network structures become irrelevant. On the other hand, assuming an extremely high innovation intensity, knowledge spillovers and thus network structures become less important, as in essence learning becomes a independent individual process.

In Figure 11.4 we report simulated knowledge growth rates assuming different innovation intensities, for example, ranging $p$ from 0.001 to 0.01 and 0.1. As can be clearly seen for $p>0.1$, which means ($log \ p>-1$), innovation intensity is sufficiently high that clustering has little impact on speed of knowledge accumulation. Analogously, the impact of a central star is significantly reduced as speed of knowledge is only slightly higher for the 1000-star-network when compared to SW-networks (see Figure 11.4).

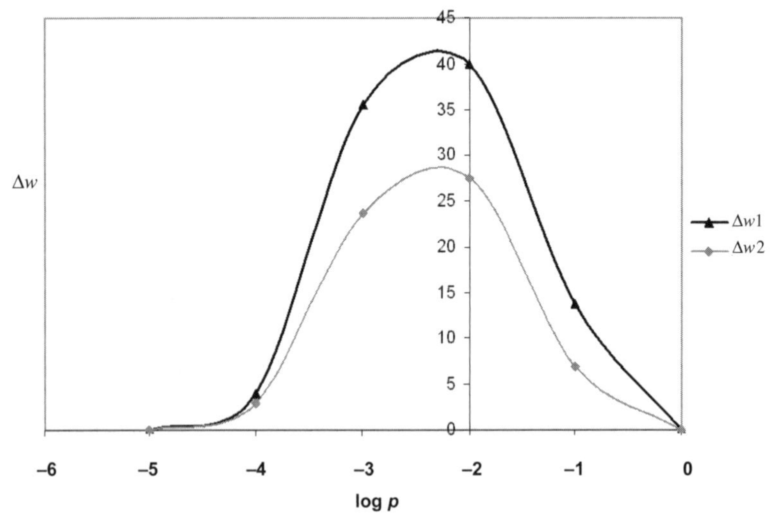


*Figure 11.4. Impact of network structures under different innovations intensities*

The lower line ($\Delta w1 = SWN_{10} - SWN_0$) displays the difference between two SW-networks where the first is a SW-network created with $\alpha = 10$ while the second SW-network was constructed with $\alpha = 0$. The second curve ($\Delta w2 = 1000 - star_{10} - SWN_0$) shows the difference for 1000-star-network with $\alpha = 10$ and a SW-network with $\alpha = 0$.

## 11.5. CONCLUSION AND OUTLOOK ON FUTURE RESEARCH

Stimulated by new evolutionary economic approaches to innovation and technical progress, this chapter aims to contribute to a better understanding of technological progress via explicitly modeling the process of knowledge diffusion in a given network of firms.

Although the importance of established informal and formal interfirm network structures for knowledge accumulation has clearly been recognized in the new ACE-literature on innovation, it is still fair to conclude that only very few studies exist analyzing the role of networks in knowledge spillovers and knowledge accumulation. In this regard the chapter certainly contributes to the existing literature.

In particular, the chapter contributes to theoretical studies in the innovative field of networks and economics that explore the emergence of stable and efficient R&D networks in a game-theoretical framework. In particular, the fundamental assumption that the number of direct network ties has a positive impact on firms' profit, made by Goyal and Joshi (2003), is challenged by our results. Results of our detailed simulations clearly imply that although at the macro level the average local network size significantly increases speed of knowledge accumulation in the complete firm network, at the micro level individual firms with a larger number of ties do not accumulate knowledge at a higher speed when compared to firms with an average number of network ties. Even a central star does not accumulate knowledge at a higher speed compared to the average firm in the network as long as networks are connected. Only if a network is disconnected do firms differ in their speed of knowledge accumulation. However, the absolute speed is extremely low for unconnected networks when compared to connected networks. Thus, individual firms have no incentives to maintain a large number of direct information ties. On the contrary, a free-rider problem might even arise regarding the establishment and maintenance of network ties. These results have major implications for the analyses of stable and efficient network structures. In particular, the major results of Goyal and Joshi (2003) might change in the framework of our model. We consider these implications as an interesting starting point for future research in the field of economics of networks and knowledge spillovers. Thus, future research might focus on how or under which condition this kind of free-rider problem occurs and influences the emergence of network structures.

Furthermore, given the fact that the majority of studies in new growth theory ignore the process of knowledge diffusion, our theory has also potential implications for regional economic growth theory. For example, models of the new economic growth theory imply that catching up generally occurs, since speed of knowledge transfers between leading and follower regions are monotonically increasing in the technological gap between a leading and a follower region (Barro, 1995; Grossman and Helpman, 1991). However, empirical studies hardly confirm the neoclassical hypothesis on catching up (Rogers, 2003). In response to the lack of empirical support of the neoclassical catching up hypothesis, some scholars suggest a non-monotonic relation between knowledge spillovers and technological gap (Verspagen, 1991; Rogers, 2003). Basically, the idea behind the assumption of a non-monotonic relation is that if the technological gap is too high, implying that the follower region is unable to decode the knowledge of the leading regions, little learning occurs. However, all of the existing approaches on catching up focus on the individual firm level. In this regard our theory extends existing theories of catching up as it understands knowledge accumulation basically as a collective process. Accordingly, beyond the absorption capacity of individual firms, speed of knowledge accumulation and hence catching up are crucially determined by interfirm network relations within the follower region. Note that in the framework of our model, assuming a low innovation intensity at individual firm level, catching up only occurs if information networks are extremely dense or extremely centralized or are characterized by an extremely large average local network size. Accordingly, our model also has interesting implications for regional development policy. In particular, beyond policies aiming to improve the firms' capacity to adopt knowledge from the leading region, such as improving trade openness and establishing international business links or sponsoring international academic exchange and studies abroad, it highlights the importance of policies improving establishment of interfirm network ties within the follower region. Examples for the latter are promotion of establishment of business associations or business meetings (exhibitions), provision of library services, technical journals, and so on.

Moreover, our study provides a theoretical foundation of existing empirical studies using only vague measures of structural (network) relations among firms or other indicators of social infrastructure as proxies for social capital (Knack and Keefer, 1997) as it generates testable hypotheses regarding the relation of quantitative network indicators of business networks with the average growth rate of knowledge and thus ceteris paribus with average technological progress observed for a finite set of firms.

However, to focus on the role of information networks in knowledge spillovers, the chapter applies a rather simple model neglecting other important factors of technological progress, for example, innovation processes resulting from the firms' in-house R&D. We claim that networks also play a role regarding innovation processes; however, this has not been analyzed in this chapter and thus, we consider this as one interesting topic for future research. In particular, it would be interesting to analyze how knowledge accumulation speeds up assuming a combined heterogeneity of local network size and investment in absorption capacity, that is a network including central stars specialized in absorption of external knowledge.

Finally, our approach simply assumes that accumulated knowledge is the key factor of technical progress, although beyond knowledge technical progress often requires investment in new capital goods. This investment is often characterized by a fundamental uncertainty, that is, firms must form beliefs regarding future states of the world without knowing ex ante the set of all possible future contingencies. Therefore, the firms' decision to invest in innovation can be better captured by agent-based approaches assuming strong substantive and procedural uncertainty than by dynamic optimization models with Bayesian updating or even perfect foresight. Social networks also have a significant impact on agents' belief formation and thus on firms' investment decision regarding innovative projects. These aspects of the impact of social networks on innovation have not been considered in this chapter; however, this as another interesting topic for future research.

# 11A. APPENDIX

## 11A.1. Indicator Table

*Table 11A.1. Network indicators*

| Alpha | | 0 | 1 | 2 | 3 | 4 | 5 | 6 | 7 | 8 | 9 | 10 |
|---|---|---|---|---|---|---|---|---|---|---|---|---|
| Network type | Indicators | | | | | | | | | | | |
| SMW-1000 | $\gamma$ | 0.62 | 0.72 | 0.76 | 0.80 | 0.82 | 0.83 | 0.83 | 0.74 | 0.44 | 0.20 | 0.12 |
| | $L$ | 1.74 | 2.00 | 2.03 | 2.30 | 2.04 | 2.57 | 3.15 | 5.77 | 3.81 | 3.43 | 3.35 |
| | $\sigma$ | 2.31 | 2.35 | 2.74 | 2.80 | 2.77 | 2.79 | 2.93 | 2.63 | 3.03 | 2.90 | 2.67 |
| | $lc$ | 6.90% | 5.89% | 8.40% | 7.50% | 5.40% | 11.50% | 18.09% | 100.00% | 100.00% | 100.00% | 100.00% |
| SMW-3000 | $\gamma$ | 0.63 | 0.71 | 0.77 | 0.80 | 0.82 | 0.83 | 0.80 | 0.61 | 0.26 | 0.08 | 0.03 |
| | $L$ | 1.76 | 1.91 | 2.06 | 2.13 | 2.23 | 2.43 | 11.71 | 5.19 | 4.08 | 3.80 | 3.76 |
| | $\sigma$ | 2.24 | 2.48 | 2.66 | 2.71 | 2.78 | 2.79 | 2.78 | 2.90 | 2.87 | 2.50 | 2.32 |
| | $lc$ | 2.62% | 2.82% | 2.87% | 2.95% | 3.14% | 4.73% | 94.76% | 100.00% | 100.00% | 100.00% | 100.00% |
| SMW-5000 | $\gamma$ | 0.63 | 0.71 | 0.77 | 0.80 | 0.82 | 0.82 | 0.78 | 0.53 | 0.18 | 0.04 | 0.01 |
| | $L$ | 1.73 | 1.92 | 2.06 | 2.14 | 2.22 | 2.67 | 9.66 | 5.12 | 4.21 | 4.01 | 3.97 |
| | $\sigma$ | 2.23 | 2.47 | 2.63 | 2.73 | 2.77 | 2.80 | 2.79 | 2.92 | 2.76 | 2.38 | 2.28 |
| | $lc$ | 1.68% | 1.81% | 1.88% | 2.11% | 2.09% | 4.86% | 99.25% | 100.00% | 100.00% | 100.00% | 100.00% |
| 100-star | $\gamma$ | 0.56 | 0.64 | 0.69 | 0.72 | 0.76 | 0.78 | 0.80 | 0.72 | 0.46 | 0.22 | 0.14 |
| | $L$ | 2.44 | 3.11 | 2.78 | 2.79 | 2.87 | 3.19 | 4.68 | 4.98 | 3.75 | 3.33 | 3.26 |
| | $\sigma$ | 5.49 | 5.92 | 6.37 | 6.93 | 7.18 | 6.68 | 6.79 | 6.22 | 6.63 | 8.89 | 9.06 |
| | $lc$ | 45.80% | 51.80% | 38.90% | 48.50% | 45.40% | 52.70% | 67.20% | 100.00% | 100.00% | 100.00% | 100.00% |
| 500-star | $\gamma$ | 0.39 | 0.41 | 0.45 | 0.48 | 0.53 | 0.58 | 0.62 | 0.64 | 0.55 | 0.49 | 0.48 |
| | $L$ | 2.40 | 2.40 | 2.30 | 2.30 | 2.24 | 2.26 | 2.23 | 2.26 | 2.14 | 2.07 | 2.06 |
| | $\sigma$ | 19.89 | 20.49 | 22.07 | 23.15 | 24.48 | 23.95 | 24.57 | 24.08 | 26.91 | 29.00 | 29.32 |
| | $lc$ | 100.00% | 98.70% | 95.00% | 100.00% | 100.00% | 98.20% | 100.00% | 100.00% | 100.00% | 100.00% | 100.00% |
| 1000-star | $\gamma$ | 0.34 | 0.34 | 0.35 | 0.36 | 0.38 | 0.42 | 0.47 | 0.54 | 0.63 | 0.71 | 0.72 |
| | $L$ | 1.99 | 1.99 | 1.99 | 1.99 | 1.99 | 1.99 | 1.99 | 1.99 | 1.99 | 1.99 | 1.99 |
| | $\sigma$ | 31.43 | 31.43 | 31.43 | 31.44 | 31.44 | 31.44 | 31.45 | 31.45 | 31.45 | 31.45 | 31.45 |
| | $lc$ | 100.00% | 100.00% | 100.00% | 100.00% | 100.00% | 100.00% | 100.00% | 100.00% | 100.00% | 100.00% | 100.00% |
| 3000-star | $\gamma$ | 0.33 | 0.34 | 0.34 | 0.34 | 0.35 | 0.37 | 0.39 | 0.44 | 0.50 | 0.58 | 0.59 |
| | $L$ | 2.00 | 2.00 | 2.00 | 2.00 | 2.00 | 2.00 | 2.00 | 2.00 | 2.00 | 2.00 | 2.00 |
| | $\sigma$ | 54.66 | 54.66 | 54.66 | 54.66 | 54.66 | 54.66 | 54.67 | 54.67 | 54.67 | 54.67 | 54.67 |
| | $lc$ | 100.00% | 100.00% | 100.00% | 100.00% | 100.00% | 100.00% | 100.00% | 100.00% | 100.00% | 100.00% | 100.00% |
| 5000-star | $\gamma$ | 0.33 | 0.33 | 0.34 | 0.34 | 0.34 | 0.36 | 0.37 | 0.40 | 0.45 | 0.52 | 0.53 |
| | $L$ | 2.00 | 2.00 | 2.00 | 2.00 | 2.00 | 2.00 | 2.00 | 2.00 | 2.00 | 2.00 | 2.00 |
| | $\sigma$ | 70.63 | 70.63 | 70.63 | 70.63 | 70.63 | 70.63 | 70.63 | 70.63 | 70.63 | 70.63 | 70.63 |
| | $lc$ | 100.00% | 100.00% | 100.00% | 100.00% | 100.00% | 100.00% | 100.00% | 100.00% | 100.00% | 100.00% | 100.00% |

*Note*:
$\gamma$ = clustering coefficient; $L$ = characteristic path length; $\sigma$ = centralization; $lc$ = largest component

*Source*: Own calculations

## 11A.2. A Construction Algorithm for Information Networks

To construct an information network, the modified $\alpha$-model (Watts, 1999) is applied which is able to generate hybrid network combining properties of scale-free, small-world and random networks.

According to this procedure, first a basic measure of the propensity that two vertices connect, $\mu_{ij}$, is assumed. Given the basic probabilities of inter-firm relationships, $\mu_{ij}$, a specific property of a social network relation is clustering, i.e., the fact that the likelihood of a connection among two firms is correlated with the existing connections among firms. In detail, the higher the number of overlapping connections between a pair of firms, the higher the probability that these two will form a connection as well.

How exactly clustering occurs is a very interesting topic in itself. However, we leave this interesting question for future research and simply assume that clustering occurs and can be implicitly incorporated into our network construction via defining the following transformation of the propensity measure, $\mu_{ij}$:

$$R_{ij} = \begin{cases} 1, & b_{ij} \geq z_i \\ \left[\dfrac{b_{ij}}{z_i}\right]^{\alpha}(1-\mu_{ij})+\mu_{ij}, & z_i > b_{ij} > 0 \\ \mu_{ij}, & b_{ij} = 0 \end{cases} \tag{11A.1}$$

In equation (11A.1), $b_{ij}$ denotes the number of overlapping ties between firms $i$ and $j$. According to the $\alpha$-model of Watts (1999), the parameter $\alpha$ determines the clustering of the network. For the special case of $\alpha = 0$, a highly clustered network results. Note that, for $\alpha = 0$, $R_{ij}$ becomes 1 whenever two vertices have at least one common connection, $b_{ij} > 0$.

On the other hand, the larger $\alpha$ the more $R_{ij}$ converges against the basic propensity, $\mu_{ij}$. Thus, as long as we assume that $\mu_{ij}$ is sufficiently small for all pairs, a random graph results.

Given the definition of the propensities $R_{ij}$, the following construction algorithm can be defined:

1. Compute probabilities, $\mu_{ij}$, for all pairs $(i,j) \in N^2$.
2. Randomly select a firm $i$. .
3. Compute $R_{ij}$ for all other vertices $j \in N$, where $R_{ij} = 0$, if $i$ and $j$ have already a connection.
4. Sum $R_{ij}$ over all $j$ and normalize each to obtain $Q_{ij} = R_{ij} / \sum_{k \neq i} R_{ik}$. $Q_{ij}$ can be interpreted as the probability that $i$ will connect with $j$. Thus, two mechanisms can be applied to select a connection, $j$, randomly with probability $Q_{ij}$. (a) Divide the unit interval $(0,1)$ into $(n-1)$ half-open subintervals with length $Q_{ij}$. Generate a uniform random variable on $(0,1)$. It must fall into one of the intervals, $Q_{ij}$. Connect $i$ with $j$, the interval that the random variable falls into; (b) randomly select a vertex $j$, with probability $1/(n-1)$, randomly select a uniform variable on $(0,1)$, if it is lower or equal than $Q_{ij}$ connect $i$ with $j$. Otherwise start the process again.

This procedure (1) to (4) is repeated until the predetermined number of edges $M = \sum_i z_i$ has been constructed. The vertices $i$ are chosen randomly, but once a vertex $i$ has been chosen it may not be chosen again until all other vertices have taken their turn.

Barabási and Albert (1999) provided a model which constructs scale-free networks; starting with a small number of vertices $b_0$ and adding a new vertex at every step. The new vertex will then be connected to $b$ other vertices, where the probability in connecting to a vertex depends on the number of already existing edges of this vertex. This principle is called preferential attachment, which has similarities to $b_{ij}$ in the $\alpha$-model of Watts (1999).

The $\alpha$-model presented in this chapter is used to generate small-world networks.

An extension of the $\alpha$-model allows us to analyze scale-free networks, including a number of $s$ 'stars', which are agents that hold a higher degree than the average agent.

The construction algorithm for the network with stars is a nested combination of the original $\alpha$-model of Watts (1999, p. 47) where the density of the network is maintained to allow for a comparison of the network types:

1. Random selection of $s$ stars characterized by $z_s$ information ties.
2. Recalculation of the degree for non-stars and construction of the network by using the $\alpha$-model algorithm until $M - s\,z_s$ edges are distributed.
3. Application of the $\alpha$-model algorithm, selecting only stars to distribute the remaining network ties, i.e., only the stars are allowed to choose ties.

This algorithm keeps the idea of clustering according to existing ties, which is similar to Watts' approach, which seems to be logical for the stars as well. In detail, we assumed that only one star exists, where we vary the number of ties this star forms.

## NOTES

1. Although their empirical test did not provide significant evidence for an impact of their selected social capital indicators on economic growth (Knack and Keefer, 1997).
2. Alternatively, the process of absorbing external knowledge could also be interpreted as original generation of new knowledge, for example, as a creative process via learning-by-doing or via a firms' own research and development activities.

3. However, the model of knowledge accumulation derived here also applies if we assume new knowledge is generated via learning-by-doing instead of assuming new knowledge is exogenously generated in a science sector or leading region.
4. A main interest in this regard is how the firms' ability to absorb knowledge spillovers affects the firms' investment into their ability to absorb external knowledge outside of the network. Obviously, for the latter a free rider problem arises in the presence of knowledge spillovers. However, we postpone this interesting topic for later research and do not investigate the free-rider problem inherent in the firms' investment into absorption capacity in this chapter.
5. However, in another paper (Henning and Saggau, 2008) we apply the seminal work of Solomonoff and Rapoport (1951) and Rapoport (1953), who were one of the first to analyze how diffusion of information is determined by global network structure, to derive a more accurate approximation of the size of *r*-neighborhoods.
6. The detailed algorithm is described in Appendix 11A.2.
7. Of course, as one anonymous referee pointed out, other indicators, for example, the maximal accumulated knowledge in the network, are also conceivable. However, we argue that average accumulated knowledge is an appropriate indicator as far as the impact of knowledge accumulation on regional economic growth is concerned. As reported below, in our specific case maximal accumulated knowledge does not differ significantly from average knowledge, thus both indicators have the same economic implications. We thank one anonymous referee for this comment.
8. Please note that for all undertaken simulation analyses growth rates did not significantly change after 100 time periods as can be seen in Figure 11.1. Therefore, calculated long-term growth rates $(w)$ presented in Table 11.1 as well as in Figures 11.2–11.4 generally correspond to growth rates calculated in time period 100. Moreover, as we undertook for every network parameter constellation 100 simulation runs, long-term growth rates $(w)$ presented in Table 11.1 as well as in Figures 11.2–11.4 are the average long-term growth rates calculated over this 100 simulations. Analogously, we calculated the variance of the long term growth rate across firms within the network, where in Table 11.1 the reported variances $\sigma_w^2$ correspond again to the average variance calculated over the 100 simulations undertaken for each network parameter constellation. Finally, the standard error of the average long-term growth rate (error) presented in Table 11.1 has been calculated based on the 100 repeated simulation runs for each network constellation.
9. We thank an anonymous reviewer for suggesting the additional calculation of correlation coefficients to underline our main finding

# REFERENCES

Antonelli, C. (1996), 'Localized Knowledge Percolation Processes and Information Networks', *Journal of Evolutionary Economics*, **6**(3), 281–95.

Arrow, K. (1962), 'The Economic Consequences of Learning by Doing', *Review of Economic Studies*, **24**(80), 155–73.

Barabási, A.-L. and R. Albert (1999), 'Emergence of Scaling in Random Networks', *Science*, **286**, 509–12.

Barro, R. and X. Sala-i-Martin (1995), *Economic Growth*, New York: McGraw-Hill.

Bollobás, B. (2001), *Random Graphs*, 2nd edn, Cambridge: Cambridge University Press.

Burt, R.S. (1982), *Toward a Structural Theory of Action: Network Models of Social Structure, Perception, and Action*, New York: Academic Press.

Cantner, U. and A. Pyka (1998), 'Absorbing Technological Spillovers: Simulations in an Evolutionary Framework', *Industrial and Corporate Change*, **7**(2), 369–97.

Cohen, W. and D.A. Levinthal (1989), 'Innovation and Learning: the Two Faces of Research and Developement', *Economic Journal*, **99**, 569–96.

Cooper, C. and A. Frieze (2003), 'A General Model of Web Graphs', Department of Computer Science, King's College, Unversity of London, mimeo.

D'Aspremont, C. and A. Jacquemin (1988), 'Cooperative and Noncooperative R&D in Duopoly with Spillovers', *American Economic Review*, **78**, 1133–7.

Dawid, H. (2006), 'Agent-based Models of Innovation and Technological Change', in L. Tesfatsion and K.L. Judd (eds), *Handbook of Computational Economics Volume 2: Agent-Based Computational Economics*, Handbooks in Economics Series, The Netherlands: North-Holland/Elsevier, pp. 1235–72.

Deffuant, G., F. Amblard, G. Weisbuch and T. Faure (2002), 'How Can Extremism Prevail? A Study Based on Relative Agreement Interaction Model', *Journal of Artificial Societies and Social Simulations*, **5**(4).

Dopfer, K. (2001), 'Evolutionary Economics: Framework for Analysis', in K. Dopfer (ed.), *Evolutionary Economics: Program and Scope. Recent Economic Thought Series*, Boston, Dordrecht and London: Kluwer Academic Publishers.

Dosi, G. and S. Winter (2002), 'Interpreting Economic Change: Evolution, Structures and Games', in M. Augier and J.G. March (eds), *The Economics of Choice, Change and Organization*, Cheltenham, UK and Northampton, MA, USA: Edward Elgar, pp. 337–53.

Erdös, P. and A. Renyi (1959), 'On Random Graphs', *Publicationes Mathematicae Deberecen*, **6**, 290–97.

Fagerberg, J. and B. Verspagen (2002), 'Technology Gaps, Innovation-diffusion and Transformation: an Evolutionary Approach', *Research Policy*, **31**, 1291–304.

Feldman, M.P. and D.B. Audretsch (1999), 'Innovation in Cities, Science-based Diversity, Specialization and Localized Competition', *European Economic Review*, **43**, 409–29.

Frank, O. and D. Strauss (1986), 'Markov Graphs', *Journal of the American Statistical Association*, **81**(395), 832–42.

Goyal, S. and S. Joshi (2003), 'Networks of Collaboration in Oligopoly', *Games and Economic Behavior*, **43**, 57–85.

Grossman, G. and E. Helpman (1991), *Innovation and Growth in the Global Economy*, Cambridge, MA: MIT Press.

Henning, C. and V. Saggau (2008), 'Learning in R-Neighborhoods: the Impact of Network Structure on Knowledge Spillovers and Accumulation', mimeo.

Henning, C. and V. Saggau (2009), 'Information Networks and Knowledge Spillovers: Simulations in an Agent-based Model Framework', Technical Report, Institute of Agricultural Economics, University of Kiel available at http://www.advanced-eval.eu.

Henning, C., V. Buskens, H. Flap, S. Bäumer, A. Henningsen, A. Castaldo, A. McKay, H. Tietje, G. Henningsen, C. Aßmann and J. Mumm (2008), 'Empirical

Network Studies in High and Low Performing Rural Communities: Slovakia and Poland', *Regional Report RR4-1*, University of Kiel.

Jackson, M.O. (2005), 'The Economics of Social Networks', *Working Paper 1237*, California Institute of Technology, Division of the Humanities and Social Sciences.

Kleinberg, J.M., R. Kumar, P. Raghavan, S. Rajagopalan and A.S. Tomkins (1999), 'The Web as a Graph: Measurements, Models and Methods', *Lecture Notes in Computer Science*, 1627, 1–17.

Knack, S. and P. Keefer (1997), 'Does Social Capital Have an Economic Payoff? A Cross-country Investigation', *Quarterly Journal of Economics*, **112**, 1251–88.

Kumar, R., P. Raghavan, S. Rajagopalan, D. Sivakumar, A. Tomkins and E. Upfal (2000), 'Stochastic Models for the Web Graph', *FOCS*, Proceedings of the 41st Annual Symposium on Foundations of Computer Science.

Levene, M., T. Fenner, G. Loizou and R. Wheeldon (2002), 'A Stochastic Model for the Evolution of the Web', *Computer Networks*, **39**, 277–87.

Nelson, R.R. (1995), 'Recent Evolutionary Theorizing about Economic Change', *Journal of Economic Literature*, **33**(1), 48–90.

Nelson, R.R. and E.S. Phelps (1966), 'Investment in Humans, Technological Diffusion and Economic Growth', *American Economic Review*, **56**, 69–75.

Nelson, R.R. and S.G. Winter (1982), *An Evolutionary Theory of Economic Change*, Cambridge, MA, and London: Belknap Press.

Nelson, R.R. and S.G. Winter (2002), 'Evolutionary Theorizing in Economics', *Journal of Economic Perspectives*, **16**(2), 23–46.

Paci, R. and R. Usai (2000), 'Technological Enclaves and Industrial Districts: an Analysis of the Regional Distributions of Innovative Activity in Europe', *Regional Studies*, **34**(2), 97–114.

Pareto, V. (1896), *Cours d'Économie Politique*, Paris: Droz.

Pennock, D.M., G.W. Flake, S.Lawrence, E.J. Glover and C.L. Giles (2002), 'Winners Don't Take All: Characterizing the Competition for Links on the Web', *Proceedings of the National Academy of Sciences*, **99**(8), 5207–11.

Pyka, A. and P. Saviotti (2001), 'Innovation Networks in the Biotechnology-based Sectors', *Discussion Paper Series*, Universität Augsburg, Institute for Economics.

Rapoport, A. (1953), 'Spread of Information Through a Population with Socio-structural Bias: I. Assumption of Transitivity', *Bulletin of Mathematical Biophysics*, **15**, 523–33.

Rogers, M. (2003), *Knowledge, Technological Catch-up and Economic Growth*, Cheltenham, UK and Northampton, MA, USA: Edward Elgar.

Romer, P. (1986), 'Increasing Returns and Long-run Growth', *The Journal of Political Economy*, **94**(5), 1002–37.

Romer, P. (1992), 'Two Strategies for Economic Development Using Ideas and Producing Ideas', *Proceedings of the World Bank Annual Conference on Development Economics*, pp. 63–91.

Romer, P. (1993), 'Idea Gaps and Object Gaps', *Journal of Monetary Economics*, **32**, 543–73.

Rosenberg, N. (1990), 'Why Do Firms Do Basic Research (with Their Own Money)?', *Research Policy*, **19**, 165–74.

Sako, M. (1999), 'From Individual Skills to Organizational Capability in Japan', *Oxford Review of Economic Policy*, **15**, 114–26.
Solomonoff, R. and A. Rapoport (1951), 'Connectivity of Random Nets', *Bulletin of Mathematical Biophysics*, **13**, 107–17.
Spence, M. (1984), 'Cost Reduction, Competition, and Industry Performance', *Econometrica*, **52**, 101–21.
Verspagen, B. (1991), 'A New Empirical Approach to Catching Up or Falling Behind', *Structural Change and Economic Dynamics*, **2**(2), 359–80.
Wasserman, S. and K. Faust (1994), *Social Network Analysis: Methods and Applications*, Cambridge: Cambridge University Press.
Wasserman, S. and P. Pattison (1996), 'Logit Models and Logistic Regressions for Social Networks: I. An Introduction to Markov Graphs and *p**', *Psychometrika*, **61**, 401–25.
Watts, D.J. (1999), *Small Worlds: the Dynamics of Networks Between Order and Randomness*, Princeton, NJ: Princeton University Press.
Watts, D.J. and S.H. Strogatz (1998), 'Collective Dynamics of "Small-world Networks"', *Nature*, **393**, 440–42.
Wilhite, A. (2006), 'Economic Activity on Fixed Networks', in L. Tesfatsion and K. Judd (eds), *Handbook of Computational Economics: Agent Based Computational Economics*, Amsterdam: North-Holland/Elsevier.

# 12. Interaction between economic and social variables: the transformational growth matrix*

**Edward Nell**

## 12.1. INTRODUCTION

The object here is to explore the interactions between economic growth and change, on the one hand, and changes in social, environmental, political and population variables, on the other. These interactions are likely to affect social and economic well-being, for better or worse, and very possibly quite strongly. Economic growth could be supported and enhanced – or it could be undermined, even reversed. The economy is 'embedded' in society, after all; the object will be to show this in a measurable way, and to show as precisely as possible why and how this matters.

Keeping the analysis simple, but still realistic, economies here will be assumed to be made up of sectors – industry, agriculture, services – and social classes – workers, landlords, business owners, bankers.[1] There are economic interactions between sectors and social classes; analyzing these is part of the theory of growth and fluctuations. But we want to focus on a different kind of interaction, also involving both sectors and classes, but this time between economic advances and the resulting pressure or development of social variables. When sectors and classes interact along the social dimensions, we shall argue, it is likely to change the patterns of development – and it may lead to stagnation and failure to develop.[2,3]

## 12.2. THE TRANSFORMATIONAL GROWTH MATRIX

To examine these questions we must set up quite a general framework, in which we can study how different kinds of economic change can interact in various ways with many aspects of the social order. But in what follows we will keep the discussion of the purely economic side as simple as possible, allowing us to define and examine a wide range of social, political and demographic variables. We will stick to straightforward cases of economic growth resulting from capital accumulation and technological advances. At this point we will present a full spectrum of non-economic variables, though later we will simplify this, too. Even so, we will see that the interaction between the economic side of a country and the other aspects of its social order turns out to be complicated and important.

To display the variables and their interactions in the most general way, we will set them out as a matrix, in which the coefficient will indicate the relationships. (Since we are examining growth, we call this the Transformational Growth Matrix.) First we will list and describe the variables to be considered. These will appear in the row and column vectors. Usually a variable will be a composite, made up of a number of different but related elements that tend to move together, so that it can be represented by appropriate proxies.[4] Measurement scales will have to be chosen or developed, and they will necessarily be approximations. However, we will not deal with the empirical issues here. Our aim is to present the approach, and outline the kinds of relationships that we can see between economic advances and social, political and demographic variables.

### 12.2.1. Indicators for the Variables

First, the variables:

**Economic**

- Economic Growth (EconG): GNP levels and growth, level and growth of employment, standard measures of sectoral growth; human development index, for comparison with purely economic.

**Environmental issues**

- Environment (EnvH): Pollution of soil, waste disposal air pollution – gases and particulate matter; acid rain; waste heat and energy discharge and the effects on climate; water quality and availability.

**Social issues**

- Socialization of Adolescents (AdlSoc): preparing adolescents for adult working life, contact between adolescents and non-parental adults, apprenticeship and other training programs, school drop-out rates, measures of substance abuse.
- Education (Educ): literacy rates, school enrollments, education spending as a percentage of government budget, of GNP, primary, secondary, and college graduation rates, research programs, specialized training programs, newspapers and books published, library book loans, net

school enrollment male and female (primary, secondary, tertiary), literacy, ratio of female to male literacy.
- Health: infant mortality, mother's condition in childbirth, life expectancy, morbidity and prevalence of disease, access to hospitals, availability of medicines, hospitals, doctors per thousand population, indicators of public health.
- Household Standard of Living (HStndL): not only the level of the average standard of living, but also its distribution – the degree of inequality. Under 5 infant mortality, shared household income ratio between highest 20% and lowest 40%, population using improved drinking water and sewage facilities. Public goods, crime rates by income distribution, radios and televisions per capita. Gini coefficients will give an overall picture; poverty rates for different poverty levels, and measures of concentration of wealth and ownership of land will portray the extremes.

**Political**
- Social Infrastructure (SocInf): transportation, communications, police and the criminal justice system, public infrastructure – roads, bridges, sewers and water supply, harbours, airports, garbage and waste management; public administration, land management and zoning, military and defense spending.
- Effective and Democratic Government (EffGov): Representative and responsive government, civil order, size of middle class, percentage voting, effectiveness of the legal system and the courts, training of the police, the working of a free press, human rights and religious freedom.

**Demographics**
- Population (PopP): Size, growth, age distribution, median age, birth and death rates, natural reproduction rates, fertility, percent under 15, percent over 65, life expectancy at birth. Sex ratios, if available.

PopP, AdlSoc and Educ together give us people along with their skills, what they know and what they can do. EconG and EnvH tell us what is being done, what is being produced, who is working, in what ways, and with what effects on the world in which the society is set. SocInf measures what the state and the society as a whole provides as a framework to undergird and regulate social life and economic activity. Health and HStndL show how what is being produced benefits the people, in both public and private dimensions. It gives us a measure of the benefits being delivered and their distribution. And finally EffGov tells us how order is maintained and disputes resolved.

### 12.2.2. The Matrix

The object here is to show how EconG interacts with the rest; we argue that this will be the key to successful development. Accordingly the top row of Table 12.1 will show how EconG depends on each of the other variables, and the first column will give the impact of EconG on the other variables. For example, EconG may be stimulated or supported by EconG itself – or it may not. It will normally benefit from improvement in the EnvH, as well as the four social variables, AdlSoc, Educ, Health, and Household StndL. Improvements in the Political variables, SocInf and EffGov can also be expected to benefit EconG.

The next line below shows EnvH as depending on EconG, EnvH itself, AdlSoc, Educ, Health, StndL, SocInf, EffGov, and PopP; below that we will have AdlSoc depending on each of the others, and so on, for Educ, Health SocInf, HStndL, EffGov, and PopP, respectively.

Each depends on the others, and the interdependence can be positive, negative, or zero. And, of course, the dependence can change, either as the result of the pressures of globalization, the changes brought about by development, or by policy, or as a mix of all these.

The bottom row of Table 12.1 shows the way PopP depends on the other variables. Higher EconG, for example, could go either way. By bringing in improved technology, it would improve medicine, and lower death rates, so increasing PopP. This is the likely short-term response. But by bringing increased economic opportunities, especially for women, it could lead to lower fertility, reducing PopP, though it may take time for this to emerge. In the same way, a better EnvH will lead to fewer deaths from respiratory disease and foul water, but a healthy environment might also lead to more chances for enjoyable leisure, reducing fertility. Good AdlSoc should lead to fewer unwanted pregnancies and smaller families, representing deliberate choices, thus lowering fertility. A higher standard of living, at least initially, increases population pressure, because it reduces deaths. But in the long run, a higher HStndL will lead to reduced fertility as women take advantage of greater opportunities with confidence that their smaller families will survive and live healthier lives. A positive relationship between these economic variables and PopP can be seen in many developing countries today, reflecting the fact that better diet and public health will increase longevity and lower childhood mortality, while the long run effects have yet to show themselves.

The matrix is not designed to make general statements; a separate matrix must be developed for each country, and it can be expected to change over time. Indeed, these changes will mark the development of the country. Each case must be investigated empirically, and the investigation must be updated regularly.

Yet when we assemble the data in the right way, some surprising general patterns can be seen. The results of empirical study can be written as the set of equations below, arranged in an array (see Table 12.1). On the left in a column we have the amounts of each of the variables; they are each set equal to the combined effects on them of the others, shown on the right. The plus or minus mark in each cell indicates whether the variable on the left is related positively or negatively to the variable at the top of each column. Strong relationships are indicated in boldface. (The particular configuration shown here reflects a stylized summary of some of the problems developing economies face now. Later we will consider the way these variables are related in the developed countries.) All the variables are endogenous, although most will also have an exogenous component.

The matrix developed here should make it possible to see patterns. An advantage of our approach is that these can be seen even when we are not able to specify the relationships numerically. Sometimes all we can say is that variables are related positively, negatively, or not at all. In such a case all we can enter are '+', '–', and '0' in the appropriate cells of the matrix. But even with this limited information, not only can we identify significant causal linkages, we see how they interact and feed back on one another. As we see here, simple visual inspection – no mathematics needed – can sometimes tell us whether the interactions will end up in a vicious or a virtuous cycle.

As a first approximation, the relationships can be taken as linear.[5] The justification is that the changes in the variables will be small.

*Table 12.1. Signs of the coefficients*

| | EconG | ENV | AdlSoc | Educ | Health | StndL | SocInf | EffGov | PopP |
|---|---|---|---|---|---|---|---|---|---|
| EconG = f ( | ___ | + | + | **+** | **+** | + | **+** | + | –) |
| EnvH = f ( | **+or–** | (+) | + | + | ___ | ?+ | + | + | –) |
| AdlSoc = f ( | +or– | 0 | ___ | + | + | + | + | + | –) |
| Educ = f ( | + | + | + | (+) | **+** | + | + | + | –) |
| Health = f ( | +or– | + | + | **+** | (+) | + | + | + | –) |
| StndL = f ( | **+?** | + | + | + | + | ___ | + | ? | –) |
| SocInf = f ( | +or– | + | ?+ | ? | + | ? | ___ | + | –) |
| EffGov = f ( | +? | + | + | + | + | + | + | (+) | –) |
| PopP = f ( | **+or–?** | +or– | – | – | +or–? | **+or–** | + | ?– | ___) |

There should also be a constant term in each equation, to capture the influences not accounted for by the stated variables.[6] This will be important later.

If the impacts shown are all positive, and if each impact is interpreted to represent a fraction of the total change of the variable, then basing the system on suitable initial conditions, it might be reasonable to expect a unique solution. That is, solving the equations would tell us how large, relative to each other, the variables must be. Since such a solution will determine relative amounts, it would be possible to use this system to examine the impact of a policy change – which is, indeed, the main point. If, for example, the degree of change in EconG were imposed from outside, the system would allow us to calculate the effects on all the other variables.[7] (Note that the case where the coefficients in a row or column sum to unity is especially useful; it gives rise to Markov chains in which successive adjustments converge to a unique solution.)

With nine equations and nine variables we have 81 relationships to consider – or 72, if we ignore the question of self-reinforcing relationships. It can all be presented neatly, as a matrix, with the nine variables arranged in rows and columns (see Table 12.2). The first row shows for example, how EconG depends on the other variables, while the first column shows how the other variables depend on EconG. The second row shows how EnvH depends on the other variables, and the second column shows how the others depend onEnvH. The third row and column then show AdlSoc, the fourth Educ, the fifth, Health, and so on, finishing with PopP.

*Table 12.2. Matrix of coefficient signs*

| | EconG | EnvH | AdlSoc | Educ | Health | StndL | SocInf | EffGov | PopP |
|---|---|---|---|---|---|---|---|---|---|
| EconG | ____ | + | + | + | + | + | + | + | – |
| EnvH | **+or–** | ____ | + | + | ?+ | + | + | + | – |
| AdlSoc | +or– | + | ____ | + | + | + | + | + | – |
| Educ | ?+ | ?+ | + | ____ | + | + | + | + | – |
| Health | –?+ | + | + | + | ____ | + | + | + | – |
| StndL | **+or–** | + | + | + | + | ____ | + | + | – |
| SocInf | +or– | + | + | ?+ | ? | + | ____ | + | – |
| EffGov | +? | + | + | + | + | + | + | ____ | – |
| PopP | **+,– ?** | +,– ? | – | – | -or+ | + | – | – | ____ |

Let us look at the variables and how they might relate to one another in various economic conditions, taking them in succession. Important cases include countries that depend on Primary Exports, Dualistic economies, economies trying to industrialize using out-dated technologies and second-hand equipment, and economies still relying on traditional and craft technologies.

**Economics**

Reading across the top row shows how Economic Growth depends on the other variables. These relationships will tend to hold in all of the cases. An improved Environment will tend to support Economic Growth; it should lead to more productive agriculture and to a healthier labor force. Better Socialization of Adolescents will mean a more skilled workforce. Both improved Education and better public and private Health measures will raise productivity and reduce sick days. A better Social Infrastructure will translate into a more secure workforce, while a higher Household Standard of Living provides larger markets and better informed consumers, and promotes better health. It also supports but does not guarantee better socialization of adolescents. A more Democratic Government helps to ensure a stable civil order and a reliable and uncorrupt system of justice. Finally, Economic Growth will be made more difficult by Population pressure,

And it works in reverse; just as improvements in these variables promote EconG, decline or reductions will hamper economic advance. If adolescents are not properly socialized, they will not fit into an urban work force, and they will not function well as citizens. This will be reflected in weaker productivity and a decline in the Household Standard of Living, as relatives will be under pressure to support them. Poor education and health will only compound these difficulties. All this will put pressure on social infrastructure, and will create tensions within democratic institutions.

**The Environment**

The Environment will very likely come under pressure from EconG in two cases, Primary Exporting and Dualistic economies, but may not be so pressured in other cases. Faster growth tends to generate increased pollution and contributes to global warming, especially in Primary Exporting and Dualistic economies. Pollution is, famously, an ‘externality’, that is, a cost which neither buyer nor seller pays, unless forced to by regulation or law. This is unlikely in weakly integrated systems. But faster growth also provides the resources and the new technologies to clean up and preserve the environment, although this may be difficult in economies undergoing Outdated Industrialization (think of Peru or Argentina in the 1960s and 70s, or parts of India even today). Prosperity also elevates the regard placed on a sustainable and healthy environment. For these reasons some have argued that starting from a low level, Economic Growth will first tend to worsen the Environment, but at higher levels further economic growth will improve the environment. This is sometimes called an ‘Environmental Kuznets Curve’ – analogous to Kuznets’ original hypothesis that historically economic growth first worsened, then improved the distribution of income. The evidence, however, is inconclusive, both in regard to the environment and for the original claim. As for the other variables, better Education and Health probably have little effect; at best they may contribute marginally to a better Environment. But better Social Infrastructure, a higher Standard of Living and greater Democracy will all tend to encourage improvement in the Environment. On the other hand, in general, when Population increases the Environment will tend to suffer.

**Social variables**

- The Socialization of Adolescents will tend to be altered by EconG in virtually any developing economy. Higher EconG will lead to an outflow of families from rural areas into the cities, where they will lose the traditional support of neighborhood and kin. The older generation will lack the skills and knowledge to provide guidance to the young. In Primary Exporting and Dualistic economies EconG may not create many new opportunities; youth unemployment may become a major social issue. On the other hand in Small-Scale Craft and Industrializing economies, higher growth will provide both the tax revenues and employment opportunities in the cities, making it possible to offer education and training to the young. The effect of the other variables is straightforward, except, perhaps, in one case. Higher Population growth will put a strain on Socialization, making it more difficult, but a better Environment and improved Social Infrastructure, a higher Standard of Living and a more Democratic Government all tend to encourage better socialization of the young. Better Education will certainly improve AdlSoc, and better Health is likely to. A warning, however: in the short run improved Education could lead to a 'generation gap' between youth and parents. This is a standard theme in Bollywood movies, and is evident even in today's Ireland.
- Education: Economic Growth can go either way; growth can promote education by demanding greater skills and a higher quality of labor. But it could also draw children and the unskilled into low-level long-hour jobs, keeping them out of school. Which effect it has depends on the kind of growth being promoted. In general the positive result is more likely in the strongly integrated economies, the negative in the weakly integrated ones. Better AdlSoc will make it easier; improved social infrastructure and a higher standard of living will tend to improve education. A more Democratic Government will strengthen it. But a cleaner and better Environment, by itself, may not have much impact one way or the other on education – although people may learn a good deal by cleaning up! Health strongly and positively impacts education – better health means better learning. Note the chain of positive linkages: a better Env leads to

better Health, which leads to better learning, which, in turn, is likely to promote a better Env! These are the kinds of connections to look for. A rise in Pop pressure, on the other hand, will generally create problems for education.

- Health: In the well-integrated economies, EconG will provide more resources; and employers will want a healthy labor force, so Health should improve; but even in these economies, and certainly in Primary Exporting and Dualistic ones, economic expansion might create too much disruption, leading to crowding and congestion that will reduce the quality and availability of health care. AdlSoc and Education will improve it, the latter quite strongly. Better SocInf and a higher StandL will both improve health, and greater EffGov will open the way for people to demand better health measures. Pop pressure can reduce health.
- The Household Standard of Living should improve with advances in EconG. However, Economic Growth can lead to such an intense concentration of income and wealth in the hands of a small group that everyone else is actually left worse off. It will also tend to be improved by increases in the other variables, but it will come under pressure from increases in Population.

**Political variables**

- The Social Infrastructure will be put under pressure by increased EconG, but at the same time, growth will bring increased resources. In the weakly integrated economies, the former effect is likely to predominate, in the strongly integrated the latter. Population will press on the Infrastructure, but it will tend to be strengthened as a result of increases or improvements in all the other variables.
- Effective and Democratic Government should be encouraged by EconG, but things are not so simple; there can be difficulties. Well-balanced economic development, encouraging the growth of a middle class, as in the integrated economies, will certainly be supportive of democracy, (think of India or Chile today). But there are other patterns of economic development. The kind of Economic Growth that results in a high concentration of income and wealth, or that focuses on an extractive industry, oil or minerals, or a plantation crop, may not be so congenial. Indeed, famously, such an economic structure favors an authoritarian or dictatorial government. As for the other variables, EffGov will be made more difficult by Population pressure, but will normally be encouraged by improvements in all the other variables.

**Demographics**

Population pressure depends on both births and deaths. Economic and social improvements will generally reduce deaths, thus increasing Pop initially, but in the long run such improvements will lead to a decline in family size. Reading across the first row, we see:

- that the effects of Economic Growth and an improved Environment will tend to go both ways, in the short run probably increasing Pop, but in the long run ultimately reducing it;
- that Population pressure will tend to be reduced by improved Socialization of Adolescents (fewer out-of-wedlock births, later marriages);
- that Educ will tend to lower Pop, through knowledge of birth control and increased awareness of opportunities for women;
- that improved Health will reduce deaths, which will tend in the short run to increase Pop, but as better Health decreases infant mortality and childhood deaths, fewer births will be needed to ensure surviving children and fertility will tend to fall;
- that better Social Infrastructure will tend to reduce Population pressure (by providing for old age and sickness, reducing the need to have large families to assure care in old age);
- that a higher Standard of Living will increase PopP initially because it will reduce mortality and deaths during childbirth – but in the long run it will lead to lower fertility;
- that Democratic Government will probably reduce PopP – for example, by offering more opportunities for women, who will then be inclined to have fewer chidlren.

### 12.2.3. Analysis

Just by glancing at the matrix we can see that the largest number of +or– and ? cases are to be found under Population and Economic Growth.

Consider PopP, reading along the bottom row: under present-day conditions it is likely that PopP will be increased by improved economic growth, a better environment and a higher standard of living. As a result, PopP itself (now read down the vertical column) will react back negatively not only on those variables, but also on the others. Greater PopP will make it harder to socialize adolescents, will create crowding and congestion, hindering education and economic progress, causing health problems and environmental stresses; moreover, it tends to overtax the social infrastructure, bid wages down and otherwise lower the standard of living, and so make democratic government more difficult. That is to say, an economic advance could undermine itself, by generating population pressures that will undo it. This is the modern version of Malthus, and the 'Iron Law of Wages', where wage gains lead to population increases which eventually pressure wages back down to subsistence levels (Clark, 2007). If there is to be development, PopP must be controlled (think of incentives to have fewer children in China).

On the other hand, it works in reverse, too. If Population pressure can be reduced, all the other variables, both social and economic, will be improved. So we need to develop policies to ensure that increases in the economic variables will not increase Population pressure. (But PopP control must not go too far; France and Italy are facing an aging population that is declining in numbers. That is one reason for permitting socially troublesome immigration.)

Now look at the column under 'EconG'. This shows the effects of a rise in Economic growth, with greater investment in new technologies raising productivity, developing new sectors and bringing increased employment. These effects increase the resources available to society. This should lead to improvements in the other variables. But economic investment does not necessarily bring general economic and social improvement. On the contrary, it will always destroy as well as create, and, especially in weakly integrated economies, it can cause terrible problems – destroying the old ways of life (as corporate farming does, for example), driving people off the land in search for work, thereby undermining the way the young are socialized. New resources are created, but in a weakly integrated economy, those who feel the destructive impact may have no access to the new resources. Moreover, as we have seen, economic decisions respond to the market; pollution costs are 'external' (costs paid by neither buyer nor seller), so unregulated industrialization normally leads to widespread environmental damage, especially air and water pollution. If the new industries are unregulated they will often have unsafe or unhealthy working conditions, creating new health hazards. We have already discussed how the migration of labor that takes place in order to supply the new industries with workers may result in haphazard housing developments, with unhealthy sewage and waste disposal, and contaminated water. These shifts of population can overburden school systems already under pressure. Economic development generally leads to at least some expansion of social infrastructure, but the expansion is not necessarily proportional, so the institutions may become overburdened. Finally, economic growth need not necessarily lead to a rise in the general standard of living; if the benefits are concentrated and the costs spread widely, most people could end up worse off.

It might seem that these are the relationships we would expect to find in a developed economy. But that is not quite so. Certainly in a developed economy the Economic and the Social, Environmental and other variables do support each other. But in a fully developed economy the support of the social and other relationships would tend to be *independent* of the current changes in the economy, certainly in the short run. That support would not vary with the current level of EconG. The Soc, Env and other variables would certainly tend to support economic development both in the short and the long run, but the positive development of those variables would be independent of any but the largest fluctuations in the economy. This of course is made possible by the fact that a developed economy has a high level of productivity, and so can support social, environmental, etc., development without regard to current variations in the economy. More on this point later.

Some variables will be fast-acting, others will exert their influence only over longer stretches of time. Economic growth will act quickly, as will the Standard of Living; in both cases the changes will be felt through markets. But changes in Social Infrastructure will be felt a little more slowly, while the impact of changes in the Socialization of Adolescents, Population Pressure and Democratic Government will take a long time to develop.

The Population variable is critically important because it has a strong long-run impact on the others. An increase in PopP will worsen all the rest, and they will in turn react on each other. PopP can change rapidly, if the death rate falls or rises, but the changes are slower when the change is due to changes in fertility.

The Environment/Economic relationship need not be positive (+); indeed, in present conditions it appears to be negative – that is, higher Economic Growth leads to a worsening of the Environment. The worsening of the Environment then leads to lower performance in many of the other variables, ultimately reacting back to reduce or impair EconG.

But if policies could be developed to ensure that Economic Growth led to a better Environment, this could be crucially important. For then the better Environment would improve all the rest, and, as we have seen, it is fairly reasonable to think that the other variables will be positively related to each other (+). Then, assuming that population growth will depend negatively (–) on the others, a positive Environment/Economic relationship will tend to bring about a pattern in which the growth of each of the other factors reinforces the rest in a positive (constructive) spiral. We will explore these relationships in a moment.

### 12.2.4. Sustainable Globalization

At this point we can derive an interesting implication of our approach, one that provides an important contribution to the current debate over globalization. Opening up new areas of trade, building new factories, outsourcing and flows of hot money – the processes of globalization, in short – all tend to generate rural-to-urban migration; they call for workers to develop new skills; they require additional infrastructure, they generate pollution, create needs for new public health measures, etc. In general they lead to social changes. But these social changes react back on the globally driven economic processes. As we have seen this raises the question whether this interaction is *sustainable*, that is, whether, given its impact on developing societies (and perhaps also on the advanced world) the process will support itself, and will be carried on, or whether it will generate counter forces that will tend to bring it to an end.

Using the ideal matrix (see Table 12.3) we can define a precise condition that shows what is necessary for development to be sustained, answering the question, when and whether the development process, driven by globalization, can be sustained. Of course, to do this the equations have to be written out with actual numbers, even if they are only estimated numbers. For this purpose we should treat PopP separately, since the issues there are on a much longer time scale. We should also separate out EffGov. (It might also be useful to examine Env on its own, but it could be included.) Then, given suitable conditions, the remaining equations can be solved, and we have

economic impact on society = social impact on the economy

This holds in equilibrium, and it says that when the equations are in balance, the economy's contribution to the growth of the social variables just balances the society's contribution to the growth of the economy. Each reinforces the other. This is the condition for 'sustainable development'. When there is an economic advance it will change the social variables in the same direction; but the social variables will act reciprocally back on the economic realm, also moving it forward, and the two effects will be just the

*Table 12.3. Matrix of ideal coefficient signs*

| | EconG | EnvH | AdlSoc | Educ | Health | StndL | SocInf | EffGov | PopP |
|---|---|---|---|---|---|---|---|---|---|
| EconG | ____ | – | – | – | – | – | – | – | – |
| EnvH | – | ____ | – | – | – | – | – | – | – |
| AdlSoc | – | – | ____ | – | – | – | – | – | – |
| Educ | – | – | – | ____ | – | – | – | – | – |
| Health | – | – | – | – | ____ | – | – | – | – |
| StndL | – | – | – | – | – | ____ | – | – | – |
| SocInf | – | – | – | – | – | – | ____ | – | – |
| EffGov | – | – | – | – | – | – | – | ____ | – |
| PopP | – | – | – | – | – | – | – | – | ____ |

right magnitude to keep the balance between the two realms (Nell et al., forthcoming). Economic advance leads to better education, improved public health and more expansive housing (higher StndL). But, in turn, the improved education, public health and housing have arrived at just the right level (not too much, not too little) to support that degree of economic advance.

If this condition does not hold, we do not have an equilibrium; either society will be contributing more to the economy than it receives back, or vice versa. Of course, an equilibrium balance can only be defined if it is possible to measure the impacts, so that we can write equations. But even when measurement is not possible we can see that if the elements of both rows and columns are positive, the economic impact on society and the social impact on the economy reinforce one another. They may not be in exact balance – without numbers we have no way of knowing – but we can say that they work in the same direction.

Look back at the earlier version of the matrix, where many elements in the EconG column were negative, but all the elements in the row were positive. Under those conditions the economic impact on society not only could not possibly be in balance with the social impact on the economy, the two could not possibly be mutually reinforcing. One will be likely to undermine the other, or worst of all, each will tend to undermine the other. The Econ variable will depend positively on good education, on effective public health, on a clean environment; but economic advances will put schools under strain, will create crowding and disease in the cities, while polluting the environment. These deteriorating conditions will then undermine the economic advance. Something very like this happened throughout Africa following independence.

## 12.3. DYNAMICS – AND DEVELOPMENT TRAPS

To carry the argument further, it will be useful first to simplify our approach, and then to explore the dynamics – the patterns of interaction – more fully.

So we will simplify by looking only at the interactions between certain parts of the matrix, holding everything else constant, rather like the 'partial equilibrium' analysis in economics. (Our approach will be open to some of the same criticisms as 'partial equilibrium', but it allows us to isolate the problems peculiar to each of the important sets of variables.) We will combine the social variables into one composite, and look at the interaction of Soc and Econ.[8] Then we can hold the Soc relationships constant, and examine the interaction of Econ with Env, with EffGov, and with Popl. In each case we will explore how these interactions can turn into various kinds of vicious circles and development traps, modeling the interactions in terms of simple stability dynamics.[9] Such modeling will help us to see exactly which aspects of the interactions cause problems (subject, of course, to our simplifying assumptions). Having identified problematic aspects and hopefully having clarified the dynamics, we might be able to suggest policies.

The various models below basically partition the matrix into simplified components – Econ and Soc, Econ and EffGov, Econ and PopP. 'Soc', for example, will be an aggregate of the variables of the matrix, such as Educ, Health, SocInf and AdlSoc. In each case we take Econ as it appears in the matrix, and then either treat the other elements as constant, and explore the relation between Econ and another variable, for example, EffGov or PopP, or combine several variables together into a composite variable, for example, Soc, made up by combining the Social Variables. Then we show how these components of the matrix can interact so as to lead to development traps.

By a 'development trap' we mean a set of relationships in which important variables are related in such a way that any advance forward sets up offsetting movements in other variables that undermine that advance. For example, in Africa, and in Bangladesh some years back, aid and economic growth improved health – which led to a population explosion, putting additional pressure on land and water, whereupon health deteriorated again.

Development traps are especially serious when the configuration of the matrix is unfavorable, but it is important to see that traps can emerge even when the overall configuration is favorable. Of course, a favorable configuration makes it much easier to devise policies to avoid the traps.

Let us now explore the dynamics. This is a difficult subject in economics, but it is increasingly apparent that it is the key to many of the most difficult problems in the field (financial instability, unemployment, inflation, business cycles, etc.) – and in our case here, it is the key to understanding how globalization impacts on development. But at this point we have to draw on some mathematics. We are looking at how incentives lead agents in the different sectors to interact, and these interactions are channeled by the structure of the system in ways that can lead to outcomes nobody expects – and sometimes nobody wants!

We will start with Econ and Soc, where the latter is a composite made up of Educ, Health, AdlSoc and SocInf. The main question is, will the incentives created by the interaction of Econ and Soc tend to lead the society to the position where the two mutually support one another? Or will the incentives drive the system away from that point, something nobody wants! Or perhaps the interaction will just leave things stagnant?

### 12.3.1. A Simple Two Equation Example

The coefficients of the matrix represent the slope of an implied linear function connecting the two variables; thus the coefficient showing the impact of EconG on Health is the slope of a linear function showing how Health varies as EconG increases or decreases. The coefficient showing the effect of Health on EconG is similarly the slope of the function showing how EconG can be expected to vary as Health gets better or worse. Our first example will examine the interaction of the variables governed by these linear functions.

To simplify, let us leave out the environment and democratic politics, and take the social variables as a group, represented by a simple index, Soc. Then we can illustrate the general principles with a simple case in which there are just two equations and two unknowns:

$$\text{Econ} = S(\text{Soc}) \text{ and}$$

$$\text{Soc} = E(\text{Econ}),$$

where *S*( ) and *E*( ) are the two functions. The first says that various levels of Soc support or, in a stronger interpretation, generate or help to generate corresponding levels of Econ, where higher levels of Soc lead to higher levels of Econ. The second says that various levels of Econ generate corresponding levels of Soc. But in this case, Econ could either damage or support Soc. If it damages it, then the effect will be negative, that is, the impact of Econ will lower the level of Soc; if it supports it, the effect will be positive, so the impact of Econ will raise Soc.

Let us first consider the linear case with one equation negative, one positive. We can write our equations:

$$\text{Soc} = A - B(\text{Econ}), \text{ and}$$

$$\text{Econ} = C + D(\text{Soc})$$

*B* and *D* are the coefficients drawn from the matrix, saying how Econ affects Soc, and how Soc affects Econ. Note that besides the coefficients, we must consider constant terms (which are not part of the matrix); these terms describe what Soc or Econ would be in the absence of effects from the other. (The equations have intercepts, as well as slopes.) The first equation says that increases in Econ will bring reductions in Soc. The second says that increases (declines) in Soc will bring increases (declines) in Econ. If there are two equations, one with a positive and one with a negative slope, there has to be an intersection. Of course it might be negative! But it exists. One relation is positive – upward sloping – and one negative, downward sloping;

so there is an intersection (see Figure 12.1) somewhere. If it is in positive space, it can be considered an 'equilibrium', that is, the social and the economic will be mutually supportive. There could equally well be an intersection where one or both of the variables was negative; in this case the relationship would be destructive rather than supportive. (In ordinary language this says that these variables affect one another, in ways described by the equations, and that there is a point where the impact of Econ on Soc just balances the opposite impact of Soc on Econ.)

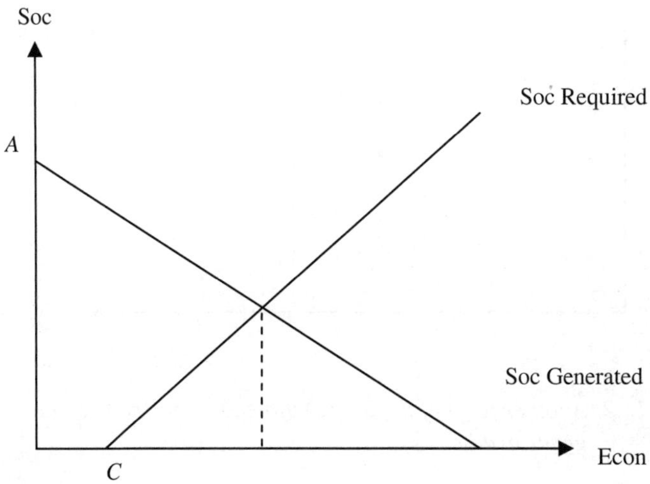


*Figure 12.1. Intersection between required and generated Soc as functions of Econ*

Solving for the level of Econ, we substitute the first equation in the second and rearrange:

$$\text{Econ} = [C + DA]/\{1 + DB\}$$

Now we can see that if the negative relationship were to turn positive, the intersection would be at a much higher level of both Econ and Soc. In that case:

$$\text{Econ} = [C + DA]/\{1 - DB\}, \text{ which is clearly greater.}$$

This is illustrated in Figure 12.2. But it should be intuitively obvious also. If Econ has a weaker negative effect on Soc, the line will be flatter; if it has no effect the line will be horizontal. But as the downward sloping line swings up, the intersection will be further out, that is, at a higher level of Econ. Note that it is possible for the Soc generated by Econ to always lie above the Soc needed line (in the positive quadrant); in such a case it would never be a constraint on economic advance – but this is not likely). This would be the case if $DB = 1$; if $DB > 1$, this would also be true, but there would be an intersection in negative space.

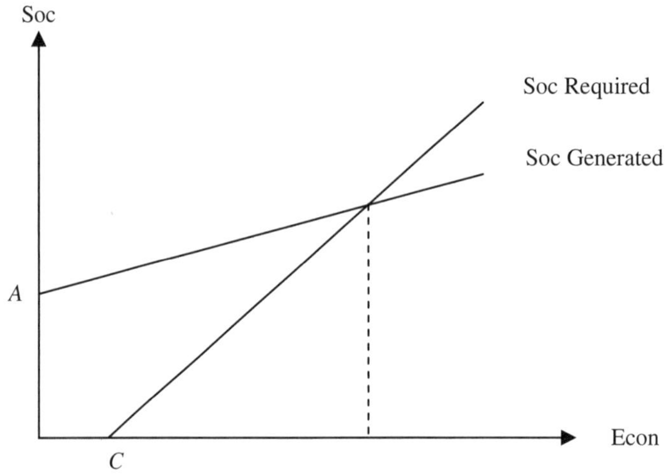


*Figure 12.2. Another form of the intersection between required and generated Soc*

Next suppose the society is not in that equilibrium – let us say that the level of Econ is a little less than the intersection or equilibrium level. Can we expect social or market forces to drive the system back to the balancing level? Will there be appropriate incentives?

Let us recall what the equilibrium means. It is the level at which the Soc generated by Econ would be just equal to the Soc required to support Econ. This is an important relationship, in regard to being able to maintain a program of economic expansion, whether market driven or planned. If the level of Soc generated or supported by a particular level of Econ is equal to or greater than the level required to support that Econ, then that economic activity can continue or move ahead. But if the Soc generated is less than the level needed to support that rate of Econ advance, the Econ will have to be cut back. But we started from the assumption that the level of Econ was just a little lower than the mutually supporting level. If Econ is cut back then the system is moving away from equilibrium – the relationships are working perversely.

This can be seen most easily looking at Figure 12.3. There are two lines, one representing Soc generated by Econ, the other Soc needed by Econ, with Econ on the horizontal axis, Soc on the vertical. We assume that both lines are positive, and that they intersect in the positive quadrant. But where are the intercepts, and which line is steeper? In Figure 12.2 the Soc generated lies above the Soc required at all levels of Econ below the intersection. Since this is so, Econ can easily be increased, so the society would be likely to move to the equilibrium. Above the equilibrium, Soc required will be greater than that generated, so Econ will tend to fall back. But suppose, as in Figure 12.3, that Soc required is high even when Econ is minimal, but rises slowly, while Soc Generated is very low at low levels of Econ, but rises rapidly.

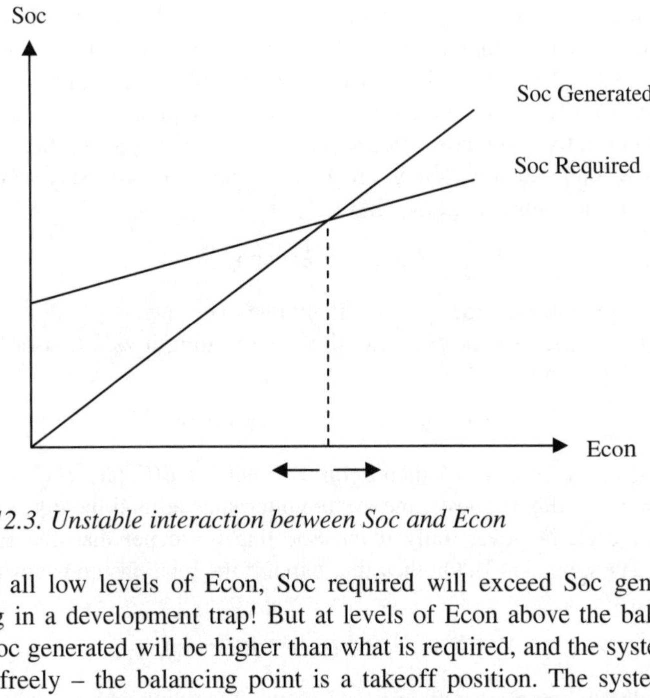


*Figure 12.3. Unstable interaction between Soc and Econ*

Then at all low levels of Econ, Soc required will exceed Soc generated, resulting in a development trap! But at levels of Econ above the balancing point, Soc generated will be higher than what is required, and the system can expand freely – the balancing point is a takeoff position. The system will find it difficult to reach or stay in its equilibrium, even though this equilibrium is well defined.

Now we can set out a simple example of what we have been saying all along. When Econ has the wrong kind of impact on Soc, the effects will react back and undermine Econ. This is a vicious circle. To see exactly how the 'undermining' (or, alternatively, the supportive process) works, as we have been discussing it, we need to express the impacts of the variables in a 'period' analysis. That is, we divide up time according to how the effects of the variables on each other work out. Mathematically, that means we set it out in Difference equations. These are equations in which the variables are 'dated', which means that the values of the variables are the values that they hold in certain specific time periods.

Here we assume that Econ will play itself out in period 0; but its impact will be felt on Soc in the next period, period 1. However, the effects of Soc on Econ will all take place in period 1. So we have:

$$\text{Soc}_1 = E(\text{Econ}_0) \text{ and}$$

$$\text{Econ}_1 = S(\text{Soc}_1)$$

The first says that impact of Econ on Soc takes time; the impact of Econ now will be felt in the following period's Soc. (Econ growth will shift population from the countryside to the cities, and next period the schools will be crowded and health facilities overrun. Think of Mexico City, or Cairo, or Sao Paulo.) The second equation says that the support of Soc for Econ is needed currently – Soc now affects Econ now. (Today's health facilities keep today's workers healthy; today's roads and bridges move today's goods and services.) Then substituting, we have

$$\text{Econ}_1 = S[E(\text{Econ}_0)],$$

which will tell us how the system will evolve over time.

Let us go back to our example, this time writing it as a first-order linear difference system:

$$\text{Econ}_1 = C + DA - DB(\text{Econ}_0).$$

If $DB(\text{Econ}_0) < C + \text{DA}$ then $\text{Econ}_1 > 1$; but if $DB(\text{Econ}_0) > C + DA$, then $\text{Econ}_1 < 1$. As this suggests, the system alternates around the equilibrium; it will converge, however, only if the Soc line is steeper than the Econ line (Allen, 1968, pp. 81–3). On the other hand, if the relationship is positive, this becomes

$$\text{Econ}_1 = C + DA + DB(\text{Econ}_0),$$

which clearly increases indefinitely. This would be self-sustaining growth.

**A non-linear case**

The matrix gives us fixed coefficients, implying that the underlying relationships are linear. But we do not have to stay with that assumption, if there are good reasons to think the variables are related in a more complicated way. The important thing is to consider plausible relationships, while keeping the analysis simple enough that we can visualize the dynamics.

We should be careful, however, when interpreting these functions – they are being used to examine dynamics, and we are assuming that they are reliable, grounded in contracts, obligations or social mores. Yet they may not be well grounded, or the grounds may be changing; it is entirely possible that some of the relationships we are considering may shift unexpectedly with social and cultural changes. We have argued that treating them as mathematical functions will be useful; it will show us the various possible patterns of interaction over time. But it should be remembered that, at times, this will be a stretch. In particular, it would be unwise to assume that these relationships are always 'reversible'. That is, if the system moved along one of the functions from *A* to *B*, it could reverse itself and return from *B* to *A*. Assuming reversibility is tantamount to holding that time does not matter, an issue hotly debated by economists. But if time matters, when reversing, things may end up at a point different from *A*. Nevertheless, let us look further.

A plausible non-linear case: the relationships might both be ones that increased slowly at first, then rapidly, then slowly again. That is, the dependent variable rises slowly, but at an accelerating rate, then rises rapidly, but decelerates, until it is increasing only slowly again, and then flattens out. (Further increase of the independent variable will have no effect on the dependent.) These are known as 'sigmoid curves'. Suppose this described the effect of Econ on Soc – as Econ increased, moving along the horizontal axis in the diagram, the Soc which each level of Econ could support would first increase slowly, then rise rapidly, and finally slow down again. But the effect of Soc on Econ would also show the same form. As Soc increased, moving along the vertical axis, the Econ it could support would first rise slowly, then more rapidly, and then slowly again.

This may be hard to grasp intuitively, but can easily be visualized; the diagram plots the curves with Soc on the vertical axis and Econ on the horizontal. The two curves start from the origin and intersect twice – the second intersection marking the point beyond which increases in the independent variables have no further effects on the dependent ones. Below the first intersection, reading from the horizontal axis, the curve showing Econ supported/generated by Soc lies above the curve showing the Soc supported/generated by Econ. After that point, it is just the other way around. The curve showing Econ supported by Soc lies below the curve showing Soc supported by Econ.

Let us interpret this. A level of Econ is only viable – can only be maintained – if the level of Soc that it supports is as large, or larger, than the level of Soc that it needs (that is, the level that is needed to support it). As

Econ increases from a very low level, the Soc that it generates or supports will be low at first, and then rise rapidly, while low levels of Soc will only support low levels of Econ. This means we have a 'development trap' here: at low levels of Econ, the Soc generated or supported will be less than the Soc required to support those levels of Econ. Since the system starts out poor, it is caught; by itself it can never get going, even though if it did, it would reach a point where it would begin a pattern of self-sustaining upward movement towards a high-level position of mutual support.

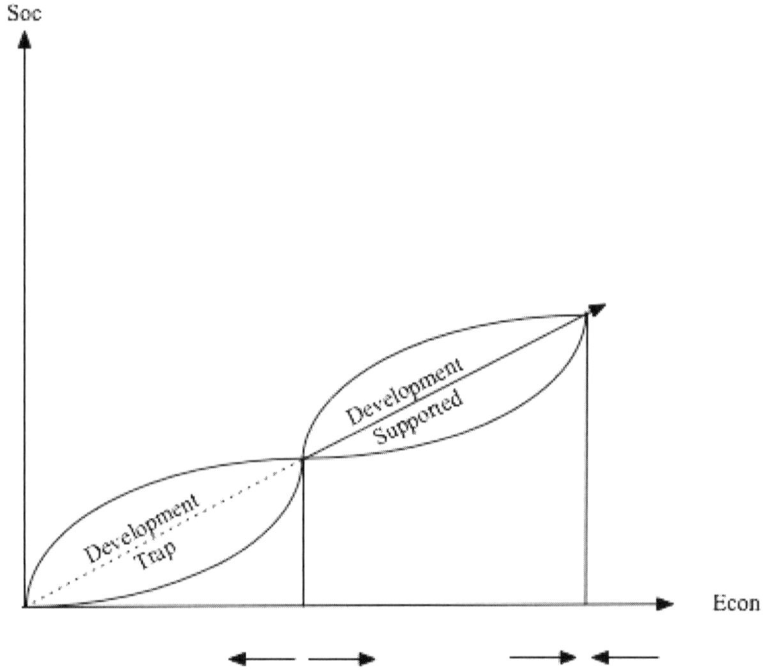


*Figure 12.4. Development trap and development support*

**Another version of the non-linear relationship**

This time let us consider not the levels of Econ and Soc, but their rates of growth; let us also include Env along with Soc, and assume they move together.[10] Both are negatively impacted by Econ growth. But in the absence of pressure from Econ, SocEnv will grow on its own. When Econ growth speeds up, rural-to-urban migration increases, putting pressure on education and health, and overstressing social infrastructure. In addition, pollution increases and environmental damage rises. Hence SocEnv will stop growing or even decline. But a stagnant or depleted SocEnv will then, after a time lag, react back on economic growth, slowing it down. But slower economic growth, in turn will reduce rural-to-urban migration. But with slower growth and lower migration, the social system will be able to absorb the earlier migrants and clean up the environmental damage; SocEnv will resume its growth. Health and education will improve, while the environment recovers. At this point growth can resume, and the cycle will start all over again. This, of course, is analogous to the famous 'prey–predator' model. Growth is the 'predator', it feeds on its 'prey', society and environment; but if it devours them too much, it cannot continue, and must slow down. Once it does so, however, society and environment can recover, and when they do, growth can resume (for the Lotka–Volterra approach, cf. Goodwin, 1966[11]).

Four possible patterns of interaction between Econ and Soc have been examined: simple linear ones, lagged linear interactions, sigmoid non-linear relationships, and a prey–predator model. Many other possibilities could have been explored, but these are more than just plausible. They show how the interaction can either undermine or augment economic development. The development of the economy cannot be considered in isolation.

### 12.3.2. Interaction Between Government and the Economy

We can set Soc aside, continue to hold our other variables constant, and turn to a study of the interaction between EconG and EffGov, that is, between economic advance and increases or decreases in the degree of effectiveness of government. (There are, of course, many other kinds of interaction between government and the economy.) Admittedly, measuring the degree of government effectiveness will be difficult, and there will be some unavoidable arbitrariness. But measures have been proposed and we can draw on them, bearing in mind that the relationships under examination cannot be considered exact.

Note that we do not insist that effective government is necessarily democratic. China, for example, has been amazingly successful, though it is notoriously not democratic. Neither is Singapore, another success story. Two issues are paramount: providing voice to those who are injured, so they can demand to be compensated, and allowing pressures to develop that will lead to renewal, to the renovation of institutions, clearing out calcified administrative structures and restoring flexibility.

Let us consider an interesting problem that could arise even though there might be positive relations between EconG and EffGov. On the one hand, under appropriate circumstances a rise in EconG can be expected to generate an increase in the effectiveness of government, EffGov. Economic growth will tend to bring an increase in the middle class, and also give rise to a prosperous upper level of the working class. Both will push for greater representation, and will try to advance their causes politically. Both will push to educate their children, and both will demand better public services. EconG and EffGov are positively related, in that an increase in EconG tends to generate a rise in EffGov.

On the other hand, an improvement in the effectiveness of government (and very often in the degree of democracy) will (usually) tend to encourage an increase in EconG. Better administration, more adequate provision of public goods and infrastructure, more reliable law and order, all will contribute to furthering EconG. So here, too, EffGov and EconG are positively related, but in this case, an increase in EconG depends on a corresponding increase in EffGov.

We have two positive relationships between EconG and EffGov; it might seem that no difficulties could arise. Not so. Consider a low level of EconG; if the degree of EffGov generated exceeds that required the level is sustainable. Suppose it rises, and it is still the case that the degree of EffGov generated is greater than required, but not by as much. Then move to quite a high level; here the degree generated is less than required; in between there will a point at which they just balance. We can see all this on a simple diagram.

Very roughly, what it means is that at levels of EconG below the point of intersection, the degree of EffGov generated exceeds that required – so the way is open for EconG to increase further. But at levels above the intersection, the EffGov required exceeds that generated, so EconG cannot be sustained, and will have to decline (see Figure 12.5).[12]

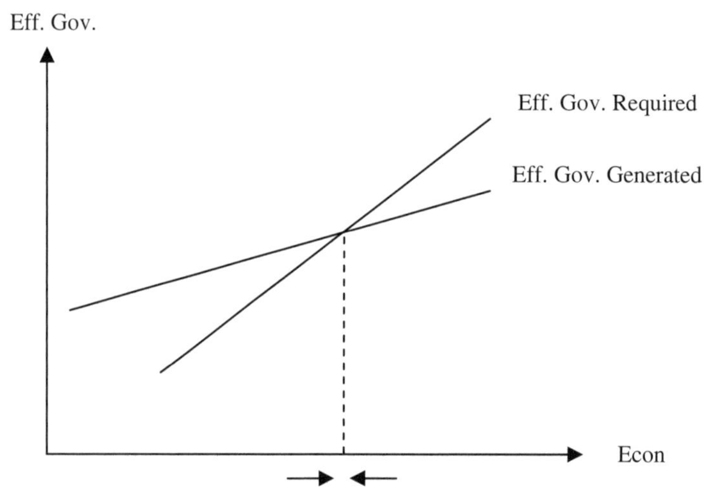


*Figure 12.5. Effective Government and Econ*

Now suppose that the slopes of the lines are reversed, and that at levels of EconG below the intersection the required EffGov exceeds the generated EffGov. EconG will not be sustainable; it will have to fall to zero. (For instance, key sectors of the developing country may be easily monopolized, leading to stagnation; democratic politics would be needed to break up the trusts.) By contrast, however, at levels of EconG above the intersection, generated EffGov exceeds required – at such high levels of economic advance social dislocation will be high, but so will opportunities; money will flow into politics, and class and sectoral conflicts will be intense. When the level of EffGov generated exceeds the level required economic expansion can move up indefinitely, no matter how high.

As noted government policy will be called upon to direct and orient economic development; but government action will surely require support from Soc. But government action that favors economic development will very likely bring improvements in Soc. That is, EffGov will tend to generate Soc, while also requiring higher Soc. So EffGov and Soc will vary together; so it might seem that would be no problems. However, for reasons we have already seen in the case of Econ and Soc, this is not so.

Look at Figure 12.5, replacing 'EffGov' with 'Soc': the two lines – Econ generates Soc, Econ requires Soc – are drawn so they intersect in the positive quadrant. If the 'requires' line is flatter, then at levels of Econ below the intersection the system is in a trap; at these levels of Econ more Soc is required than is generated, and the position is unsustainable. (The economy needs more education, more health care, better infrastructure than it is getting. Absent these, the level of economic activity cannot be sustained.) Above the intersection, however, the situation is the opposite; more Soc is generated than is needed to support the economy. This could just lead to cab drivers with PhDs. But, more optimistically, if matched with surpluses in other variables, it could be the start of a takeoff into self-sustained growth.

### 12.3.3. Interaction Between Population and Economic Growth

The discussion so far has dealt with short or intermediate term relationships. Let us now consider some possible longer term interactions – between economics and population pressures. These are, of course, much more hypothetical; many external factors can change and introduce unexpected influences. The relationships themselves may change because of new technologies, or new socio-political conditions. Nevertheless, it may still be illuminating to 'hold these matters constant in our minds', and consider the relationships. They are after all, the relationships underlying the pros and cons of the debate over Malthus. Remember, Malthus argued that reform and policy-induced poverty reduction would not work; higher wages and higher living standards would simply lead to increases in population, driving living standards down again. Population increased geometrically, but food supplies and higher living standards could only increase arithmetically; the former would inevitably overwhelm the latter. But in fact economic activity, and so living standards, also grow geometrically, and the patterns of interaction are more complex, and result in quite a different picture.

At a minimum we have two relationships, enough to illustrate the issues. There are two variables, economic growth and population growth; one relationship shows the effects of Pop on Econ, the other shows the effects of Econ on Pop.

The two relationships are:

- Econ depends inversely on Pop; as Pop declines, Econ rises. Reduced pressure on natural resources allows for more investment; reduced pressure on family resources allows for more investment in children, producing more highly educated and healthier workers. On a diagram with Pop on the vertical axis and Econ on the horizontal, this curve slopes down from left to right.
- Pop depends on Econ, first rising with higher Econ (better diet, better health), then peaking and falling (smaller families), finally flattening out at a low or zero level. That is, as Econ rises from a low level, it makes better health and diet possible, so Pop grows faster, but as Econ goes higher still, women become educated and reduce their fertility, so Pop slows down and growth declines to a low level. On the same diagram, this curve rises from near the origin to a peak, then falls, and flattens out.

As is evident in Figure 12.6, there could easily be three intersections of these curves. At least one would be unstable, according to the usual analysis of economists. If the first curve started very high and did not fall steeply, while the second rose only a little before starting to fall, there could be no intersection at all.

This has implications for the Malthusian debates. Contrary to Malthus it is clear that both Pop and Econ grow geometrically. But it is also apparent that there is no reason to expect them to grow at the same rate. Instead the question is, will they support each other? At intersection points, Pop supports Econ to the same extent that Econ supports Pop – they are mutually consistent. This raises the question, are there forces that pull them together, so that they will tend over time to grow in a supportive balance? This does not mean that they must grow at the same rate; in fact, there may be a number of equilibrium points, and some may be 'unstable', (by economists' definitions – which may not always be appropriate!) The equilibrium positions will generally not lie on the 45 degree line (the line along which

Pop growth = Econ growth). Malthus feared that Pop would normally grow faster than Econ. In general this will not be true, nor need they grow at the same rate; on the contrary, in advanced countries, normally, Econ > Pop, which implies that average income per capita will be rising.

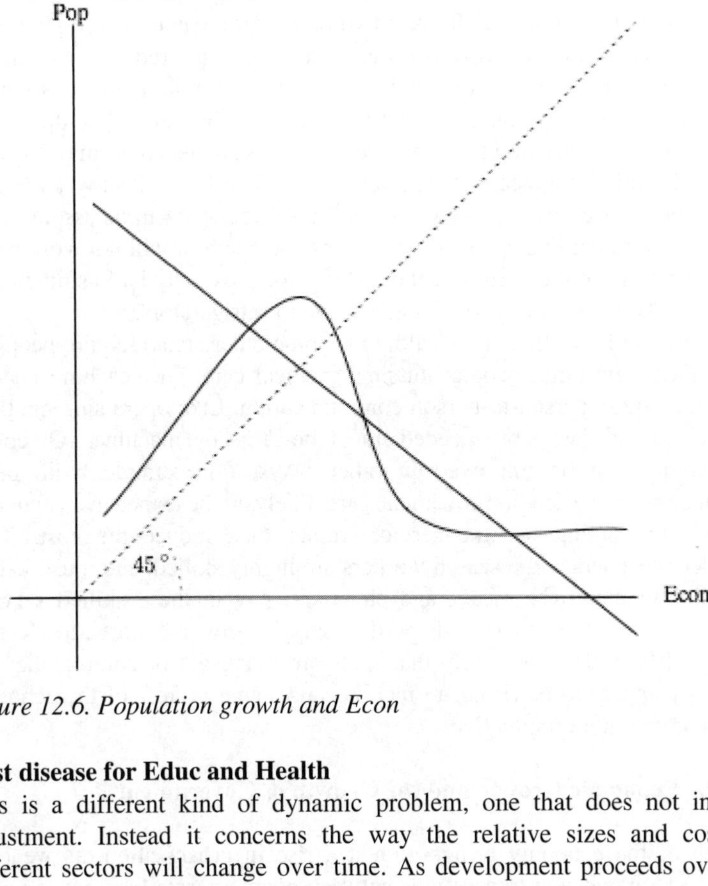


*Figure 12.6. Population growth and Econ*

**Cost disease for Educ and Health**

This is a different kind of dynamic problem, one that does not involve adjustment. Instead it concerns the way the relative sizes and costs of different sectors will change over time. As development proceeds over the long run the costs of Educ and Health and some government services will appear to rise relative to other costs. It may begin to seem that these services are becoming more and more difficult for the economy to afford. This is an illusion, as many economists have argued. In reality, they are easier for the society to afford; what makes them seem relatively more expensive is that productivity in other sectors has been growing more rapidly, compared to the services in question. Slower than average productivity growth in a given sector or industry implies a rise in the costs of that sector relative to those in others. Productivity in certain services such as Education and Health cannot increase rapidly – some jobs just cannot be performed faster – but those who work in these sectors must be highly trained so their wages and salaries must keep pace.

Consider an example: an opera company is putting on Così Fan Tutte, the orchestra plays and the singers sing; they are good and do it well. Nearby there is an assembly plant in which skilled workers put together refrigerators from imported components. It takes two hours for a batch of refrigerators to be assembled from start to finish; that is also the time required to sing the opera. Let us suppose that the number of workers and the number of singers and musicians are the same, and that they are paid the same; then the cost of an opera performance and a batch of refrigerators are also the same. Now the time and motion engineers reorganize the work at the assembly plant, and with suitable incentives, it speeds up, and a refrigerator can be assembled in one hour. But it still takes two hours to sing the opera; it will not work trying to speed up the singing. So now the refrigerators cost only half as much; that is, the cost of the opera has doubled, relative to refrigerators.

Services in Education and Health (and some other areas) require people to spend time with other people; nursing, medical care, and teaching all take time and require person-to-person communication. Like opera singing, these services cannot easily be speeded up or be done by machine. (Of course productivity can be improved in other ways, for example, with better equipment – but such improvements are likely to be expensive, and may improve the product or the service, rather than reduce the cost.) Care providers, teachers and research workers are highly skilled, and must be paid accordingly; moreover as average pay rises, pay in these skilled services must keep pace – even though productivity is growing more slowly than average. It will therefore seem that costs are rising out of control; they are not. They appear to be rising, in fact, because other sectors of the economy are becoming more productive.

### 12.3.4. Economic Growth and the Growth of Government

Growth of the economy brings with it a rise in urbanization, as we have seen.[13] The number of transactions between people normally depends on the density of the population in a given area – given the transport and communications system. Urban population density is obviously higher than rural, and urban transportation and communications are normally much superior. So a rise in urbanization typically leads not only to an increase in transactions, but to a more than proportional increase. Again, typically, this tends to reduce transaction costs, and also leads to economics of scale and scope. The presence of such economies, and also of externalities resulting from concentration, is well-known to promote agglomeration, which in turn will tend to generate increases in productivity (Acs, 2006). The externalities and spillover effects are particularly strong in regard to 'human capital', skilled workers and especially the professional classes (Simon and Nardinelli, 1996). So an increase in urbanization could be expected to lead back to a rise in productivity, which could, in turn, have a positive effect on growth.

These are common observations, and figure frequently as assumptions in discussions of the reasons for migration to urban areas, and for locating industry in urban areas.

However, urbanization will not continue indefinitely; a shift from low or irregular growth to strong and regular growth will lead to a rise in urbanization, setting off a rate of migration from the countryside that will continue for a long time. But the migration will slow down and come to a halt when the gains from additional migration are offset at the margin by the rising costs of congestion. At this point industry will seek to locate its expansion elsewhere – perhaps back in the countryside, perhaps in a new area of agglomeration, or possibly overseas – and migrants will find it sufficiently difficult to find accommodation, jobs, health care, etc., that they will look for ways to survive in the informal and illegal economy.

As urbanization increases, transactions increase more than proportionally. If we think of this in terms of a network, the in-movement of migrants increases the number of nodes per unit of space (the same can be said for the formation of new businesses). This can be thought of as an arithmetical increase in the nodes in a given area of living space. But, as a first approximation, the network consists of the direct relations between the nodes, and this increases per unit space in a much faster rising series:

Number per unit space: 1 2 3 4 5 6 7 8 9 …

Relations per unit space: 0 1 3 6 10 15 21 28 36 …

The expenses of government arguably will depend not on the number of people, but on the relationships and activities that arise between them; it is to encourage and support these connections and activities that governments build infrastructure (roads, sewers, light and power, water, etc.), provide police and courts, undertake regulation, and support education and public health. (Of course not all the possible direct relations will become actual; also, besides the direct relations, there can be higher order relationships.) So, as a very simple first approximation, government expenditure will tend to be proportional, not to the number of people, but to the connections between them. It will therefore rise with urbanization, but will rise faster than the urban population; however, it will then slow down and stop rising when urbanization slows down and stops.

So as population shifts from rural and lightly populated areas to urban intensely populated areas, the number of transactions and activities in the urban areas increases at a faster rate than the population intensity; government expenditures will then rise with the transactions activity.

These models show not only the variety and complexity of possible interactions between the variables of the Transformational Growth Matrix, but they demonstrate that the problems of the economy cannot be separated from those of the society, its politics and its environment (see also Keuning, 1996, 1997). Economics as a subject cannot be isolated, except temporarily for the purposes of argument, from the other social sciences.

'The economy' is supposed to be generally independent of the rest of society; it produces the goods and services that support the rest of society, but only insofar as these needs are manifested through the market; and it is not itself directly or immediately dependent on the rest of society. Indirectly, and in the long run, yes, of course, the economy depends on and interacts with the social system. But not in the short run, and not immediately or directly. So when 'the economy' is well-developed, as in the advanced countries, the matrix will exhibit this independence; for the short run case, many of the cells representing the interaction between EconG and the social variables will show zeroes. But this will never be the case for a developing economy.

### 12.3.5. Advanced Socio-economic Development

This suggests a way of defining 'economic development'. Typically in traditional societies, there will be a balance between Econ, Env and Soc for small changes in established economic practices. But substantial and innovative economic advance will create turmoil and have a negative impact on the social variables. Successfully developing economies will exhibit a positive relationship, a virtuous cycle. Then economic development can be said to reach a high or 'advanced' level when social and environmental activities can be supported on an independent basis, 'funded', so that they do not depend on the success or failure of current economic activities. That is when 'the economy' emerges, as an aspect of the society (partially) independent of the rest.

We can rewrite the matrix again, now showing that in a fully developed economy many short-run connections can be severed, so that the different areas are independent of one another. This will be represented by '0's. In an advanced economy a rise in EconG means an increase in growth and in productivity. So in such an economy we can expect the acceleration principle to work; EconG will therefore have a positive effect on itself. An improved Env will surely support EconG, but better AdlSoc is unlikely to have a much more immediate impact. Improved Educ, Health, a higher HStndl and better SocInf may all have an encouraging effect. Better political institutions are unlikely to have much effect in the short run, but they might.

Now look at the effects of higher EconG on the other variables, bearing in mind that we are thinking of the short to medium term, i.e. the next year or so. Of course, higher EconG can be expected to show up as higher HStndl. But otherwise it will *not have any great impact on any of the other variables*. The sectors that these variables represent are already supported and developing according to plan, independently of whether or not the economy is running strongly, that is to say, independently of the business cycle. If they are supported by taxes the expenditures they require will be sustained by deficit spending during downturns; to the extent they are private, funding will carry them through difficult times.

Table 12.4 suggests that once a country is developed, further progress is likely to come chiefly through the political arena. Effective and responsive government, EffGov, will have a positive effect on all the social variables. A more sensitive, better functioning government, especially one responsive to the public, will be able to offer improved services to the economy, to monitor the environment more carefully, to provide programs to counsel adolescents, to promote education and health, improve the distribution of income and social services, thereby raising the household standard of living. And it will most likely work to improve social infrastructure, and finally it is likely to react back on itself, and move towards improved and more democratic practices. All of these will be furthered or supported by strong and effective approach to demand management – which could be developed around

*Table 12.4. The case of advanced development*

| | EconG | EnvH | AdlSoc | Educ | Health | HStndL | SocInf | EffGov | PopP |
|---|---|---|---|---|---|---|---|---|---|
| EconG | + | + | 0 | + | + | + | + | + | 0 |
| EnvH | 0 | -------- | 0 | 0 | 0 | 0 | + | + | – |
| AdlSoc | 0 | 0 | ------ | 0 | 0 | 0 | 0 | + | 0 |
| Educ | 0 | 0 | + | ____ | 0 | 0 | 0 | + | 0 |
| Health | 0 | + | 0 | + | ------- | 0 | 0 | + | 0 |
| HStndL | + | + | 0 | + | + | -------- | + | + | 0 |
| SocInf | 0 | 0 | 0 | 0 | 0 | 0 | ------- | + | – |
| EffGov | 0 | 0 | 0 | + | 0 | 0 | 0 | +? | 0 |
| PopP | 0 | 0 | 0 | 0 | 0 | 0 | 0 | 0 | ------- |

a public service employment program, operating as an 'automatic stabilizer' as suggested elsewhere.[14]

## 12.4. Concluding Remarks

Now let us review what we have accomplished; initially we set up the Transformational Growth Matrix to show the way the variables impact on each other; now we have indicated the dynamic implications, sketching how those impacts play out – filling in the initial sketches.

1. First, we have broken down the barrier between economic and social/environmental analysis. Our approach shows how economic variables interact with social and environmental ones. Contrary to what some mainstream economists believe, not only can economics not be isolated from the rest of society, but in principle, we can show just how it impacts on the other aspects of society and how society reacts back on it. These relationships can be modeled precisely, and we can see that there are many possible positions of 'mutual support' (equilibrium, economists would say), both stable and unstable.
2. Second, this also lets us show how and to what extent the economy can become independent of the rest of society as development proceeds. The separation of the economy from society is not inherent or necessary; it emerges as a result of development and will normally remain partial and incomplete.
3. Third, we have provided a method not only for examining this theoretically, but one which can be applied practically. It is flexible and can be used with ordinal or cardinal measures, even without numbers at all; this could be important in practice, since the statistics in developing areas are often poor to non-existent.
4. Fourth, we have derived the condition for a balanced mutually supportive relationship, one where, for example, the effect of Econ on Soc is just balanced by the reciprocal effect of Soc on Econ.
5. Fifth, we have shown how the matrix can be partitioned, and the coefficients used to define simple functional relationships. This makes it possible to explore whether market or, more broadly, general material incentives would tend to push the system towards the balanced position just defined – and we have seen that in very plausible cases this will not happen. Even worse, 'development traps' can be identified, where the incentives work perversely, preventing development from moving forward, or setting vicious cycles in motion, undermining economic advances.

6. Finally, we have shown that active policies will be needed, and can be defined, to avoid traps and to establish the relationships that will be mutually supportive. We have already suggested what those policies should be, and we will consider them further in a moment.

Our argument suggests that the mainstream view that the economy can be investigated separately from society is seriously in error. The economy rests on social foundations, and the society rests on the economy. They are interdependent, and that interdependence can be modeled with a great deal of precision; that is the central message of our condition for sustainable globalization.

## NOTES

* This chapter is partly based on *Humanizing Globalization*, forthcoming, co-authored by Edward Nell, Federico Mayor and Karim Errouaki.

1. On this view economies are not made up of abstract, rational, self-seeking 'individuals'; we see the agents in the economy as products of socialization, therefore having identities, skills and commitments resulting from that socialization. Moreover, the economy has to support the institutions of socialization. The interactions between sectors and classes are central in distribution theory and in the analysis of business cycles, but in our discussion here we will focus chiefly on the interaction between the economy – taken as a whole – and the other parts of the society. (For interactions between sectors, classes and banks, cf. Nell, 2004.)
2. The pattern of transactions between sectors, and between sectors and classes, in developed countries will be different from those in developing ones. In developed countries agriculture tends to employ few workers, industry tends to be large, and services even larger, but services tend to serve business more than households, are often technologically advanced and also employ many high skill workers. More than half the labor force is white collar. By contrast in developing countries, agriculture tends to be large and technologically backward, industry often employs traditional craft skills, and remains small-scale, while services may be a strange mix of advanced hotels and tourism, on the one hand, and traditional, largely household services on the other. White collar employment is low and important white collar jobs may be filled by expatriates.
3. An important special case is 'Dualism', in which a modern sector develops in a traditional society; the modern sector trades with the advanced world, but has little connection with the traditional economy, which tends to stagnate. In many cases the traditional crafts and crops will be undercut by imports from the advanced world, which may also (contradicting its professed support for free trade) deny access to the products, especially crops or other agricultural goods, of traditional economies. The middle class in the advanced sector may identify with the advanced world and therefore may fail to support the interests of the traditional sector, so that the society divides politically as well.
4. Principal Component Analysis can be used for constructing a single variable out of a set of related variables. Note that sometimes the elements making up a variable may not move together, or may not do so over certain ranges; in such cases the variable will have to be disaggregated.
5. Each equation could be written to show the current change in a variable to be equal to the sum of the impacts on it by the other variables. These impacts would be measured as

percentages of the initial amount of the variable. The impact of one variable on another, say of EconG on Env, would depend first on whether the interaction was positive or negative. Secondly it would depend on the size or amount of the variable – how large or extensive is the economic change? Each term would therefore be a coefficient multiplied by a quantity or size measure of the impacting variable. This approach is developed elsewhere (Nell et al., forthcoming).

6. It will be assumed here that there will be little or no immediate impact of a variable on itself. Such impacts do take place in economics – cf. the well-known Multiplier-Accelerator models – but this usually happens in developed economies, and is not thought to be so likely in developing ones. However, there may be self-reinforcing effects in some of these variables. For example, higher PopP probably leads at a later date to even higher PopP. EconG is also likely to be self-reinforcing. Good AdlSoc tends to be reinforcing; adolescents who have been properly socialized will develop into socially adjusted adults who want to help the next generation adjust, too. Bad socialization may perhaps be even more likely to spread its effects. EnvH could in some cases lead to self-reinforcing spirals. However it seems unlikely that SocInf or StndL will have effects of this kind, and while EffGov could conceivably, the effects are likely to be insignificant compared to other factors. In general, these effects are likely all to be positive or zero, and if positive very small, at least in the short run.
7. Estimating the coefficients will not be easy. (Preliminary estimates have been made for El Salvador and the Philipines, cf. Ozawa, 2008.) The procedure is to move step-by-step. The first step is to ascertain that there is indeed an impact; the coefficient is not zero. Next, not as easy as it looks: is the impact positive or negative? This may require calculating the net resultant of several offsetting impacts. Third, we must judge or measure by some rule of thumb (but one applied consistently) whether the impact is strong or weak? In the same vein, does it take effect rapidly or slowly? And comparisons should be made: Is the impact stronger or weaker than the impact on other related variables? Finally, can a quantitative index be developed, or a suitable proxy be found?
8. An increase in Econ means growth of monetized economic activity. It does not automatically mean an increase in economic welfare – although plausibly that will often be the case. More people are producing more of the things they want and doing more of the things they want to do. But there may also be more economic coercion, too, and more negative externalities, and these will show up in the social and environmental variables. By examining how the Econ and other variables interact we can see the extent to which an increase in Econ will lead to a rise in general welfare.
9. The matrix is a snapshot, holding at a moment of time. But we are now proposing to examine these relationships as they interact over time, which means assuming they are durable, fixed or settled enough so we can trace how they work out. Yet in many cases they may be unsettled, and liable to shift, or they may not be 'reversible'. In interpreting the matrix the unsettled quality of some of the relationships could be indicated for example, by entering a question mark with the coefficient. When a relationship is not reliable, we need to know how unreliable it is, and in what ways. If this cannot be determined, then it may be difficult to say anything definite about patterns of interaction. Nevertheless working through the possible patterns will give us an idea not only of how the variables might develop, but of how their development might affect the system as a whole.
10. If we plot the growth of Soc on the vertical axis, and that of Econ on the horizontal, the 45 degree line will mark the balancing point. Along this line the overall ratio of Econ to Soc will equal the ratio of new Econ to new Soc.
11. Another version of this story could be developed following the 'non-linear accelerator' model of Goodwin (suggested in correspondence by Matias Vernengo, University of Utah).

12. Examples might be found in ambitious African development programs following independence, which often failed at least in part because of inadequate administration and oversight.
13. The shift in population has two sources; one is migration, the other relative rates of population growth.
14. Cf. Nell and Forstater (2002); Wray (1998); also Nell et al, (forthcoming). Such programs are sometimes called 'Employer of Last Resort' (ELR) systems. They offer public service jobs at a basic wage to anyone who wants to work. The work will be in environmental cleanup, educational or healthcare support, poverty relief and the like. This provides unskilled or semi-skilled labor for a wide range of public sector projects, and it provides income for many low-end households. In a boom, labor will be attracted out of the ELR into higher paying work in the private sector; in a slump, labor will flow back into it. This will act as a buffer stock, tending to stabilize wages and it will provide countercyclical support for aggregate demand.

## REFERENCES


Acs, Z. (ed.) (2006), *The Growth of Cities*, Cheltenham, UK and Northamton, MA, USA: Edward Elgar.

Allen, R.G.D. (1968), *Macro-economic Theory: a Mathematical Treatment*, London: Macmillan; New York: St. Martin's Press.

Clark, G. (2007), *A Farewell to Alms*, Princeton, NJ: Princeton University Press

Goodwin, R.M. (1966), 'A Growth Cycle', in C.H. Feinstein (ed.), *Socialism, Capitalism and Economic Growth*, Cambridge: Cambridge University Press

Keuning, S. (1996), *Accounting for Economic Development and Social Change*, Amsterdam: IOS Press.

Keuning, S. (1997), 'Sesame: an Integrated Economic and Social Accounting System', *International Statistical Review*, **65**(1), 111–21.

Nell, E.J. (2004), 'Monetizing the Classical Equations: a Theory of Circulation', *Cambridge Journal of Economics*, **28**(2), 173–205.

Nell, E.J. and M. Forstater (2002), *Reinventing Functional Finance*, Cheltenham, UK, and Northampton, MA, USA: Edward Elgar.

Nell, E.J., K. Errouaki and F. Mayor (forthcoming), *Humanizing Globalization*,

Ozawa, S. (2008), 'Preliminary Estimates of the TG Matrix: El Salvador and the Phillipines', New School For Social Research.

Simon, C.J. and C. Nardinelli (1996), 'The Talk of the Town: Human Capital, Information, and the Growth of English Cities, 1861 to 1961', in Z.J. Acs, *The Growth of Cities*, Cheltenham, UK, and Brookfield, USA: Edward Elgar.

# 13. Financial fragility, mean-field interaction and macroeconomic dynamics: a stochastic model

**Corrado Di Guilmi, Mauro Gallegati and Simone Landini**

## 13.1. INTRODUCTION

In recent decades, a considerable stream of research, following the complexity approach (Rosser, 2004), has developed a series of models that import concepts and tools from hard sciences to economics. They represent an attempt to identify an alternative framework to the representative agent hypothesis and to its underlying simplified solution to the aggregation problem (Kirman, 1992). Theoretical research has moved in two main directions: first, the development of agent-based models, solved by means of computer simulations (Axtell et al., 1996; Axelrod, 1997); second, formulations of stochastic frameworks for the aggregation of micro-variables (Aoki, 1996, 2002; Aoki and Yoshikawa, 2006). Despite major advances, the problem of how to analytically determine an explicit and closed solution for this class of models, as commonly performed in traditional economic analysis, remains substantially unsolved. Indeed, a considerable methodological problem arises, since the introduction of heterogeneous (in time and space) agents prevents the common tools of the economist being used. To overcome this obstacle, different aggregation methods have been proposed. Yet they are still waiting for an application that, using explicit functions and formulations, succeeds in proving their usefulness.

With this work we seek to fill this gap. Starting from the pioneering works of Aoki, we develop a model of financial fragility, along the lines of Greenwald and Stiglitz (1993) and Delli Gatti et al. (2005), in a dynamic stochastic framework, where the interaction of heterogeneous agents in conditions of uncertainty gives rise to economic fluctuations.

Delli Gatti et al. (2005) rebuilt the model of financial fragility presented in Greenwald and Stiglitz (1990, 1993) with the introduction of indirect interaction of heterogeneous agents and solved it numerically. As amply shown in that work, a complex system structure appears to be particularly suitable to model a financial fragility approach in which, given the existence of different financial structures, the distribution of agents matters (Forni and Lippi, 1997). The financial instability hypothesis, since its first formulation (Minsky, 1963), considers firms heterogeneous as regards the proportions of short-term debt on total sources of finance. The quantitative outcomes of the model replicate a number of stylized facts, strengthening the idea that the economy would be better represented as a complex dynamic system rather than a mere sum of identical perfectly informed agents.

From a methodological point of view, the recent works of Masanao Aoki introduced into economics the concept of mean-field interaction, by means of which analytical modelling of interaction among heterogeneous agents becomes possible. Mean-field interaction can be defined as the average interaction model that approximates the interactions among agents that could not otherwise be analytically treated (Opper and Saad, 2001). Agents are clustered in a set of states, with regard to one particular feature (the micro-state, for example, the level of production for each firm) that determines the characteristics and the evolution of the aggregate (the macro-state, for example, the total level of output). The focus is not on the single agent, but on the number or proportion of agents that occupy a certain state at a certain time. These levels are governed by a stochastic law which also defines the functional of the probability distributions of aggregate variables and, if they exist, their equilibrium distributions. The stochastic aggregation is then made effective through master equation techniques, that allow us to describe the dynamics of probability flows and hence determine the aggregate effects of underlying fluctuations in agents' configurations, and therefore the consequent changes at the macro-level.

The main result of this chapter is the development and use of a framework for aggregating heterogeneous agents that proves capable of originating fluctuations of total production around a long path trend. Consistent with the inspiring financial fragility models, aggregate output is an inverse function of the system's degree of financial fragility, but with a different and more consistent microfoundation, given that objective functions differ for firms that have a dissimilar financial condition. Unlike the work of Delli Gatti et al. (2005), the interaction of different units, which gives rise to the complex dynamics, is analytically modelled by means of innovative stochastic aggregation tools. Indeed, with respect to Aoki's results, we manage to find a closed-form solution for a model with interacting and heterogeneous agents. In particular, we present an explicit steady-state solution for the master equation that leads to the analytical identification of an ordinary differential equation to describe trend dynamics and of a probability distribution function for fluctuations.

The structure of the work is the following: first, we specify the hypothesis for the stochastic structure of the system (Section 13.2) and for firms that comprise it (Section 13.3). In section 13.4, we develop the framework, setting the dynamic instruments required for aggregation, and solve the model, determining the two equations that drive production trends and business cycles. Some results of the model's computer simulations are presented in section 13.5, followed by concluding remarks in section 13.6.

## 13.2. THE PROBABILISTIC STRUCTURE

We set up a model in continuous time for a system of heterogeneous and interacting agents, partitioned into groups or states. In this section we state the hypothesis regarding the definition and structure of the states. Our system is structured into two states. Along time, a single firm can be in one of them, depending on its financial soundness, quantified by its equity ratio, that is, the ratio of net worth to total assets. We use $0$ to identify the state of firms with an equity ratio $a_i(t)$ no lower than the threshold $\overline{a}$, and $1$ for the state of firms which have an equity ratio lower than the threshold and are thus exposed to the risk of demise. The twofold partition permits us to isolate the effect of the expected bankruptcy costs on aggregate dynamics. For the analytical treatment, all the $a_i$ are approximated by the two variables $a^1$ and $a^0$. It is thus feasible to obtain the mean-field approximation of interactions among agents. More precisely, $a^j : j=0, 1$ can be regarded as a statistic of all the equity ratios for each state.

The choice to let the system work in continuous time is due, on the one hand, to analytical reasons, since it gives the option to use a set of analytical tools that cannot be employed in discrete time. Continuous time also appears to be more consistent with a complexity approach (Hinich et al., 2006).

The economy is populated by a fixed number of firms $N$, each indexed by $i$. Let us define the occupation numbers $N^j$ for $j=0, 1$ as the number of firms, respectively, in state $0$ and state $1$ and $n^j$ as their percentage. By assumption, the dynamics of these occupation numbers follow a continuous-time jump Markov process. *A priori* probability of being in state $1$ is indicated by $\eta$, such that:

$$p(1)=\eta \Leftrightarrow p(0)=1-\eta$$

Firms exit from the system only for bankruptcy. In order to maintain constant the number of firms $N$, we assume that each bankrupted firm is immediately substituted by a new one. New firms, by assumption, enter the system in state 1 (that is with a low equity ratio). Therefore failures of firms do not modify $N^1$.

In order to model the probabilistic flows of firms from one state to another, we have to properly define transition probabilities and transition rates. The former are the probabilities of a single firm switching from one state to the other in a given instant. Namely, $\zeta$ is the transition probability of moving from state 0 to 1 (firms whose financial position is deteriorating, with equity ratio that becomes lower than $\bar{a}$) and $\iota$ indicates the probability of the opposite transition (firms whose equity ratio improves to become greater than $\bar{a}$). Moreover, we use $\mu$ to indicate the probability of bankruptcy.

The particular configuration assumed by agents, jointly determined by these probabilities, thus gives rise to a particular macro-state at aggregate level. This macro-state can be identified by the occupation number. The set of macro-states is therefore represented by all the possible occupation numbers $N^j$. Given that $N$ does not change, it is enough to observe one of the states. Therefore, we can take as state variable the numbers of firms in 1, defining $N_k$ as the number of firms occupying it in a given instant, with $0 \leq N_k \leq N$. Once a particular macro-state $N_k(t)$ is verified, it can be modified by a 'birth' from state 0 to state 1, and by a 'death' from state 1 to state 0. Thus, in order to describe the dynamic behaviour of the system, we need to specify the aggregate probability of observing, in a unit of time, a 'jump' of an agent from one state to another, and a consequent variation in occupation numbers, given the particular starting macro-state. This measure of probability is quantified by transition rates. We specify a transition rate for entries *into* state 1, $\lambda$, and a transition rate for exits *out* from the same state, $\gamma$, according to the following formulation:

$$\begin{aligned} \lambda &= \zeta(1-\eta) \\ \gamma &= \iota\eta \end{aligned} \tag{13.1}$$

Therefore, the transition rate is given by the probability of a firm switching from one state to another, weighted by the probability of being in the starting state. Multiplying the result by the actual occupation numbers, we obtain the probability of observing this transition in a unit of time:

$$\begin{aligned} b(N_k) &= P[N_{k+1}(t') \mid N_k(t)] = \lambda(N - N_k) \\ d(N_k) &= P[N_{k-1}(t') \mid N_k(t)] = \gamma(N_k) \end{aligned} \tag{13.2}$$

where $b$ and $d$ indicate, respectively, 'births' (transition to $N_{k+1}$) and 'deaths' (transition to $N_{k-1}$) of the stochastic process and $t'^{+}$.

The probability of bankruptcy for a distressed firm is indicated with $\mu$. It represents a key variable in determining the evolution path and the dynamics of fluctuation in the economic system, as detailed in the following section. The rate of exit from the system is then quantified by $\mu\eta$, which, given the hypothesis, also represents the rate of entry into the system.

The mechanism of the system[1] is depicted in Figure 13.1.

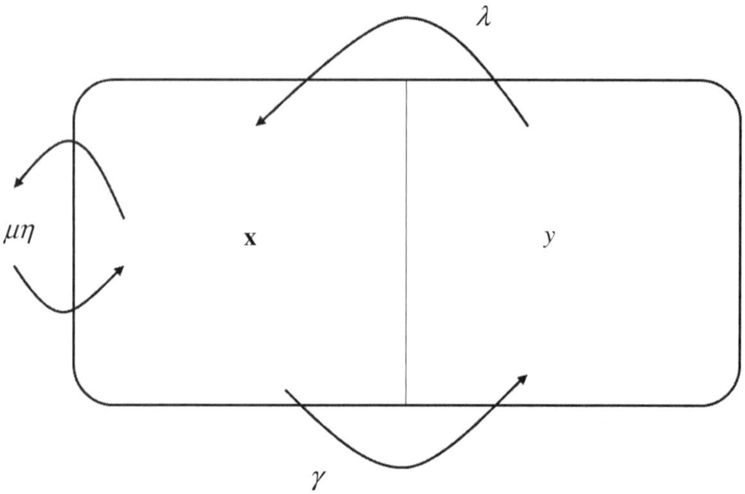


*Figure 13.1. System structure*

## 13.3. THE FIRMS

### 13.3.1 Hypothesis

Firms' behaviour is adapted from the original models of Greenwald and Stiglitz (1990, 1993), as modified by Delli Gatti et al. (2005). The adjustments are mainly due to the convenience of keeping the computational mechanism as simple as possible in order to highlight the aggregation problem and the proposed solution. At the same time, the framework maintains consistency with the original bankruptcy costs approach and a degree of heterogeneity among firms that is suited to the stochastic dynamics described in the previous section.

In Delli Gatti et al. (2005) the effect of firms' financial fragility on aggregate production is made effective through the credit market mechanism, that reduces the supply of credit when a firm fails. In this work, financial variables and production influence each other through feedback effects from the system to the agents and *vice versa*. Indeed, aggregate production is determined by the occupation numbers, and the probability of observing a change in state is itself influenced by the general financial situation of the economy. Interaction is not direct, but is represented as a mean-field interaction, that is to say, mediated at a meso-level of aggregation.

The economy is supply-driven: each of the $N$ firms sells all the output that it (optimally) decides to produce. The produced good is perishable. Firms are identical within each state. Firms employ only one factor in the production process, indicated as the physical capital $k$, that does not depreciate. Unlike Delli Gatti et al. (2005), the total number of firms $N$ does not change over time. Firms are identical within each state. In what follows the apex refers to the state while the firm index is in subscript.

According to these hypotheses the aggregate production function of the economy is given by:

$$Y(t)=N^1 y^1+N^0 y^0 \tag{13.3}$$

where $y^1$ and $y^0$ indicate the optimal level of production for firms in the two states. The significance and dynamic structure of the occupation numbers $N^1$ and $N^0$ are detailed above. In the following we define the mechanism for determining firms' production levels. The production function of a generic firm $i$ is:

$$q_i(t)=2[k_i(t)]^{1/2} \tag{13.4}$$

where $q$ is the physical output. Therefore, the demand function for capital of a single firm will be:

$$k_i(t)=\frac{1}{2}[q_i(t)]^2 \tag{13.5}$$

Basing on equation (13.5), firms adjust their capital stock to optimize their production level, investing an amount equal to $I_i(t)$, which can be either positive or negative, since a firm that reduces its production also has to diminish its physical stock.[2]

As assumed by Greenwald and Stiglitz (1993), firms are fully rationed on the equity market, such that they can finance their investments only with internal sources $(A_i)$ or with loans $(B_i)$. Equity is given by the profits that firms retain over time such that the law of motion of $A_i$ is given by:

$$A(t')=A(t)+\pi(t')$$

Variation in the stock of debt $(\delta B_i(t'))$ in a period will then be:

$$\delta B_i(t') = I_i(t') - A_i(t) \tag{13.6}$$

In order to maintain balance sheet identity, we have $K_i(t) = A_i(t) + B_i(t)$. Under the assumption that firms and banks sign long-term contractual relationships (with no set date of repayment), at each $t$ debt commitments in real terms for the $i$-th firm are $rB_i(t)$, where $r$ is the real interest rate. Supposing that the market for capital is always in equilibrium (such that the real return on net worth equals the interest rate $r$), each firm incurs financing costs equal to:

$$r[B_i(t) + A_i(t)] = rK_i(t) \tag{13.7}$$

We can assume that the interest rate is constant over time and the same for all firms since demand for credit is endogenously limited within the model and cannot grow indefinitely.

At the moment of selling, each firm faces an iid idiosyncratic real shock in price. The $i$-th individual selling price is the random outcome of a market process around the average market price $P(t)$, according to the law:

$$P_i(t) = \tilde{u}_i(t)P(t) \tag{13.8}$$

The random variable $\tilde{u}_i(t)$ has uniform distribution with $E(\tilde{u}) = 1$, where $E$ is the mathematical average. Without loss of generality its support can be fixed in the interval [0.75; 1.25]. Choice of the range for $\tilde{u}$ does not affect probabilities, given the normalization procedures detailed below. Once a firm fails, it faces bankruptcy costs $C_i(t)$ growing with firm size, quantified by sales volume, and given by:

$$C_i(t) = c[P_i(t)q(t)_i]^2 = c[P(t)\tilde{u}_i(t)q_i(t)]^2 \ : 0 < c < 1 \tag{13.9}$$

Greenwald and Stiglitz (1993) use a linear function but their results, as they state, hold for any function convex in $q$. The introduction of bankruptcy costs may be justified by the behaviour of managers, who act to avoid failure for two main reasons (Greenwald and Stiglitz, 1990). First, given the impossibility of identifying the cause of default in bad luck or in managers' incompetence, bankruptcy may generate stigmatization of managers' behaviour and, as a consequence, a reduction in their future earnings. Second, the imposition of a penalty for failure constitutes an incentive, since managers' contracts cannot state a participation in losses. As a further consequence, bankruptcy costs grow with size, since the number of employed managers is determined by the scale of operation.

### 13.3.1.1. Transition probabilities

A firm fails when its own capital $A_i$ goes to 0. Given that the only exogenous variable in the model is the stochastic price shock $\tilde{u}_i(t)$, a bankruptcy condition may be defined as a function of the price shock:

$$\tilde{u}(t') \leq \frac{P(t)}{P(t')}\left[\frac{rK_i(t)}{q_i(t)} - a^1(t)\frac{k_i(t)}{P(t')q_i(t)}\right] \equiv \overline{u}_i(t') \tag{13.10}$$

Substituting equation (13.5) into the above expression and, without loss of generality, normalizing reference price $P(t)=P(t')$ to 1, the r.h.s. of equation (13.10) becomes:

$$\overline{u}(t') \equiv \frac{q^1(t)}{2}\left[r - a^1(t)\right] \tag{13.11}$$

Having the random variable $\tilde{u}$ support [0.75; 1.25], we can quantify the critical thresholds of shock prices for having bankruptcy as:

$$\begin{cases} \overline{u}_i(t) = 0.75 & \textit{if } \overline{u} < 0.75 \\ \overline{u}_i(t) \leq \tilde{u}_i(t) & \textit{if } 0.75 \leq \overline{u} \leq 1.25 \\ \overline{u}_i(t) = 1.25 & \textit{if } \overline{u} > 1.25 \end{cases} \tag{13.12}$$

It is then possible to indicate the probability of failure $\mu(t)$ for a firm as a function of $\tilde{u}(t)$:

$$\mu(t) = F(\overline{u}(t)) = \frac{\overline{u}(t) - 0.75}{0.5} = 2\overline{u}(t) - 1.5 \tag{13.13}$$

Equation (13.13) permits endogenous determination of the equity ratio threshold $\overline{a}$. It can be interpreted as the minimum equity ratio which ensures a firm's survival, that is for which the probability of bankruptcy is equal to zero,[3] and hence can be expressed as:

$$\overline{a}(t') = r - \frac{1.5}{q^1(t)} \tag{13.14}$$

Analogously, the transition probabilities $\zeta$ and $\iota$ can be expressed as dependent variables of the price shock $\tilde{u}_i(t)$, with the opportune critical values, indicated, respectively as $\overline{u}_\zeta(t)$ and $\overline{u}_\iota(t)$:

$$\tilde{u}_i(t) \leq \frac{q^0(t)}{2}\left[r+\bar{a}(t)-a^0(t)\right] \equiv \bar{u}_\zeta(t)$$
$$\tilde{u}_i(t) > \frac{q^1(t)}{2}\left[r+\bar{a}(t)-a^1(t)\right] \equiv \bar{u}_\iota(t) \tag{13.15}$$

The range of variation of the two thresholds is truncated as in (eq:baru), explicit formulation for transition probabilities can now be straightforwardly calculated:

$$\zeta(t) = p\left[\tilde{u}(t) \leq \bar{u}_\zeta(t)\right] = 2\bar{u}_\zeta(t) - 1.5 \tag{13.16}$$

$$\iota(t) = 1 - p\left[\tilde{u}(t) \leq \bar{u}_\iota(t)\right] = -2\bar{u}_\iota(t) + 2.5 \tag{13.17}$$

### 13.3.2. Firms' Objective Function and Aggregate Production

Each firm acts to maximize its profit function:

$$\max_{q_i(t)} F(q_i(t)) = E\left\{\left[P(t)u_i(t')q_i(t)\right] - rK_i(t) - C_i(t)\mu(t')\right\} \tag{13.18}$$

We suppose that firms allow for the present level of failure probability, hence $E[\mu(t')] = \mu(t)$, and that $E[P(t')] = P(t') = P(t) = 1$, without loss of generality. The first order condition is:

$$1 - rq_i(t) - 2cq_i(t)\mu(t) = 0$$

Consequently, there are two different optimal levels of production, one for firms in state 1 and one for firms in state 0, respectively:

$$q^{1*} = (r + 2c\mu)^{-1}$$
$$q^{0*} = r^{-1} \tag{13.19}$$

given that $\mu = 0$ for firms in state 0. The aggregate output of the system given by equation (13.3) can now be expressed as:

$$Y(t) = \frac{N^1(t)}{r + 2c\mu(t)} + \frac{N^0(t)}{r} \tag{13.20}$$

As can be seen, fluctuations have two main sources: the first concerns the failure probability $\mu$ and the second is related to the dynamics of the occupation numbers. To highlight the impact of financial fragility, we may express equation (13.20) in the following way:

$$Y(t)=\frac{N}{r}-\xi(t)N^1(t) \tag{13.21}$$

where $\xi(t)=\frac{1}{r}\left(1+\frac{r}{2c\mu(t)}\right)^{-1}$. The second member of the r.h.s. in equation (13.21) is the product of the two independent random variables $\xi(t)$ and $N^1$. The latter can be considered a macroeconomic indicator for the financial fragility of the system; it is weighted by $\xi$, which is a function of probability $\mu$ that, depending upon $a^1$, reflects financial conditions of firms in state 1. Therefore the dynamics of aggregate production is negatively correlated to the micro- and macro-level of financial distress in the economy.

## 13.4. STOCHASTIC DYNAMICS

### 13.4.1. Master Equation

In order to describe the dynamics of aggregate production, we need to specify the stochastic evolution of micro-states, which determines the evolution of occupation number probabilities. For this task we need to set up and solve the master equation. A master (or Chapman–Kolmogorov) equation can be defined as a first-order differential equation that describes the dynamics of the probability of a system occupying each of a determinate set of macro-states. It 'describes the time evolution of the probability distribution of states, not the time evolution of the states themselves' (Aoki, 2002, p. 7). Hence it permits us to quantify the variation of probability fluxes in a small interval of time for continuous-time Markov processes. According to this definition, the probability distribution of having $N_k$ firms in state 1 in a given instant will follow this scheme:

$$\frac{dP(N_k)}{dt}= \text{(inflows of probability fluxes into 1)} - \text{(outflows of probability fluxes out of 1)}.$$

To specify the dynamics of joint probabilities and thereby the stochastic evolution of the system, we make use of the following master equation:[4]

$$\frac{dP(N_k)}{dt}=b(N_{k-1})P(N_{k-1})+d(N_{k+1})P(N_{k+1})-\{[(b(N_k)+d(N_k))P(N_k)]\} \tag{13.22}$$

with boundary conditions:

$$\begin{cases} P(N,\, t) = b(N^1)P(N^1 - 1,\, t) + d(N)P(N,\, t) \\ P(0,\, t) = b(1)P(1,\, t) + d(0)P(0,\, t) \end{cases} \tag{13.23}$$

These conditions ensure that the distribution functions only consider meaningful values, that is to say $N^1 \in [0;\, N]$.

A master equation is a balance flows equation that sums the probability of reaching the number $N_k$ of firms in state 1 with a 'death' from $N_{k+1}$ or with a 'birth' from $N_{k-1}$, less the probability of already being in the macro-state $N_k$ and observing a transition to or from micro-state 1. It fully describes the dynamics of our system. Below we show that, by means of this analytical instrument, it is possible: first, to determine the endogenous steady-state value of the probability $\eta$ that we have so far treated as exogenous; second, to describe the trend and fluctuations of occupation numbers and hence of aggregate production.

### 13.4.2. Stationary Points and Equilibrium Probability

In this section we define an endogenous formulation for the probability $\eta$ of being in state 1. By definition, steady state implies that the probability of influxes equates the probability of out-fluxes for each state. This condition is known as detailed balance and is obtained by equating the master equation to 0. Analytical details are provided in Appendix A. Stationary probability can be derived by applying Brook's lemma (Brook, 1964) that quantifies the equilibrium probability $P^e(N_k)$ which ensures that detailed balance holds for each pair of macro-states:

$$P^e(N_k) = P^e[N(0)]\left(\frac{\iota}{\zeta}\right)^{N_k}\binom{N}{N_k}\prod_{h=1}^{H}\frac{\eta(N - N_h)}{[1 - \eta(N_h)]} \tag{13.24}$$

Thanks to Hammersley and Clifford's theorem (Clifford, 1990), it is possible to treat the Markovian space as a Gibbs space, expressing $P^e(N_k)$ in Gibbs form. Then, by following Landini (2005, ch. 5) the probability $\eta$ of a firm being in state 1 can be expressed as a function of the occupation number of that state and quantified by:

$$\eta(N^1) = N^{-1}e^{\beta g(N^1)} \tag{13.25}$$

where:

$$\beta = \ln\left[-\frac{y^1(t)-\overline{y}(t)}{y^0(t)-\overline{y}(t)}\right]\left[y^1(t)-y^0(t)\right]^{-1}$$

$$g(N^1) = -\frac{1}{2\beta}\frac{dH(N^1)}{dN^1} = -\frac{1}{2\beta}\ln\left(\frac{N^1}{N-N^1}\right)$$

$\overline{y}(t)$ is the average production $Y(t)/N$. The probability of being in state 1 in a given instant appears to be dependent on three factors: the number of firms already occupying the state, $N^1$; parameter $\beta$, which quantifies the impact on total output of the financial distress of the system; and function $g(N^1)$, which measures the average difference in the optimal levels of production. The situation and consequent behaviour of a firm is then linked to the state of the economy which, in turn, is determined by the number of firms that reduce output due to expected bankruptcy costs and by the level of this reduction, captured by $g(N^1)$. Equation (13.25) expresses the indirect interaction among firms and the feedback effects between macro-, meso- and micro-level.

### 13.4.3. Master Equation Solution: Stochastic Dynamics of Trend and Fluctuations

Applying the master equation solution (13.22) we can quantify and express in explicit form the stochastic dynamics of aggregate production and also decompose it into trend and cycle components. As a result, we can identify a long-run path dynamics (that eventually leads to a steady-state equilibrium, if it exists), and the fluctuations around this trend. In order to obtain such information, we assume that the fraction of firms in state 1 in a given moment is determined by its expected mean $(m)$, the trend or *drift*, and, according to Aoki (2002), by an additive fluctuation component of order $N^{1/2}$ around this value, that is to say the *spread*:

$$N_k = Nm + \sqrt{N}s \tag{13.26}$$

As aggregate output is determined by the proportion of firms in the two states, the dynamics of $N^1$ describes the dynamics of production. Moreover, using equation (13.26), the solution of the master equation will return the expected long-run path of production and a probability distribution for business fluctuations.

Since an analytical solution for master equations can be obtained only under very specific and restrictive conditions (Risken, 1989), we can solve it using one of the approximation methods detailed in Aoki (2002) and Landini (2005) (see Appendix B). The asymptotically approximated solution of the master equation is given by the following system of coupled equations:

$$\frac{dm}{d\tau} = \lambda m - (\lambda + \gamma)m^2 \tag{13.27}$$

$$\frac{\partial Q}{\partial \tau} = [2(\lambda + \gamma)m - \lambda] \frac{\partial}{\partial s}[sQ(s)] + \frac{[\lambda m(1-m) + \gamma m^2]}{2}\left(\frac{\partial}{\partial s}\right)^2 Q(s) \tag{13.28}$$

Equation (13.27) is a deterministic ordinary differential equation (the macroeconomic equation, in Aoki's words) which displays a logistic dynamics for the trend or drifting component. Equation (13.28) is a second-order stochastic partial differential equation, called *Fokker-Planck equation*, that drives the spreading component (that is the fluctuations around the trend) of the probability flow. Dynamics to the steady state value $m^*$ is clearly convergent. Setting the l.h.s. of the macroscopic equation (13.27) to 0, we can calculate the steady-state value for $m$:

$$m^* = \frac{\lambda}{\lambda + \gamma} \tag{13.29}$$

Hence, directly integrating equation (13.27):

$$m(\tau) = \frac{\lambda}{(\lambda + \gamma) - ke^{-\psi\tau}} : \begin{cases} k = 1 - \dfrac{m^*}{m(0)} \\ \psi = \dfrac{(\lambda + \gamma)^2}{\lambda} \end{cases} \tag{13.30}$$

This differential equation describes the dynamics of fraction $m$ of firms occupying state 1 at each point in time. It is fully dependent on transition rates. Solution of the equation for the spread component (see Appendix C) permits the distribution function $\theta$ to be calculated for spread $s$, thus determining the probability distribution of fluctuations:

$$\theta(s) = C\exp\left(-\frac{s^2}{2\sigma^2}\right) : \sigma^2 = \frac{\lambda\gamma}{(\lambda + \gamma)^2} = m^* \frac{\gamma}{\lambda + \gamma} \tag{13.31}$$

which looks like a Gaussian density. Fluctuations then also depend only on transition rates. Given the relationship between $m$ and total production, the dynamics of our economy is now fully described since we have a differential equation for output dynamics, its equilibrium value, and a probability function for business fluctuations around the trend.

### 13.4.4. Output Dynamics

Once the equilibrium distribution of the drift has been quantified, we are now able to obtain the steady-state aggregate production, $Y^e$:

$$Y^e = N\left[\frac{1}{r} - \frac{\lambda}{\lambda+\gamma}\frac{2c\mu}{r(r+2c\mu)}\right] = N\left[\frac{1}{r} - \frac{\lambda}{\lambda+\gamma}\left(y^0 - y^1\right)\right] \tag{13.32}$$

As shown by equation (13.32), the dynamics depends on the difference among firms' optimal production levels and on the transition rates. The first component is given by the exogenous parameter $c$, that reflects institutional conditions, and by the probability of bankruptcy $\mu$, that is the result of the relative financial condition of 'bad' firms. Indeed, the probability of demise depends on the distance between their equity ratio $a^1$ and the 'safety' level $\bar{a}$. The second component, recalling equations (13.1) and (13.16), is basically determined, on the one hand, by relative financial soundness or distress of firms of the two groups and, on the other, by the general financial situation of the system, revealed by the number of firms in each state. Substituting equations (13.16) and (13A.3) of Appendix A in equations (13.1), under detailed balance condition we can express the transition rates $\lambda$ and $\gamma$ as a function of the occupation numbers and shock price thresholds:

$$\lambda = \left(N^{-1}e^{\beta g(N^1)}\right)\left(2\bar{u}_\zeta - 1.5\right) \tag{13.33}$$

$$\gamma = \left[1 - \left(N^{-1}e^{\beta g(N^1)}\right)\right]\left(-2.5\bar{u}_\iota + 1.5\right) \tag{13.34}$$

Transition rates, hence the whole dynamics and final equilibrium of the system, are determined by a macro-factor, represented by $\eta$, and a micro factor, represented by probabilities $\zeta$ and $\iota$. The joint effect of these variables gives rise to a mechanism that can be termed financial contagion. In particular, keeping in mind equations (13.15), the effect of the probability of bankruptcy at micro-level (reduction in optimal production $q^1$) appears to be amplified by the system's level of global financial distress. Distribution of agents, far from being neutral, is clearly the main determinant of the economic outcome. Moreover, since the system is governed by inherent uncertainty, all relationships have to be expressed as probability functions. Therefore the system dynamics appears to be fully stochastic, and the steady-state level of production can with difficulty be defined as a natural equilibrium.

## 13.5. SIMULATION RESULTS

To illustrate in greater detail the mechanism of the system and check the sensitivity of the results to variations in the parameters, we performed some simulations with Matlab software. The simulations highlighted the role of financial fragility in determining the evolution path for output and the model's capacity to generate multiple equilibria.

In order to get a treatable analytic approximation of mean-field interaction, equity ratios for firms in the two states are quantified by:

$$a^0(t) = \bar{a} + \varepsilon\sigma(t)$$
$$a^1(t) = \bar{a} - \varepsilon\sigma(t) \qquad (13.35)$$

where $0 < \varepsilon \leq 1$ and $\sigma(t)$ is the standard deviation in equity ratio distribution at time $t$. Parameter values are set to: $c = 0.3$, $\varepsilon = 0.1$.

The obtained series of $m$ and of aggregate output are displayed in Figure 13.2. Trends are represented by continuous black lines, determined by means of equation (13.30). Fluctuations in $n^1$, which determine business cycles, follow the stochastic distribution expressed by equation (13.31). These two equations fully describe the economy's behaviour. The dynamics of $m$ is convergent.

The final equilibrium percentage of 'bad' firms is positively related with interest rate. Indeed, a higher level of interest rate implies a higher value of $m^*$ (and a lower level of steady state production), since it determines greater financing costs for firms, raising the probability of entering state 1 and lowering the probability of exit.

As demonstrated by equation (13.31), the percentage of heavily indebted firms also influences the amplitude of business cycles, amplifying the role of the risk of bankruptcy and then raising volatility and uncertainty. Figure 13.3 shows that a higher interest rate leads to a wider range of oscillation for output fluctuations due to the higher number of firms that occupy state 1. Indeed, the share $n^1$ constitutes a factor of uncertainty since the optimal level of output for 'bad' firms is subject to stochastic variations, due to the presence in their objective function of the probability of demise $\mu(t)$. Given equations (13.11) and (13.20) and considering the mean-field approximation (13.35), one can verify that firms' financial conditions, proxied by equity ratios, have a growing impact, as $n^1$ increases, not only on the level of output but also on its volatility. A higher level of financial distress in the system thus raises uncertainty, hence the higher risk involved in economic activity. The model appears suitable to provide indications for stabilization policies since the level of output and the amplitude of business fluctuations can be modified by handling the interest rates.

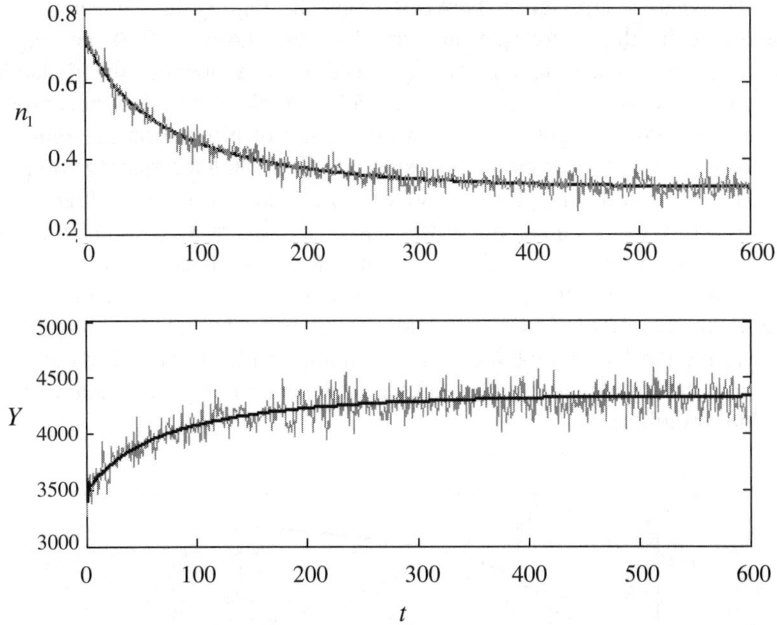


*Figure 13.2. Trends and fluctuations for* n[1] *(upper panel) and aggregate production (lower panel)*

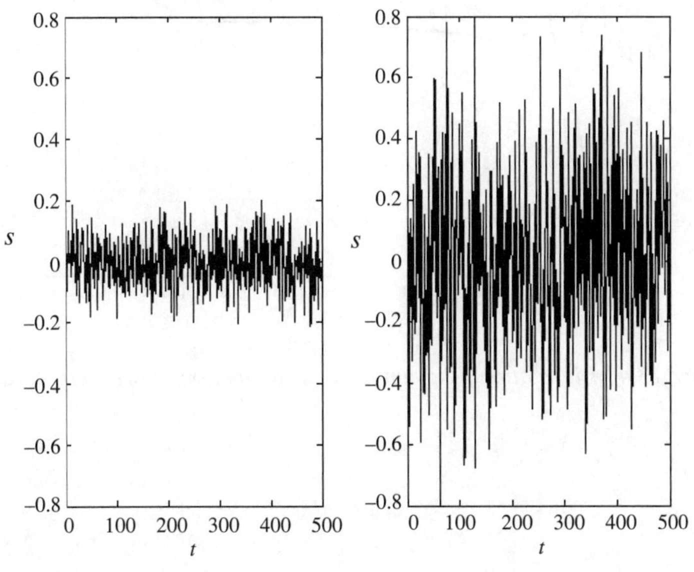


*Figure 13.3. Spread for* r = *0.1 (left panel) and* r = *0.05 (right panel)*

The positive correlation between financial fragility and uncertainty is confirmed by the bifurcation diagram (Figures 13.4 and 13.5). For higher values of $r$, as ceiling effects on transition rates operate, the dynamics cannot be explosive. For interest rates below $10\%$, the system generates a chaotic dynamics. Figure 13.5 shows the detail of bifurcation diagrams for two different initial levels of $m$, showing that a higher starting value of $m(0)$ may result, also for an interest rate close to 0, in a higher $m$. Moreover, higher values of $m(0)$ will also generate a wider range of possible outcomes in the chaos region. Therefore, uncertainty about the effect of a variation in the interest rate turns out to be positively correlated to the financial fragility of the economy. As may be noted, although the underlying stochastic structure is rather simple, being structured in only two possible microstates, the model is able to generate complex dynamics with multiple equilibria.

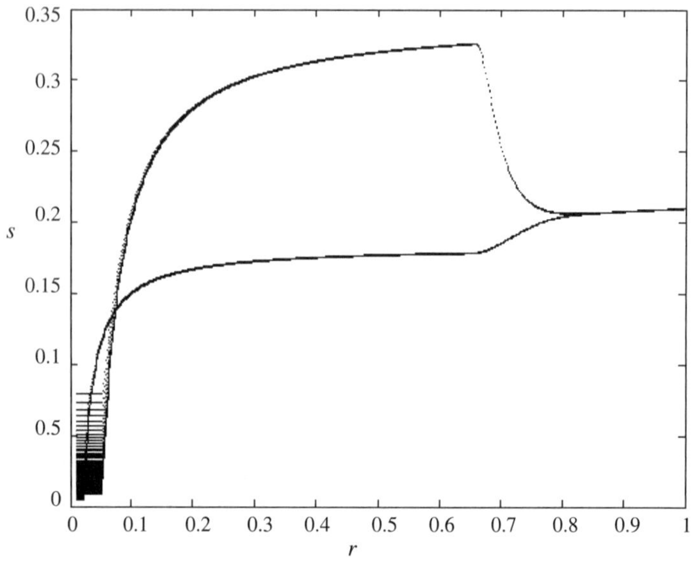


*Figure 13.4. Bifurcation diagram for* m *as a function of the interest rate* r

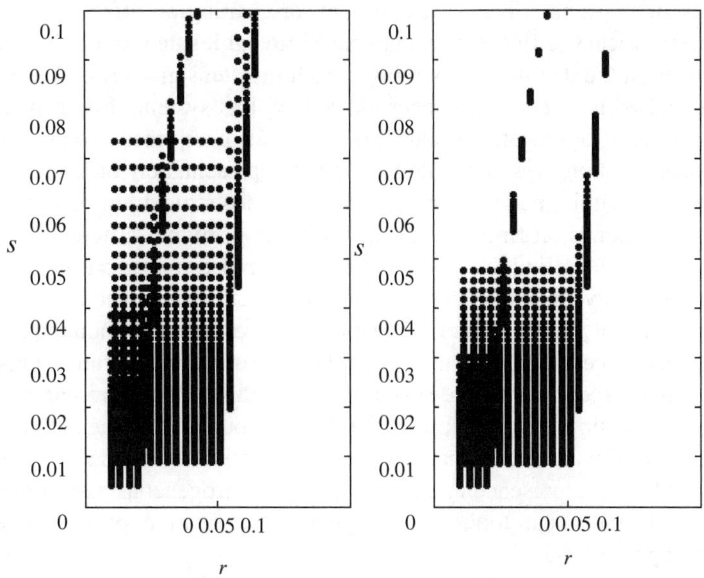


*Figure 13.5. Spread for* r = *0.1 (left panel) and* r = *0.05 (right panel)*

## 13.6. CONCLUDING REMARKS

Herein we developed an innovative framework for the aggregation of heterogeneous agents, originally conceived by Aoki, and applied it within a financial fragility model. The main result was endogenous generation of fluctuations of total production around a long-path trend, with growth paths and temporary variations dependent on firms' financial conditions. In particular, given a steady-state solution for the master equation, it is possible to identify an ordinary differential equation and a stochastic equation in order to describe, respectively, trend dynamics and fluctuation probability. The macro-level outcomes were obtained without formulating an *ad hoc* hypothesis about the dynamics of the system or its starting (or final) conditions. Importantly, the long-term trend can hardly be termed a natural level of production since, even though the proportions of firms in the two states asymptotically tend to a stationary value, this dynamics is purely stochastic.

Equilibrium probability formulations include micro- and macro-factors, permitting analytical representation and evaluation of the effect of indirect interaction among firms. The probability of a firm being forced to reduce production due to the risk of failure proves dependent also on the financial fragility of the other firms in the system, originating an effect that can be defined as stochastic financial contagion. Since aggregate production is itself dependent on the debt-to-equity ratio of each firm, this gives rise to feedback effects between micro- and macro-levels of the system. Micro-financial variables and aggregate production dynamics are then connected in functional relationships that allow detailed representation of transmission mechanisms within the system. At micro-level, the structure of optimization processes depends on firms' financial soundness, proving different for each type of firm. Modelling the links between financial fragility, business cycles and growth dynamics is then consistently microfounded, given the heterogeneity of firms' financial variables and the interaction among agents, and between agents and the macro-level of the system. This may open up interesting prospects for future developments of this stream of research.

This promising method, presented here through implementation in a financial fragility model, appears suited to application in any macroeconomic context where the presence and interaction of heterogeneous agents prevent the use of traditional tools for analytical identification of the system's emerging properties.

## 13A.1. APPENDIX A

We sketch here the basic steps for deriving the steady-state probability, referring the interested reader to the cited references. Stationary probability can be obtained by applying Brook's lemma which defines the local characteristic of continuous Markov chains. Hammersley and Clifford demonstrate that, under opportune conditions, for each Markov random field there is one, and only one, Gibbs random field, and define the functional form for the conjunct probability structure once the neighbourhood relations have been identified (Clifford, 1990). The expected stationary probability (eq:brook) of the Markovian process for $N^1$, when detailed balance holds, can then be expressed by:

$$P^e(N_k) \propto Z^{-1} e^{-\beta N U(N_k)} \tag{13A.1}$$

where $U(x)$ is the *Gibbs potential* and can be defined as a functional of the local dynamic characteristics of the state variable $N_k$. In particular we have:

$$e^{\beta g(N^1)} + e^{-\beta g(N^1)} = N \tag{13A.2}$$

Using the above formulation (Landini, 2005; Di Guilmi, 2008) the probability $\eta$ can be expressed explicitly as a function of the state variable $N^1$:

$$\eta(N^1) = N^{-1} e^{\beta g(N^1)} \tag{13A.3}$$

where $g(N^1)$ is a function that evaluates the relative difference in the outcome as a function of $N^1$. $\beta$ may be interpreted as an inverse measure of system uncertainty. The uncertainty among the different possible configurations in a stochastic system can be evaluated through a statistical entropy measure (Balian, 1991). Parameter $\beta$ can be quantified by maximizing the statistical entropy of the system (Jaynes, 1957). In our case the problem is configured as follows:

$$\begin{cases} \max H(N^1, N^0) = -N^1(t)\ln\left[N^1(t)\right] - N^0(t)\ln\left[N^0(t)\right] \quad s.t. \\ N^1(t) + N^0(t) = N \\ N^1(t) y^1(t) + N^0(t) y^0(t) = Y(t) \end{cases} \tag{13A.4}$$

The first of the two constraints ensures the normalization of the probability function. The second ensures that all the wealth in the system is generated by firms in the two kinds of states. With suitable Lagrange multipliers equal to, respectively, $\delta_1 = 1 - \alpha$ and $\delta_2 = -\beta$, we get a closed solution for $\beta$:

$$\beta(t) = \ln\left[-\frac{y^1(t) - \overline{y}(t)}{y^0(t) - \overline{y}(t)}\right]\left(y^1(t) - y^0(t)\right)^{-1} \tag{13A.5}$$

Large values of $\beta$ associated with positive values of $g(N^1)$ cause $\eta(N^1)$ to be larger than $1-\eta(N^1)$, making the transition from state 0 to state 1 more likely to occur than the opposite one. In binary models and for great $N$, the equation of the potential is:

$$U(N^j) = -2\int_0^{N^j} g(z)dz - \frac{1}{\beta}H(\underline{N})$$

where $H(\underline{N})$ is the Shannon entropy with $\underline{N} = (N^1, N^0)$. In order to determine the stationary points of probability dynamics we need to determine its peak (if it does exist). $\beta$ is an inverse multiplicative factor for entropy: a relative high value of $\beta$ means that the uncertainty in the system is low, with few firms exposed to bankruptcy risk. For values of $\beta$ around 0, and higher volatility in the system, in order to determine the peak of probability dynamics we need to find the local minimum of the potential. Aoki (2002) shows that the points in which the potential is minimized are also the critical point of the aggregate dynamics of $P^e(N_k)$. Deriving the potential with respect to $N^1$ and then setting $U' = 0$:

$$g(N^1) = -\frac{1}{2\beta}\frac{dH}{dN^1} = -\frac{1}{2\beta}\ln\left(\frac{N^1}{N - N^1}\right) \tag{13A.6}$$

and using equation (13A.5), we get an explicit formulation for $g(N^1)$ in the stationary condition:

$$g(N^1) = \frac{y^0 - y^1}{2}$$

that quantifies the mean difference (for states) of the outcome.

## 13A.2. APPENDIX B

The master equation (13.22) must be modified, according to equation (13.26), and expressed as $\dot{Q}(s)$, a function of $s$:

$$\dot{P}(N_k) = \frac{\partial Q}{\partial t} + \frac{ds}{dt}\frac{\partial Q}{\partial s} = \dot{Q}(s) \tag{13A.7}$$

with transition rates reformulated in the following way:

$$b(s)=\lambda\left[N-Nm-\sqrt{N}s\right] \tag{13A.8}$$

$$d(s)=\gamma\left[Nm+\sqrt{N}s\right] \tag{13A.9}$$

Since

$$\frac{ds}{dt}=-N^{1/2}\frac{dm}{dt} \tag{13A.10}$$

equation (13A.7) can be expressed as:

$$\dot{Q}(s)=\frac{\partial Q}{\partial t}-N^{1/2}\frac{\partial Q}{\partial s}\dot{m} \tag{13A.11}$$

Now we rewrite again the master equation (13.22) and the transition rates by means of lead and lag operators. These operators make the two probability flows (in and out) homogeneous. Specifically the transition probabilities (13.1) become:

$$L[d(N_k)P(N_k,\, t)]=d(N_{k+1})P(N_{k+1}) \tag{13A.12}$$

$$L^{-1}[b(N_k)P(N_k,\, t)]=d(N_{k-1})P(N_{k-1}) \tag{13A.13}$$

so that the master equation will be expressed in this way:

$$\dot{Q}(s)=(L-1)[d(s)Q(s)]+(L^{-1}-1)[d(s)Q(s)] \tag{13A.14}$$

Using the modified transition rates (13A.12) and expanding the thus obtained master equation in inverse powers of $s$ to the second order we get:

$$\begin{aligned}
&N^{-1}\frac{\partial Q}{\partial \tau}-N^{-1/2}\frac{dm}{d\tau}\frac{\partial Q}{\partial s}=\\
&N^{-1/2}\left(\frac{\partial}{\partial s}\right)[d(s)Q(s)]+N^{-1}\frac{1}{2}\left(\frac{\partial}{\partial s}\right)^2[d(s)Q(s)]+\\
&-N^{-1/2}\left(\frac{\partial}{\partial s}\right)[b(s)Q(s)]+N^{-1}\frac{1}{2}\left(\frac{\partial}{\partial s}\right)^2[b(s)Q(s)]+\ldots\\
&=N^{-1/2}\left(\frac{\partial}{\partial s}\right)\{[d(s)-b(s)]Q(s)\}+N^{-1}\frac{1}{2}\left(\frac{\partial}{\partial s}\right)^2\{[b(s)+d(s)]Q(s)\}+\ldots
\end{aligned} \tag{13A.15}$$

where $\tau=t/N$. At this point, in order to match the component of the same orders of powers of $N$ between equations (13A.7) and (13A.15), we need to rescale the variable $\tau=tN$. Knowing that:

$$d(s)-b(s)=(\lambda+\gamma)(Nm+\sqrt{N}s)-\lambda N=(\lambda+\gamma)N_k-\lambda N$$

$$d(s)+b(s)=(\lambda-\gamma)(Nm+\sqrt{N}s)+\lambda N=(\lambda-\gamma)N_k+\lambda N$$

and taking the derivatives up to the second order, it is possible to obtain what Aoki (2002) defines as *diffusion approximation*:

$$N^{-1}\frac{\partial Q}{\partial \tau}-N^{-1/2}\frac{dm}{d\tau}\frac{\partial Q}{\partial s}=$$

$$(\lambda+\gamma)Q(s)+N^{-1/2}\left[d(s)-b(s)\right]\left(\frac{\partial}{\partial s}\right)Q(s)+N^{-1}\frac{1}{2}[b(s)+d(s)]\left(\frac{\partial}{\partial s}\right)Q(s) \tag{13A.16}$$

Applying the polynomial identity principle to equation (13A.16) for powers of $N$ of order $-1$ we get a formulation for the *Fokker-Planck* equation:

$$N^{-1}\frac{\partial Q}{\partial t}=-b'(m)s\frac{\partial Q}{\partial s}+b(m)\frac{1}{2}\left(\frac{\partial}{\partial s}\right)^2 Q(s)-b'(m)sQ(s)$$

$$+d'(m)s\left(\frac{\partial}{\partial s}\right)Q(s)+d(m)\frac{1}{2}\left(\frac{\partial}{\partial s}\right)^2 Q(s)-d'(m)Q(s) \tag{13A.17}$$

$$=\left[d'(m)-b'(m)\right]\left(\frac{\partial}{\partial s}\right)Q(s)+\frac{1}{2}\left[d(m)+b(m)\right]\left(\frac{\partial}{\partial s}\right)^2 Q(s)$$

The generic asymptotic approximated solution for the master equation will then be given by the solution of the following coupled dynamic system of equations:

$$\begin{cases} \dfrac{dm}{d\tau}=\rho(m) \\ \dfrac{\partial Q}{\partial \tau}=-\rho'(m)\left(\dfrac{\partial}{\partial s}\right)[sQ(s)]+\dfrac{1}{2}\alpha(m)\left(\dfrac{\partial}{\partial s}\right)^2 Q(s) \\ s.t.\ \rho(m)=b(m)-d(m),\ \alpha(m)=b(m)+d(m) \end{cases} \tag{13A.18}$$

In order to arrive at an explicit solution we introduce a modification in the transition rates of equations (13.1), supposing that the probability $\eta$ is equal to the observed frequency of firms occupying state 1. The new transition rates are then:

$$\begin{cases} b_n = r(N_k + 1 | N) = \zeta \dfrac{N_k}{N} \dfrac{N - N_k}{N} \\ d_n = l(N_k - 1 | N) = \iota \dfrac{N_k}{N} \dfrac{N_k - 1}{N} \end{cases} \tag{13A.19}$$

where the factor $N_k / N$ allows us to interpret, respectively, the probability transition $\zeta$ as a constant of proportionality between the birth rate per individual and the deviation from the upper bound $N - N_k$ and the probability transition $\iota$ as a constant of proportionality between the death rate per individual and the deviation from the lower bound or $N_k - 1$. One can thus set the two functions:

$$\begin{aligned} \lambda(N_k) &= \lambda \frac{N_k}{N} \\ \gamma(N_k) &= \gamma \frac{N_k}{N} \end{aligned} \tag{13A.20}$$

Substituting the transition rates (13A.20) in the master equation (13.22) and collecting terms with $\lambda$ and $\gamma$, after some simple but tedious algebraic passages, we obtain:

$$\begin{aligned} \frac{dP}{dt} &= N^{-2}\{\gamma[N_k(N_k + 1)L(P) + 2nP] + \\ &- \lambda\left[(N_k - 1)(N - N_k + 1)L^{-1}(P) + (N - 2n + 1)P\right]\} \end{aligned} \tag{13A.21}$$

where $L(P)$ and $L^{-1}(P)$ are lead and lag operators, reformulated in the following way according to Aoki (1996) and Landini and Uberti (2008):

$$L(P) = \sum_{z=1}^{\infty} \frac{N^{-z/2}}{z!} \left( \frac{\partial}{\partial s} \right)^z Q(s) \tag{13A.22}$$

$$L^{-1}(P) = \sum_{z=1}^{\infty} \frac{(-)^z N^{-z/2}}{z!} \left( \frac{\partial}{\partial s} \right)^z Q(s) \tag{13A.23}$$

Substituting the above indicated operators into equation (13A.21), it becomes:

$$\begin{aligned} \frac{dP}{dt} &= N^{-2}\left\{ \Sigma_{z=1}^{\infty} \left[ D(N_k) + (-)^z B(N_k) \right] \frac{N^{-z/2}}{z!} \left( \frac{\partial}{\partial s} \right)^z Q(s) \right\} + \\ &+ N^{-2}\{[2\gamma N_k - \lambda(N - 2n + 1)]\ Q(s)\} \end{aligned} \tag{13A.24}$$

where:

$$\begin{cases} B(N_k) = \lambda(N_k - 1)(N - N_k + 1) = \lambda N(N_k - 1) - \lambda(N_k - 1)^2 = B(m) \\ D(N_k) = \gamma N_k(N_k + 1) = D(m) \end{cases}$$

(13A.25)

The specification of the drift displayed in equation (13.26) implies that:

$$\begin{cases} N_{k+1} = Nm + \sqrt{N}(s + N^{-1/2}) \\ N_k = Nm + \sqrt{N}s \\ N_{k-1} = Nm + \sqrt{N}(s - N^{-1/2}) \end{cases} \qquad (13A.26)$$

Using these specifications in equation (13.26), we obtain:

$$\begin{cases} B(m) = \lambda\left[N^2 m(1-m) + N^{3/2}s(1-2m) + N(2m - s^2 - 1) + 2N^{1/2}s - 1\right] \\ D(m) = \gamma\left[N^2 m^2 + N^{3/2}2ms + N(m + s^2) + N^{1/2}s\right] \end{cases}$$

(13A.27)

Now, expanding to the second order equation approximation equation (13A.24), that is to say for $z = 1,\ 2,$ we get:

$$\begin{cases} z=1: \quad N^{-1/2}\left[D(m) - B(m)\right] = \\ \quad N^{3/2}\left[-\lambda m(1-m) + \gamma m^2\right] + N\left[2ms(\lambda+\gamma) - \lambda\langle s\rangle\langle s\rangle\right] + \\ \quad + N^{1/2}\left[s^2(\lambda+\gamma) + (\gamma - 2\lambda)m + 1\lambda\right] - 2\lambda s + N^{-1/2}(\gamma s - \lambda) \\ z=2: \quad \frac{N^{-1}}{2}\left[D(m) + B(m)\right] = \\ \quad N\left[\lambda m(1-m) + \gamma m^2\right] + N^{1/2}\left[2ms(\lambda+\gamma) - \lambda s\right] + \\ \quad + \left[s^2(\gamma - \lambda) + m(\gamma + 2\lambda) - \lambda\right] + N^{-1/2}2\lambda s + N^{-1}(\gamma s + \lambda) \end{cases}$$

(13A.28)

and substituting it into equation (13A.25), it gives back the following approximated master equation:

$$\frac{dP}{dt} = \left\{N^{-1/2}\left[-\lambda m(1-m)+\gamma m^2\right]+N^{-1}\left[2ms(\lambda+\gamma)-\lambda s\right]\right\} \frac{\partial}{\partial s}Q(s)+$$
$$+\left\{-N^{-3/2}\left[s^2(\lambda+\gamma)+(\gamma-2\lambda)m+\lambda\right]-N^{-2}2\lambda s+\right.$$
$$\left.-N^{-5/2}(\gamma s-\lambda)\right\} \frac{\partial}{\partial s}Q(s)+\frac{1}{2}\left\{N^{-1}\left[\lambda m(1-m)+\gamma m^2\right]+\right.$$
$$\left.+N^{-3/2}\left[2ms(\lambda+\gamma)-\lambda s\right]\right\} \left(\frac{\partial}{\partial s}\right)^2 Q(s)+$$
$$+\frac{1}{2}\left\{N^{-2}\left[s^2(\gamma-\lambda)+m(\gamma+2\lambda)-\lambda\right]+\right.$$
$$\left.+N^{-5/2}\lambda s+N^{-3}(\gamma s+\lambda)\right\} \left(\frac{\partial}{\partial s}\right)^2 Q(s)+$$
$$+\left\{N^{-1}\left[2m(\lambda+\gamma)-\lambda\right]+N^{-3/2}\left[2s(\lambda+\gamma)\right]-N^{-2}\lambda\right\} \tag{13A.29}$$

Given that:

$$\frac{dP}{dt}=\frac{\partial Q}{\partial t}-N^{-1/2}\frac{dm}{dt}\frac{\partial Q}{\partial s} \tag{13A.30}$$

in order to match the higher order terms in powers of $N$, we have to rescale time as $t = N\tau$:

$$\frac{dP}{dt}=\frac{\partial Q}{\partial t}-N^{-1/2}\frac{dm}{dt}\frac{\partial Q}{\partial s} \Leftrightarrow N^{-1}\frac{dP}{d\tau}=N^{-1}\frac{\partial Q}{\partial \tau}-N^{-1/2}\frac{dm}{d\tau}\frac{\partial Q}{\partial s} \tag{13A.31}$$

Then we have to equal the two formulations thus obtained for the master equation: equation (13A.29) and equation (13A.31). This can be done by matching the terms that have the same power of $N$. Then we collect terms of order $N^{-1}$ in equation (13A.29) so as to match them with $\partial Q/\partial\tau$ of equation (13A.31) and those of order $N^{-1/2}$ to set them equal to $N^{-1/2}\dot{m}(\partial Q/\partial s)$. All the other terms asymptotically vanish as $N \to \infty$. In this way we get:

$$-N^{-1/2}\frac{dm}{d\tau}\frac{\partial Q}{\partial s}=-N^{-1/2}\left[\lambda m(1-m)-\gamma m^2\right]\frac{\partial}{\partial s}Q(s) \tag{13A.32}$$

$$N^{-1}\frac{\partial Q}{\partial \tau} = N^{-1}\left[2m(\lambda+\gamma)-\lambda\right]\frac{\partial}{\partial s}\left[sQ(s)\right] + \frac{N^{-1}}{2}\left[\lambda m(1-m)+\gamma m^2\right]\left(\frac{\partial}{\partial s}\right)^2 Q(s) \tag{13A.33}$$

Asymptotically approximated solution of master equation is given by the following system of coupled equations:

$$\frac{dm}{d\tau} = \lambda m - (\lambda+\gamma)m^2 \tag{13A.34}$$

$$\frac{\partial Q}{\partial \tau} = \left[2(\lambda+\gamma)m-\lambda\right]\frac{\partial}{\partial s}(sQ(s)) + \frac{\left[\lambda m(1-m)+\gamma m^2\right]}{2}\left(\frac{\partial}{\partial s}\right)^2 Q(s) \tag{13A.35}$$

## 13A.3. APPENDIX C

Below we determine a solution for the Fokker-Planck equation in terms of $Q(s)$. Using $\theta(s)$ to indicate the stationary probability for $Q(s)$ and setting the equilibrium condition $\dot{Q}=0$ (that implies $\dot{\theta}=0$), it is possible to obtain:

$$-\left[2(\lambda+\gamma)m^* - \lambda\right] s\theta(s) = \frac{\left[\lambda m^*(1-m^*)+\gamma m^{*2}\right]}{2}\left(\frac{\partial}{\partial s}\right)\theta(s) \tag{13A.36}$$

Rewriting (13A.36) more conveniently as:

$$\frac{2\left[\lambda - 2(\lambda+\gamma)m^*\right]}{\left[\lambda m^*(1-m^*)+\gamma m^{*2}\right]}s = \frac{1}{\theta(s)}\left(\frac{\partial}{\partial s}\right)\theta(s) \tag{13A.37}$$

and integrating it with respect to $s$, we obtain:

$$\log\theta(s) = C + \frac{\lambda - 2(\lambda+\gamma)m^*}{\lambda m^*(1-m^*)+\gamma m^{*2}}s^2$$
$$\Updownarrow \tag{13A.38}$$
$$\theta(s) = C\exp\left[\frac{\lambda - 2(\lambda+\gamma)m^*}{\lambda m^* + (\gamma-\lambda)m^{*2}}s^2\right]$$

Then, substituting $m^* = \lambda/(\lambda+\gamma)$ , we get the final result:

$$\theta(s) = C\exp\left(-\frac{s^2}{2\sigma^2}\right) : \sigma^2 = \frac{\lambda\gamma}{(\lambda+\gamma)^2} \tag{13A.39}$$

# NOTES

1. The probabilistic dynamics shown here shares some features with the compartmental models. For a reference see Bischi (1999).
2. Consequently, negative investment implies negative variation of debt, that is disinvestment is used to repay debt.
3. We can now quantify the upper bound of the demand of money. Given the optimal levels of capital for each cluster of firms, $k^1$ and $k^0$ , the quantity of demanded credit reaches its maximum when $a^1$ and $a^0$ reach their minimum. $a^1$ cannot go below $r-2.5/q^1$, at which value $\mu$ becomes equal to 1. The minimum level for $a^0$ is, by definition, $\overline{a}=r-1.5/q^1$. For these values we have:

$$\lim_{a^0\to\overline{a}} B^0 = \frac{(q^0)^2}{2}(1-r+1.5/q^1)$$

$$\lim_{a^1\to\overline{a}} B^1 = \frac{(q^1)^2}{2}(1-r+2.5/q^1)$$

Consequently, the maximum level of the demand of debt $B=B^0+B^1$ is:

$$\max(B)=N^0\left[\frac{(q^0)^2}{2}\left(1-r+\frac{1.5}{q^1}\right)\right]+N^1\left[\frac{(q^1)^2}{2}\left(1-r+\frac{2.5}{q^1}\right)\right]$$

that cannot grow indefinitely since $q^0=1/r$ and $q^1<q^0$ as demonstrated below.

4. For details on derivation see Aoki (2002, ch. 3), Landini (2005, p. 252) and Kelly (1979).

# REFERENCES

Aoki, M. (1996), *New Approaches to Macroeconomic Modeling*, Cambridge: Cambridge University Press.

Aoki, M. (2002), *Modeling Aggregate Behavior and Fluctuations in Economics*, Cambridge: Cambridge University Press.

Aoki, M. and H. Yoshikawa (2006), *Reconstructing Macroeconomics*, Cambridge: Cambridge University Press.

Axelrod, R. (1997), 'Advancing the Art of Simulation in the Social Sciences', *Santa Fe Institute Working Papers*, no. 97-05-048.

Axtell, R., R. Axelrod, J.M. Epstein and M.D. Cohen (1996), 'Aligning Simulation Models: a Case Study and Results', *Computational and Mathematical Organization Theory*, **1**(2), 123–41.

Balian, R. (1991), *From Microphysics to Macrophysics*, Volume I, Berlin/Heidelberg/New York: Springer-Verlag.

Bischi, G.I. (1999), 'Compartmental Analysis of Economic Systems with Heterogeneous Agents: an Introduction', in A. Kirman and M. Gallegati (eds), *Beyond the Representative Agent*, Cheltenham, UK, and Northampton, MA, USA: Edward Elgar, pp. 181–214.

Brook, D. (1964), 'On the Distinction Between the Conditional Probability and the Joint Probability Approaches in the Specification of Nearest-neighbour Systems', *Biometrica*, **51**(3–4), 481–3.

Clifford, P. (1990), 'Markov Random Fields in Statistics', in G.R. Grimmet and D.J.A. Welsh (eds), *Disorder in Physical Systems: a Volume in Honour of John M. Hammersley*, Oxford: Clarendon Press, pp. 19–32.

Delli Gatti, D., C. Di Guilmi, E. Gaffeo, G. Giulioni, M. Gallegati and A. Palestrini, (2005), 'A New Approach to Business Fluctuations: Heterogeneous Interacting Agents, Scaling Laws and Financial Fragility', *Journal of Economic Behavior and Organization*, **56**(4), 489–512.

Di Guilmi, C. (2008). *The Stochastic Dynamics of Business Cycles: Financial Fragility and Mean-field Interaction*, Frankfurt am Main: Peter Lang Publishing Group.

Forni, M. and M. Lippi (1997), *Aggregation and the Microfoundations of Dynamic Macroeconomics*, Oxford: Oxford University Press.

Greenwald, B. and J.E. Stiglitz (1990), 'Macroeconomic Models with Equity and Credit Rationing', in R. Hubbard (ed.), *Information, Capital Markets and Investment*, Chicago: Chicago University Press.

Greenwald, B. and J.E. Stiglitz (1993). 'Financial Market Imperfections and Business Cycles', *Quarterly Journal of Economics*, **108**(1), 77–114.

Hinich, M.J., J. Foster and P. Wild (2006), 'Structural Change in Macroeconomic Time Series: a Complex Systems Perspective', *Journal of Macroeconomics*, **28**(1), 136–150.

Jaynes, E.T. (1957), 'Information Theory and Statistical Mechanics', *Physical Review*, **106**(4), 620–30.

Kelly, F. (1979), *Reversibility and Stochastic Networks*, New York: John Wiley and Sons Ltd.

Kirman, A.P. (1992), 'Whom or What Does the Representative Individual Represent?, *Journal of Economic Perspectives*, **6**(2), 117–36.

Landini, S. (2005), *Modellizzazione stocastica di grandezze economiche con un approccio econofisico*, PhD thesis, University Bicocca, Milan.

Landini, S. and M. Uberti (2008), 'A Statistical Mechanic View of Macrodynamics in Economics', *Computational Economics*, **32**(1), 121–46.

Minsky, H. (1963), 'Can "it" Happen Again?', in D. Carson (ed.), *Banking and Monetary Studies*, Homewood: Richard Irwin, Reprinted in H. Minsky, *Inflation, Recession and Economic Policy*, New York: ME Sharpe, 1982.

Opper, M. and D. Saad (2001), *Advanced Mean Field Methods: Theory and Practice*, Cambridge, MA: The MIT Press.

Risken, H. (1989), *Fokker-Planck Equation. Method of Solutions and Applications*, Berlin: Springer Verlag.

Rosser, J.B. (ed.) (2004), *Complexity in Economics*, Cheltenham, UK, and Northampton, MA, USA: Edward Elgar.

# Index